# Psychology of Adjustment

# Psychology
## of Adjustment

*Second Edition*

## James M. Sawrey
## Charles W. Telford

San Jose State College
San Jose, California

Allyn and Bacon, Inc.                                  Boston

FIRST PRINTING . . . . APRIL, 1967
SECOND PRINTING . . . . FEBRUARY, 1968

PRINTED IN THE UNITED STATES OF AMERICA

LIBRARY OF CONGRESS CATALOG CARD NUMBER: 67-17144

# Preface

THE FACETS OF PSYCHOLOGY that contribute to self-understanding and to the understanding of one person by another are numerous. Any book purporting to deal with the psychology of adjustment must cover a great variety of social and psychological topics; this book deals with the ones that seem most pertinent to the enhancement of the understanding of personal-social behaviors. Emphasis is on both the means by which socially significant behaviors develop and the nature of complex individual behavior.

We have tried to use established principles of psychology in discussions of adjustive behavior; thus we have relied heavily on theory and research in the areas of motivation and learning. Significant personal-social behaviors are viewed as derived from learning in a social setting. In such a setting, much of the reinforcement for behavior is social, as opposed to immediately physical, in nature. When social reinforcers are employed in the development of behavior, the learning that occurs can be called "social" learning. The nature of such social learning and the nature of reinforcements in social learning situations are given extensive treatment.

The introduction and the first chapter of this book provide an orientation to and description of the general aspects of adjustive behavior. The remaining chapters of Part I are descriptive of the adjustment problems encountered by individuals and the means of problem solution by which these problems are frequently attacked. The second part of the book deals with basic psychological processes involved in personal-social living. The first two parts of the book are arranged so as to describe the nature of the behaviors to be studied before attempting to account for their development and function. The broader aspects of adjustment and personality are considered in the third part of this book while the fourth part deals with some positive principles by which effective and satisfying existence may be enhanced.

This book is designed to introduce interested persons to the principles of personal and social adjustment. As a book for general use, people interested in the psychology of adjustment and effective living should find it meaningful and useful in their efforts to understand themselves and others more adequately. It should be useful as a college textbook in courses concerned with principles of adjustment, mental health, personal adjustment, personality, and related areas.

We, as the authors, are equally responsible for the content and organization of this book, and agree that the most fruitful approach to understanding behavior is to utilize the principles of learning and motivation that have been developed through psychological research. We are deeply indebted to the many psychologists who have contributed to the scientific literature of learning, motivation and adjustment. In addition to the individuals known and given appropriate recognition for their works, we thank the others who have influenced us in a variety of ways reflected in this book. These contributors are acknowledged though they remain anonymous and in many cases are unknown.

Material assistance in the preparation of the manuscript as well as the encouragement and support by our wives, Una Mae Sawrey and Aldene Telford, has been given generously. For this we are most grateful.

James M. Sawrey

Charles W. Telford

# Contents

# Introduction

Man has always searched for the "good life." Theologians, philosophers, and, more recently, social scientists and psychologists have tried to define the concept and discover those conditions and experiences which contribute to its realization. In the past, psychological conceptions of mental health, good adjustment, and the "good life" were dominantly negative in their emphasis. Mental health was considered to represent an absence of pathology. Mental pathology was originally explained in terms of evil spirits or retribution for one's sins. More recently the concept of mental disease or mental illness was substituted for the demonological and retributional doctrines. The concept of mental health as the absence of mental illness was a considerable advance over the supernaturalistic and moralistic ones. When a person showing personal and social inadequacies is called "mentally ill," he is thereby classified with other types of sick or disabled people and is provided the benefits accruing to the physically disabled. Society assumes some responsibility for the care and treatment of sick people and those people labeled "mentally ill" thus have extended to them the humane treatement accorded the physically "sick." This certainly constitutes an advance over the moralistic attitude.

However, there were disadvantages to applying the medical model of disease to mental pathology. It also has some unfortunate connotations that have led many workers to discard it in favor of one that places less emphasis on cure and more on prevention, less on pathology and more on the realization of potential. Abnormal or maladaptive behavior was considered the result of a disease caused by such things as germs, viruses, organic lesions, and trauma, or their "mental" equivalents. It was therefore the disease that needed to be treated. The disease analogy placed an emphasis on nosology—the classification of diseases—and on precise diagnosis. The notion that an illness may remit without being "cured," as well

1

as many other physical disease concepts, was applied to mental illness. The medical model led to a great emphasis on the categorization of people in terms of presumed underlying diseases, formal diagnosis of illness, and prescriptive treatment. If deviant behavior was caused by mental illness, the attainment of mental health by curing the illness should ensure "normal" conduct and a good life. It was assumed that social intercourse and personal life would be harmonious and personally satisfying but for the disrupting influences of mental pathology.

There is increasing dissatisfaction with the negative emphasis provided by the demonological, moralistic, and medical concepts in attempting to understand the full range of human functioning. There has been a marked trend recently toward the study of normal and superior individuals as well as the developmental sequences and processes that lead to psychological maturity, superior integration, and adjustment. This increased interest in normal and superior functioning has resulted in several attempts to conceptualize psychological and social normality and supernormality more adequately. Superior adjustment and creativity are conceived of today as the expression of superior psychological health rather than as the absence of pathology.

As early as the 1930's there were attempts to conceptualize normal psychological development and functioning. More recently, psychoanalysts have tried to extend traditional Freudian concepts beyond their original psychopathological frame of reference. The most active current movement in this direction is that of the "social learning" theorists. According to social learning conceptions, all adjustment—normal as well as abnormal— is to be understood in terms of the same basic concepts. The development and maintenance of maladjustive behavior is considered to involve the same processes and principles of learning as the acquisition and perpetuation of normal or superior behavior. There is no discontinuity between normal and abnormal behavior. The social learning theorists contend that the behavioral deviations of maladjusted, neurotic, or psychotic people are ways of acting that have been learned in social contexts and are largely the result of the social reinforcements provided by their society, just as the delinquent has learned his self-defeating behavior patterns in his family and/or subculture.

In so far as possible we have used the concepts and language of social learning in accounting for the origins and development of normal as well as abnormal behavior. We do not reject the data or concepts originally derived and developed within a different frame of reference. However, we find the social learning explanations and terminology to be the least ambiguous, most parsimonious, and most flexible for a wide variety of behavioral and experiential phenomena.

We have tried to interpret many psychoanalytic and phenomenological concepts within the framework of conventional learning principles, and we hope we have done so without losing either the phenomena or their meanings. When we interpret defensive and aggressive behavior or nu- rotic and psychotic symptoms as the outcome of ordinary developmental, motivational, and associative processes we are not throwing out the baby with the bath. Conventional developmental, motivational, and learning concepts, to the extent that they are equal to the task, must account for all of the dynamic and affective components as well as the cognitive and motor aspects of the phenomena under consideration.

This volume, like every book in psychology, attempts to forward man's understanding of himself and others. Textbooks in psychology attempt to bring together and to present in some reasonably consistent and coherent form what many know about certain aspects of man. Every book represents a selection of data, a point of view concerning man, and the presentation of these within the conceptual framework that seems most reasonable to the authors. The conscious and unconscious biases of the authors as well as the current state of knowledge concerning man are reflected in the pages that follow. While our unconscious biases must remain unacknowledged, an indication of our major conscious commitments may be helpful.

One bias, the preference for the terminology and concepts of "social learning," has already been mentioned. Although we are not sure that conventional learning interpretations always account adequately for all the phenomena to which we have applied them, we do believe that they have the greatest explanatory power of any alternative conceptual system.

The authors are committed to a dynamic, but not to either a psycho-analytic or a phenomenological, frame of reference. We have handled the purposive, goal-oriented, actively striving aspects of behavior and experi- ence in terms of conventional motivational learning concepts. We have not found it helpful to postulate a libido, an *elan vital*, or a unique drive impelling one to "self-realization," "self-actualization," or "competence" in order to account for man's development of his positive-valued abilities into actual skills and competences. We accept the reality of the phenomena encompassed by these concepts but feel that these phenomena can be accounted for more satisfactorily within a conventional motivational-learn- ing context. We also conceive of man's striving for personal identity as progressive performance along positively-valued dimensions of experience without assuming the existence of a unique drive impelling him toward these goals.

We accept the inevitability of a "fact-and-value" frame of reference when dealing with the problems of human adjustment. The "mental hygienist" is, to some degree, a moralist functioning in a world of science.

He implicitly or explicitly defines the "good life," and relates relevant psychological information to the attainment of that goal. Unfortunately our knowledge of man is least adequate in those areas which are most relevant to prescriptions concerning behavior within the social-moral field. Our knowledge of man has an extremely jagged advancing border. In areas such as the simpler sensory, motor, learning, and motivational processes great progress has been made. However, in the more complex areas of social processes, personality, and moral development we lag far behind. Such a situation is not favorable to understanding man as a whole, and certainly not for making authoritative pronouncements about what man ought to do.

However, societies and men have to act—and they do so, either un-intelligently, blindly, and on impulse or, to some degree, intelligently, deliberately, and in an informed way. Theoretically "man as psychologist" and "man as man" can be compartmentalized, but the mental hygienist is both psychologist and man. He is both scientist and advocate. He must deal with what is desirable as well as with what is. He must deal with the full range of human experience and behavior in a scientific way and then relate his scientifically derived information to the achievement of personally and socially valued goals.

We further believe that human behavior and experience can be understood most adequately in terms of their biological and social origins and sequences. Man is a product of his biological endowment and his unique ontological and social development. Biological endowment and environment interact in development just as the individual and the situation combine in the determination of behavior.

We believe in the continuity of normal and pathological behavior. We see defense mechanisms and neurotic behavior as exaggerated or distorted adaptive devices that in less extreme forms are a part of normal personality functioning. Defensive and nondefensive behavioral function-ing constitute a continuum and merge into each other. Neurotic conflict is not different in either kind or content from the conflicts that are a part of normal living. The more adequate individual weathers these conflicts and derives from their satisfactory resolution a sense of personal adequacy and integrity. Moreover, such experiences increase his capacity to achieve according to his own internalized values and in ways consistent with the standards of the "significant others" in his life.

Our primary interest is in the normal, healthy individual. However, much of the existing terminology and many of the concepts are best suited to dealing with aberrant, neurotic, or psychotic behavior. If we consider the abnormal as the normal "writ large" the study of deviant behavior will throw light on the ordinary behavior of everyday people. Consequently, when we deal with maladaptive behavior, neurotic syndromes, and psychotic symptoms it is not because of any primary interest in these as such, but because of the insights they provide in the understanding of the behavior of normal people.

# Part I

# Adjustment Processes

*Chapter* 1

# The Adjustive Process

We shall forego the time-honored practice of beginning with a formal definition of that which we are to study. While adjustment sometimes refers to a condition of static equilibrium between an organism and its surroundings, it also refers to the *process* of making changes within oneself and/or one's environment in order to achieve and maintain the optimum relationship between the two. While this latter meaning is closer to our usage, it still is too restrictive. Adjustment and maladjustment can refer to the process of relating person and environment, but they can also refer to the harmonious or conflictual relationships within and among the many behavioral patterns, belief systems, and sentiments making up the functioning personality. Adjustment involves an inner-inner as well as an inner-outer (individual-environmental) relationship.

Adjustment as a process involves the complex interaction of an intricate set of behavioral, ideational, and emotional systems with each other. In turn, this dynamic matrix of personality components is continuously interacting with the ever-changing circumstances of one's life. Satisfactory or ideal adjustment does not correspond to any unique state of the individual and/or his environment. Neither does it constitute a single process or even an identifiable set of processes or relationships between the individual and his surroundings along a single dimension.

Adjustment is multidimensional and can be described only in terms of a number of interacting variables. Traits or processes as human adjustment variables can be conceived of either as ranging from a theoretical zero point to some maximum or as having both positive and negative values on each side of a theoretical neutral point. Each dimension can be described in unidimensional terms, whereas the entire process is always multidimensional.

### DIMENSIONS OF HUMAN ADJUSTMENT

Although many long lists of personality traits and adjustment variables have been developed, we shall conceptualize adjustment in terms of six dimensions. We call these dimensions (1) selective awareness, (2) tolerance, (3) autonomy, (4) personal integration, (5) behavior and impulse control, and (6) self-realization.

## Selective Awareness

Adjustment, as a broad concept, involves growing accustomed to or ceasing to respond to certain aspects of one's environment. This is the process of sensory or negative adaptation. It consists of a diminution or cessation of response to nonsignificant, constantly or regularly recurring stimuli. We cease to attend to constant noises and familiar sights and odors that are of no particular significance to us. This cessation of response to nonsignificant stimuli leaves us free to note and concentrate on the significant aspects of our environment so that we may handle them appropriately. It is a universal and a useful aspect of adjustment. Adjustment involves a cessation of response to certain stimuli and an intensification of response to other stimuli. This is the selective awareness dimension of adjustment.

The infant's stimulus selectivity is determined by his inherent organic make-up and the characteristics (size, intensity, color, movement) of the stimuli about him. Attention is initially determined and sustained by the objective stimulus variables. Experience determines which stimuli are significant or nonsignificant, important or unimportant. Stimuli are observed or disregarded without attention to their inherent physical properties. The mentally deficient child is lacking in his capacity to make these distinctions and continues throughout his lifetime to respond dominantly to stimulus properties as they relate to his organic make-up.

The brain-injured individual is often characterized by a lack of appropriate stimulus selectivity. He is said to be distractible (*Strauss and Lehtinen, 1950*). This distractibility involves an undue fixation of atten-

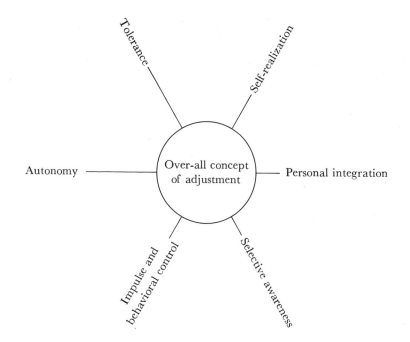

*Figure 1. The components of adjustment.*

tion upon irrelevant external stimuli as well as difficulties in figure-ground differentiation (distinguishing between the significant and nonsignificant components of perception). The attention of the brain-damaged person is caught and held by things that the normal person ignores. Conversely, the defective individual disregards the more significant stimuli which may have less inherent attention-attracting properties. These people display a "forced responsiveness" and are more "stimulus bound" in their behavior than normal people (*Strauss and Lehtinen, 1950*).

Adjustment involves the diminution or cessation of response to certain stimuli and an increased responsiveness to other stimuli, depending upon their relative significance. The capacity for differentiating stimuli and responding appropriately on this basis is one index of an individual's adaptability.

Selective awareness applies to affective (emotional) and ideational (thought) processes as well as to sensori-motor processes. A person can be distracted by irrelevant thoughts and inappropriate emotion just as his attention can be diverted by competing stimuli. High levels of anxiety can reduce a person's perceptual accuracy and keep him from maintaining an effective problem-solving orientation to life's problems. So far as the inter-action among sensori-motor, ideational, and affective processes is con-cerned, the selective awareness dimension represents a continuum ranging from the most rigidly stimulus-tied processes, at one extreme, to completely fantasy or emotion dominated awareness, at the other. In between these extremes we have all degrees of reality-tied awareness with appropriate ideational and emotional accompaniments.

## SELECTIVE AWARENESS

| Rigid and limited stimulus-bound awareness | Reality-oriented awareness | Fantasy- and emotion-dominated awareness |
|---|---|---|

## Tolerance

The process of human adjustment also demands a degree of acceptance of things that can be neither ignored (adapted to) nor changed. In the present state of our knowledge and in our culture, the color of one's skin can hardly be considered a nonsignificant characteristic; nor can it be permanently changed to a significant degree. Skin color, along with many of our physical attributes, can at best be "accepted," and then realistic levels of aspiration can be set up within the limitations thus dictated.

There are also limits to the extent to which physical and mental handicaps can profitably be denied and limits to levels of aspiration set up in disregard of disabilities, even when the goals could possibly be achieved. For example, while it may be possible for many orthopedically handi-capped individuals to become ballet dancers, it is probably better for them to accept a relatively low level of accomplishment as dancers and strive for achievement and recognition in areas where their orthopedic disabilities will be less of a handicap. The tremendous time and energy required to become a ballet dancer may result in a neglect of other areas of endeavor, such as painting or science, where they could succeed more easily.

A person without any particular handicap is sometimes unable to accept the difficulties inherent in the normal process of development. To set out on a new learning venture requires one to yield to the possibilities of failure as well as the promise of success. The acceptance of failure, the ability to tolerate error, the willingness to go ahead in spite of the im-perfections in oneself are prerequisites to the acquisition of newer and better patterns of adjustment.

Life, in general, requires the acknowledgement of certain limitations and the renunciation of certain specific goals. This means that an acceptance of the inevitable is a part of a satisfactory over-all adustment process.

At the high end, tolerance can take the form of an indiscriminate and unreflective acceptance of oneself and of other people and their activities. The person with a medically defined disability may "over-accept" his limitation and develop an unrealistically low self-concept, perceiving himself as more handicapped than his disability really dictates. The person who sees himself as unrealistically handicapped and dependent and consequently maintains low levels of aspiration is more tolerant and accepting of his limitations than is appropriate. The opposite end of the tolerance continuum gets into the extreme rejection-denial range. This is the perfectionistic range, where the individual cannot accept imperfection either in himself or in others. The disabled person who functions at this end of the scale denies his handicap by showing himself and the rest of the world that he is as good as or better than anyone else. He elects to compete and prove himself in the area of his disability.

## TOLERANCE

Indiscriminate acceptance                                    Extreme rejection
of self and others                                           and denial

## Autonomy

Adjustment as conformity has been criticized by many students of our contemporary culture. Conformity to the ways of the majority as the goal of adjustment assumes that the majority is always right. A high level of conformity is conducive to a stable social structure. If the stability of the larger social system is regarded as the final goal and if the individual's welfare is seen as requiring harmony with a given social system, then such a criterion of adjustment is basic and defensible. Because of the tremendous range of social systems and cultures and the variety of individual behavior patterns required to live in harmony with them, it is inconceivable that these systems are all equally "good" in terms of other dimensions of adjustment. When one views the various forms of social organization under which man lives or has lived, the thought occurs that a whole society could be maladaptive or "sick." Conformity to its standards would then constitute "mental illness" or personal maladjustment in a more inclusive sense. In such a broad context, the autonomous person who attempted to modify the culture rather than conform to it might be the "better adjusted."

There are limits to which individual autonomy is tolerated in any society. Psychosis (insanity), delinquency, and criminality are deviations from codified or uncodified social norms. If a man is permitted freedom in society, he must conform to a certain extent to the written and unwritten laws and expectancies of his culture. If he is to survive and remain a significant person, either within a given social structure or as a modifier of that system, he must conform to some degree to the demands of that culture. In a statistical sense, all of our creative, political, social, religious, artistic, and scientific leaders are nonconformists, but not all nonconformists are, either actually or potentially, creative leaders.

Although we would not accept social conformity as *the* criterion of "good" adjustment, neither would we exclude it from the dimensions as satisfactory adjustment. A certain balance between autonomy and social conformity is an important component of an over-all concept of human adjustment.

Autonomy ranges from rigid and extreme social conformity at the one extreme to an equally rigid and compulsively independent and "inner directed" pattern of behavior at the other. All degrees of personal autonomy and social control of behavior are found between these extremes.

## AUTONOMY

Rigid social conformity                                Compulsive "inner direction"

### Personal Integration

An important characteristic of people for adjustment is the degree to which their beliefs, feelings, and behavior are congruent with each other. Some people have highly integrated, rigid, and almost completely closed behavioral and attitudinal systems. Other people are poorly integrated, in the sense that they maintain highly inconsistent and unstable belief systems, have vacillating emotional reactions toward the same or similar situations, and behave in contradictory ways in the same or highly similar situations. In between these extremes we find people with varying degrees of stable integration and congruence of the various components of their personalities. Most people have a certain fixity to their personality make-ups but are still open to learning and subject to change.

## PERSONAL INTEGRATION

A "closed system" of highly integrated and rigid personality components

Diffusion or disorganization of unstable personality components

## Behavior and Impulse Control

Behavior and impulse control ranges from severe repression of impulse and restriction of behavior, on the one extreme, to the wholesale, immediate, unreflective, and uninhibited overt expression of impulse and feeling, on the other. The first extreme constitutes a paralysis of action, with repression so strong as to permit impulse expression only in symbolic ways. The opposite extreme involves immediate over-reaction, with a minimum of restriction and control. The distance between these extremes represents varying degrees of repression, suppression, and free expression of impulse, with behavior held in abeyance and controlled appropriately to the time and place.

## BEHAVIOR AND IMPULSE CONTROL (EGO CONTROL)

| Extreme constriction of behavior and repression of impulse | Uninhibited or compulsive overt expression of impulse |
|---|---|

## Self-Realization

The definition of "good adjustment" or ideal personality development as self-realization is partly a protest and partly an affirmation of faith concerning human nature. It is a protest against the acceptance, social conformity, and, to a lesser degree, the personal happiness concepts of adjustment. These criteria by themselves seem to present us with the "well-adjusted" man as the socially conforming accepting, self-satisfied person without problems. This is too neutral a definition to satisfy many people. They feel that there is a "higher" criterion for the desirability of behavioral patterns. If adjustment, as a condition, is the goal, we then ask, "adjustment to what?" If acceptance is the goal, we ask, "acceptance of what?" If happiness or self-satisfaction is the criterion, we inquire, "what are we happy about?" or "with what are we satisfied?"

The proponents of self-realization insist that when social conformity takes the form of exploitation, domination, and a restriction of individual development a refusal to conform is a sign of mental health. In some situations, they consider it to be a sign of mental illness not to protest. Discomfort, pain, grief, and anxiety are necessary for the continued growth of the individual. Excessive protection may make the individual feel secure, self-satisfied, and happy; but if he is to continue to grow and develop, he needs to become a bit anxious, insecure, and sufficiently dissatisfied with himself to do something about it. This is the form that the protest component of the concept of "adjustment as self-realization" typically takes.

Self-realization as an affirmation of faith assumes that man's basic behavioral trends are "good" and if these inherent tendencies and potentialities are permitted to express and develop themselves to their maximum, all will be well. Such a belief implies a faith in the inherent goodness of human nature. It assumes that a spontaneous and uncorrupted expression and development of man's inner propensities works out ultimately for the good of the individual and presumably also for society. "Sin" is failure to do all that one is capable of doing. Good adjustment involves the free expression of one's inner nature, rather than its suppression (*Maslow, 1956; Rogers, 1961*).

Ideal adjustment defined as self-realization assumes a large reservoir of innate socially-relevant behavioral tendencies which, if permitted to unfold and develop spontaneously, will take care of man's social and personal needs. The most systematic interpretations of the evidence accumulated over the last thirty years are opposed to this conception. The human infant is believed to inherit relatively little, if anything, in the way of socially relevant behavioral trends. He has a long period of infancy and a large capacity for learning. The presence of other people inculcates in him the social behavior patterns which constitute a large segment of his action potential.

It is generally believed that the child's attitudes, beliefs, ideals, and most of his motives are social products. They represent the acceptance and internalization of the social judgment and values of his culture. Once having been internalized, these attitudes, beliefs, and value systems become autonomous and operate independently of his immediate environment. Self-realization within such a conceptual framework consists in the expression and further development of one's self consistently with the already established, but previously acquired, behavioral trends. This process is detailed more fully in later chapters.

Such an interpretation of self-realization does not diminish its importance but it does deny its independence of society. The social trends which one realizes represent earlier acquisitions from either direct or vicarious contacts with the general culture, subculture, groups of people, or even a particular person. They do not derive directly from man's instinctive behavioral trends. This means that one's self-actualization or self-realization is within a social context and has imbedded with it the elements of social conformity, acceptance, and personal happiness.

The *complete* realization of one's potential is not only an impossibility but would also be socially undesirable. No one knows the limits of his own or another's potential. Certainly a person of normal mental and physical endowment has the capability of becoming an accountant or an embezzler, an honest citizen or a thief, a statesman or a demagogue. The list is endless, just as one's potentialities are infinite in variety. Of the infinite number of potentialities, those which are realized in order to contribute to personal and social welfare are determined by the unique cultural and personal circumstances of the individual. The "good personality" and the "well adjusted person" are not the result of the unmodified and unrestricted expression of one's inner nature; nor are they the indiscriminate development of one's potential. They result from the selective development of one's potential along culturally appropriate and personally satisfying lines.

The degree of self-realization attained by each individual can be conceptualized as ranging from a theoretical complete realization of one's potential to the minimum necessary for survival. We have already suggested that complete realization of one's inherent potentialities is impossible and that to strive to attain this goal in even a limited area will result in the neglect of other areas of potential. The partial development of much of one's potential is a prerequisite to making the best use of one's potentialities in the more highly valued areas.

## SELF-REALIZATION

| Complete realization of one's potential | Minimal achievement in proportion to potential |
| --- | --- |

### THE MULTIDIMENSIONAL CONCEPT OF ADJUSTMENT

With so many dimensions and criteria of adjustment, we may question the usefulness of the concept as a global description or overall characterization of an individual. Instead of trying to decide "what good adjustment really means," or arbitrarily defining the term and giving it a specific (perhaps operational) meaning for the purpose of discussion, it may be better to accept the fact that there are many facets and dimensions to the adjustment process. If we do this, we can then consider specific dimensions and recognize the relative nature of each. This will provide a multidimensional definition of adjustment from which we can determine a series of questions concerning each of these dimensions. Questions of the following type are appropriate within this context: (1) How much is this person distracted or bothered by constant environmental factors to which either the average or the "ideal" person normally becomes accustomed? (2) To what degree is this person fighting irremediable social circumstances in his life? (3) Does this person's trouble stem from social nonconformity or from rigid over-conformity? (4) To what extent are these activities satisfying experiences for the individual? (5) How well are the person's individual needs and desires being satisfied? (6) To what extent is the individual realizing his potentialities?

These questions are suggested as a substitute for a single question concerning a person's "adjustment" in general. We are forced by more specific designations to indicate: adjustment to what, adjustment in what way, adjustment in what dimension, adjustment according to what standard? Within this context it is meaningless to try to indicate a level of adjustment as a single value.

## Adjustment as Normality

One connotation of the term "adjustment" is the term "normal"; to be normal is to be on the norm and the norm is average. The equation of the well-adjusted individual with the average individual is, to some extent, the consequence of an overemphasis on social conformity. If to be well adjusted is good, and to be adjusted is to be normal, and to be normal is to be average, then it is good to be average. According to such a conception, to strive for better adjustment is to try to be average.

Here we have the same problem concerning the word "normal" as we had with the term adjustment. At least the three following interpretations of "normal" can be identified: (1) the usual or the average, the statistical norm, (2) neither abnormal nor subnormal in some arbitrarily defined way, (3) an ideal standard, a standard worthy of emulation. The first two meanings which equate the normal with either the average or the absence of abnormality, are variations of the statistical or social conformity meaning of adjustment. This has already been discussed.

### THE IDEALISTIC CONCEPT—NORMALITY

This leaves the concept of "normal" or "good adjustment" as an *ideal pattern of life* or a pattern of behavior to be considered. We feel that some variation of this concept of normality or "good adjustment" is the most useful one. The conception of adjustment as an ideal pattern of life, is actually an infinite number of possible patterns which meet certain criteria of "goodness."

The concept of "good adjustment" as an "ideal way of living" has considerable attractiveness, particularly if we introduce some variations into the traditional concept. One proposed modification, previously discussed, is to emphasize adjustment as a process rather than as a goal. This involves a shift in emphasis either from the adjusted individual to the *adjustable individual,* or from the adapted person to the *adaptable* person. An additional shift is from the emphasis on the attainment of certain fixed points along a dimension or series of dimensions of adjustment as a goal to an emphasis on the direction of change and rate of movement toward an ideal.

Within this frame of reference, "good adjustment" is seen as a positive movement along either a continuum or a series of continua toward a goal or series of goals that represent maximum adjustability or adaptability according to the changing demands of the situations confronting the individual. Some of these desirable achievement goals represent medians between extremes; others represent continuous movement in a single direction. Adjustment as positive movement along these continua can be represented somewhat as follows.

To the extent that the individual is, on the one hand, developing the habit of disregarding the irrelevant aspects of his environment and ceasing to respond to nonsignificant stimuli impinging on his senses and, on the other hand, becoming increasingly sensitive, attentive, and responsive to the significant components of his environment, he is becoming well adjusted. The progressive development of these traits represents positive movement along a selective-sensitivity continuum. This dimension involves the "selective awareness" variable.

Progressive movement along the tolerance dimension involves an acceptance of those things that cannot be changed, efforts to change those things that should and can be changed, and an increasing ability to distinguish one of these categories from the other. Since these categories are never static, emphasis will be upon the continuing revision of the limits of these groups. That which cannot be changed in childhood may be subject to change in adulthood. Maturity and increased knowledge and skill produce continuous modifications of the boundaries of these categories.

Changes along the autonomy dimension in the direction of better adjustment are best represented as movements toward a region intermediate between two extremes. One extreme constitutes a rigid social conformity pattern. Persons functioning at this end of the continuum find deviations from the social norm so threatening that their own minor behavioral deviations and even the perception of differentness in other people are anxiety-arousing. At the other end of the continuum is the compulsive noncomformist. This is a person who avoids social conformity in order to conform either to his own self-concept or to what he thinks others expect of him. Over-regimentation and compulsive nonconformity both preclude active progressive adjustment in accordance with one's personal and social demands.

Improved adjustment for people showing either of these two behavior patterns consists in a shift toward a more intermediate position within the autonomy dimension. Such a movement will result in a more flexible and adaptable person who will be able to conform or be individual according to the demands of a situation and his own self-concept. He will be able to modify his own behavior and beliefs in the face of changing situational requirements without losing his individuality.

An intermediate position somewhere between the two extremes of the personal integration dimension would seem to be the most appropriate one. The most adequate adjustment requires a well integrated personality with an openness to change and a flexibility of inner organization that makes it possible for the individual to meet the varying demands of the situation without sacrificing his own integrity.

Maximum adjustment in terms of behavior and impulse control requires that the make-up of the individual allow impulse satisfaction in open, ordered, and tempered ways. Behavior controls are dominantly conscious and directed at coping with the environmental demands, rather than defensive in nature. Unacceptable thoughts, feelings, and behavioral tendencies are supressed rather than repressed.

Living up to one's potential in selected areas and developing and acting consistently with one's self-concept move a person along the self-realization dimension in a positive direction.

There is increasing support for an idealistic conception of psychological normality and individual adjustment. Good adjustment as movement toward an ideal is a dynamic concept. It is a process of becoming rather than the attainment of a static condition. This concept of adjustment stresses what *can be* rather than what *is*, either in terms of the individual or as judged by society's norms. It emphasizes the growing, developing, maturing, self-fulfilling aspects of the individual as he lives within a given social order and participates in and contributes to his culture. Normal adjustment involves the progressive approximation to a culturally defined ideal in such areas as rationality, integrity, and maturity.

The idealistic conception of adjustment involves a constantly changing frame of reference. Satisfactory adjustment is not the same for the child, the adolescent, the adult, or the aged individual. Good adjustment requires adaptability and flexibility rather than stereotyped behavior patterns.

## Implications of the Concept of Normality as Adjustment

The idealistic concept of adjustment is value-oriented. It assumes certain criteria of good and bad or better and worse in adjustment. This value commitment is not unique to the idealistic conception.

Any discussion of the adjustment process that goes beyond the descriptive level inevitably becomes involved, knowingly or unknowingly, with the question of values (what is good or which is better). This problem is not peculiar to psychology. On the purely descriptive scientific level, the physician can study the cell growth of a cancer just as easily and profitably as he can the growth of a normal nerve cell. The burglar's learning to "crack a safe" may be just as revealing of the principles of learning as if he were learning to operate a lathe. Tracing the development of a psychosis or a neurosis may tell the psychologist as much about the process of adjustment as studying the more normal behavior patterns.

As soon as one turns practitioner and begins to recommend, advise, or help people, value decisions take place. Whether one's acts contribute to normal nerve growth or a cancer, a criminal act or a socially useful skill, a disabling illness or a wholesome adjustment, makes a great deal of difference. When we do something to remove or to retard the rate of growth of cancer, recommend that someone learn socially useful rather than socially destructive skills, take preventative or remedial measures to ward off or treat a psychosis, we are making value decisions. The values involved—that it is better to live than to die, to be comfortable than in pain, to be a useful citizen than a criminal, and to be mentally healthy than to be psychotic— are so universally a part of our culture that we take them for granted. These values remain implicit and are seldom challenged. The value problem becomes explicit, however, when we go beyond the level of "treating illness" or "removing handicaps," when we go beyond the statistical norm in a positive direction, or when we indicate how a reasonably normal person can be made better. Our traditional religious terms—virtuous, good, and without sin—are recognizably value-laden. Our modern equivalents of maturity, integration, adequate self-concept, and self-realization are no less value-oriented. Implicit in our use and understanding of these terms is the notion that immaturity, personality disintegration, inadequate self-concept, and failure to realize one's potential are "bad."

Some implicit value judgments involved in therapy are: I believe you are ill or in trouble (bad), I think you should be changed (for the better), I am able and willing to help you change in desirable ways (I know how you should be changed to make you a better person). These values may be fairly universal and implicit, or they may be limited to a certain culture or subject to challenge by other cultures, or even by other individuals in the same culture.

The idealistic conception of adjustment is also culture-bound. If values are social products to which the individual has made a personal commitment, a value-oriented criterion of adjustment is necessarily socially oriented and culturally limited. We may deduce the probable behavioral consequences of holding certain value systems, but the available experimental and observational data will be limited to those cultures and values actually studied. The dimensions of adjustment selected as significant and the relative importance given to each dimension is socially determined.

In an open and permissive culture in which there is considerable "looseness" in organization and social expectancy, the self-realization dimension may be highly valued. In such a society, a high level of individual initiative and uniqueness of personality may be permitted and reinforced. In more rigid and formally organized cultures, the social mores and formal codes may specify in great detail what one can or cannot do. In such cultures, social conformity has high value, whereas deviant personality traits, unusual behavior, and atypical social activities may be intolerable. A person's skin color, race, kinship, parental occupation, or place of birth may define what he shall do, how he shall do it, and the areas within which he can make choices. It is the culture in terms of its tacit values that selects out as significant a limited number of adjustment dimensions. Within the framework of this value system, forces are brought to bear on the developing child that mold him in accordance with these social dictates. Out of an infinite number of possible developmental trends that the individual has the potentiality to actualize, each culture defines and reinforces a limited number as most worthwhile. Sometimes these selected potentials are narrowly and rigidly specified; at other times they are broadly defined. Adjustment criteria always involve a conception of the good life and the good life is culturally defined.

The multidimensional concept of adjustment implies the involvement of multiple criteria of good functioning rather than a single unitary definition of adequate adjustment. The particular set of dimensions selected for study in this book discloses the nature of the authors' value commitments. Within the framework of these commitments, the principles of perception, motivation, and learning are used to indicate how these values arise and are transmitted from generation to generation, how they become internalized in terms of personal ideals and attitudes, and what their behavioral consequences are.

## Range of Adjustive Reactions

An example of the possible range of adjustive reactions to a single type of frustration may make clearer the social evaluations of these reaction patterns.

A young married woman with a strong maternal motive finds that she is apparently incapable of bearing children. This threatens her concept of herself as wife and potential mother. She becomes anxious, and in order to reduce her anxiety and to resist a change in her self-concept, she may react to the frustrating situation in one or more of the following ways:[1]

DIRECT OVERT ATTACK

    (1) Have a thorough examination and diagnosis by a competent physician.

    (2) Prevail upon her husband to have an examination for possible sterility.

    (3) Follow through prescribed surgical, medical, or behavioral procedures recommended.

SOCIALLY ACCEPTABLE SUBSTITUTE REACTIONS (COMPENSATORY ACTIVITIES)

Either in place of the above or after failure of it to remedy the situation she may:

    (1) Adopt children.

    (2) Become a children's nurse, pediatrician, or teacher.

    (3) Adopt and keep pets or establish a veterinary hospital.

    (4) Join or found an antivivisection society or society for the prevention of cruelty to animals.

BORDERLINE DEFENSIVE REACTIONS

    (1) Insist upon the blessings of childlessness (rationalization).

    (2) Place the blame for her sterility upon her own parents' neglect of her in childhood (projection).

    (3) Revert to the behavior of a young adolescent (regression).

    (4) Resort to daydreams in which the children in the neighborhood become her own (fantasy).

    (5) Develop an aversion to children (reaction formation).

SOCIALLY UNACCEPTABLE OVERT REACTIONS (COMPENSATORY REACTIONS)

    (1) Indulge in sexual promiscuity.

    (2) Contract multiple marriages.

    (3) Engage in anxiety-driven social or economic aggressiveness.

    (4) Resort to alcoholism or drug addiction.

[1] Adapted and modified from *Masserman*, 1946.

SOCIALLY AND PERSONALLY HANDICAPPING PSYCHOSOMATIC AND NEUROTIC
ADJUSTMENT PATTERNS

(1) Display a functional amenorrhea (abnormal cessation of menstruation).

(2) Suffer from "morning sickness" without pregnancy.

(3) Experience "pseudo-pregnancy" distortion of the abdomen and other signs of pregnancy without actual pregnancy).

PSYCHOTIC (MENTALLY ILL) PATTERNS OF ADJUSTMENT (DELUSIONS)

(1) Experience delusions of persecution concerning the seductive behavior of men.

(2) Have delusions of being drugged and raped.

(3) Believe that she will give birth to a Messiah.

(4) Experience delusions of motherhood.

The reactions to frustration listed above range all the way from the socially approved to the personally and socially unacceptable behavior patterns. They also range from the normal adaptive, through borderline and neurotic, to the frankly psychotic personally and socially maladaptive reaction patterns. Within these limits there exists a bewildering array of adjustments to frustration.

We can only theorize as to why people differ so widely in their reactions to stress. Some of the probable differentiating factors are: (1) inherited and acquired constitutional organic, endocrinological, and biochemical differences, (2) prior idiosyncratic experiences that predispose the individual to develop certain types of defenses, (3) social conditions peculiar to a given historical period, culture, subculture, or social class.

Irrespective of the level of adjustment involved, whenever the adaptive process requires the development of new ways of acting, certain elements are likely to be present. These will now be indicated.

### ANALYSIS OF THE ADJUSTMENT PROCESS

Except on the basic homeostatic and instinctive levels, the behavioral adjustments of the individual are learned. All forms of learning are involved in the acquisition of these adjustment patterns. The basic patterns for the learning of adjustments are fairly simple, but their ramifications are infinite. The basic elements common to the development of new

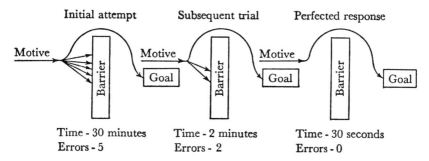

*Figure 2. Diagram of the typical Adjustment process.*

ways of adjusting are: (1) motivation; (2) obstacles or barriers; (3) variable response; (4) success or partial success; (5) partial or complete satisfaction of the motive; (6) with repetition of the preceding elements, the perpetuation of the successful and elimination of the unsuccessful responses; and finally (7) integration and consolidation of the selected responses into characteristic ways of acting.

## Motivation

It is assumed that an individual's characteristic ways of acting (adjustment patterns) are acquired as a means of satisfying his motives, wishes, and desires. He may be hungry, thirsty, and cold (organic states) and respond to these conditions in ways that he has learned are satisfying; he may feel lonely, inferior, insecure, and threatened (social motives) and respond to these conditions in ways that he has learned from experience. Adjustment patterns represent the individual's habitual ways of either avoiding stressful situations or alleviating the conditions under which they occur. The nature and the varied manifestations of man's motives are discussed more fully in Chapters Seven and Eight.

## Obstacles or Barriers

If all of man's motives were immediately and completely satisfied as soon as they became operative, life would be very simple. If all of his organic needs were continuously taken care of, if his social demands were always adequately met, nothing new would be learned in order to alleviate those conditions. However, most living organisms, including man, encounter obstacles to the attainment of their satisfaction. These obstacles may be in the environment or they may be inadequacies within the person. Time, distance, or the unavailability of food and water may constitute environmental barriers for the satisfaction of hunger and thirst. Unresponsive, cold, and punishing adults may make acceptance, love, and prestige unattainable for the child. The adolescent may be without appropriate clothes to gain popularity. Poverty, inadequate educational opportunities, and social isolation may represent external obstacles to the satisfaction of one's motives. If these operate from the beginning of a child's life, they are "privations." Privations constitute one important class of obstacles to man's achievement of satisfaction.

Very often the *loss or withdrawal* of opportunities or resources previously enjoyed will be felt more keenly as frustrating obstacles than the continued absence of the same opportunities when they have never been enjoyed. The individual who loses his friends after having enjoyed their friendship experiences the loss much more than the individual who has never had friends. The lowering of one's social status is more disturbing than the inferior position of the person who has never known or aspired to anything better. *Deprivation* may be more frustrating to the individual than privation. Deprivations constitute another important class of environmental obstacles.

*Personal obstacles* to the satisfaction of one's motives may take many forms. Physical handicaps such as specific bodily deformities, a generally inadequate physique, sensory defects, or mental deficiency may represent obstacles to achievement. Illness or insufficient knowledge, skill, or strength may likewise prevent the realization of one's ambitions. A person's fear of failure or of public ridicule may operate as a barrier to achievement. One's conflicting motives, "self-concept," or "conscience" may also constitute functional barriers to satisfactory living.

It is obvious that external and internal barriers or obstacles are interrelated. Motive strength or intensity also enters into the determination of the extent to which internal deficits and external obstacles prevent achievement. What constitutes a barrier is the result of the dynamic interaction of environmental obstacles, personal characteristics, and motivational factors. For example, the mastery of the multiplication tables represents a minor challenge to a child of average intelligence, but to a child with an I.Q. of 30 these same tables may constitute an insurmountable barrier. A crooked nose may be perceived as a social calamity by the aspiring young movie star, but to the young prize fighter it is an honored mark of his profession. For the average boy severe burns on his legs may preclude any athletic achievements, but to a Glenn Cunningham they represented a challenge to be overcome by tremendous drive and hard work. It is obvious that environmental obstacles and personal limitations cannot be defined objectively and universally. They are always relative to the intricate inter-relationship of the many factors determining behavior.

## Variable Response

A motivated individual thwarted in his attempt to achieve a goal may give up and renounce the goal, but more often he persists in his efforts. Approaches to a problematic situation may vary all the way from a relatively blind, motor, trial-and-error attack, at one extreme, to a deliberate, rational, ideational, insightful approach, at the other. When a naive individual finds his efforts thwarted he can do little else but make a random, haphazard try-and-try-again attack on the situation. The more experienced person is able to transfer experience from similar situations and make a more systematic and logical approach. The very experienced individual may be able to make an ideational analysis of the difficulty, set up and systematically try out various hypotheses concerning the most fruitful approach to the problem, and arrive at a satisfactory solution with very little motor trial and error.

The following examples may make the variable response component of the adjustment process clearer. A lonely boy, in order to satisfy his affiliative motives, wishes to join a group of children at play. He first asks if he can join the group and is told that he cannot (his affiliative motive is thwarted). The boy may then (1) try to force his way into the group, (2) threaten to retaliate if he is not permitted to join them, (3) plead to be permitted to play with them (4) cry, (5) try to purchase acceptance by giving them money, candy, or playthings or promising to do things for them, (6) try to convince them that it will be to their own advantage to let him play with them, (7) try to get adults to intercede in his behalf. The range of variability in attack is limited only by the boy's repertoire of responses, his ingenuity in devising new approaches, and his persistence.

Failing in the more direct approaches, the boy may resort to various defensive maneuvers to protect himself against the ego-deflating implication that he is not wanted because he is an inferior person. These defenses may take the form of rationalization (the game isn't worth playing; the boys don't know how to play), projection (the boys are really poor players and are afraid that a newcomer will always win), identification (the boy attaches himself to the best player in the group, follows him around, and basks in his superior achievements), or fantasies (the boy imagines that he is a superb performer and that all the other boys plead with him to play with them). He may also resort to any of the additional defensive devices described in later chapters. There is a good deal of trial and error or trial and success in the development of the adjustment behavior patterns.

## Success or Partial Success

One of the approaches to the obstacle preventing motive-satisfaction is found to be successful or partially successful in overcoming or circumventing the barrier. The success may be either real or imaginary. It may constitute goal-achievement or goal-renunciation. Partial success may take the form of a substitution of goals. Success can be evaluated only within the subjective frame of reference of the individual.

## Motive-Satisfaction

Success and motive-satisfaction are two sides of the same coin. From the individual's standpoint, success is either motive-satisfaction or motive-reduction and, conversely, motive-reduction or motive-satisfaction is success. Motive- or drive-reduction is rewarding (positively reinforcing) and tends to perpetuate those activities leading to it.

## Selection and Elimination of Response Patterns

As indicated above, those adjustment patterns which are most often successful and are therefore either maximally or most regularly positively reinforced, will be selected and perpetuated, and the less successful responses will be eliminated either because of lack of positive reinforcement (rewards) or because they are negatively reinforced (punishments). With practice there occurs a gradual selection and fixation of certain behavior patterns and an elimination of other competing ways of dealing with stressful situations.

## Consolidation and Integration of Adjustment Patterns

The selected behavior patterns eventually become integrated and consolidated into fairly stable and consistent ways of dealing with stressful situations. Some individuals develop habits of dealing with their adjustment problems by direct attack. Others meet frustrations by withdrawal or compromise. Ways of handling stressful situations are also complicated by various ego-defensive mechanisms, which will be discussed later. With some people, these adjustment patterns become encapsulated, rigid patterns that are prohibitive of further growth. Such individuals are not flexible; they are driven to either attack, withdraw, or avoid threatening situations irrespective of the appropriateness of the behavior. Other people are flexible enough to be able to fight or flee, to compromise, to comply, or to do whatever seems most appropriate.

Habitual ways of meeting frustrations become interwoven with the attitudes, feelings, and beliefs that constitute personality traits. Personality traits are aggregations of behavioral trends, beliefs, attitudes, and ideals. These groupings combine, at a still higher level, to constitute one's "style of life" and, when recognized by the person himself, they constitute his "self-concept."

### SUMMARY

The process of human adjustment involves a constant interaction between the person and his environment, each modifying the other. Through increased knowledge about the world in which he lives, man is able to change the world, and, by changing the world in which he lives, he changes himself. Adjustments range all the way from those on the elementary physiological level, which are essential for individual survival, to infinitely complex forms of social interactions. We are concerned primarily with the more socially relevant forms of adjustment.

Man's patterns of social adjustment are motivated and learned in essentially the same way as are other acquired reaction tendencies. Adjustment can be understood within the same conceptual framework as other forms of behavior.

Adjustment is a continuous activity and is best understood as an ever-changing process rather than as a static condition to be attained and maintained.

Adjustment is a multidimensional concept. Six different aspects or dimensions of adjustment are: (1) the selective awareness component, (2) the tolerance component, (3) the autonomy component, (4) the personal integration component, (5) the behavior and impulse control component, and (6) the self-realization component. We believe that the multidimensional idealistic conception of "good adjustment" is the most satisfactory one. Such a conception is frankly culturally limited and value-oriented.

### REFERENCES

Maslow, A. H. Personality Problems and Personality Growth. In Moustakas, Clark E. (ed.), *The Self*. New York: Harper & Brothers, 1956.

Masserman, Jules H. *Principles of Dynamic Psychiatry*. Philadelphia: W. B. Saunders Company, 1946.

ROGERS, CARL R. *On Becoming a Person: A Therapist's View of Psychotherapy.* Boston: Houghton Mifflin Company, 1961.

STRAUSS, ALFRED A., and LEHTINEN, LAURA E. *Psychopathology and Education of the Brain-Injured Child.* New York: Grune and Stratton, 1950.

*Chapter* **2**

# Defensive
# Behavior Patterns

POETS, NOVELISTS, AND PLAYWRIGHTS, as well as ordinary laymen, were familiar with many of the behavior patterns commonly called "defense mechanisms" long before psychologists formally catalogued, labeled, and analyzed them. In *King Lear,* when Shakespeare observed that "Wisdom and goodness to the vile seem vile, filth savors but themselves," he was describing the process of projection. In *Hamlet,* when he observed, "The lady doth protest too much, methinks," he was indicating the mechanism of reaction formation. When the man on the street calls someone an "Alibi Ike," he refers to the person's habitual tendency to rationalize away or project outwardly the causes of his own shortcomings.

Freud, the father of psychoanalysis, first formally named and described the defense mechanisms. He conceived of these behavior mechanisms as operating on an unconscious level. According to Freud (1938), the individual threatened with ego-deflation and its consequent anxiety *represses* the anxiety-laden experiences and *unconsciously defends his self-esteem* by devices of denial, disguise, and distortion as found in the various defense mechanisms; hence repression and unconscious motivation are

31

basic concepts in the psychoanalytic understanding of the defense mechanisms.[1]

Non-psychoanalytically oriented psychologists have adopted the psychoanalytical systematization of the defense mechanisms without subscribing to the belief that either these mechanisms or their motivations are necessarily unconscious. It is believed that most, if not all, of the defense mechanisms can function at all levels of awareness from fully conscious deliberation, through all the intermediate degrees of awareness, to the completely unconscious. Of course, it is possible, by definition, to confine the concept of "defense" to the unconscious category; however, setting limits to this category in terms of its degree of consciousness is difficult and probably serves no useful purpose.

Freud developed his concepts of defense mechanisms largely from his studies of neurotic individuals. In the fully developed neurotic the defensive behavior patterns are full-blown and thoroughly ingrained. In such individuals the defense mechanisms are largely unconscious and quite impervious to logical attack. The psychoanalysts have not been interested in tracing the acquisition of the defense mechanisms. They have been more concerned with the motivation and the nature of the mature devices. A longitudinal study of the origin and development of these behavior mechanisms would undoubtedly disclose a gradual shift from the fully conscious, through all levels of awareness, to the completely unconscious level. Processes and motives can function at all levels of awareness from one extreme to the other. This means that a dichotomy on the basis of whether the individual is or is not aware of the process and its motivation is unrealistic.

We can conceive of a person's originally using defensive behavior knowingly for the purpose of disproving to others evidences of his inferiority. Initially he tries to deceive others as to the real state of affairs as he perceives it. If his defenses are successful (reinforced) he continues to use them; their use becomes habitual; he finally comes to believe them; and they become an integrated component of his personality. They may

---

[1] Freud was not consistent in his handling of the concept of repression. He originally sponsored the notion that repression occupied a unique position among the "psychic processes." It was thought to be continually operative in the "ego's" struggle against painful or unendurable ideas or experiences. Whatever threatened the ego tended to be repressed into the unconscious and the various defense mechanisms (regression, reaction-formation, projection, etc.) developed as a means of handling subsequent threatening experiences. Later, Freud seemed to reduce repression to the level of a "special method of defense" along with the other specific methods. One solution of this apparent inconsistency is to conceive of repression operating in a relatively pure form as a defense mechanism resulting in uncomplicated amnesia. In other situations repression produces various perceptual, memorial, and ideational distortions and disguises resulting in the many other defense mechanisms.

eventually function entirely on an unconscious level. We conceive of the defense mechanisms as learned reaction patterns that are acquired and maintained much as other behavior patterns are learned.

## DEFENSE MECHANISMS AS DESCRIPTIVE CATEGORIES

The term "mechanism" suggests a machine or entity that does something. When we talk of "defense mechanisms," a group of entities or forces that defend the individual against threatening agents is typically envisaged. When thus conceived, defense mechanisms tend to become animistic or self-activating entities. The original psychoanalytic discussions of the behavior mechanisms encouraged these animistic implications. It is very difficult to use the psychoanalytic concepts of the id, the ego, and the super ego, or the unconscious, the censor, the libido, or even the Oedipal and inferiority complexes, without reifying them (making a *thing* out of a process) to some extent. In reifying these concepts we elevate processes or activities to the level of forces or powers, or even to little men within the man, that control his behavior. When so conceived, these terms are assumed to be *explanations* rather than descriptions of behavior. When Freud (1938) refers to the libido as a "force which expresses itself" in various ways, when the unconscious is at times referred to as a place and at other times as an entity, we can only conceive of it as an explanatory concept.

Non-psychoanalytic psychologists have adopted the original psychoanalytic "defense mechanisms" but have used them predominantly as descriptive names either for things that people do or for behavioral trends, rather than as *explanations* of why people do these things. One way to emphasize the descriptive nature of the terms and to eliminate the explanatory implications is to avoid using the noun forms of these words. If instead of speaking of *the unconscious,* we talked either about unconscious processes and activities or about activities and processes which function without the person being aware of them, there would be less of a temptation to terminate the discussion with the feeling that when we have named a process we have explained it. In other words, to say that a person is rationalizing, regressing, projecting, compensating, identifying, or repressing emphasizes the descriptive nature of these terms. The problem of why these activities occur still has to be investigated. When we use the corresponding nouns and speak of rationalization, regression, projection, compensation, identification, and repression it is much easier to think of them as entities that *do things.*

We shall use the defense mechanisms as classifications of behavior and consider the names as descriptive rather than explanatory in nature. We shall also discuss separately, in this and in a later chapter, the question of the origins and motivations for these activities. In general, we shall consider these defense mechanisms learned ways of acting, the motivation for which is not essentially different from that of other learned activities. We do not consider the origin of the defense mechanism to require the postulation of any unique motivations or learning principles for their understanding. We shall account for the origin, nature, and persisting characteristics of these activities by means of the same motivational and learning concepts that account for acquired behavior in general. We shall treat, in a descriptive way, the origin and functioning of these behavior patterns in this and the two succeeding chapters, and defer until later the systematic discussion of the fundamental motivational and learning principles involved.

### GENERAL CHARACTERISTICS OF THE DEFENSE MECHANISMS

According to Freud (1938), the defense mechanisms are: (1) unconscious, (2) defenses against anxiety, and (3) self-deceptive. These are still accepted as the most important characteristics of defense mechanisms but, as already indicated, they are relative rather than absolute. In other words, defense mechanisms possess in varying degrees the characteristics of being unconscious, anxiety-reducing, and self-deceptive. In the early stages of their inception, defense mechanisms may be quite conscious and deliberate, protecting more against social deflation than against anxiety; they are designed to deceive others rather than the individual himself. As the mechanisms develop in effectiveness they become more unconscious, more anxiety-reducing, and more self-deceptive, until in the full-blown neurotic the Freudian characterizations become quite appropriate.

## Unconscious Nature

Although many of today's psychologists do not emphasize the unconscious nature of the defense mechanisms, in their fully developed forms unconsciousness is one of their essential characteristics. When a person deliberately claims that he bought a new automobile because it would be more expensive to repair and maintain his old one, when he knows that the real reason was his desire to outdo his neighbor, he is simply lying. He is deliberately falsifying in order to deceive other people. On the other hand, when the individual feels threatened by implications that he is acting from unworthy motives, then he habitually and unconsciously presents the more worthy motives as the real ones and actually believes that they are true. He is deceiving himself as well as others.

When a person physically attacks another who is threatening his activities he may be making a direct, straightforward attempt at problem solving. He is conscious of what he is doing and why he is doing it. His acts are a direct, honest facing of the realities of the situation. There is no defense mechanism involved in his behavior. A defense mechanism is involved when a frustrated individual directs displaced aggression against a perfectly innocent second party and perceives his attack as being either justifiable or as having been actually provoked by the innocent party. When a person makes a mistake and recognizes that the fault is his, but deliberately tries to place the blame on someone else, he is simply trying to falsify the situation and mislead others. This is a defensive maneuver but not a defense "mechanism." When he actually comes to believe that all his failures are the results of his "never getting the breaks," or that his lack of success is due to the machinations of other people, when neither of these things is true, he is making use of a defense mechanism (projection).

It will be noted that, in most of the instances cited, it is not the acts themselves that become unconscious, but rather the motivation that evokes them and the individual's perception of the situation. At times the process as well as its motivation is unconscious. The individual using defense mechanisms may be aware of what he is doing but he is unaware of his motivation. He may also be unaware of the fact that his *perception* of the situation (as threatening or thwarting) is his own projection, just as the motivation responsible for his projection is not "known" to him. Thus he can have various degrees of awareness of both process and motive. This idea has been developed more fully by Goldin (1964). This will be illustrated more completely in our discussion of projection. The usual explanation of why the person is unaware of his true ego-deflating motives is that they have been repressed. The assumption of some repressive mechanism seems to be essential to the understanding of the unconscious motivation of the defense mechanisms. We are still far from an adequate understanding of just how repression functions.

## Behavior Mechanisms as Defenses Against Anxiety

A threat is, by definition, anxiety-arousing. Whenever an individual is threatened by evidences or implications of personal inadequacy or unworthiness of any sort, he becomes anxious. Anything that serves to deny or diminish the threat of ego-deflation, represented by the evidences of personal failure, will be anxiety-reducing; thus, if any or all of the defense mechanisms function efficiently, they automatically and unconsciously operate as defenses against anxiety. They either prevent anxiety from arising or reduce anxiety when it is aroused.

Anxiety is considered to play a central role in current concepts of the defense mechanism as well as in the more serious neurotic and psychotic states. Anxiety is an unpleasant emotional state involving an ill-defined fear of the future; it includes an element of threat. The anxious individual is afraid that something terrible is going to happen but he is often unable to say what it is or why it should happen. The anxious individual is tense, fearful, and disturbed. He is driven to do something to reduce the unpleasant state of affairs. In this way, anxiety can operate as an acquired source of drive and can motivate behavior. Anxiety-reduction is satisfying to the individual and can serve as a reinforcement in learning. It is an important concept in the explanation of motivation and learning, as well as of the acquisition and perpetuation of defense mechanisms, neurotic reactions, and psychotic behavior.

## Defense Mechanisms as Self-Deceptive

We have already indicated some of the self-deceptive characteristics of the defense mechanisms. Like awareness of one's motives, awareness of self-deception may be present in all degrees. When the mechanisms are fully developed, as in the typical neurotic individual, self-deception is quite complete. Extent of self-deception and degree of unconsciousness vary together. When a person is aware of the real motivation of his acts he, almost by definition, is not "kidding" or deceiving himself. He is simply trying to deceive others. When he begins to believe his own rationalizations and accepts his ego-inflating, but untrue, reasons for his behavior as the "real" ones, he has repressed the motivation for his acts and deceives himself as well as others. In a certain sense, the individual becomes the victim of his own motivation. As long as a person is aware that he is using a "trick" to deceive others he is in control of the situation, but as soon as he begins to "fool" himself, his "trick" is controlling him or a segment of his behavior.

Defense mechanisms involve the partial or complete denial, distortion, or disguise of motives, acts, or thoughts that are self-belittling or self-degrading. They involve a distortion of reality in one way or another. These distortions represent the effects of a person's dynamic motives, values, and self-concept on the way he perceives and judges the world in which he lives. Motives, particularly unconscious motives, affect the way he thinks, acts, and perceives the objects in his environment. These effects constitute parts of his defense against threats.

Defense mechanisms are a means of bolstering self-esteem through self-deception. This self-deception involves the *denial* of ego-deflating impulses, traits, or memories; or through *disguise* the unacceptable motives, characteristics, or ideas are distorted, displaced, or converted in such ways that we do not recognize them for what they are. We shall now discuss some of the more common defense mechanisms.

## RATIONALIZATION

Rationalization refers to the process of presenting more ego-inflating reasons in place of ego-deflating "true" reasons to account for one's practices or beliefs. It has been suggested that for most of our acts we have both *real reasons* and *good reasons*. The "good reasons" are the rationalizations. Goodness of motives is culturally determined. However, prior to the inculcation of social values, one motive is as "good" as another. The child learns that certain reasons for doing things are "better" (more socially acceptable) than others. He learns that rewards and punishments, praise and reproof are often administered for his motives, or the declaration of his motives, rather than for his acts. The child in our culture is not very old before he learns that to act from impulse, or emotion, or desire, or revenge, is not socially approved. He learns that a group of "unworthy" motives exist. People who act from these motives are less worthy individuals than are those who act from better motives. He also discovers that "rational" motives are "good" motives.

The Western cultures have developed a great faith in the rationality of man and in the desirability of his behavior resulting from rational motives. Man is supposed to be the reasoning animal. Rationality is the thing that distinguishes him from the lower animals. Animals act from impulse, whereas man's behavior is (or should be) guided by reason. Western man further believes that morality (the good) and reason (the right) must coincide. As the result of this supposed congruence of morality and reason, we muster a secular and humanistic support for a moral and theological code. Because of these commitments in our culture there is a considerable reinforcement of the rationalization of one's behavior (*Thelen, 1965*).

A second cultural value that motivates the rationalization of one's behavior is the belief in free will and individual responsibility. If the individual is personally responsible for his acts and his behavior is the manifestation of his "free will," irrational or socially unacceptable behavior must derive from an evil or perverted will. Since the "will" is thought to be the very essence of the individual, the nature of this entity and the goodness of its motives are the most important thing about him. If his intentions are pure and his motives are good, it is evidence of his inherent goodness. Evidences of irrationality, implications of evil intent, or suggestions of lack of good will constitute threats to a person's social prestige and self-respect. Such threats to social- and self-esteem are anxiety-arousing and stimulate self-defensive reactions among which rationalization is prominent. Western culture's emphasis on the importance of "good will" and individual responsibility is conducive to rationalization as a defense mechanism.

Rationalization is a means of logically justifying what we do and believe. A large section of our beliefs and practices is culturally derived. We are born into and grow up in a given family, in a certain community, and within a subculture that is a part of a larger culture. These cultural units provide us with a set of beliefs, attitudes, and values, which we unconsciously absorb and uncritically accept. They seem to be self-evident and not in need of justification or support.

When we move out of our own cultural units we find that other people do not share many of our beliefs and attitudes. Our opinions are challenged. We then respond to any attack on our practices as we do to an attack on our physical self. We perceive this attack as a threat to our self-esteem and react in self-defense by searching for logical support for our beliefs. We look for plausible excuses for not changing.

Our initial attempts at self-justification are not very successful. Our appeals to the universality and the self-evident nature of our beliefs are not very convincing arguments to those whose contradictory beliefs belie the claims. With practice, however, we become more adept at justifying our cherished beliefs and prejudices on a rational basis. We come to recognize that the fact that an idea is ancient and widely accepted does not prove its validity. We also recognize that to accept a belief simply because other people accept it is not very complimentary to our rationality. Consequently, we discover or fabricate a set of logical reasons for believing and acting as we do and, in time, come to believe our own rationalization.

Self-deception of this sort is easy because we are often not aware of our reasons for believing or acting as we do. The origin of our beliefs is unknown to us, but we assume that either we or those from whom we acquired the beliefs originally accepted them for good and sufficient reasons. Our problem is simply to discover or rediscover their underlying rationality. We are less likely to feel threatened when these beliefs are questioned if we are certain of their basic rationality. When we are certain that an examination of the facts will prove us to be right, we are less likely to strenuously defend and justify our beliefs than when we feel less secure. There is no need for us to conceal or distort contrary evidence or to give undue weight to arguments that support our own beliefs when we feel sure that, even with the most complete and thorough presentation of opposing views, ours will still prove to be true. With a firm and secure conviction in the rightness and reasonableness of our beliefs we do not feel vulnerable, and we do not become self-defensive when these beliefs are questioned.

Self-defensive rationalization is most extensive in the area of our religious, moral, and political beliefs, which are least subject to objective verification and proof. Opinions in these areas are also quite likely to be subject to considerable emotional involvement. They are not only "right" or "wrong," they are also "good" or "bad." When our profound and passionate beliefs are questioned, we rise to the defense much more vigorously than when our less emotionally toned opinions are questioned.

## Citing the Incidental Cause

Rationalizations are never complete fabrications. They are plausible, at least to the one doing the rationalizing. They are not obviously contradicted by known facts. They usually contain some elements of truth. Sometimes the rationalization consists of putting the main emphasis on a causal factor that is really only a minor or incidental one. Most acts have multiple causes. Most behavior has multiple motivation. It is therefore quite easy, in justifying one's acts, to place the major emphasis on the most noble motive that may be responsible for the behavior. By a shift in emphasis, the threat imposed by the presence of the less worthy motives can be minimized.

The failing college student, after declaring his intention to stay at home and study Saturday afternoon, turns up at the football game. When someone questions the wisdom of his choice, he declares that he was so tired by prolonged study that watching the game will refresh him and make it possible for him to accomplish more in the remaining hours of study than if he had stayed home and worked all afternoon. The "real" reason for his behavior was his fondness for football games; however, an affective reason for not studying is much less socially and personally acceptable than recuperation from fatigue. He *was* tired, but in placing the major emphasis on this minor contribution he is rationalizing.

A man buys a new car because his next-door neighbor bought one, but he claims that the reason was the excessive expense involved in the upkeep of his old car. Another man joins an expensive golf club for social prestige and fraternization but justifies it to his wife on the basis of the professional contacts he has to make. In these cases, fatigue, expense of upkeep, and the possibility of professional contacts were actually present but were not the principle determining factors.

## "Sour Grapes"

This name is self-explanatory to anyone familiar with Aesop's fable of the fox who, when unable to reach the grapes, declares that they are really sour and not worth having. According to this mechanism those things which we are unable to attain are really not worth striving for.

The student dismissed from college because of poor scholarship claims that a college degree is really meaningless and that education is greatly overrated. A really mature person does not need formal education. The unsuccessful athlete, turned scholar, belittles athletics. The homely girl insists that "beautiful but dumb" is the rule. The people of average intelligence derive satisfaction from their belief that the intellectually gifted are queer, socially withdrawn, or physically weak. These are examples of the "sour grapes" form of rationalization.

## "Sweet Lemon"

This mechanism carries rationalization one step beyond the "sour grapes" level. The sour grapes device says that the unattained goal is really not worthwhile; the "sweet lemon" form of rationalization says that failure to attain the original goal is actually the most desirable outcome. A student is unsuccessful in college and claims that his failure is really a blessing in disguise. He steps right into a job that is much better than any he could possibly have obtained if he had finished college.

The foreman, with the plant owner's son working under him, claims that even though the boy is incompetent, his presence serves to keep the other workers "up on their toes" and increases the output of his department. The foreman insists that he is glad he has the boy in his department. The foreman throws a halo over his incompetent assistant because he selected him and it would reflect on his judgment if his choice were admittedly a poor one.

The "sweet lemon" mechanism is also called the "Pollyanna" form of rationalization.

## Rationalization with Other Defense Mechanisms

All of our classifications of behavior traits and processes are arbitrary and overlapping. Many of our defensive behaviors are mixtures of several conventionally labeled ones. For example, a student cheats on an exam and justifies his behavior by saying that everyone else does it and that he must do it in order to be graded on an equal basis with the others. If this student really sees others as cheaters when, in fact, they are not, he is projecting. Projection is a defense mechanism by itself. His justification of his own behavior on this basis is rationalization. Some have called this "rationalized projection."

One explanation for the origin of certain psychotic symptoms is the rationalization of irrelevant, irrational behavior and bizarre ideas as being imposed by someone or something else. The person's thoughts are being forced upon him by hypnosis, radar, radio, or television waves. This device, involving both projection and rationalization, relieves the individual of anxiety concerning his own responsibility for his bizarre thoughts and behavior. In delusions of presecution, the individual projects his own hostile and aggressive impulses outwardly and then rationalizes his aggressive behavior as self-defense. His failures are due to the machinations of others, and his fears are caused by others' plotting to kill him. These devices are self-defensive. They relieve the individual of any personal responsibility for his difficulties. They involve projection, fantasy, and rationalization to various degrees.

## Rationalization of Group Behavior

The activities of groups of people are rationalized in essentially the same ways and from the same basic motives as the behavior of individuals. Individuals identify to some extent with most groups to which they belong. They consequently respond to threats to the group in much the same way that they respond to threats to themselves. Many "defense mechanisms" may be called into play in defense of group activities. We find people rationalizing institutional and group practices just as they rationalize their individual acts, beliefs, and attitudes. When suggestions or accusations of group or institutional snobbishness, prejudice, tyranny, and misuse of power are made, the group justifies its activities as being motivated by a desire to reward and encourage excellence, defend the truth, and protect the individual either from himself or from malign groups.

On the national level, "good" reasons must rationalize the behavior of nations in order for them to "save face" in the eyes of the world. What one part of the world sees as "colonial aggression," another segment of the world sees as "protective custody." One nation's "oppression" is another's "liberation." All nations perceive themselves as "peace-loving" people threatened by "warmongers" in other nations, and consequently are forced to arm, threaten, or even attack in "self-defense" (rationalization and projection).

## Levels of Awareness and Self-Deception

Earlier, it was indicated that defense mechanisms are: (1) defenses against the anxiety aroused by threats, (2) unconscious in various degrees, and (3) self-deceptive. Rationalization, by definition, is defensive. It is probably one of the *least unconscious* of the defense mechanisms. It often involves more social- than self-deceptiveness. Most of the fully-developed, unconscious, self-deceptive rationalizations probably begin in a conscious effort at social-deception.

The individual accused of having acted from unworthy motives may originally recognize the truth of the accusations but try to save his "social face" by falsifying his motives. He attempts to bolster his social status by claiming more worthy motives. If he believes that he is successful, he feels less threatened, his anxiety is reduced, and his rationalizing is reinforced (rewarded). With practice he becomes adept in rationalizing and successful in deceiving others. In time, he comes to believe his own rationalizations. When this occurs he forgets (or represses) his original motivation; he loses sight of the fact that his behavior is ego-inflating. His rationalization then becomes habitual, unconsciously motivated, and self-deceptive. This stage is, however, the end product of a learning process involving motivation, variable attacks, reinforcement, selection, and perpetuation of the successful (reinforced) responses (*Goldin, 1964*).

### *PROJECTION*

"To project" means to throw or cast forward. "Projection" as a behavior mechanism contains the element of casting forward, but only that "throwing or casting out" of personal traits that are "defensive" in nature is a "defense mechanism." In its broader sense, projection consists in ascribing one's own motives, attitudes, feelings, and behaviors to other people. When the motivation for attributing one's own characteristics to others is ego-inflation, or the prevention of ego-deflation, or the defense of a "self-concept," the projection is defensive.

## Non-Defensive Projection

Projection is not always defensive. It may be purely "predictive." In the predictive form, projection involves one's attempts to describe or forecast the behavior or characteristics of others by ascribing one's own characteristics to them. No conflict, no threat, and no defense occurs. It represents a nondefensive kind of projection derived from the correct or incorrect assumption that other people perceive, think, feel, and act in the same way that we do.

Research studies have quite consistently shown a relationship between the possession of certain traits and the ascription of these traits to others.

For example, self-critical people perceive others as also being critical of them (*Sears, 1937; Murstein and Pryer, 1959*). There is a correlation between the "happiness" ratings of the pictures of others and self-ratings of happiness (*Murstein and Pryer, 1959*). In elections most people believe that the candidate whom they favor will win the election (*Murstein and Pryer, 1959*). People tend to over-estimate the proportion of other people holding opinions similar to their own (*Wallen, 1941; Murstein and Pryer, 1959*).

The results of these studies are fairly consistent, but their interpretation is less straightforward. These research findings, as well as everyday observations, indicate that we perceive the world in terms of what we are. Those who are honest and virtuous see others as honest and virtuous. The deceitful see others as deceitful. We perceive our own moral lapses reflected in others. When we are afraid we read fear on the faces of others. This attribution of our own traits to others may not be defensive.

Positive correlations between our own traits and our belief that other people possess these same traits may arise from correctly perceiving similarities between oneself and others, or from incorrectly inferring such similarities. If an average middle-class, American-born, white, Protestant Democrat rates his associates as being like himself he may be right more often than not. If, on the basis of common interests and backgrounds, his associates are considerably like himself, ascribing his own characteristics to them may be either an accurate perception or a naive wholesale attribution of his own characteristics to them, which happens to be more often correct than wrong because of his selection of associates. Of course, the naive attribution of one's own "life style," or scale of value to other people may be quite an error when one is dealing with people not sharing the same personal attributes. Accurately or inaccurately perceived similarities are not necessarily the result of a projective mechanism. The naive assumption that people in general are like us in terms of beliefs, feelings, and behavior may simply represent a lack of information. In the above cases, the observed judgments or perceptions reveal the intellectual and informational characteristics of the individual rather than the dynamics of his personality.

## Defensive Projection

Similarities between one's own characteristics and the judged or perceived (misperceived) characteristics of others may be defensively motivated. Processes so motivated may operate on various levels of awareness and involve varying degrees of self-deception. The student caught cheating may point to and exaggerate the cheating of others in an attempt to prevent the lowering of his own status in the eyes of the world. He may be fully aware of his own behavior and quite conscious that his accusation, "everyone is doing it," is only an attempt to lessen his own culpability.

On a slightly different level, a student whose cheating goes undetected by others may actually misperceive cheating by others. This misperception operates to diminish his own feelings of guilt. The individual cheater may go one step farther and condemn others for cheating (even though they are not), and insist to himself and to others that their cheating makes it necessary for him to do the same (rationalized projection). Our competitive culture probably encourages and reinforces this type of projection. A person's limitations are minimized by discovering and exaggerating the greater shortcomings of others.

A person may (as in the above instances) transfer the blame for his shortcomings, mistakes, and misdeeds to other people or things. In doing so, he defends himself against feelings of failure, stupidity, and guilt. "It wasn't my fault; he pushed me first." "He made me do it." "I just had bad luck." "The examination was unfair." "The teacher is too hard." The poor workman blames his tools; the tennis player misses his shot and looks inquiringly at his racquet. The other man gets the job because he is the boss's favorite and has more "pull." The unemployed person, the victim of a vicious economic system, says, "I never had a chance."

These projections may be used with varying degrees of awareness of their motivation. All, to some degree, diminish social disapproval, punishment, or self-devaluation. They help the individual maintain self-esteem and social esteem in the face of failure or threatened ego-deflation.

When projection functions on the most uncritical, unconscious, and self-deceptive level, the individual attributes to others his own unrecognized and unacceptable impulses, thoughts, and desires. On this level he does not recognize, or he completely denies, the existence of his own undesirable characteristics and misperceives these same characteristics in others. The homosexual sees everyone else seducing him and is oblivious to his own homosexual tendencies. The stingy person perceives himself as quite generous but sees others as penurious. The individual is able to deny his own objectionable characteristics and relieve himself of any anxieties concerning his inadequacies; thus he is relieved of both his objectionable traits and his feeling of guilt concerning them (*Goldin, 1964*).

When projected traits are perceived in others, the projector sees these people as forcing themselves and their objectionable traits on him. Paranoid symptoms may represent this type of projection in its most extreme form. The individual has ascribed his own self-accusations to others and now hears someone else accusing him. He hears threats of punishment for crimes of which he now feels entirely innocent. He has projected "self-criticism" to the outside world and then finds it returned to him by the world.

**IDENTIFICATION**

Identification is another defense mechanism that everyone uses to some extent. Implications of personal inferiority may be lessened if a person becomes a part of an organization, or attaches himself to another individual of superior status. The rewards of group identification are somewhat different from those of identification with other individuals (*Brady and Mahoney, 1964; Smith, and Suinn, 1965*).

## Group Identification

An individual's social status is partially *earned* and partially *assigned*. Social status may be earned as the result of one's own achievements, or it can derive partly from his family and other group memberships. His father's occupation, the prestige of his family, and the achievements of his siblings all contribute to his *assigned* social status. As a child grows up he initiates group memberships and enjoys various increments of social esteem from these identifications. He basks in the reflected glory of his school, class, church, professional organizations, fraternity, and social clubs. He participates in the growth and achievements of his football team, his company, or his department within the company. He identifies, in various degrees, with his clique, gang, community, city, state, and nation, and he enjoys a certain assigned social prestige from these group identifications. He acquires a sense of personal adequacy and security from his memberships and these in turn enhance his own self-evaluations.

## Identification with Other Individuals

In addition to identifying with groups, individuals identify with other people in varying degrees. In general, we tend to identify with people who possess characteristics that we admire and would like to possess. In some cases the possession of another's characteristics is not the desired end so much as the goals and satisfactions that can be attained by the individual possessing these characteristics. For example, the young boy may identify with and model himself after his favorite prize fighter because he desires the expensive cars and flashy clothes that he believes prowess in fighting makes possible.

## The Process

The general factors involved either implicitly or explicitly in the process of identification are as follows (*Bronfenbrenner, 1958; Kagan, 1958; Bandura, 1965; Smith and Suinn, 1965; Baxter et al., 1965*): (1) A person observes that someone else (a model, M) possesses or commands certain things (money, power, affection, prestige) that he would like to have. (2) The person believes that if he were like the model, M (possessed certain of his characteristics), he could achieve these desired ends. (3) The person sets out to be similar to M. (4) Whenever the person perceives or is told that he is similar to M, his identification responses (whatever he does to be like M) are rewarded (reinforced).

(5) For the identification to continue indefinitely the person must attain, at least partially, the desirable things that the model possesses and that he hopes to possess. (6) Identification involves the entire personality; "imitation" usually refers to specific acts or skills. The personal and emotional involvement in identification brings about a change in the individual's self-concept.

## Distortions

The patterning of one's behavior after another is not always appropriately selective. The aspiring young fighter may copy the swaggering gait, the manner of speech, and the eating and sleeping habits of his hero rather than following his training and conditioning program, which might be more appropriate. The young girl who wears the same clothes, combs her hair in the identical style, eats the same food, uses the same soap, and frequents the same places as her favorite heroine basks in her idol's reflected glory and achieves a degree of identification, even though these are minor accompaniments of her heroine's success.

The stronger the motivation for identification, the more the individual is apt to overdo, exaggerate, or overgeneralize in his attempts to copy his model. If the level of motivation is sufficiently high, anxiety is evoked. Under these circumstances, the individual copies indiscriminately the irrelevant details of the model's characteristics. If manner of dress becomes the object of imitation, the idol's dress or certain features of it are copied to such an extent that it may seem ludicrous. Such a person may lose status as a result of his over-strenuous efforts to attain it.

The individual strongly motivated to identify with another may over-idealize his model. When this happens he may in effect model himself after an idealized version of the person rather than copy the person himself. Such identification may cease when the discrepancy between the real person and the idealized version is discovered. This is commonly referred to as "discovering the idol's feet of clay."

A person may increase the extent of his identification with another by changing his conception of himself to be more like his concept of his model, or by changing his conception of his model to be more like his own self-concept. The end result of these modifications is to increase the perceived similarity between the person and the model. To the degree that identification with the model is achieved, the person's own self-concept is elevated. When he changes his conception of his model to make it more congruent with his conception of himself, the process also involves projection.

## The Choice of Models

A person's choice of models is largely the result of social influences. For example, the average high school boy's tendency to identify with his father is positively related (r equals .39) to the fact that the mother approves of the father (*Helper, 1955; Bronfenbrenner, 1958*). The mother's approval of her husband makes him a desirable model in the son's eyes; at the same time, her approval of the son's identification with the father reinforces and encourages further identification. It has also been shown that boys with dominant and masculine mothers identify very little with their fathers (*Payne and Mussen, 1956; Distler, 1965*).

On a broader level, the young adolescent's dominant identifications are typically a reflection of the fluctuating ideals and aspirations of his culture and his gang and his own acceptance of these aspirations. His choice of screen characters (the ones with whom he presumes to identify) is more closely related to his aspirations than to the status he currently occupies (*Maccoby and Wilson, 1957*). The most intense identifications occur when he has strong needs for affection or power, feels personally incapable of gratifying these needs, and perceives another person who commands these goals.

### UNDESIRABLE MODELS

Why should we identify with undesirable models such as gangsters, villains, and aggressors, who represent threats to us and to our way of life? Freud (1938) spoke of this as "identification with the aggressor." It has also been called "defensive identification" (*Mowrer, 1950*). It is said to represent the outcome of a desire to possess the power or threat value of the villain or the aggressor. A feeling of power or mastery over the environment makes the individual more secure and less subject to anxiety concerning possible aggressive attacks by others. By identifying with the aggressor he acquires his power, thereby reducing the element of threat (*Distler, 1965*).

## Unconscious Factors

Much of the above discussion makes identification seem more deliberately conscious and less defensive and self-deceptive than the other "defense mechanisms." Identification is defensive to the extent that it represents an attempt to deny one's inadequacy and to obtain a spurious social status and ego-inflation through shining in someone else's reflected glory. It becomes self-deceptive when the individual vicariously participates in his hero's superior status. Identification is unconscious when a person does not recognize what he is doing or why he is doing it.

Identifications may at times be only momentary, transient, and fanciful. Much of our enjoyment of novels, movies, radio, and television derives from a fanciful identification with the character portrayed. We share the adventures, triumphs, the thrills, and experiences of the fictional characters.

## Similarities Due to Factors Other Than Identification

Identification leads to either imaginary or real similarities between people, but not all similarities are due to identification. Common innate mechanisms account for some similarities. When one person starts, another starts also because both are responding to the same loud sound. People walk erect because of common structures rather than because every infant wants to be like his parents. Common experiences account for other similarities (such as acquiring a common language). Some people imitate others to avoid accidents and social embarrassment, and to save time in learning. The observation of others helps in the acquisition of skills and indicates proper social procedures to the naive. In none of these is the individual's primary motivation the enhancement of his feelings of adequacy or the reduction of anxiety incident to the vicarious borrowing of strength from someone else.

## Age Changes in Identifications

Defensive identification normally decreases with age, maturity, increased competence, and a greater feeling of security on the part of the individual. Anxiety arising from a general feeling of inferiority or inadequacy with respect to environmental demands or expectancies is the basic situation giving rise to the development of defense mechanisms of all types. As the individual becomes more competent, as he acquires an inner security, and as he develops a more adequate self-concept, the necessity for identification as defensive behavior diminishes.

## Nondefensive Identifications

Although we have described identification as a defense mechanism, nondefensive identification can occur. When a person correctly perceives some of his own characteristics in another person, and then erroneously assumes that he and the other individual also have other characteristics in common, a certain degree of identification (or projection) is involved. This observed similarity between oneself and another may occur on a purely intellectual and perceptual level without any motive of ego-enhancement or defense. Nondefensive identification is often the result of over-generalization. Like projection, identification based on misperceived similarity can be either defensively motivated or the result of errors in judgment.

### EMOTIONAL INSULATION AND SOCIAL ISOLATION

## Defensive Emotional Insulation

One defense against conflict, tension, and anxiety is to build a shell of emotional passivity around oneself. When one has found active emotional involvement in interpersonal relationships to be too threatening and anxiety-arousing, one may become cold, detached, and aloof as a protective device. Rebuffed by associates, betrayed by friends, jilted by a lover, one withdraws from all emotional involvements. Since giving affection carries the risks of further rejection and disappointment, a solution is neither to accept nor to give affection.

Such defenses may make it possible for the individual concerned to meet others with a superficial "correctness." The social amenities are observed. Many acquaintances are made and superficial friendships are formed, but whenever genuine affection begins to develop, the person feels threatened and retreats to less emotionally involved relationships. Such a person is often lonely and feels a need for love but is unable to give or accept it when the opportunity arises. Individuals so motivated may have a wealth of social *contacts* but still remain affectionally isolated.

## Intellectualization of Social Relationships

Sometimes an intellectualization of one's social relationships may be a defensive means of cutting off normal emotional involvements. It may take the form of cynicism, criticism, or attempts at intellectual analysis and understanding of situations. This detachment protects one from conflicting loyalties, confusing identifications, and personal hurt. The *cynical* approach to threatening situations is to believe that emotional involvements are childish, "soft," and foolish. The truly mature, sophisticated person sees problems coldly, rationally, and analytically! All emotional commitments are equally stupid. The cynic may paradoxically even react emotionally to any implication of emotional involvement on his part.

The more purely intellectualized approach is typified by the "dopester," the one who knows, the one who has the intellectual insights. He is the bystander who analyzes motives, describes movements, assigns reasons, and suggests strategies, but does not become personally committed. He is emotionally detached, rational, and an uninvolved observer.

The critic sometimes elects to play a defensive role. He censures people, finds their weakness, points out their defects, and evaluates their performances. He does this impartially, unemotionally, and without personal commitments or loyalties. Experiences that would normally invite personal loyalties, or that might be strongly emotional or conflictual, are kept isolated and/or insulated.

Intellectualism is dealing with problems and situations cut off from their emotional aspects. It operates as a barrier against anxiety and is contrasted with normal enthusiastic probing of a situation. Intellectual dogmatism may function as a defense mechanism (*Long and Ziller, 1965*).

### DEFENSIVE BEHAVIOR AS ADAPTIVE

Our discussions of defensive behavior usually stress the negative or pathological aspects of defense mechanisms so completely that it is easy to overlook their positive values. Defensive behaviors are not activities engaged in solely by the socially and personally inadequate minority. Everyone uses defensive behavior to some extent. Man is so constituted that for him to live facing stark reality, without any distortion, evasion, or denial, would be too much to endure. A certain "softening of the facts" of life is necessary to make it endurable for even the most competent and secure people. Defensive behavior patterns do have their positive values, and these values are often overlooked.

The defense mechanisms are patterns of adjustment. They are a type of "problem-solving" behavior. The individual, finding his desire for status threatened by evidences of inadequacy, resolves the conflict by explaining away the facts (rationalizing) or by ascribing the inadequacy to someone else (projecting). Although the solution may be of the "blind alley" type, it does handle the immediate situation for the individual and make it possible for him to attend to more important problems. A failure to resolve the conflict in some way will result in continued tension, preoccupation with the problem, and a failure to use his resources to deal with more impelling demands such as earning a living.

The defense mechanisms also operate to keep the pain of intolerable inferiority, unendurable ideas, and threatening perceptions from overwhelming one. This is one of the most important functions of the defensive behavior patterns. They protect the individual from intolerable levels of anxiety. When threats mount and the anxiety level rises, defensive behavior reduces the apparent threat and the level of anxiety drops.

Relatively low levels of anxiety can be tolerated by the individual and may be conducive to constructive and creative effort. Low anxiety levels can motivate learning and constructive problem solving. When stresses are minimal the behavioral effects are alertness, attentiveness, and vigilance. As the stresses build up, anxiety increases to the point where the individual becomes apprehensive and agitated, and finally behavioral disorganization and panic result. A low anxiety level may sustain creative efforts and behavioral progress and lead to the attainment of a reality-anchored feeling of security. Adequate defenses may operate as safety devices, keeping the individual from being constantly upset. They safeguard the integrity and adequacy of one's self-concept.

Although defense mechanisms may themselves at times be maladaptive, by keeping the anxiety level within tolerable limits, they may *prevent more serious maladjustments from developing.* The neuroses (or psychoneuroses) and the psychoses (or insanities) are often conceived of as adjustment to, or defenses against, intolerable and overwhelming anxiety. As already indicated, when stress builds up, threats mount, and the anxiety level becomes unbearable, disorganized panic ensues. The final resolution of the panic reaction may be the development of the many neurotic or psychotic behavior syndromes, which are more severely maladjustive than are the defense mechanisms. The development of adequate minor defenses may protect some people from the more serious psychotic or neurotic defenses.

The defense mechanisms have positive values for the individual. They diminish his feelings of guilt and shame. They help him to maintain a more adequate self-concept. With well functioning defenses, he feels less threatened and more secure, less inferior and more adequate; he is less conscience-stricken and more self-confident. Even when defenses are insufficient to keep some feelings of anxiety from arising, the "total situation" is less painful and more endurable than if a person were entirely free of defensive devices (*Haan, 1965*).

### THE MALADAPTIVE ASPECTS OF DEFENSE MECHANISMS

Most of the maladaptive aspects of the defense mechanism have been either suggested or implied in our discussion of the specific behavior patterns. We shall now discuss the negative aspects of the defense mechanisms more fully.

The frame of reference from which we evaluate the outcome of the defense mechanism is largely culturally determined. It is tied up with what we consider to be "the good life." In America we have idealized the aggressive, straightforward, outgoing behavioral patterns. Our maxims and proverbs say: "The world steps aside for the man who knows where he is going," or "If at first you don't succeed, try, try again." A high value is placed on the extrovertive, offensive behavior patterns. The defensive, avoidance, and withdrawal behaviors are considered undesirable. In a more contemplative culture, where the "material world" is renounced and where autistic behavior is seen as "good," the evaluations of many of our "defense mechanisms" would be quite different.

Our ethical and moral codes condemn anything that smacks of deception, distortion, evasion, or falsification. When we describe the defensive behavior mechanisms in these terms we are, by definition, categorizing them as "bad." Our evaluation of behavior patterns is from a particular cultural and personal frame of reference and will not necessarily hold for all societies and individuals. We shall discuss four ways in which defensive behavior may become handicapping:

(1) The defense mechanisms are not the most effective means of solving problems. They are primarily devices for the circumvention of real problems. They constitute an evasion rather than a real meeting with the situation. The defensive behavior patterns always contain autistic (wish-fulfilling) elements. They transform problems into a more acceptable form. Defensive attempts at problem solving are always second choices. The person's first preference would be to meet and solve problems in an aggressive, straightforward, socially approved way, but either his aptitudes or his self-concept or environmental threats prevent him from doing so. He then resorts to a less satisfactory but better-than-nothing solution to his problems.

(2) The defense mechanisms typically involve a denial or distortion of "reality." The individual either represses or distorts his percepts, thoughts, wishes, desires, and motives. He makes the world over into his own image or, at least, closer to what he would like it to be. His world is, to some degree, a fanciful one.

It is obvious that all perception, thought, and feeling contain autistic and projective elements. The individual, in using these defense mechanisms, simply exaggerates the fanciful components. When his conception of reality becomes too distorted he is "maladjusted."

(3) Each person consciously and/or unconsciously develops tactics for handling his own desires and the forces operating in his environment. In doing so, he develops defense mechanisms that become his habitual ways of meeting inner conflicts and outer stresses. These ways of acting represent part of his personality. Because of their tendency to become unconscious, defense mechanisms are likely to develop into *fixed and rigid behavior patterns*. The constantly defensive individual becomes a victim of his own defenses and loses flexibility. He is driven to rationalize, project, and identify in a compulsive fashion. Behavior patterns become crystallized into a way of life. These early acquisitions become prohibitive of subsequent learning and inhibit spontaneous growth; they tend to be reactionary and resistive of change. We hang onto our defenses just as the man with a broken leg hangs onto his crutches.

(4) The defense mechanisms *preclude objective self-evaluation*. The person who habitually rationalizes, projects, and identifies with others when faced with ego-deflating facts deprives himself of opportunities for and incentives to self-improvement. As long as he remains oblivious to or lacks responsibility for his mistakes and shortcomings, he is not going to do anything to remedy the situation. Without any self-criticism he feels reasonably self-satisfied and not in need of change.

The defense mechanisms are handicaps when they become our only way of handling threats. If a person can meet problems in a straightforward, offensive, or defensive-avoidance pattern, depending upon the demands of the situation; if he can keep a reasonable contact with reality even though there are autistic components to his perception and ideation; if he can remain flexible in spite of a basic core of defensive behavior traits, he is not a slave to his defenses.

### SUMMARY

The defense mechanisms are considered as descriptive categories rather than as explanations of behavior. The original psychoanalytic systematization of the defense mechanisms characterized them as unconsciously motivated, self-deceptive, and operating against anxiety. These three characteristics are still accepted, however the degree of unconscious motivation may vary.

Some of the most common defense mechanisms are: (1) Rationalization—presenting more socially acceptable but fictitious reasons in place of the less socially approved "real" reasons for one's behavior. (2) Projection —defensive ascribing of one's unworthy motives, attitudes, and behaviors to other people or things. (3) Identification—the attempt to improve one's status by shining in the reflected glory of a superior individual or group. (4) Emotional or social isolation—avoiding possible ego-deflation by building a shell of social and emotional insulation around oneself.

Defensive mechanisms are adaptive devices that often have considerable value for the individual.

### REFERENCES

BANDURA, A. Vicarious Processes: A Case of No-Trial Learning. In Berkowitz, L. (ed.) *Advances in Experimental Social Psychology*, Vol. II. New York: Academic Press, 1965.

BAXTER, J. C., LERNER, M. J., and MILLER, J. S. Identification as a function of the reinforcing quality of the model and the socialization background of the subject. *J. pers. soc. Psychol.*, 1965, **2**, 692–697.

BRODY, M. W. and MAHONEY, V. P. Introjection, identification, and incorporation. *Inter. J. Psychoanal.*, 1964, **46**, 57–63.

BRONFENBRENNER, U. The measurement of skill in social perception. In McClelland, D. C., et al., *Talent and Society*. New York: Van Nostrand, 1958.

DISTLER, L. S. Patterns of parental identification: an examination of three theories. University of California: Unpublished dissertation, 1965.

FREUD, SIGMUND. *A General Introduction to Psychoanalysis*. Garden City, New York: Garden City Publishing Company, 1938.

GOLDIN, P. C. Experimental investigation of selective memory and the concept of repression and defense: a theoretical synthesis. *J. abnorm. soc. Psychol.*, 1964, **69**, 365–380.

HAAN, NORMA. Coping and defense mechanisms related to personality inventories. *J. consult. Psychol.*, 1965, **29**, 373–378.

HELPER, M. M. Learning theory and self-concept. *J. abnorm. soc. Psychol.*, 1955, **51**, 184–194

KAGAN, J. The concept of identification. *Psychol. Rev.*, 1958, **65**, 296–305.

LONG, B. H., and ZILLER, C. Dogmatism and predecisional information search. *J. appl. Psychol.*, 1965, **49**, 376–378.

MACCOBY, ELEANOR E., and WILSON, W. C. Identification and observational learning from films. *J. abnorm. soc. Psychol.*, 1957, **55**, 76–87.

MOWRER, O. H. *Learning Theory and Personality Dynamics*. New York: The Ronald Press Company, 1950.

MURSTEIN, BERNARD I., and PRYER, RONALD S. The concept of projection: a review. *Psychol. Bull.*, 1959, **56**, 353–374.

PAYNE, D. E., and MUSSEN, P. H. Parent-child relations and father identification among adolescent boys. *J. abnorm. soc. Psychol.*, 1956, **52**, 358–362.

SEARS, R. R. Experimental studies of projection: II. Ideas of reference. *J. soc. Psychol.*, 1937, **8**, 389–400.

SMITH, T. L., and SUINN, R. M. A note on identification, self-esteem, anxiety, and conformity. *J. clin. Psychol.*, 1965, **21**, 286.

THELEN, M. H. Similarities of defense preferences within families and within sex groups. *J. proj. tech. pers. Assess.*, 1965, **29**, 461–464.

WALLIN, R. Individual estimates of group attitudes. *Psychol. Bull.*, 1941, **38**, 539–540.

# Chapter 3

# Avoidance, Withdrawal, and Compromises

IN THE COURSE OF ORDINARY LIVING, people learn that certain objects and situations in their environments are to be avoided because they produce pain. Very early in life, children learn to avoid objects, persons, and situations that are associated with painful stimulation of one kind or another. Learning to avoid injury associated with pain is a necessary component of life. One way of coping with situations that represent a threat to the organism is to anticipate and avoid the situation. Another is to withdraw from situations that are dangerous or potentially dangerous. Not only physically dangerous things, but psychologically painful or distressing situations must be dealt with by the individual. Avoidance of and withdrawal from physically hazardous situations may result in a direct overt avoidance or escape response. Some fear-evoking or threatening situations may be dealt with in a similar fashion, but there are many psychologically subtle means of coping with such situations. Amnesia, regression, fantasy, neurosis, and many psychotic syndromes may be interpreted as having strong elements of withdrawal and avoidance.

### SIMPLE, OVERT WITHDRAWAL
### AND AVOIDANCE

When confronted with a noxious or threatening situation, an individual typically either attacks the situation or flees from it. Feared or anger-evoking stimuli tend to elicit movement directed either *toward* or *away from* them. When an individual's dominant patterns of behavior are *against threat*, he is said to be aggressive. Aggressive behavior patterns will be discussed in the next chapter. The person whose movements are predominantly *away from threat* is frequently said to be timid or withdrawn. The response patterns of avoidance and withdrawal may be subtle, complex, and self-deceptive or they may be rather straightforward and deliberate.

Not all quiet and retiring people are defensively withdrawn. Many laymen as well as clinicians have become so impressed with the possible pathological effects of excessive repression and introversion that they see all quiet, unpretentious, and meditative people as mentally ill. Because some of our major psychotic syndromes are dominantly withdrawal behavior patterns, nonaggressive and introvertive people are sometimes in danger of being considered sick.

A fifth-grade boy was referred for psychological services because his teacher perceived him as pathologically withdrawn and in need of help. Jerry, the oldest in a family of four children, was ten years and seven months of age. His school work was slightly below average. His grade placement on achievement tests ranged from 4.0 to 5.1. He had an I.Q. in the 90–100 range on various individual and group intelligence tests. In the classroom Jerry never volunteered to recite, but when called upon he responded readily. He participated in most individual and group class activities without noticeable hesitation or embarrassment.

Before and after school and during recess periods, Jerry's activities were decidedly of a solitary nature. He would sit at his desk and read, draw, or play with his model airplanes. On the playground he usually played alone or with one or two other quiet boys. He seldom made overtures toward other boys or groups. When invited to join a group in play, he would usually do so and seemed fairly adequate in such group activities. There was no evidence that Jerry was rejected by other children, but he was rarely sought out by them and practically never joined in group activities of his own initiative.

In direct interview, Jerry related well to the examiner. He responded readily and frankly to all questions but volunteered nothing beyond answers to specific questions. His responses to a sentence-completion test were nonsignificant. He showed a mild concern in the areas of play and work, but his completions disclosed nothing outside the normal range. On the Rogers Test of Personal Adjustment and the Murray Thematic Apperception Test, Jerry's responses were all quite normal, and they largely supported the general impressions and information obtained by direct interview. No areas of significant emotional disturbance or of personal concern were discovered. At this point the examiner saw Jerry as a quiet, soft-spoken, but fairly adequate individual with few, if any, personal or social problems.

A visit to the boy's home disclosed a middle class family. The parents were soft-spoken, quiet, and retiring. They were very cooperative and genuinely interested in their child's welfare. They wanted Jerry to get better grades in school but were reasonably satisfied with him. His leisure-time activities at home were similar to those observed at school. He took responsibility for the supervision and care of his younger brothers and sister.

The general findings indicated that Jerry was displaying in his school behavior a family pattern of quiet, somewhat submissive, retiring activity that was neither defensive in motivation nor maladaptive in outcome. The teacher was over-concerned with possible symptoms of defensive withdrawal among her students and tended to perceive a quiet child as a "sick" child. The significance of withdrawn behavior must be seen within the cultural, subcultural, and family background of the child. There is no one-to-one relationship between bits of behavior and motives. A given act can result from more than one possible motive, and a given motive can produce a great variety of acts. We cannot infer motives from isolated acts or vice versa.

Withdrawal is often a defensive mechanism. When punishment or threat of punishment becomes excessive, isolation may develop as an escape and a tension-reducing device. Simple overt avoidance is frequently the most obvious and the most available means of handling threats and conflicts. Withdrawal may be either an appropriate response to realistically appraised danger or an overgeneralized reaction to people or to any situation in which the individual feels inadequate. Defensive withdrawals, if excessive, may become maladaptive. Withdrawal as a response to threat is a means of social isolation, which reduces or eliminates emotional tensions and anxieties resulting from social frustrations.

### CAUSES OF WITHDRAWAL

As indicated in the case cited above, some children develop a somewhat solitary way of life that may be misinterpreted as defensive withdrawal.

When the significant adults in the child's world are quiet and nonaggressive, when retiring and sedentary activities are expected and reinforced, the child will normally follow the family pattern. The preference of intellectually gifted children for reading and solitary play rather than for more social and competitive games may be partially a reflection of the quiet leisure-time and sedentary professional activities of their parents (*Terman, 1926*).

Prolonged illness, physical handicaps, and previous social isolation may predispose the child to avoid social and competitive activities. Seclusive adjustment may develop as the most satisfactory behavior patterns that a weak, or handicapped, or socially unsophisticated person can achieve. As long as such people find this adjustment satisfactory, do not feel inferior because of their behavior, and do not become so socially withdrawn that they deprive themselves of opportunities for individual development and self-expression, moderate social withdrawal may be the best possible adjustment for them. In many cases, a certain degree of social isolation may be the most intelligent compromise. The person whose socially-isolated behavior results from a prolonged series of reality-oriented learning experiences is not necessarily maladjusted.

The more severe, defensive withdrawal behavior patterns are emotionally induced and serve an anxiety-reducing function. In the broadest terms, the individual who perceives others as sources of pain and discomfort and who finds that social isolation is less painful or less threatening than social contact, will develop withdrawn and seclusive habits of adjustment. Abusive discipline, continual physical punishment, verbal mistreatment, and the withholding or withdrawal of affection as the dominant methods of control in childhood are conducive to the development of rebellion and aggression on the one hand, or fear, timidity, and withdrawal on the other. We are now concerned with the latter reactions.

There is some evidence that inconsistencies in treatment, or changes in a customary level of treatment, are more conducive to anxiety and withdrawal than are perpetually painful or punishing situations. A given level of abuse or punishment is less disturbing to a child if the abuse is a part of the social culture to which he is subjected than if he is the only individual in his family and community who is so treated. Punishment is universal and apparently inevitable; it is perceived as a part of a rough world, but it can and must be endured. When a child is sometimes punished and sometimes rewarded, or when he is punished and another is not, the possibility of punishment-avoidance is indicated. There is evidence that predictable punishment is more tolerable and less anxiety-arousing than random and unpredictable punishment (*Sawrey, 1961*). It seems likely that severe and inconsistent punishment is particularly conducive to withdrawal behavior. If the individual finds that avoidance or withdrawal from fear- or anxiety-arousing social situations reduces these emotions, these behaviors will be perpetuated.

A CASE OF DEFENSIVE WITHDRAWAL

Gwendolyn, age ten, was referred to the school psychologist because of chronic withdrawal. Her teacher reported that she refused to recite, her school work was poor, and she was considered to be emotionally disturbed. Gwendolyn appeared in the office frightened and on the verge of tears. Her teacher of the previous year had also reported that Gwendolyn was uncommunicative, timid, frightened, and unhappy. Her I.Q. from group intelligence tests ranged from 109 (Otis) to 125 (Verbal C.M.M.). Her achievement test scores were considerably above the level of her school grades. She practically never recited in class and her written work was below average. She seemed inhibited and unsure of herself. Her medical history was nonsignificant and the report of a recent physical examination stated, "Gwendolyn _____ is an unusually strong and well-developed girl. She shows no physical defects, no evidence of any diseased conditions or illness."

Gwendolyn had few contacts with her schoolmates. She was usually alone and didn't participate in extracurricular activities. Either her father or a housekeeper left her at school each morning and called for her after school, so she didn't have the simple social contacts gained in walking to and from school. The other girls in her class referred to Gwendolyn as "retiring and quiet."

Gwendolyn's mother was dead and several conferences with her father provided little information. The housekeeper was also uncommunicative. A shrug of her shoulders, a nod of the head, and a few monosyllabic replies were all that could be obtained from Gwendolyn in direct interview. A sad, pathetic, unhappy look was her most constant characteristic.

A home visit disclosed a large, well-furnished, comfortable home. The members of the family, the father, Janet, the older sister, and the maternal grandmother were all affable. The grandmother had lived with the family since the death of the girls' mother two years before. Janet was a vivacious, social, and popular girl who had never experienced any particular problems. Gwendolyn took piano lessons, practiced an hour a day, and occasionally attended concerts and music recitals.

The father, at first, answered all questions concerning Gwendolyn's early history by saying, "She has always been fine. Everything is all right." When the school situation continued to deteriorate, the father came to to the school and confided to the psychologist that Gwendolyn was an adopted child and that her early life had been very unusual. He related the following:

Mr. _____ (Gwendolyn's father) was a member of the American army of occupation stationed in West Germany following the Nazi surrender in World War II. Early one morning while driving a jeep along a narrow street, he found two little girls being taken into custody by a policeman. The policeman was trying to carry a kicking, clawing, biting girl of three to a nearby patrol wagon. Mr. _____ tried to find out the cause of the commotion. From bits of broken English and his meager understanding of German, he discovered that the children's father had been killed during the war and the mother had disappeared a week before. Since that time this three-year-old and her sister, two years older, had lived from refuse picked up on the streets and from garbage cans. The policeman discovered the two children at an early morning hour, cold and weak from lack of food, and was trying to take them to a relief center. The older sister was docile and yielding but Gwendolyn resisted and fought back. Mr. _____ persuaded the policeman to let him take the children to the center. He sat down on the doorstep, held Gwendolyn until she quieted down, and finally she went willingly with him to the center. Mr. _____ visited the girls daily and when his wife joined him in Germany, they legally adopted Gwendolyn. At the end of Mr. _____'s term of duty, they return to the United States with the girl. Gwendolyn had been raised here as their second, but adopted, daughter.

While in the relief center in Germany, Gwendolyn had moved about very little, talked hardly at all, and acted like a frightened, hunted animal. In her adoptive parents' home, she still failed to respond. She feared everyone about her and was constantly on guard. She spent most of her waking hours under her bed. Most of the time, she could be coaxed only to the edge of the bed where she was fed.

It was three years before Gwendolyn began to act like a normal child. To the infinite patience and minimum coercion of her foster parents she gradually responded with affection. She came to idealize her father and would do anything for him. Gwendolyn's progress had been satisfactory until the death of her adoptive mother when she was eight. At that time the maternal grandmother came to live with the family and a housekeeper was hired to do the housework.

With this change in the family constellation, Gwendolyn began to regress. She had periods of depression, kept more to herself, and her school work deteriorated. She became quite concerned about her father's welfare, and seemed afraid that something might happen to him. She would say, "Father, I really do belong to you, don't I?" He would reassure her but she would demand constant reassurance.

Although the maternal grandmother tried to treat the two girls alike and never discriminated against Gwendolyn, she idolized Janet. She would say, "You are looking more like your mother every day," or "Your hair is just the color of your mother's," or "You look just like your mother did when she first met your father." Gwendolyn would leave the room when such remarks were made. It seemed quite clear that her basic feelings of insecurity were being reinstated by the changed circumstances in her home.

Here we have a case of defensive withdrawal whose primary cause is a profound feeling of inferiority dating from a series of traumatic experiences in early childhood. The girl developed a great dependence upon her foster father. The death of her mother, the favoritism of her grandmother, the obvious social superiority of her sister, and the fear of losing her father, all represented threats with which she was unable to cope, and which contributed to the reinstatement of her withdrawal tendencies.

A conference with the members of the household resulted in every effort to give Gwendolyn the assurance that she belonged to and was accepted into the family group without reservation. Everything was done to indicate to her that the family members all loved her for herself and for what she was. The grandmother was the least understanding, but did co-operate to the extent of refraining from constantly mentioning Janet's resemblance to her mother.

She began to feel assured of the genuine affection of those about her, as she had before her mother died. The following summer an extended trip for the 'Happy Three," as the father called them—Gwendoyn, Janet, and the father—did much to reinstate Gwendolyn's feeling of security. The next year her school work and social adjustment showed considerable improvement.

Gwendolyn would probably never be as tolerant of threat as her sister, Janet. Fifteen years later, however, she was happily married and the mother of a fine baby boy. She gave every evidence of stability, and was described by her friends as "a fine wife and an understanding mother."

### REGRESSION (RETROGRESSION)

Regression, as a behavior mechanism, is defined (a) as a return to earlier and less mature behavior, or (b) as a manifestation of more primitive behavior after having learned and behaved in a more mature fashion. Some writers have used the term "retrogression" to refer to the first meaning of regression, a return to earlier habits when more recently acquired ones are blocked. They have called the childish or more primitive behavior following frustration "primitivation." Primitive behavior does not necessarily refer to a person's earlier behavior.

It seems doubtful that the second category of regression actually occurs. Under conditions of high frustration, when the individual's current repertoire of responses is inadequate, there seem to be two alternatives open to him. One of these is to fall back on older response patterns— behavior that has been replaced by more recent and more adequate ways of acting. The other alternative is to develop new ways of handling the frustrating situation (learning.) How "more primitive" behavior, which has never actually been a part of a person's repertoire, could show itself under conditions of stress is not clear. There are two ways to account for the appearance of the supposedly new "more primitive" behavior patterns. The new response may represent a hypothesis or new trial-and-error attempt at problem-solving. It is a frontal attack on the problem, not defensive in nature, and is "primitive" only if it happens to be less promising and less insightful as an approach to the problem than the activities it replaces. Some reversions to earlier behavior patterns, during attempts at straightforward problem solving, may be a return to *more complex* activities. They are not always simpler than the responses they replace (*Masserman, 1946*).

An alternative explanation of the occurrence of new, "more primitive" responses under frustration is that the new activity represents a "throwback" or atavistic return to some hypothetical racially or culturally more primitive behavior. Such a conception postulates the existence of a reservoir of inherited behavior patterns that are potentially arousable under adequate environmental stress. That these inherited tendencies display themselves for the first time rather late in life is a doubtful hypothesis.

We shall use the term regression (retrogression) to mean a return to earlier, less mature, and less appropriate behavior than that which the individual is currently capable of performing. Our discussion of the concept of primitivation has indicated that the term "earlier" in this definition of regression is really superfluous. If a person's *present* repertoire of responses is inadequate to meet the frustrating situation, and if a direct problem-solving (learning) approach in which new solutions might emerge is precluded, the only behaviors that can occur are *earlier* ones. *Regression*, as a defense mechanism, refers to a return to less mature behavior after having learned more mature forms of behavior. It is considered to be anxiety-reducing. Defensive regression tends to be rigid, compulsive, and persistent; reversions to earlier activities during attempts at learning and problem solving remain flexible and modifiable.

## Examples

A wide variety of lower animals have been shown to return to older habits when newer and more efficient ones are thwarted (*Mowrer, 1940; Hamilton and Krechevsky, 1933; Hilgard, 1957*). Examples of regression in human areas are: the wife who goes home to mother whenever marital conflicts arise in her own home; the boy rejected by girls of his own age who returns to his mother for love; the person who breaks down and cries until others soften their demands on him. After the arrival of a new baby into the family, a three-year-old boy ceases talking and walking, becomes enuretic, and has to be fed by someone else when he had previously walked, talked, fed himself and been toilet-trained.

Extreme frustration, experimentally induced during children's play activities, has been shown to reduce subsequent play to a much less mature and constructive level. The children differed tremendously in the extent of their regression, but on the average they regressed to a play level of about one and one half years below their previous play patterns (*Barker et al.,* *1941*).

Catastrophic loss may induce regressive behavior in an adult. A wealthy man loses his fortune in a stock-market crash and is so crushed that he becomes entirely dependent upon his friends, relatives, or charity for his livelihood. He does nothing to recoup his losses or start a new life for himself. He regresses to a childish dependence upon others.

The person who loses his legs in an industrial accident and spends the rest of his life as a whining, complaining, dependent individual, who expects and demands continued sympathy, attention, and care from others, is another example of a regressive individual. The loss of a husband or wife may be met by a prolonged period of mourning, weeping, and protestations of helplessness, and result in the development of a childish overdependence upon friends, relatives, lawyers, doctors, or counselors rather than the acceptance of increased responsibility.

Men exposed to the stress of prolonged combat during war may finally show almost total collapse, regressing to the condition of a terrified child (*Grinker and Spiegel, 1945*).

Even more dramatic regressive phenomena may be seen in some psychotic conditions. Wallin (1949) describes a woman of normal intelligence who, on the death of her husband, was left with considerable wealth and three adolescent daughters. Following the death of her husband, she began to dress and act like her daughters. She adopted her daughters' circle of friends, mingled with them socially, and displayed typical adolescent behavior. Within a short time the mother began to act and dress even more childishly. She became more dependent upon others for her care. Soon she was dressing in short dresses and pigtails and spent most of her day rocking in a chair. She began acting like a six- or seven-year-old child. She talked childishly, played with toys, and enjoyed playing infantile jokes on others. Within an additional few months she regressed to a three- or four-year-old level. She had to be fed, soiled herself, ceased reading, and talked poorly. A few months later she behaved like an infant, stayed in bed, ceased talking, whined, cried, and played with a rolled-up towel as if it were a doll. At the time of her death some years later in an institution, she had regressed to the point where she maintained a purely vegetative existence.

Many of the symptoms of senile dementia (a psychosis of old age) are regressive in character. The "second childhood" characterization of this condition is suggestive of some of its regressive aspects. This regression of senility is partially the result of organic deterioration. The return to the infantile grasping reflex is typical of the reversion to earlier behavior patterns found in senile dementia; it presumably has an organic basis.

## Significance of Regression

Regression is a type of defensive withdrawal response to threat and anxiety. The individual, feeling threatened and inadequate, attempts to return to an adjustment level or condition where his inadequacies are less apparent. In the midst of insecurity he seeks to return to a period or condition of past security. His equilibrium is destroyed and he reverts to a simpler level of adjustment in an attempt to reestablish his equilibrium. By adopting a younger and less demanding definition of himself, he excuses his behavior to himself and to others and thereby achieves some degree of self-enhancement. The threats to his self-esteem and his social self are no longer so great. He receives some degree of comfort and reassurance in his implied redefinition of himself. Since he is young and helpless others will expect less of him.

Regression, like most defense mechanisms, can function at all levels of awareness. At one extreme, a person may revert to more childish levels of behavior in a conscious bid for special consideration as a young and helpless individual. Helplessness and immaturity are socially acceptable excuses for not assuming responsibility, for failure to achieve, and for demanding special attention, consideration, and sympathy. The individual may be quite aware that his regressive behavior is calculated to achieve these results. At the other extreme, the regressive behavior of the three-year-old, the disorganized and childlike behavior of the terrified soldier, and the functional component of the reversions of the psychotic individual to the life of an infant are probably unconsciously motivated. The individuals displaying these behavior patterns normally have no insight into what they are doing or why they are doing it.

## Conditions Conducive to Regression

If favorable experience with childish behaviors continues beyond the age when such behavior is appropriate, regression is encouraged. The infant learns that fussing and crying are a means of obtaining attention and solicitude. If at an older age shouting, whining, and throwing temper tantrums are still successful means of obtaining pampering and indulgences, such childish behavior patterns are encouraged. The child who is overindulged and over-protected when young, and then finds life at a later age very demanding and threatening will be inclined to meet hardships and discouragement by returning to his golden period of early childhood. Elizabeth Aker Allen indicates this desire when she says:

> Backward, turn backward, O Time in your flight.
> Make me a child again just for tonight!
> Mother come back from the echoless shore,
> Take me again to your heart as of yore.

There is some evidence that the selective nature of memory is conducive to regressive behavior. Most of the experimental studies indicate that there is a tendency for people to remember more of the pleasant than the unpleasant experiences of their pasts (*Dudycha and Dudycha, 1941*). This selective retention of pleasant memories results in adolescents' seeing childhood as a period of bliss, and adults' thinking of adolescence and childhood as times of great happiness. The excessively rosy retrospective view of earlier periods of life has been called the "Old Oaken Bucket" delusion after the song which says: "How dear to this heart are the scenes of my childhood, when fond recollection presents them to view."

### WITHDRAWAL FROM REALITY

We have shown how overt timidity and shyness result in social isolation, which develops as a means of reducing emotional tension and anxiety caused by social frustrations. This social isolation does not typically involve any particular distortion of, or withdrawal from, reality. Regression as a form of *defensive* physical withdrawal usually implies some distortion of reality. In fantasy as a defense, there is still more distortion. There is an attempt at partial or complete withdrawal, which takes the form of the substitution of an imaginary world for the real one.

## Fantasy and Daydreaming

Daydreaming is apparently a universal human activity (*Singer and McCraven, 1961*). Much of the average person's daydreaming is casual ideation related to immediate concrete situations, transient problems, and interests; it has only a limited future reference. Such daydreaming is closely tied to reality and is neither autistic (wish-fulfilling) in nature nor defensive in purpose. Much fantasy of this type contributes to problem solving and is personally and socially useful.

In addition to the casual, unsystematic, reality-anchored fantasy, day-dreaming also may be systematic and defensive. Systematic daydreams tend to follow certain lines for a given person. Themes tend to be repeated and are related to the persisting needs of the individual. Such systematic daydreams are dominantly wish-fulfilling in nature and are defensively motivated. They take characteristic forms sufficiently often to be given names. The two most common are the "conquering-hero" and the "suffering-hero" forms.

### THE CONQUERING-HERO DAYDREAM

In this type of revery the central figure or hero is the dreamer himself and the motive dominating the dream is the desire for prestige or esteem. The dreamer envisages himself performing outstanding feats of daring, strength, skill, or self-sacrifice. The aspiring young athlete sees himself going into the baseball game in the last half of the ninth inning with the score tied and all bases full. He hits the home run that brings in all of the men and wins the game. He then receives the acclaim that he desires. The individual in his daydreams may become an opera star, concert performer, dancer, noted scientist, or skillful financier. The unfulfilled desires and unrealized ambitions of the dreamer manifest themselves in the systema-tized daydream. The conquering-hero daydream is a means of obtaining vicarious compensatory satisfactions. It either provides a sense of increased adequacy or diminishes one's feeling of inadequacy. When a person feels threatened by inadequacy and his level of anxiety mounts, he may be able to reduce his anxiety through imaginary achievements.

### THE SUFFERING-HERO DAYDREAM

The motivation for the suffering-hero type is not obvious at first glance. To picture oneself as jilted by one's sweetheart, mistreated by parents, mis-understood by one's friends, and persecuted by society would seem to be ego-deflating in nature. However, the motive of self-enhancement is prob-ably operative in this type of daydream just as it is in the conquering-hero form. The suffering-hero daydream always contains an element of self-vindication or ego-enhancement.

In his dream, a young boy feels unjustly punished or restricted by his parents and pictures himself as goaded to the point where he is forced to run away from home, whereupon, he takes a job to support himself, has an accident, and is terribly hurt. His sorrowful parents then come to him and admit that they really should not have punished him. He was right and they were wrong. He thus returns home a vindicated, if wounded, hero.

In another dream of this type, after being spurned by his best girl, the boy leaves home and goes to another city where all the girls flock to him. He marries the most gorgeous girl that he can imagine. He then returns to his home town to display his prize to his former sweetheart.

When a person, in his revery, greatly exaggerates the extent of his persecution by others, his self-esteem may be enhanced either by his subsequent vindication when their persecution is *proven* to be unjust or by the implication that he must really be a very important person to warrant such attention. The suffering-hero form of daydream thus protects the person against implications of inferiority and enhances his self-esteem just as the conquering-hero daydream does.

### BORROWED FANTASIES

The average individual does not fabricate all of his daydreams; he has many of them supplied ready-made by others and participates in them vicariously. These prefabricated daydreams are the fictions supplied by novels, short stories, movies, radio, television, and stage shows. In stories of romance, adventure, and great achievement the reader or viewer can vicariously live adventurously or romantically, or become skilled and highly esteemed. The popularity of the Horatio Alger from-rags-to-riches-success-story in America is a reflection of our cultural values and the aspirations of our youth. The fact that a large segment of popular fiction is known as "escape literature" is evidence of its fanciful wish-fulfilling nature.

When an individual derives satisfactions vicariously from fiction, a combination of identification and fantasy is involved. The person selectively identifies with the fictional characters and then in fancy enjoys their power, prestige, and accomplishments.

### REASONS FOR THE WIDESPREAD USE OF FANTASY

One reason for the popularity of revery as a defense device is its availability. It can be engaged in by anyone at any time provided he is not too preoccupied with other activities. No one else need know that one is daydreaming. It requires no equipment, practically no energy, no permission from others, and but little time. Daydreaming is one of the most universally available of the defense mechanisms.

Another advantage of daydreaming as compared with overt behavior is the absence of risk. When a person has performed an overt act he can never "undo" it. He can do it again, he can say he is sorry he did it or wish he had not done it, but he can never revoke the performance of the act. This means that the performance of every overt act carries some risk. It could be a mistake. It may have unfortunate, irrevocable consequences. Imaginary acts avoid these risks. In fantasy, one's choice can always be right, and mistakes do not occur. One's knowledge and skills are always completely adequate.

An additional advantage of imaginary achievements is the absence of any accompanying or resulting unpleasantness. In fantasy, pleasures exist without pain, success comes without effort or fatigue. Time is collapsed or annihilated; consequently one's needs can be immediately and completely taken care of with no compensating disadvantages.

## Schizophrenia as Psychotic Withdrawal

Schizophrenia is the most common form of psychosis. Although the fundamental nature of schizophrenia has yet to be fully determined, this psychosis is commonly described as the most extreme form of withdrawal from the world of reality to a realm of fantasy. To define schizophrenia as simply a withdrawal behavior pattern certainly oversimplifies the matter, but the various schizophrenic syndromes do contain large withdrawal components.

### CHARACTERISTICS

There are many subvarieties of schizophrenia that exhibit a tremendous diversity of symptoms. Some workers are so impressed by this that they doubt the usefulness of a single category for all forms of the disorder. However, the majority of workers feel that the different varieties of schizophrenia have enough in common to justify giving them a common name, and assume that the many forms have a common origin.

Some lines of research indicate that organic and biochemical factors are either contributory or basic causes of schizophrenia (*Coleman, 1964*). However, this psychosis has traditionally been classed with the functional (impaired performance not caused by pathological structural changes) as opposed to the organic psychoses (mental illness attributed to organic, usually brain, pathology). Schizophrenia is generally conceived of as a disturbance of one's relationships with people. As a result of this disturbance the individual withdraws from social participation, retires into himself, and lives largely in his own private world of thoughts and fantasies. This withdrawal is accompanied by a general, and often progressive, personality disorganization and a breakdown of rational thinking and adaptive behavior. Whether the personality disorganization, bizarre ideation, and irrational behavior are the result of unsatisfactory social relationships (defenses against threats) or the disturbed social relationships and withdrawal are caused by the personality, ideational, and behavioral disorganization is still in doubt. The consensus seems to favor the first of these alternatives, that disturbed social relationships are the primary factors and that the social withdrawal and inappropriate affect, disturbed ideation, and bizarre behavior are their natural consequences.

Historically, four subgroups of schizophrenia have been recognized. However, recently there have been two opposite movements with regard to classification of the groups. Some workers propose to do away with any classification of schizophrenia into subclasses. In fact, they conceive of all mental illness as essentially the same in quality, although differing quantitatively and in external manifestations. Such a unitary concept of mental illness sees psychosis as differing only in degree from "normal" personality organization. Mental illness ranges from mild degrees of personality disorganization and slight impairment of adaptive control, through chronic detachment of the individual from his environment and a "freezing" of a set of handicapping coping devices into the classical "neurotic syndromes," to the extremes of personality disorganization displayed in acute psychotic reactions and in the progressive deterioration of chronic psychosis. This sequence is perceived as a continuum differing only in severity and reversibility (*Menninger, 1963*). It is also suggested that we dispense with the conventional names assigned to the classical syndromes of mental illness. However, if we are to deal with adjustment patterns and coping devices conceptually, the use of some type of classification is inevitable. If we go beyond the endless minute descriptions of an infinite number of individual cases, the grouping of people into categories in terms of behavior syndrome is necessary as an economizing principle, if for no other reason.

Recently, because of the great heterogeneity of schizophrenic patients, and the failure of diagnosis in terms of classical categories to have any prognostic or therapeutic implications, a two-fold process-reactive classification has gained rather wide acceptance. Malignant-benign, chronic-acute, and chronic-episodic are alternative terms that have been suggested to describe these two syndromes.

Process (malignant or chronic) schizophrenia is characterized by a long-term progressive deterioration of the adjustment patterns of the individual, a poor premorbid social adjustment, a gradual and insidious onset, and an absence of any clear precipitating factors. Signs of the illness are present early in life and include social isolation with little interest in others, emotional blunting, affective flattening, disturbances in thinking, excessive fantasy in childhood, and interest patterns that are lacking in intensity and direction. The process schizophrenic's social history is one of rather general inadequate sexual, social, and occupational adjustment. The prognosis for process schizophrenics is poor.

The typical reactive (benign, acute, episodic) schizophrenic, on the other hand, has a relatively normal premorbid personality and social adjustment pattern. His developmental patterns are within the normal range. His sexual, social and occupational interests and activities have not been noticeably deviant. The early prodromal signs present in the process schizophrenics are usually absent. The onset of psychotic reaction patterns is sudden, and precipitating stresses or experiences can usually be identified. The reactive schizophrenic is more amenable to treatment than the process schizophrenic, and prognosis is relatively good (*Heron, 1962; Zigler and Phillips, 1962; Coyle and Coyle, 1965; Donovan and Webb, 1965; Johnson, 1966; Spohn and Wolk, 1966*).

Many recent investigators have taken exception to the proposition that the process-reactive distinction represents a true dichotomy. They believe that classic process and reactive schizophrenia represent the extremes of the continuum and that all gradations exist between its end points (*Zigler and Phillips, 1962; Johnson, 1966*). It has also been shown that process and reactive schizophrenics can be differentiated in terms of the family patterns from which they come and the types of schedules of social reinforcement (rewards and punishments) that they have experienced (*Coyle and Coyle, 1965; Donovan and Webb, 1965*). There is also considerable evidence that the process-reactive distinction is applicable to all psychopathology and is not peculiar to schizophrenia. Some selected case studies will help clarify the distinction between process and reactive schizophrenia.

A CASE OF REACTIVE SCHIZOPHRENIA

One of the authors was asked to see a fifteen-year-old high school boy whose changed behavior was causing his parents considerable concern. Peter was a physically normal boy of better than average intelligence. He had recently refused to attend school. In fact, he could hardly be induced to leave his home. He had to be continually urged even to get out of bed and dress himself. He spent most of the day sitting in the kitchen, and conversed only in monosyllables.

Peter's history was not particularly revealing. He was the only boy in the family, the second of five children. His father was a high school teacher; his mother kept house and gave private music lessons. The father was the dominant parent. The sisters all seemed to be well adjusted, and there was no history of mental illness in the family lines.

Peter had always been a better than average student. His participation in social and athletic activities had been quite normal. He was on the high school tennis team and went out for track. Early in the second semester of the previous school year he was injured in a car accident. His left foot was crushed and he spent several weeks in the hospital. Although the general prognosis was favorable, his left foot was stiff and it was doubtful that he would ever be able to participate in competitive athletics. He had missed so much school that it would be necessary for him to repeat his second semester courses.

Peter's specific trouble had begun at the end of summer vacation, about six months before he was first seen by the author. He had not wanted to return to school in September. After considerable urging he had started school, but had done practically nothing except to attend classes sporadically and answer questions in monosyllables. When his teachers insisted that he turn in his homework, he handed in sheets of paper with a few random scribblings on them.

When the author visited him in the kitchen of his home, Peter was dressed in old, dirty slacks and a ragged sweater. He wore no socks, and his shoes were unlaced and run-down. At first he would not talk. When he finally responded to questions nothing more than a "yes," "no," "It's O.K.," or "I don't know," was elicited. He spoke in a flat monotone. His face was expressionless throughout the interview.

Peter was referred to a psychiatric clinic, which recommended hospitalization. After nine months of individual and group psychotherapy, he was able to return home and re-enter school. In the two years since, he has had no recurrence of his trouble. The sudden onset of the disorder, reasonably normal pre-psychotic adjustment, dominance of the male parent, and the presence of precipitating factors all indicate that Peter's psychosis was at the reactive end of the process-reactive continuum. His good response to therapy is also consistent with the generally favorable prognosis for the reactive types.

A CASE OF PROCESS SCHIZOPHRENIA

Alice, a female of 22 years of age, was admitted to the psychiatric ward of a general hospital six months ago. Attempts at psychotherapy were unsuccessful and she continued to deteriorate. During this time she talked a good deal, but most of what she said was incoherent. Her speech was interspersed with spells of silly and inappropriate laughter. At times she became quite excited, jumped up and down, and ran around the room. Occasionally she sat in a corner of the ward muttering to herself, grimacing, smiling, and periodically bursting forth with silly laughter. Ward attendants gained the impression that the patient experienced hallucinations, but the reports were so disconnected that it was impossible to tell whether or not this was true. The facial grimacing, talking to herself, repetitive and apparently meaningless gestures, and an abnormal interest in the eliminative processes have increased during the six months that Alice has been hospitalized. The over-all picture is that of a young lady slowly regressing into a bizarre fantasy world.

Alice was described by her teachers as a "timid withdrawn child." Despite average intelligence, she repeated one grade and dropped out of high school at the end of her freshman year after failing two courses. Her parents reported that they were quite concerned when Alice had two "spells" during her last year in school. During these "spells" she refused to leave her room and for an entire day sat on the floor muttering to herself, seemingly out of contact with the external world. When she was eighteen, Alice left home and found employment as a waitress. She lived alone in a rented room. In two years she worked at six different places. Her employers uniformly reported her to be "moody," uninterested in her work, and unable to get along with the other employees.

Two years prior to her hospitalization, Alice became careless in her speech, dress, and work, and had prolonged spells of shallow laughter. When asked what was funny she would either say that she did not know or give some childish, irrelevant answer. When she became unable to work or to live alone, her parents took her home and cared for her until her hospitalization.

Alice's parents, teachers, and employers described her as excessively rigid and methodical in all areas of her life. She was perfectionistic in many small and relatively unimportant ways. She was overcritical of other people, and brooded over her own shortcomings. She was the younger of two daughters. Her father was a semiskilled laborer who was periodically out of work because of a series of chronic illnesses. The mother worked regularly as practical nurse, provided the principal support for the family, and was the dominant parent.

This case falls somewhere near the extreme process end of the reactive-process schizophrenic continuum. Alice shows, in rather extreme form, the process characteristics of gradual onset, chronicity, poor pre-psychotic adjustment, and absence of any apparent precipitating factors. These characteristics, combined with her failure to respond to six months of treatment, all indicate a poor prognosis.

SIGNS OF WITHDRAWAL

The aspects of the development and manifestation of the schizophrenic syndrome that fit into the withdrawal pattern are as follows:

(1) The process schizophrenic breakdown commonly comes as the culmination of a history of unsuccessful social and personal adjustments (*Jenkins, 1952; Lundin, 1965*). The typical childhood home atmos-

phere of the schizophrenic is described as oppressive, hostile, in-consistent, and either subtly or directly dominating or indifferent (*Sheiver et al., 1957*). Such a background is conducive to with-drawal as a defense.

(2) Disturbed family relations and unhealthy family patterns are com-mon features of schizophrenic individuals. The mothers of schizo-phrenic patients have typically been found to be perfectionistic, moralistic, rejecting, dominating, over-anxious, and over-possessive (*Coleman, 1964; Clandy, 1951; Gerard and Siegel, 1950; Freeman and Grayson, 1955*). Although the fathers of schizophrenics are generally described as inadequate and either indifferent or passive (*Coleman, 1964; Despert, 1938; Hajdw, 1940*), there is evidence that the family patterns of male and female schizophrenic patients are different (*Fleck et al., 1963*). A "weak, ineffectual father" is more significant for the offspring than a "weak, ineffectual mother" because of the differing traditional sex roles of the mother and father. Similarly, a "cold, unyielding" mother is more of a problem than is a "cold, unyielding" father. The weak father as a parental model is a contradiction and more a source of conflict for the son than for the daughter, whereas the cold mother affects the girl as an inap-propriate model.

(3) An aberration of family communication known as the "double bind" has been found to characterize many families of schizophrenics. For example, in the double bind situation, the parent keeps telling the child, "Don't be so obedient," or to be more independent or mature, and yet will not permit him to do so. What is done contradicts what is said. The child is so dependent on the parent (binder) that he is unable to acknowledge the contradiction, but he feels that he can neither ignore nor fail to respond in the paralyzing situation. The disorganizing effect of the double bind varies with the emotional relation between the victim and the binder. Schizophrenia is con-sidered to be a means of escape by withdrawal from an untenable situation. In the realm of fantasy, meanings and reality can be altered and the ambiguities of the world reduced. The causes of the flight from reality are found in the nature of the social realities with which the patient has lived (*Fleck, 1960; Lundin, 1965; Laing, 1964*).

(4) A relative lack of the social give-and-take necessary for normal reality testing is found in the social histories of many schizophrenics. The lack of normal family relationships results in a failure to develop the necessary social skills and emotional attitudes necessary for healthy social participation. The preschizophrenic often acquires unrealistic conceptions of his own social roles and develops a self-concept con-siderably at variance with others' conception of him. Because of a lack of constant checks on his own frame of reference there develops an ever-widening gap between the schizophrenic and other people.

His thought and language patterns become progressively more individual and he becomes "an emotional stranger in a strange land" *Ellsworth, 1951; Moran, 1953; Whiteman, 1954*).

(5) Many schizophrenic behavior characteristics are regressive in nature. Some investigators have considered regression the basic mechanism underlying schizophrenic reactions (*Coleman, 1964; Brown, 1940*). The schizophrenic's thinking regresses form an abstract, conceptual level to a primitive "concrete" form (*Kasanin, 1945; Levy, 1943; Johnson, 1966; Goldstein, 1943*). His deterioration in personal, social, and ethical behavior is also part of a general picture of regression.

(6) Many other schizophrenic symptoms are defensive in nature. The schizophrenic's emotional apathy can operate as a protective shell to prevent disappointment and frustration. Regressions, as previously indicated, reduce his level of expectancy, diminish his disappointments in life, and justify his acceptance of a position of dependency. His wish-fulfilling fantasies provide him with compensatory achievements and status symbols. His delusions of being controlled or influenced by other people or things enables him to escape responsibility for his own inadmissible thoughts and inadequate behavior. Delusions of persecution project his own hostile impulses to other people, and he places the blame for his defensive behavior on his enemies. Delusions of grandeur compensate for the psychotic's feelings of inadequacy and deny his inferiority. Hallucinations may similarly represent the projection of the person's own unacceptable thoughts, wishes, and impulses into the external world, thus freeing him of any responsibility for them and justifying his bizarre behavior.

### ADJUSTMENT BY AILMENT

No one will admit that he wants to be ill. Illness, by definition, is bad. However, illnesses, or the symptoms of illness, have their advantages. Sickness can operate as a defense mechanism because of its social effects. Some of its consequences, which are conducive to its utilization as a defense, are as follows:

(1) Illness operates as a socially acceptable excuse for evading many of life's problems.

(2) It serves as a means of avoiding responsibility and provides a plausible excuse for the absence of achievement.

(3) Illness is a means of obtaining a relaxation of discipline and of avoiding blame and punishment.

(4) Increased attention, sympathy, and care are normal consequences of being ill.

(5) Bizarre, unusual, or baffling illness may provide a patient uniqueness or status.

(6) Illness may be perceived as a punishment, which relieves anxiety that springs from a sense of guilt.

MALINGERING

Illness, or the development of the symptoms of illness, may be either consciously or unconsciously motivated. Malingering is the conscious feigning of illness or physical disability. It always involves deliberate deception. In the conversion reactions (hysteria), neurasthenia, and less certainly in the psychosomatic disorders, the motivation for illness is largely unconscious. It is quite possible that habitual conscious malingering may gradually shift to the more unconsciously motivated hysterical, neurasthenic, and psychosomatic manifestations. If this occurs, there then exist all levels of consciousness in the motivation of the functional manifestation of the symptoms of physical illness or organic disability. Malingering constitutes the most highly conscious level of motivation; the hysterical, neurasthenic, and psychosomatic symptoms are more unconsciously motivated.

The child who pretends to have a headache in order to avoid attending school when he is unprepared is malingering. The girl who feigns illness on the night of her dreaded recital is doing likewise. There are few people who have not at some time pretended that they were sick as a means either of avoiding threatening and potentially unpleasant situations or of obtaining special consideration of some sort. In cases involving disability claims or lawsuits for compensation following accidents, the possibility of malingering is always present.

In such cases three or four possibilities are always operative: (1) the disability may be a genuinely organic one; (2) the disorder may be either purely functional (neurotic); or (3) the individual may be simply pretending (malingering) in order to obtain either compensation or some other advantage; (4) organic, functional, and malingering components may all be present simultaneously in varying degrees. They are not mutually exclusive.

Malingering is a conscious maneuver designed to defend one's status and either prevent ego-deflation or contribute to one's status. It is a means of obtaining protection, exemptions, special privileges, and rewards via deliberate deception.

## Psychosomatic Disorders

There is some question concerning the defensive nature of psychosomatic disorders. Psychosomatic disorders are commonly defined as psychogenic or functional disorders having organic or physiological symptoms and (potentially) producing harmful structural alterations. In contrast to *neurosis*, the organic or physiological symptoms in the psychosomatic disorders do not relieve anxiety and do not symbolize a repressed desire or wish (*English and English, 1958*). If the term psychosomatic disorder is limited to those organic malfunctions of psychogenic origin which *do not reduce or relieve anxiety*, it seems to eliminate those symptoms which operate directly as defenses. Defense mechanisms are generally considered to operate as anxiety-reducing devices. Since every physical illness and every symptom of physical illness may be utilized by the individual experiencing them for defensive purposes, and since many people suffering from psychosomatic disorders do use their symptoms in that way, we shall discuss them in this chapter.

If the term is taken literally, the category of psychosomatic disorders is much broader than the definition given above. The term when defined literally can be used to refer to any disturbance in which functional (usually emotional) maladjustment results in organic changes or dysfunction of some physiological system. This broad definition would include every disorder in which psychic (functional) and somatic (organic) factors both play a part. This would include practically everything a person does. In practice, the term is not given such a broad meaning.

In common usage, the psychosomatic disorders are those organic dysfunctions having functional (usually emotional) causes. The term is further limited to the malfunctioning of those organs or parts of the organs controlled directly or indirectly by the autonomic nervous system. The autonomic nervous system controls the smooth muscles and glands of the body. Thus the more common psychosomatic disorders involve primarily the gastrointestinal tract, the circulatory, respiratory, and genito-urinary systems, and various other regulatory processes. The classical neurotic syndromes (hysteria, neurasthenia, and psychasthenia) are excluded from the psychosomatic category, although the line between these two groups is often a tenuous one (*White, 1956*).

DISTINGUISHING CHARACTERISTICS

A listing of some of the characteristics of psychosomatic disorders as indicated by the common usage of the term may help us go beyond the stage of formal definition.

(1) As already indicated, psychological (functional) as well as somatic (organic) factors are necessary for a given disorder to be called "psychosomatic."

(2) Emotion is typically the functional or psychological component that acts as the precipitating factor.

(3) Certain personality types are predisposed to psychosomatic disorders. Some workers believe that certain types of personality are associated with particular psychosomatic disorders. For example, outwardly calm and efficient but repressed people develop ulcers, whereas overanxious and insecure people develop asthma. This latter concept of specificity is less generally accepted than the first, more general, proposition. This will be discussed more fully later in the chapter.

(4) Most psychosomatic disorders tend to come and go; they are phasic in their manifestations.

(5) As compared with the neuroses, the psychosomatic disorders are less defensive, less symbolic, and less directly anxiety-reducing. The defensive function of the psychosomatic symptoms are secondary rather than primary gains for the patient. The psychosomatic disorders often represent organ-involvement in a biological pattern of offense or defense in response to threat. (Stomach ulcers are the direct result of the hypersecretion of gastric juice which may be incident to prolonged worry or anxiety.)

### COMMON PSYCHOSOMATIC DISORDERS

Every part of the body that has smooth muscle or glandular components (controlled by the autonomic nervous system) can be involved in the psychosomatic disorders. Since almost all of the organs of the body do have some components under autonomic nervous system control, they are all subject to emotional involvement. This means that all bodily reactions in either health or disease may involve a psychological (functional) factor of varying intensity. The conditions most commonly recognized as psychosomatic in nature are: the common allergies (exzema, hay fever, asthma), ulcers, colitis, and hypertension (high blood pressure).

*Eczema.* Mr. R. P., age 30, had suffered from eczema on his neck and the backs of his hands for the seven years of his married life. Diet, X-ray therapy, and medication had been of no avail. He was a lawyer. He had been a very good student, graduating second in his class of 85. Although he had shown great promise, he was unable to establish himself as a trial lawyer. His practice was insufficient to support him and his wife and he felt they could not afford to have children. His wife taught school and became the principal support of the family. Mr. R. P. was very disturbed by the idea of having to depend upon his wife for his livelihood. Whenever he was working on a law case he would become excited and tense. His eczema would get worse and he would scratch his hands and neck until they bled. If he bandaged the affected areas, he would pull off the bandages in his sleep. The intensity of the eczematous reaction varied directly with the emotional intensity of his day.

After seven unsuccessful years in private practice, Mr. R. P. obtained a position with a large law firm. He then had a regular salary and did not have the primary responsibility of pleading cases before the courts. Six months after securing this position, his wife stopped work. He became a much more relaxed person, and all traces of his eczema vanished.

The skin is an organ of expression as well as a receptor surface. It reflects the emotional tensions of the individual. Changes in circulation, perspiration, and pilomotor activity are all subject to emotional influences. In a reactive individual the degree of eczematous reaction may be directly related to his state of emotional tension.

*Asthma.*   Harold is 27 years old, single, unemployed and living with his parents. He has suffered from asthma most of his life. His first attack occurred when he was hospitalized for influenza at the age of two. His asthmatic attacks were infrequent but became increasingly severe at the age of six and reached a peak when he was thirteen. Extensive skin tests were made and he was given hyposensitization injections for the next five years. He continued having periodic attacks. He was drafted into the army but after six months was discharged because of his asthmatic attacks. Following his discharge from the army he took cortisone and ACTH, but felt that the medication made him worse. He held several jobs for short periods but he had to quit each job because his asthma became more severe.

When he was scheduled for psychological testing, his asthma also increased in severity. After a year of psychotherapy Harold started work as a free-lance commercial artist. His work increased enough so that he was supporting himself and left home. He was free of attacks for a period of six months and decided to discontinue his therapy. A year later he was still at work and had had only two minor asthmatic attacks.

The relationship between periods of environmental stress and the asthmatic attacks, the failure of the attacks to respond to medication and injections for hyposensitization, and the cessation of the attacks following psychotherapy all suggest that the asthma was at least partially functional (emotional) in origin.

*Hay fever.*   A girl of seventeen first developed hay fever at the time of her graduation from high school. Graduation meant leaving home to attend college. She had always been extremely close to her mother. During her college years her hay fever improved while she was away at school but would return each fall when her departure from home was imminent. It became very severe upon graduation from college. This time she felt that she was really leaving home for the big world, and she experienced considerable anxiety at the prospect. The girl continued her close ties with her mother for the next five years while she worked in her home town and lived at home. In her late twenties she married, whereupon her hay fever became much worse, only to disappear entirely during the period of her three pregnancies. Within a few weeks of the birth of her third child, her father died and her mother became seriously ill with little prospect of surviving. The patient's hay fever became severe and constant and has continued to the present. With each critical step in her life, with each difficulty, she desired to return to the warmth, protection, and devotion of her mother. She did not give in to her wish but reacted to the stress by an attack of hay fever.

ORGANIC AND FUNCTIONAL ASPECTS

There is still considerable difference of opinion concerning the exact role played by emotional factors as contrasted with organic sensitivity factors in the precipitation of allergic reactions. The following facts indicate that factors other than organic sensitivity to allergic agents are involved in allergic reactions:

(1) Allergic patients do not always react to the allergens to which they are sensitive.

(2) Sensitive patients often develop typical allergic attacks when there is no evidence of the presence of the provoking allergen.

(3) The allergic reactions of many patients vary directly with their emotional states.

In many cases, such as the preceding one, the relationship between emotional tension and allergic reactions is so marked as to indicate a causal relationship between the two. Suggestion and expectation can also induce typical allergic reactions in susceptible people. For example: Hay fever in rose-pollen sensitive people may be brought on by the sight of an artificial rose, and asthma may be induced by the sight of a dust cloud on a movie screen.

The other side of the picture can also be demonstrated. The injection of an allergen into a sensitive subject can induce a reaction in a person who is ignorant of the nature of the injection and who will not react to similar injections of allergens to which he is not sensitive.

The evidence indicates that in psychosomatic allergic reactions both organic sensitivity and emotional factors are usually involved. The emotional conditions affect the general resistance of the person to disease and his reactiveness to allergic agents or inflammatory processes. The sensitivity of some people is so great that a minimal amount of the allergen itself without any lowering of the threshold of reactivity by emotions will cause an allergic reaction. Such individuals will react to the allergens whenever they are present, even in very small quantities. The emotional state of the person may influence the extent of the reaction but is not necessary for its induction. The allergic reactions in such people are not called psychogenic or psychosomatic.

Some people have a relatively high threshold of reactivity. They can withstand ordinary contact with or ingestion of allergenic agents without reacting to them provided their resistance is at a normal level. However, when emotional conditions lower the threshold for allergenic reactions, they react to levels of stimulation to which they are normally resistant. With such people, whether an attack of hay fever or asthma results from inhalation of a standard dose of pollen depends upon the accompanying emotional state of the person. During emotional stress the skin and mucous membranes show increased sensitivity to those foods, pollens, and toxic agents to which the individual is sensitive.

Not all people react alike to stress. In susceptible individuals experiencing psychosomatic disorders, the arterioles and other small blood vessels of the skin, the mucous membranes of the nose, and the gastrointestinal tract dilate. The involved tissue becomes engorged with blood, swells, and becomes turgid. Such engorged and swollen tissues are particularly susceptible to the effects of mechanical and chemical stimulation or to those foods, pollens, and drugs to which the individual is sensitive. Some specific examples will illustrate these effects.

In one instance the tone of the minute blood vessels in the skin of a person subject to hives was determined. This provided an index of the vessels' capacity to hold the contents of the blood within their walls. The subject then discussed his painfully disturbing home situation with a counselor. The capillaries of his forearm acted as though they had been dealt a blow or otherwise mechanically irritated, their tone fell, excessive fluid passed from the blood vessels into the surrounding tissues, and the characteristic wheals (local swellings) of hives developed. At a later date this same subject's skin was tested for its reaction to a measured amount of mechanical stroking, and to the chemical toxin, histamine (a toxic substance liberated from injured body cells). The subject's skin did not react to the amounts applied. Following the discussion of an emotionally disturbing topic a reapplication of the same mechanical and chemical stimuli that a few minutes before had produced no effect now caused the development of hives on the forearm. After a rest period and the counselors' providing the subject with some reassurance, his skin again failed to react to mechanical stroking or the administration of comparable amounts of histamine (Wolff, 1953; Graham, 1950).

In one case a subject with a permanent opening into the stomach, through which the digestive activity and the condition of the lining of the stomach could be directly observed, was studied over a period of several years. The condition of the stomach was found to be very sensitive to the emotional states of the subject. The following observations of the effects of emotion on gastric activity is typical of many reported.

The subject was employed by a doctor to do some housecleaning tasks, a type of work he considered beneath him. He resentfully performed the tasks. When the work was completed the doctor insinuated that the charges made were excessive and told the subject that his services were no longer required. The subject became very resentful but said nothing in reply. A short time later in the laboratory his stomach lining was found to be very red and engorged with blood, and the acid content of the copious gastric juice secreted more than doubled. The stomach contractions were very vigorous. The threshold for pain resulting from the pressure of a blunt object placed against the inside of the stomach wall was considerably lower than normal. The mucous membrane of the stomach was also found to be unusually fragile. The hyperactive state of the stomach produced "heart-burn" and stomach discomfort, which were relieved either by eating food or by the administration of antacids (*Wolf and Wolff, 1947*).

Unrelieved feelings of hostility, resentment, and guilt have been shown to be associated with increased activity, increased blood supply, swelling and, at times, small hemorrhagic lesions of both the stomach and the colon. Such lesions are considered to be the forerunner of peptic ulcers and ulcerative colitis (*Wolff, 1953; Grace et al., 1951*).

The involvement of the mucous membranes of the nose, sinuses, and bronchial tubes in emotional responses has been demonstrated in many cases of "psychosomatic" asthma and hay fever.

One subject suffered from seasonal "hay fever." The observations were performed in March, when he was without nasal complaints. An examination of the nasal mucous membranes showed them to be relatively pale, with no swelling, obstruction, or significant secretion. A dose of 2 mg. of mixed ragweed pollen was introduced into each nasal chamber. No swelling, hypersecretion, obstruction, or increased redness appeared during the hour of observation following instillation of the pollen.

The following day, initial observations of the nasal mucous membranes showed a similar normal condition. The subject was then asked to describe the events surrounding the discovery of diabetes in his daughter, a condition for which the patient somehow felt personally responsible. After about ten minutes of discussion of his daughter's condition, another dose of 2 mg. of mixed ragweed pollen was introduced into each nasal chamber as before, whereupon he began to sneeze and his eyes "watered." The mucous membranes of his nose were now a deep red color; there was considerable swelling and hypersecretion with marked obstruction to breathing, and a small bleeding point appeared on a mucous membrane on one nostril. Ninety minutes later there was still considerable hyperfunction in the nasal passages. Thus the administration of a measured amount of pollen had no observable effect on a calm nonemotional subject, whereas the same amount of pollen produced prompt and vigorous reaction in the same subject when he was emotionally aroused (*Holmes et al.*, 1950). Similar instances of the combined effects of the allergic reactivity to pollens and emotional disturbances in the production of asthmatic attacks have been reported (*Holmes et al.*, 1950).

Asthmatic and hay-fever attacks have been brought on by hypodermic injections of distilled water when the subjects believed they were receiving injections of allergens to which they were sensitive. Cessation of attacks have also been produced by similar injections of distilled water in subjects whose previous attacks have been terminated by adrenalin injections and the subjects believed they were receiving adrenalin again (*Metzger*, 1960). Every allergist can relate bizarre cases such as the young woman who was sensitive to aspirin. The cause of her aspirin-induced hives was discovered and eliminated, but the young woman continued to break out with hives every time her doctor came into the office wearing a white coat. She did not get the hives if the doctor did not wear the white coat (*Metzger*, 1958). Such cases indicate the role of conditioning (associations) and expectancy in the production of allergic reactions.

The likelihood of the occurrence of an attack of hay fever or asthma after inhalation of a standard quantity of pollen often depends upon whether or not there is a pre-existing nasal hyperfunction as a reaction to emotion-arousing situations (*Funkelstein*, 1950; *Holmes et al.*, 1950). Chronic hypertension (high blood pressure), acne vulgaris (the typical acne of adolescence), and many chronic headaches (particularly some migraine headaches) are additional disorders that are often psychosomatic in origin.

PSYCHOSOMATIC REACTIONS AS EXPRESSIVE RESPONSES

So far the psychosomatic reactions have been presented as components of man's responses to stress. The gastrointestinal tract, the respiratory and circulatory systems, and the glands of the body all participate in the emotional response to either danger or the threat of danger. The reactions of the stomach, intestines, heart, blood vessels, skin, mucous membranes, and bronchi can be considered as parts of these emotional reactions. When prolonged, these functional components may result in gastric ulcers, ulcera-

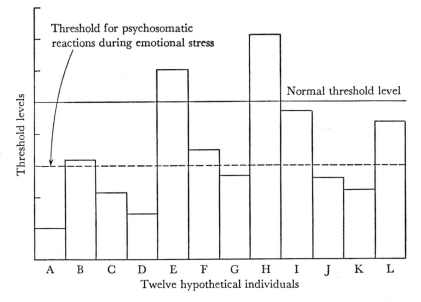

*Figure 3. Effects of changing thresholds for psychosomatic reactions. Under normal conditions only individuals E and H will display psychosomatic symptoms while under emotional stress individuals, B, F, I, and L will also respond. The rest of the individuals—A, C, D, G, J, and K—will not react psychosomatically. The height of each individual's column is his constitutional susceptibility of reactivity.*

tive colitis, and arterio-sclerosis (hardening of the arteries), which are organic tissue changes. Bodily processes are so involved in emotional responses as to produce real organic illness.

Many of the bodily aspects of emotion are protective and defensive reactions to stress. However, some of these preparatory responses are not appropriate to the actual situation, and become persistent chronic preparations for crises that never arise. Psychosomatic disorders are the results of persisting emotional disturbance and can be considered as the natural concomitants or consequences of these disturbances. According to this conception, psychosomatic reactions are neither defensive in nature nor anxiety-reducing in their effects.

PSYCHOSOMATIC REACTIONS AS DEFENSIVE RESPONSES

Most workers in the field believe that, in addition to being a direct somatic expression of emotion, psychosomatic symptoms are also defensive in nature.

The defensive aspect of psychosomatic disorders may be only a secondary gain, which the patient achieves following the development of the disorder. For the person who is inclined either to malinger or to develop neurotic (conversion) symptoms, psychosomatic disorders are made to order for his purposes. The symptoms, and eventually the facts, of organic illness or physical disability can be used as a defense against either failure or implications of personal inferiority in the ways previously indicated. The somatic components of psychosomatic illness can serve as attention-getting and sympathy-evoking devices. The psychosomatic disorders may also represent, for some people, self-punishment for real or imaginary sins and thus reduce guilt feelings.

Many psychoanalysts go still further and make a symbolic interpretation of psychosomatic disorders. Alexander (*1950*) explains the hyperactive stomach that results in peptic ulcers as a preparation for the reception of food which symbolically represents the receiving of loving care of which the individual has been deprived. According to this conception, the unconscious longing for rest, care, and affection manifests itself in terms of a preparation for food because of infantile associations between the receiving of loving care and the receiving of food (*White, 1956*). Other psychoanalysts interpret the increased tempo of gastrointestinal activity as the expression of prolonged suppressed anger (*Szasz et al., 1947*). Chronic constipation is conceived as a manifestation of the individual's unconscious desire to withhold affection or support from others. Chronic diarrhea is the symbolic ridding oneself of guilt or sin via autonomic functions (*White, 1956*). The wheezing of the asthmatic is interpreted as the blocked cry of the person trying to confess some sin. The sin is considered to be connected with sexual temptation (*French, 1939; White, 1956*). Most workers are unwilling to assign so much weight to the symbolic meanings of psychosomatic symptoms.

THE PROBLEM OF "ORGAN SELECTION"

We have nothing but speculation and hypotheses as to why the psychosomatic disorders take the form of gastrointestinal disturbances in some people, eczema in others, and asthma, hay fever, or chronic hypertension in still others. One suggestion is that each individual has an inherent weakness, vulnerability, or sensitivity in a given organ or system of the body. The person with a weak digestive system develops ulcers or colitis; the one with weak lungs develops asthma. This hypothesis assigns no specificity to the emotional components; the selection is entirely in terms of differential organ vulnerability. The various emotions are considered to have essentially the same general patterns of bodily expression.

On the other hand, we have the emotional "specificity hypothesis," in which the specificity is supposed to reside in the emotional patterns of response. Each type of psychosomatic syndrome (set of symptoms) is thought to result from a specific emotion (*Alexander, 1950; White, 1956*). According to the specificity hypothesis, there is a high correlation between type of organic (somatic) disorder and type of emotional disturbance. Up to the present no such correlation has been demonstrated.

It is claimed that during psychotherapy the psychosomatic symptoms may shift from one system to another, i.e. from migraine headache to asthma to eczema. Many cases have been reported in which similar symptoms have apparently shifted spontaneously. In times of war the case histories of servicemen suffering from psychosomatic disorders indicate that the psychosomatic syndromes seem to hold back or prevent the development of more severe neurotic or psychotic personality disorganizations (*White, 1956*). These latter observations suggest that the psychosomatic reactions constitute a form of defensive adaptation.

The incidence of allergic reactions seems to be below normal expectancy in people with well developed defenses of other types. For example, in one survey of over 7,000 cases in mental institutions (mostly psychotics), only 1 percent of the inmates showed allergic reactions as compared with 6 or 7 percent for comparable normal cases (*Metzger, 1960*). This leaves the question of why a particular person experiences a certain type of psychosomatic disorder still an open one.

### NEUROTIC REACTION PATTERNS

The neurotic (psychoneurotic) reactions include a wide array of motor manifestations such as tics, convulsions, paralyses, and compulsive acts; sensory deviations including cutaneous anesthesias and complete or partial blindness or deafness; emotional abnormalities such as irrational fears (phobias) and pathological anxieties; ideational aberrations such as obsessions and pathological doubts; dissociative reactions such as amnesias, fugues, somnambulisms, and multiple personalities; as well as vague aches, pains, pathological fatigue, and hypochondriasis (asthenic reactions).

In terms of severity, the neurotic reactions are intermediate between the minor personality disfunctions bordering on the normal and the more serious psychoses, and are about on a par with the psychosomatic disorders. They differ from the psychosomatic reactions in that they tend to be more anxiety-reducing and involve principally the sensory and cerebro-spinal nervous systems rather than the autonomic nervous system. Neurotic symptoms involve functional rather than organic impairment, whereas the psychomatic disorders often entail physical damage (skin lesions, ulcers). The regions affected in the psychosomatic disorders respect the boundaries of the anatomical and physiological systems, whereas neurotic systems do not (glove and stocking anesthesias). In the psychosomatic disorders, the agent producing the symptoms is usually a normal organic mechanism (acid in ulcers, histamine in allergy); neurotic symptoms are more often conversion reactions in which the symptoms have only a vicarious or symbolic significance.

In discussing the neuroses, the problem of classifying and naming is a difficult one. As a compromise between proposals to dispense with all names for mental disorders (*Menninger, 1963*) and the old classical rigid classifications, we shall describe and illustrate some of the more common neurotic syndromes.

## Asthenic Reactions

Asthenic reactions include a rather indefinite and changeable set of symptoms, including vague aches and pains, a constant state of fatigue that is unrelieved by rest, hypersensitivity to minor irritants, and hypochondriasis. Fatigue is usually the dominant symptom and because of this fact the term "asthenic (weakness) reaction" is in some respects a suitable designation. The following case is fairly typical.

An unmarried male, age 32, complains of the following symptoms: He suffers extreme fatigue and finds it impossible to work for more than 20 or 30 minutes at a time. The fatigue is present in the morning just as much as it is during the rest of the day. He has a poor appetite and suffers from indigestion, which he describes as "sour stomach," "gas," "heartburn," and "constipation." He has frequent headaches and blurred vision, which make it impossible for him to read for any length of time. Periodic back pains prevent him from sitting or standing in comfort. He has ringings and buzzings in his ears that are highly distracting. He is very irritated by ordinary noises. The ticking of the clock, the traffic noises, and the slamming of doors keep him hunting for quieter living quarters. He is sure that he has some obscure malignant illness. Repeated physical examinations have shown negative results, and various tonics and dietary supplements have been tried, with only short-term improvements. The patient has become a health food faddist and is sure he would have died except for his special diet.

The asthenic symptoms are thought to originate from sustained emotional tensions, but the individual ascribes his discomfort to physical ailments. These symptoms of physical illness permit the person to escape from his problems, responsibilities, and environmental stresses in the ways discussed earlier in this chapter.

## Conversion Reactions

In many ways the conversion reactions are the most dramatic of the neurotic behavior patterns. The more bizarre forms of conversion reactions seem to have gone out of style. Janet's (1920) "major symptoms of hysteria" are much less common today than they were 25 or 50 years ago, whereas the compulsive-obsessive patterns seem to be more common (White, 1956; Coleman, 1964); see Dawes (1960) for a recent striking case of conversion reaction.

The conversion reactions include functional paralyses, which may involve only one or more limbs or one whole side of the body. Other motor symptoms are the total inability to speak (mutism), inability to speak above a whisper (aphonia), tremors, and tics (involuntary spasms of localized muscle groups). Occupationally related motor disorders, like writer's cramp, may also be hysterical.

There are several varieties of functional anesthesia. Blindness may occur in one or both eyes, or the right half or the left half of both eyes, or the visual field may be restricted (tunnel vision). Functional deafness may likewise occur. Functional loss of skin sensitivity (cutaneous anesthesia) of various types have also been reported. The functional cutaneous anesthesias are distinguished from anesthesias due to organic nerve injury in that (1) they fail to conform to the anatomical distribution of nerves (i.e. a glove or stocking anesthesia is always functional), (2) reflex responses can still be evoked from stimulation of the anesthetic areas, (3) the boundaries of the insensitive areas shift from time to time in a way not characteristic of regenerating nerves, (4) under hypnosis or with partial general anesthesia the functional disorder may disappear.

The term "conversion reaction" refers most appropriately to the more bodily forms of this disorder, and takes its name from the hypothesis that anxiety, unable to manifest or resolve itself in overt behavior, is converted into or manifests itself in the blocked or distorted function of some body organ. According to this hypothesis, conversion reactions are anxiety-linked and represent the somatic equivalent of the internal emotion. Anxiety typically precedes the appearance of the conversion symptoms and diminishes on their occurrence. Consequently, conversion reactions are sometimes spoken of as "anxiety equivalents." The conversion reaction syndromes can be defensive and anxiety-reducing in the ways previously indicated.

## Dissociative Reactions

Dissociative reactions are a different sort of neurotic manifestation. The common forms of dissociative reactions are (1) amnesias, (2) fugues, (3) dual or multiple personalities, and (4) somnambulisms. In all of these there is a "cleavage" or blocking off of a part of one's memories, experiences, activities, or life from the main current of one's existence.

*Amnesia.* In hysterical amnesia there is a partial or complete inability to recall or recognize past experiences. Although amnesia is often referred to as a "loss of memory," it is not a failure to retain but an inability to recall or recognize. The fact that amnesias are often only temporary and the "forgotten" experiences can usually be recalled under hypnosis or narcosis indicates that the failure is not one of retention but of recall.

The inability to recall in amnesia is selective and usually involves ego-related material such as one's identity, one's relatives, and friends, and the events of one's past or a segment of one's past. Motor skill and habits are usually retained. The amnesic individual can still talk, walk, write, and play a musical instrument. The individual may function quite normally except where the segments of past experience for which he is amnesic are concerned.

*Fugue.* When the amnesia also involves a "fleeing" or "running away" it is called a "fugue." An individual may wander away from his home or community or he may travel by train, car, bus, or plane and then find himself in a strange place not knowing who he is, where he is, or how he got there. Such cases are frequently reported in the daily newspapers. A soldier may suddenly find himself several miles behind his line of duty traveling away from his battle station with no knowledge of who he is, how he happens to be where he is, or where he is going. An unhappily married girl leaves home to go shopping, boards a bus, and two days later finds herself in a strange city, with no awareness of her own identity and no recollection of her past life. A boy whose fantasy life is filled with adventure may awaken to find himself a member of a crew, aboard ship, and headed for the South Pacific with no knowledge of how he got there or who he is.

*Somnambulism.* In somnambulism (sleepwalking), the individual, in a dreamlike or trance state, does bizarre and inappropriate things in a purposeful fashion, but in his normal waking state has no recollection of the events. Sometimes these somnambulisms are re-enactments of past events in the person's life; or they may represent the actual or symbolic carrying out of an act that the individual would like to perform but is unable to in his ordinary waking state. The somnambulism may represent an attempt to escape from either real or imagined danger (*Sandler, 1945*).

*Dual personality.* Dual or multiple personality represents the most dramatic form of dissociation. While Robert Louis Stevenson's Dr. Jekyll and Mr. Hyde are, of course, fictional, many less spectacular actual cases of dual or multiple personality have been studied and documented. Although such cases are comparatively rare, Taylor and Martin (1944) found 76 cases reported in the literature prior to the time of their investigation. A movie has been made of one such case. (See *Masserman, 1946; Prince, 1930; Harriman, 1942; Lipton, 1943; Taylor and Martin, 1944;* and *Franz, 1933,* for case studies.)

The difference between amnesia and fugue, on the one hand, and dual or multiple personality, on the other, is one of degree. In most cases the dual personality can be viewed as the resolution of a conflict between resentful conforming and guilty nonconforming behavioral trends in the same person. In the case reported by Harriman (1942) a girl in a state of abstraction took on the personality and name of her best friend, of whose business success and economic independence she was envious.

In the case described by Lipton (1943), Maud was a happy, extroverted, noisy individual who wore gaudy, striped, high-heeled, open-toed sandals, used excessive makeup, painted her fingernails and toenails deep red, and wore girlish red ribbons in her hair. She used poor English and had a limited vocabulary and childish handwriting. She would chain-smoke, had no sense of right and wrong, and felt no guilt over her promiscuous sexual behavior. In contrast with Maud, Sara, the alternate personality, was quiet, sedate, and depressed. She dressed demurely and used no makeup or nail polish. Her favorite color was blue. Sara was a mature, intelligent individual who used good English. She did not smoke, was very awkward when she tried, and had marked guilt feelings concerning her previous sexual misdemeanors.

From the girl's previous history, it seems that the appearance of the dissociated personality, Maud, enabled Sara to gratify her sexual and other frivolous desires without conscious knowledge and without guilt feelings. The evidence suggests that Sara changed to Maud whenever her sexual desires and guilt feelings concerning her previous sexual behavior became too threatening. The alternate personality operated as a defense against excessive anxiety and served as a means of resolving a conflict.

### Anxiety Reactions

Although the state of pathological anxiety characteristic of anxiety re-actions is not a defensive reaction, it is a form of neurosis and will be discussed here along with the other neurotic reactions. Chronic anxiety may precede the development of other neurotic defensive reaction patterns or it may continue indefinitely due to the partial or complete failure of defenses to develop. A typical case will point out some of the character-istics of the anxiety neuroses.

The subject is male, 33 years of age, has been married ten years, and has two children. Following a series of physical examinations by various physicians he was advised to "take a trip," "to rest more," and to "take vitamins." After exhausting the local supply of regular practitioners he went to an irregular of some kind and after a diagnosis based on readings supposedly taken on a mechanical gadget was told that his "nerves were weak." As a child, a wagon had run over his back. Despite repeated negative findings, he felt that his back was permanently injured and that his present trouble was related to this childhood injury. Throughout the course of his treatment, the subject periodically kept returning to his injured back and his "weak nerves" as the possible cause of his trouble. He was referred to one of the authors following a course of eight electric shock treatments that he claimed had not helped.

The subject complained of being afraid—he was afraid all or most of the time. He could not say what he was afraid of, but he had a rather constant feeling of impending disaster without knowing why. The fear, or more accurately anxiety, varied in intensity from situation to situation. He was most disturbed when he was alone or in crowds. He felt least anxious when he was with some member of his immediate family, preferably his wife. He wanted his wife to be with him all the time. If she was not with him he wanted to know she was either at home or immediately available. When he was at work and knew his wife was at home he could feel reasonably comfortable, but if he knew she was away and he did not know where, he would become quite disturbed. Having one of his little children with him was preferable to being alone.

The subject was afraid to go places by himself. As it neared time to go home from work, his anxiety would mount to such a pitch that when he started for home he would be in a panic, feeling sure that something terrible would happen to him on his way. He dreaded starting across each street intersection because he was sure he would never reach the other side alive. In crowds he would sigh repeatedly, become tense, and find some excuse to move on. He could no longer drive his car; his wife usually drove for him.

The subject recognized the irrationality of his feeling but could do nothing about it. He knew all about the statistics of personal accidents and realized the low probabilities of any of his fears being realized, but facts and information did not help. He would say, "I have a fine wife and two wonderful children. I have a good job, some money in the bank, and a nice home clear of mortgage. I should be a happy man, but actually I am perfectly miserable all the time."

Over a period of six years, four years prior to our contact with him and two years during treatment, he apparently never had any other neurotic symptoms. His general health remained good. He had no other bodily complaints or symptoms. He had no specific phobias, compulsions, or obsessions. His persistent anxiety seems to fit the classical picture of anxiety neurosis or anxiety reaction.

The level of anxiety in the anxiety neuroses is pathological in the sense that it is out of all proportion to its cause. It is unrealistic and this fact is often recognized by the individual. The anxiety is often "free-floating" in the sense that it is rather constant, although varying in intensity, and is not stimulus- or situation-tied. The anxiety state is often described as a fear and is ascribed by the sufferer to a specific cause or situation. This assigning is an attempted rationalization; the causes and objects to which the emotion is attached shift from time to time and are not the real causes of the anxiety.

The unmodified anxiety reactions seem to be persistent nonadjustive behavior patterns. They develop and persist in the absence of adequate defenses. Some degree of anxiety is practically always involved prior to the development of the various defensive devices. As already pointed out, the various defensive patterns are perceived as devices for reducing anxiety and keeping it to a minimum. Persisting high levels of anxiety result from the failure of the various protective and defensive devices.

### PSYCHASTHENIC REACTION PATTERNS

Phobias (morbid or pathological *fears*), obsessions (unwanted, irrational, persistent *thoughts*), and compulsions (forced repetitive *actions* performed despite the person's recognition of their inappropriateness or irrationality) often occur together in various combinations. In phobias, the emotion of fear is the dominant element; in obsessions, the ideational component is foremost; in compulsions, the act or the impulse to act is predominant. In many cases all three may be present in varying degrees and in all possible combinations.

## Phobias

The number of possible phobias is almost infinite. Medical dictionaries often list several hundred. The names of the phobias are derived by attaching the Greek name indicating the thing feared to "phobia"; thus we have claustrophobia, a fear of closed places; acrophobia, a fear of heights; and agoraphobia, a fear of open places.

Some examples of phobias follow. A soldier is so afraid of closed places that he will spend the night in an open truck under fire rather than remain in an enclosed safe dugout. A grown woman is extremely afraid of cats, dogs, and other small household pets. A fifteen-year-old boy has an intense fear of open places. He becomes panic-stricken whenever he finds himself alone in any large open place. An adult male becomes very disturbed whenever he has to go alone more than a few blocks from his home. A young man has a strong fear of being attacked from behind.

While the forms of phobias are legion, they do have some common features. Some of these are:

(1) Most phobias orginate from early, often childhood, experiences.

(2) The phobia-inducing experience has some element of shame or guilt connected with it. It is anxiety-laden.

(3) The original experiences that gave rise to the phobia have been "forgotten." (They cannot be recalled.) This inability to recall the original traumatic experience is due to repression. For example: the incident of sexual misbehavior in a small enclosed space is forgotten, but enclosed spaces are now fear-inducing.

(4) The phobic object often symbolizes the real cause of the fear. (A fear of knives symbolizes the person's wish that her older sister would die.)

(5) Some phobias are generalized conditioned fear responses. (A fear of animals dates from being attacked by a dog when the person, as a child, ran away and entered a neighbor's backyard after having been forbidden to do so.)

(6) Phobic reactions are perpetuated because they operate as defenses and are anxiety-reducing in the following ways:

(a) Phobic reactions constitute an avoidance of the fear-evoking situation. The person tends to either avoid or withdraw from the anxiety-laden situation. The avoidance or withdrawal is anxiety-reducing and reinforcing of the behavior, thus perpetuating the avoidance-withdrawal activity.

(b) The phobia sometimes localizes and rationalizes a generalized emotional response. Prior to the development of phobias the person often suffers from a "free-floating" anxiety. This general anxiety state becomes focused on some object or class of objects and becomes a phobia. Thus an avoidable specific object or situation is substituted for an unavoidable general state of persistent anxiety.

(c) The attention-getting and sympathy-inviting outcomes of phobias sometimes operate as "secondary gains" for the individual. Phobic reactions may function to control other people. (The fear of being alone may keep the members of one's family close at hand.)

## Obsessions

An obsession is a *thought* or *idea* that keeps recurring and cannot be "shaken off." An obsessive idea is usually coercive, irrational, and, to some extent, anxiety-laden. For example: A mother is continually bothered by the idea that she may harm or even kill her baby, whom she dearly loves. A wife is obsessed with the idea that if she had only given her husband a certain medicine he would not have died. A commuter is obsessed with the notion that he will lose his commuter's ticket. He keeps thinking about losing it, looks into his pocket every few minutes to reassure himself, and heaves a great sigh of relief when the conductor has punched it. Obsessions typically occur in combination with compulsions and so the two are usually combined into the "obsessive-compulsive reactions."

## Compulsions

Compulsions are coercive, recurrent *acts* or *impulses to act* in rather specific ways. Compulsive acts are automatisms over which the individual has little control. The person is quite aware of what he is doing or feels compelled to do. He recognizes it as irrational, silly, or even dangerous, but he is unable either to stop doing it or to get rid of the impulse to perform the act. The impulse is sometimes situation-tied to the extent that it occurs whenever the situation is right. At other times the impulse or tendency to act seems to build up spontaneously until the act is performed. Performing the act affords the sufferer a measure of relief.

The catalog of compulsions or compulsive-obsessive reactions is as long as that of the phobias. Compulsions range all the way from having to count steps, posts, and cracks in the sidewalk to criminal acts such as kleptomania (compulsive stealing) and pyromania (compulsive fire-setting). All of the "manias" are technically compulsions.

As previously indicated, combinations of phobic and obsessive-compulsive reactions are more common than the pure forms. For example, a person may have a mysophobia (a morbid fear of dirt), so that he is obsessed with the idea that he is being contaminated with dangerous germs by everything he touches, and he has an accompanying hand-washing compulsion. These elements are all consistent and mutually supportive.

## Characteristics of the Psychasthenic Syndromes

Although the phobic, obsessive, and compulsive reaction patterns have much in common with the other neuroses, there are *some* features that characterize them.

(1) They have *some* dissociative characteristics. The patient recognizes that his phobias, obsessions, and compulsions are "within him"; he does not project them to the outside world. Yet he feels that these tendencies are like foreign bodies; they are not a part of his real self. These irrational fears, thoughts, and impulses intrude and force themselves upon him despite his desire to be rid of them. There is a semi-detachment of the emotions, ideas, and impulses from the self. This partial detachment of the psychasthenic symptoms from the self represents their dissociative element.

(2) Elaborate secondary defenses develop around the psychasthenic symptoms. Complicated rituals often develop as a means of avoiding the phobic objects and giving relatively harmless expression to the obsessive ideas and compulsive acts. The person often attempts to either conceal or rationalize his bizarre behavior.

(3) Overt anxiety is kept at relatively low levels. There may be an undercurrent of uneasiness, which varies in intensity from time to time, but the elaborate defenses keep acute anxiety and panic from developing.

(4) Sexual and aggressive impulses often underlie the basic conflicts.

(5) Certain personality traits are said to characterize patients experiencing the phobic-obsessive-compulsive syndromes. They are typically conscientious, idealistic, and moralistic. They tend to be overtly calm, kind, and considerate of others.

(6) These personality traits are thought to constitute a reaction-formation (display of the opposite traits) against aggressive, hostile, destructive, and "messy," sexual and hostile tendencies. The various symptoms represent the manifestations of these repressed, unacceptable impulses.

### *THE NATURE OF NEUROTIC SYMPTOMS*

Despite the great diversity of neurotic symptoms the following generalizations can be made concerning these reactions.

(1) Many of the primary neurotic symptoms are the bodily manifestations of the basic anxiety pattern itself (trembling, sweating, increased pulse and blood pressure, respiratory and gastrointestinal disturbances).

(2) Other neurotic symptoms constitute defensive reactions and strategies to ward off or diminish anxiety.

(3) Neurotic symptoms often have a symbolic significance for the individual and may provide partial or vicarious satisfaction of anxiety-linked impulses or desires.

(4) Neurotic symptoms are often sustained by the secondary gains that accrue (sick-person status brings relief from work, sympathy and care, removal to a place of safety, honorable discharge).

(5) The secondary gains play no part in the initial appearance of the symptoms. The individual does not develop the symptoms in order to enjoy the advantages. The mechanism of their perpetuation is largely unconscious. However, the appearance of the symptoms may be preceded and accompanied by a half-conscious wish for illness or for the symptoms of illness that will result in withdrawal from danger, the avoidance of responsibility, and reduction of the humiliation of failure.

### *SUMMARY*

Not all avoidance behavior is defensive in nature. Avoidance and withdrawal may be the result of the copying of family, subcultural, or cultural behavior patterns. Behavior that some people perceive as defensive may be a way of life and not a defense against threat.

Defensive withdrawal may take the forms of (1) simple overt avoidance; (2) regression—a return to less mature behavior when more recently acquired activities are blocked; (3) fantasy—withdrawal from reality into an imaginary world where one's problems are all solved (The withdrawal into a fantasy world may range all the way from wishful thinking and daydreaming and revery, at the one extreme, to schizophrenia, at the other.); (4) flight into illness—capitalizing on illness or the symptoms of illness as a means of ego-inflation. Psychosomatic disorders and the neuroses often serve as defensive adjustive devices. The more common psychosomatic disorders are eczema, hay fever, and asthma. Asthenic reactions, conversion reactions, dissociative reactions (amnesia, fugue, somnambulisms, and dual or multiple personality), anxiety reactions, phobias, obsessions, and compulsions constitute the more common neurotic syndromes.

## REFERENCES

ALEXANDER, F. *Psychosomatic Medicine: Its Principles and Applications.* New York: W. W. Norton and Company, 1950.

BARKER, R., DEMBO, TAMARA, and LEWIN, K. Frustration and regression: an experiment with young children. *Univ. Iowa Stud. Child Welf.*, 1941, **18**, No. 1.

BROWN, J. F. *Psychodynamics of Abnormal Behavior.* New York: McGraw-Hill Book Company, 1940.

CLANDY, E. R. A study of the development and cause of schizophrenia in children. *Psychiat. Quart.*, 1951, **25**, 81–90.

COLEMAN, J. C. *Abnormal Psychology and Modern Life* (3d ed.). Chicago: Scott, Foresman, 1964.

COYLE, F. A. and COYLE, G. F. An operant explanation of the process-reactive differentiation, *J. Psychol.*, 1965, **61**, 39–45.

DAWES, LYDIA G. The psychoanalysis of a case of "Grand Hysteria of Charcot" in a girl of fifteen. In E. Podolsky (ed.), *The Neuroses and Their Treatment.* New York: Philosophical Library, 1960.

DESPERT, J. L. Schizophrenia in children. *Psychiat. Quart.*, 1938, **12**, 366–371.

DONOVAN, M. J. and WEBB, W. W. Meaning dimensions and male-female voice perception in schizophrenics with good and poor premorbid adjustment, *J. abnorm. Psychol.*, 1965, **70**, 426–431.

DUDYCHA, G. J., and DUDYCHA, MARTHA M. Childhood memories: a review of the literature. *Psychol. Bull.*, 1941, **38**, 668–682.

ELLSWORTH, R. B. The regression of schizophrenic language. *J. consult. Psychol.*, 1951, **15**, 387–391.

ENGLISH, H. B., and ENGLISH, A. C. *A Comprehensive Dictionary of Psychological and Psychoanalytical Terms.* New York: Longmans, Green, and Company, 1958.

FLECK, S. Family dynamics and the origin of schizophrenia, *Psychosom. Med.*, 1960, **22**, 333–344.

FLECK, S., LIDZ, T., and CORNELISON, R. Comparison of parent-child relationships of male and female schizophrenic patients, *A.M.A., Arch. gen. Psychiat.*, 1963, **8**, 1–7.

FRANZ, I. *Persons One and Three.* New York: McGraw-Hill Book Company, 1933.

FREEMAN, R. V., and GRAYSON, H. M. Maternal attitudes in schizophrenia. *J. abnorm. soc. Psychol.*, 1955, **50**, 45–52.

FRENCH, T. M. Psychogenic factors in asthma. *Amer. J. Psychiat.*, 1939, **46**, 87–101.

FUNKELSTEIN, D. H. Variations in response to standard amounts of chemical agents during alterations in feeling states in relation to occurrence of asthma. *Proc. Ass. Res. nerv. ment. Dis.*, 1950, **29**, 566–572.

Gerard, D. L., and Siegel, J. The family background of schizophrenia. *Psychiat. Quart.*, 1950, **24**, 47–73.

Goldstein, K. The significance of psychological research in schizophrenia. *J. nerv. ment. Dis.*, 1943, **97**, 261–279.

Grace, W. J., Wolf, S., and Wolff, H. G. The Human Colon. New York: Paul B. Hoeber, 1951.

Graham, D. T. The pathogenesis of hives. *Proc. Ass. Res. nerv. ment. Dis.*, 1950, **29**, 987–992.

Grinker, R. R., and Spiegel, J. P. *War Neurosis.* Philadelphia: The Blakiston Company, 1945.

Hajdw, G. L. Contributions to the etiology of schizophrenia. *Psychoanal. Rev.*, 1940, **27**, 421–438.

Hamilton, J. A., and Krechevsky, I. Studies on the effects of shock upon behavior plasticity in the rat. *J. comp. Psychol.*, 1933, **16**, 237–253.

Harriman, Philip L. The experimental induction of a multiple personality. *Psychiatry*, 1942, **5**, 179–186.

Herron, W. G. The process-reactive classification of schizophrenia. *Psychol. Bull.*, 1962, **59**, 329–343.

Hilgard, E. R. *Introduction to Psychology.* New York: Harcourt, Brace and Company, 1957.

Holmes, T. H., Treuting, T., and Wolff, H. G. Life situations, emotions, and nasal disease: Evidence on summative effects exhibited in patients with "hay fever." *Proc. Ass. Res. nerv. ment. Dis.*, 1950, **29**, 545–555.

Janet, P. *The Major Symptoms of Hysteria* (2d ed.). New York: The Macmillan Company, 1920.

Jenkins, R. L. The schizophrenic sequence: withdrawal, disorganization, psychotic reorganization. *Amer. J. Orthopsychiat.*, 1952, **20**, 738–748.

Johnson, M. H. Verbal abstracting ability and schizophrenia. *J. Consult. Psychol.*, 1966, **30**, 275–277.

Kasanin, J. S. Developmental roots of schizophrenia. *Amer. J. Psychiat.*, 1945, **101**, 770–776.

Laing, R. D. Is schizophrenia a disease? *J. soc. Psychiat.*, 1964, **10**, 184–193.

Levy, E. Some aspects of the schizophrenic formal disturbance of thought. *Psychiatry*, 1943, **6**, 55–69.

Lidz, T., Cornelison, R., Fleck, S., and Terry, D. The interfamilial environment of the schizophrenic patient: I the father. *Psychiatry*, 1959, **20**, 329, 342.

Lipton, S. Dissociated personality, a case report. *Psychiat. Quart.*, 1943, **17**, 35–56.

Lundin, R. W. *Principles of Psychopathology.* Columbus, Ohio: Charles E. Merrill, 1965.

Masserman, J. H. *Principles of Dynamic Psychiatry.* Philadelphia: W. B. Saunders Company, 1946.

Menninger, K., with Mayman, M., and Pruyser, P. *The Vital Balance: The Life Process in Mental Health and Illness.* New York: The Viking Press, 1963.

Metzger, F. C. Allergy and Psychoneurosis. In E. Podolsky (ed.), *The Neuroses and Their Treatment.* New York: Philosophical Library, 1960.

Moran, L. J. Vocabulary knowledge and usage among normal and schizophrenic subjects. *Psychol. Monogr.*, 1953, **67**, No. 37, 40.

Mowrer, O. H. An experimental analogue of "regression" with incidental observations on "reaction-formation." *J. abnorm. soc. Psychol.*, 1940, **35**, 56–87.

Prince, M. *The Dissociation of a Personality* (2d ed.). New York: Longmans, Green, and Company, 1930.

Sandler, S. A. Somnambulism in the armed forces. *Ment. Hyg.*, 1945, **39**, 236–247.

Sawrey, W. L. Conditioned responses of fear in relationship to ulceration. *J. comp. physiol. Psychol.*, 1961, **54**, 347–349.

Sheiver, Sara B., Metzger, Emy A., and Hatt, L. R. Schizophrenia: a panel. *Amer. J. Psychoanal.*, 1957, **17**, 110–120.

Singer, J. J., and McCraven, Vivian G. Some characteristics of adult daydreaming. *J. Psychol.*, 1961, **51**, 151–164.

Spohn, H. E., and Walk, W. P. Social participation in homogeneous and heterogeneous groups of chronic schizophrenics. *J. abnorm. Psychol.*, 1966, **71**, 147–150.

Szasz, T. S., Levin, E., Kirsner, J. B., and Palmer, W. L. The role of hostility in the pathogenesis of peptic ulcers: Theoretical considerations with the report of a case. *Psychosom. Med.*, 1947, **9**, 331–336.

Taylor, W. S., and Martin, M. F. Multiple personality. *J. abnorm. soc. Psychol.*, 1944, **39**, 281–300.

Terman, L. M. Mental and Physical Traits of a Thousand Gifted Children. In *Genetic Studies of Genius*, Vol. I. Stanford, California: Stanford University Press, 1926.

Wallin, J. E. W. *Personality Maladjustments and Mental Hygiene* (2d ed.). New York: McGraw-Hill Book Company, 1949.

White, R. W. *The Abnormal Personality* (2d ed.). New York: The Ronald Press Company, 1956.

Whiteman, M. The performance of schizophrenics on social concepts. *J. abnorm. soc. Psychol.*, 1954, **49**, 266–271.

Wolf, S., and Wolff, H. G. *Human Gastric Function* (2d ed.). New York: Oxford University Press, 1947.

Wolff, H. G. *Stress and Disease.* Springfield: Charles C Thomas, 1953.

Zigler, E., and Phillips, L. Social competence and the process-reactive distinction in psychopathology. *J. abnorm. soc. Psychol.*, 1962, **65**, 215–222.

# Chapter 4

# Aggressive Behavior

THE LABEL "aggressive" can designate a great variety of behaviors. These behaviors vary in their severity or vigorousness, in how purposive they are, and in the stimulus events evoking them. When aggressive behavior is readily analyzable in terms of how and why it was acquired, and when it is easily understandable and largely socially acceptable, it does not cause great concern. Aggressive behavior has been divided, for purposes of study, into two categories: (1) behavior deriving rather directly from the learning situation provided by the social-personal environment, and (2) behavior that derives more indirectly from the experiential environment and appears to be more immediately motivated by emotional states such as anger or hostility.

Aggressive behavior is not necessarily associated with strong emotional states, but some aggressive behavior is so associated. The fact that some aggressive behaviors appear to be closely affiliated with strong emotion does not imply that there is not a strong learning component involved in them. People learn to react not only to external stimulating circumstances, but also to their own emotional reactions to these stimuli. Thus it can be seen that some aggressive behavior may be mediated by such feelings as anger and hostility while other aggressive behavior may have no such affiliation. We shall use the term "aggression" in a broad sense, to include most approach behavior, as opposed to withdrawal behavior.

It can be considered appropriate, for purposes of exposition, to classify approach behavior according to whether it is essentially hostile or cultural in nature. There is a large overlapping area between these two classifications, and it is probably true that much aggressive behavior has both elements in it. Hostile aggression involves anger, and the behavior is intended to inflict harm upon either a person or a group of people or their possessions. Cultural aggression may take the form of a vigorous attack on other people, or on situations, with the intention of controlling, manipulating, or modifying them. If hurt or harm to others is a result, it is a by-product of the aggression rather than a deliberate purpose for the aggressive behavior. "Passivity" may be an appropriate antonym for cultural aggression, whereas fearful withdrawal may more appropriately be the opposite of hostile aggression. We shall classify compensation, sublimation, and reaction-formations as aggressive behaviors even though they do not have anger or hostility as a component.

## SOCIAL-CULTURAL AGGRESSION

Many cultures, including our own, place a premium on certain forms of aggression. Ours is a vigorous, competitive culture that encourages and reinforces aggression of certain types. Initiative, enterprise, leadership, and ambition are "good." To be an aggressive "go-getter" is a praiseworthy American virtue. "Whatever we do, we should do with all our might"; "Never give up"; "If at first you don't succeed, try, try again"; "The world steps aside for the man who knows where he is going." The list of such proverbs and maxims extolling the virtues of the aggressive and strenuous life is a long one. As long as aggressiveness proceeds according to the "rules of the game," it is socially approved. Much aggressive behavior is the result of social practices that reinforce such activity; it is neither hostile in motivation nor defensive in outcome.

Some behavior judged by the general public to be aggressive and hostile in nature may really be the result of social learning and not necessarily emotion-laden. Aggressive behavior that exceeds socially approved limits may be the manifestation of response patterns acquired in a family, community, or subculture that encourages and rewards such behavior. In many lower class families and subcultures, the children, particularly the males, are taught to be fighters. The boy gains status with his father, brothers, and peers by means of his fighting prowess and not only defends himself, but seeks out opportunities to assert himself and improve his status by whipping others. Such fighting may not be emotionally motivated and is not necessarily the result of frustration. It is a way of life and a means of status seeking.

When the lower class boy moves out of his subculture, where fighting, sexual aggressiveness, and minor legal misdemeanors are rewarded, he finds that these same activities meet with resistance and punishment in a middle class culture. When his previously rewarded activities are blocked and punished, he often responds with increased aggression. Such counter aggressions may be hostile in nature, whereas the original, thwarted aggressive acts were not emotionally motivated.

## CAUSES OF HOSTILE AGGRESSION

Hostile aggression is probably always the result of some kind of frustration. However, aggressive behavior is not the only reaction to frustration. The blocking of goal-directed activity may result in learning, problem solving, avoidance, or withdrawal. All of the defense mechanisms previously discussed may be reactions to actual or threatened thwarting, but the original, primitive response to frustration is physical resistance of an overtly aggressive sort. Although the situations that produce frustration and threatened frustration change with the experiences of the individual, real or threatened frustrations remain the principal, if not the sole, cause of hostile aggression (*Glueck and Glueck, 1950; Bandura and Walters, 1959; Berkowitz, 1958, 1962*).

## THE NATURE OF FRUSTRATIONS

The original frustrations consist of the physical hampering or restricting of bodily movements. To the young infant, having the arms and legs held so that they cannot be moved is a frustrating experience. Confining the older child to a playpen, a single room, the house, or the back yard, when he has been accustomed to greater freedom, causes frustration. Although many other frustrations develop as people mature, physical thwarting of bodily activity or freedom of movement never entirely loses its force as a frustrating agent.

Whenever the sight or sound of, or contact with, certain objects, people, or experiences regularly precedes or accompanies frustrating situations, these stimuli come to operate as substitutes for the actual frustrating situations. These substitute or "conditioned" stimuli then function as "threats" and evoke the same responses as did the original frustrating situations. Threats operate in place of and in the same way as the physical thwarting of activity. The child who responds with an angry outburst whenever he is forcibly prevented from doing something he wants to do may respond similarly when he sees a person make a threatening gesture to block his activities. A movement in his direction, the sight of the rope to tie him up, or the presence of the playpen in which he is placed evokes angry resistance just as the physical restraint did at an earlier time. Threats of physical thwarting have come to function much as the actual restraints do.

When language controls become established, verbal or other symbolic stimuli may operate as frustrating agents. The admonitions "don't," "no," "stop," "you can't," "stay here," "come back" may operate as social stimuli to hamper or restrict activity just as pushing, pulling, and restraining operate as physical restricting agents. A shake of the head, a frown, or a wave of the hand may operate similarly as symbolic restraining agents or as threats of restraint. In this way social thwarting becomes an important form of frustration and evokes aggression as a response.

A parallel developmental sequence in the frustration-aggression relationship is in terms of what is thwarted or threatened with thwarting. Originally the frustrations involve the thwarting of gross physical activities like locomotion and manipulation. With the development of language and the establishment of beliefs and convictions, the activities that are hampered or threatened to be hampered come to include one's speech, plans, purposes, beliefs, ideas, and ideals. Interference or threatened interference with one's freedom of speech, expression, and beliefs may evoke aggressive retaliation just as does the hampering of one's bodily movements. With maturity and the enlargement of the area of identification, one may also respond to any attack or threatened attack on friends or relatives, on the members of one's own race, religion, church, or fraternity, or on one's city, state, or nation much as though one had been personally attacked or restrained. With the enlargement of the "self," the frustrations that evoke aggressive retaliation become very extensive.

### AGGRESSIVE RESPONSES TO FRUSTRATION

The modifications in form of the aggressive responses to frustration show progressive changes just as do the situations that evoke them. The shifts in frustrating agents can be considered substitutions of one stimulus for another (conditioning). As previously indicated, stimuli accompanying or preceding physical thwarting agents begin to operate as threats. Words, gestures, facial expressions, and intonations are substituted for the physical thwarting agents. The shifts involved in these changes are on the stimulus end of the S-R formula. These shifts are brought about by simple association or by conditioning, as discussed in a later chapter.

Modifications in the *form of the aggressive response* to frustration involve either a substitution of one response for another or modifications of the response. The change involved is in the response end of the S-R sequence. These changes go through several stages.

The original response to thwarting is a *diffuse, chaotic, emotional outburst*. The angry outburst is not purposive or directed. It consists in squirming, twisting, throwing the arms and legs about, and crying.

With maturity and experience, the aggressive response to frustration becomes less random and more *directed, purposeful*, and *retaliative*. The responses are directed at the thwarting agent, and are intended to eliminate, remove, or diminish the effectiveness of the restriction. The child physically attacks, hits, kicks, and bites the hampering agent.

With increasing experience the child learns that an *indirect attack* on the thwarting agent is often more strategic than a direct attack. Consequently, the child may hide or break a toy or other possession of his big brother in retaliation for having been thwarted. Or when big brother is restricting the child's activities, the child may appeal to his mother or father to punish the brother. Another indirect retaliation is to act as if his brother is hurting him so that the mother or father will punish the bigger boy. A two-year-old boy, when restrained from investigating the contents of his father's pockets, ran to the floor lamp, pulled out the cord, and then pretended that he was going to tip the lamp over. Another boy of three violently mussed up his freshly combed hair when his mother prevented him from going out into the yard to play. When a piece of candy was taken from a four-year-old, he ran to the sofa, dragged off all the cushions, threw them on the floor, and jumped on them. A girl of three would suck her thumb in a conspicuous manner when angry, although she had ceased to do so when not thwarted (*Goodenough, 1931*). Indirect physical retaliation to frustration is a further modification of the aggressive response to thwarting.

Indirect physical attack may take the form of the well known temper tantrum. Young children, when frustrated, may display a pattern of behavior characterized by crying, screaming, falling to the floor, thrashing and kicking, and even violent banging of the head on the floor. Parental alarm over such behavior can serve as reinforcement for it; the behavior is perpetuated either by this reinforcement or by parental acquiescence to the child's demands. Some severe tantrum behavior may also be interpreted as representing the child's failure to learn more sophisticated ways of responding to frustration. Viewed in this fashion, the diffuse, chaotic, emotional outburst characteristic of early responses to frustration appears to persist as a consequence of immaturity, and to derive from an absence of social learning rather than from its occurrence.

The next shift in the developmental sequence of aggressive responses to thwarting is from the indirect physical to the *symbolic level*. The child learns through bitter experience that neither direct nor indirect physical attack on the person restricting one's activity is always the wisest approach to the problem. If the person who is causing the frustration is larger, stronger, or more skillful, direct physical attack invites counterattack, with further frustration and increased punishment for the child. Consequently, with the development of language, a verbal attack on the thwarting agent may be substituted for the direct or indirect physical retaliation. Calling the person names, swearing at him, and "cutting him down to size" verbally are symbolic aggressive responses to thwarting. One girl of seven expressed her resentment against her mother by such remarks as "I wish I had a mother like Mary's." Just as verbal stimuli may function as thwarting agents, so the reaction to thwarting may be verbal. Making faces, sticking out one's tongue, and thumbing one's nose may also function as symbolic retaliative aggressive responses to frustrations.

The final shift in the sequence of aggressive responses to frustration is to the *indirect symbolic or verbal level*. Instead of swearing at the other person and calling him names to his face, we tell derogatory stories, start malicious rumors, and otherwise undermine his reputation. We attack the status and the good name of the person who is thwarting us instead of making a direct attack upon him. We may also attack another person indirectly by belittling or discrediting his possessions, his family, his friends, his beliefs, ideas, and ideals. Any extensions of the "self" may be subject to aggressive attack as a substitute for a direct attack on the person.

Indirect hostile responses to thwarting may even involve a form of self-punishment. The "black sheep" of the family may become immoral, delinquent, or a criminal in an indirect attack on his family who, he believes, thwarted him. His behavior serves to discredit the family and to besmirch its reputation.

## Table 1. Tabular Presentation of the Developmental Sequence of Aggressive Reactions to Frustration

| Thwarting agents | Activities or processes thwarted | Responses to thwarting |
|---|---|---|
| a. Physical restraints<br>b. Threats of physical restraint<br>c. Verbal restraints<br>d. Threats of verbal restraint | a. Physical activity (locomotion or manipulation)<br>b. Speech<br>c. Ideational processes (plans, purposes, beliefs, values) | a. Diffuse motoractivity<br>b. Retaliatory physical activity directed at the thwarting agent<br>c. Direct verbal retaliation<br>d. Indirect verbal retaliation |

## Familial Correlates of Aggression

Research studies of the backgrounds of over-aggressive antisocial individuals have consistently disclosed an early environment characterized by parental rejection, familial discord, the use of physically painful punishment or threats of physical punishment, inconsistency in treatment, parental permissiveness of aggression, a low level of parental expectation, a lack of parental supervision, parental examples of social deviance, and parental dissatisfaction with the child's role in life (*Glueck and Glueck, 1950; Weiss and Fine, 1956; Sears et al., 1957; McCord et al., 1959; Bandura and Walters, 1959; McCord et al., 1961*).

These research findings are consistent with our interpretation of over-aggression as constituting either a reaction to excessive frustration (hostile counteraggression) or a product of social learning. Parental examples of social deviance, conflict, bickering, recriminations, overt physical attacks, acceptance or tacit approval of aggression, the absence of consistent parental supervision and control, and an atmosphere of family discord in which the parents undermine the values and significance of one another are all conducive to the development of aggression as a way of life. Patterns of aggression developing under such conditions can be considered essentially non-hostile in nature.

Several of the familial correlates of aggression also constitute excessive frustrations of a hostile aggression-instigating sort. They are: the use of physical punishment, the frequent use of threats, parental rejection of the child, and parental disagreement concerning methods of child rearing resulting in inconsistent treatment.

The studies of aggression in children uniformly disclose that both social learning and excessive aggression-instigating factors in the home contribute to the development of over-aggressiveness in the child. The evidence indicates that aggression is a form of behavior developed in response to specific environmental conditions in which the familial environment is an important component.

### DISPLACED AGGRESSION

It seems reasonable that acts of direct aggression would be more satisfying to the performer than indirect forms of aggression. There is some experimental evidence to support this expectation (*Berkowitz, 1962*). As described in the preceding section, the shifts in the objects toward which aggression is directed are limited to people or things having some functional relationship with the person toward whom the aggression is directed. The person responsible for the thwarting is always the primary target of the aggression. His possessions, reputation, ideals, and friends are attacked only because hurting them will indirectly hurt him.

There is sometimes a shift in the *primary object* against which the aggression is directed. When acts of aggression against a frustrating object or person are prevented, there is a tendency for the person to attack another object or person. Sometimes the direct act of aggression against a thwarting agent is prevented by the absence of the instigating object or person, at other times, by conflict with a specific fear of punishment. Because of social disapproval and other painful consequences of openly expressing one's hostile tendencies, hostility is often perceived as a danger-ous impulse that should be suppressed, and against which defenses must be developed. In such situations a convenient, but perfectly innocent, scape-goat may become the object of aggression.

A rat who has been trained to strike at another rat when frustrated will attack a celluloid doll when no other rat is present (*Dollard et al., 1939; Berkowitz, 1958*). Experimentally frustrated human subjects rate their friends, who have not been responsible for the frustration, lower on a personality rating scale than do comparable subjects who had not been subjected to such frustrations (*Dollard et al., 1939; Berkowitz, 1958*). The person who trips over a toy on the floor may kick the cat. The person who perceives himself as being frustrated by the members of one minority racial group may express hostile aggression against all minority racial groups. The object of personal or racial hostility may even extend to all people who are significantly different from the person's own social group. In such cases the mere perception of "differentness" may arouse hostility. Some of these shifts of the objects of aggression may result from "stimulus generaliza-tion." (See later chapters for a discussion of this concept.)

When a person "bullies" those who are smaller or weaker than he is, it is usually evidence of scapegoating. When a gang or school group exhibits a persisting tendency to persecute and be cruel to weak and defenseless individuals, to their own less popular members, or to a small subgroup, we can suspect that displaced aggression is manifesting itself; thus, "teacher's pet" may become a substitute target for students frustrated by the teacher when they are afraid to attack the teacher directly.

### DELINQUENCY

Not all delinquency is hostile aggression, just as not all other forms of aggression are necessarily retaliative in nature. Some children raised in areas of high delinquency, where many families and subcultures reward and reinforce delinquent behavior, grow up with delinquency and accept it as a way of life. Fighting, lying, cheating, and stealing are accepted as the more rugged components of a rough world. These activities are accepted as essential parts of the only life they know. The individual growing up in such a culture acquires and fixates aggressive behavior patterns as his "life style."

Non-hostile delinquency may also occur as a means of status seeking and prestige-enhancement for the participants. The members of a deviant delinquent subculture perceive conformity to a violently aggressive way of life as a prerequisite to acceptance into, continuing membership in, and increased status within that subculture. So long as an individual's dominant social contacts and sources of individual satisfaction are within such a group, he will look upon aggressive, delinquent behavior as a means of obtaining positive satisfactions.

It is no doubt true that both psychological and sociological factors are significant in the etiology of delinquency (*Hathaway and Monachesi, 1963*). Our culture rewards aggressiveness, but at the same time insists on conformity and cooperation. Learning when and how to compete and when to conform is not an easy task for many children or for adults. The studies of the personalities of delinquents have yielded all too little in the way of consistent findings (*Richardson and Roebuck, 1965*), and attempts to predict subsequent delinquency have been less than promising (*Bothman et al., 1965*). The search for simple causes and cures for delinquent behavior appears doomed to failure, for the background of delinquency is a complex one.

## Delinquency as Aggressive Retaliation for Frustration

When an individual has experienced, either first-hand or vicariously, some of the better things of life and then has these desirable objects or experiences withdrawn or withheld, he may react in a hostile and aggressive manner. Aggressive retaliation for deprivation commonly takes the form of delinquent behavior. Sociologists have repeatedly documented the delinquency-breeding outcomes of poverty, and family and social disorganization (*Cloward and Ohlin, 1960; Gibbons and Garrety, 1962*). Children deprived of adequate food, clothing, and shelter; children experiencing loss of one or both parents due to death, desertion, or divorce; children who lack parental affection; children who are rejected by either peers or major social groups because of social, economic, cultural, or personal characteristics are very likely to develop "grudges." Grudges often manifest themselves in aggressive retaliation against either the real or imagined sources of deprivation, or against perfectly innocent people (scapegoats).

## PATHOLOGICAL AGGRESSION

Bettleheim, in his book *Love is Not Enough* (1950), and Redl and Wineman, in *Children Who Hate* (1951) and *Controls From Within* (1952), have dramatically described children displaying pathological aggressiveness as a way of life. These children are largely incapable of rationally controlling their own behavior. They are at the mercy of their own hostile impulses. Either they have failed to develop any inner behavior controls or their normal behavior controls have been destroyed by the inconsistencies of their social environments when they were young. They have become helpless bundles of aggressive impulses. Aggression seems to be their only way of reacting to life. On the slightest provocation they erupt into wreckless destruction or blind rage. Their slightest fears and anxieties find immediate outlet in disorganized aggression. Their slightest guilt feelings manifest themselves in aggressiveness, which often involves repeating the same acts that produced their guilt in the first place.

Despite normal general intelligence, they seem incapable of profiting by their social experiences. Having had a pleasurable social experience, they do not seem to remember the feat and realize the possibility of its repetition. They cannot delay satisfaction. If their desires are not immediately gratified, they react with hostility and violence. The causes of their failures and their hostilities are all projected outwardly. The world and everyone in it is perceived as threatening. They react to the hostile and punishing world by counterhostility.

These "psychopaths" have proved to be very resistant to treatment because of the consolidation of their intense hostility into a set of ready-made defenses against any offers of help from other people. Manifestations of affection and good will are either signs of an enemy's weakness or tricks designed to deceive them. Offers of help or assistance are met with unreasonable demands for more, and if the demands are not met the inevitable explosion of hate is set off. They seem incapable of either requesting or accepting help. These children are seriously disturbed and behave in ways that are both socially and personally destructive.

## COMPENSATORY BEHAVIOR

Compensation as a behavior mechanism refers to activity that achieves satisfaction of a motive when immediate direct satisfaction is blocked. When used in this broad sense, compensation would include all the defense mechanisms as well as most of the learning and problem-solving solutions of problematic situations. In practice, the term is reserved for the aggressive, overt meeting of thwarted motives by the excessive development of either task-related or substitute skills or abilities.

Compensatory behavior may be: (1) *compensation in kind*, as when an individual, by dint of unusual drive and effort, overcomes an initial handicap and achieves in the area of his original deficiency; (Demosthenes, originally a stutterer, is said to have practiced speaking with pebbles in his mouth. He became a famous orator.) (2) *vicarious or substitute*, as when a person develops substitute abilities for the ones he lacks (the physically handicapped boy who renounces his athletic ambitions to become a musician).

It has been said that society rewards its great compensators. This statement implies that many of our great men have achieved eminence as the result of their over-compensations for initial handicaps. One can accumulate an impressive array of historical figures for whom this hypothesis seems plausible. Napoleon, Mussolini, and Franco, all dictators, were men of small stature. Theodore Roosevelt's advocacy and exemplification of the strenuous life may have sprung from his physical frailty in boyhood. Demosthenes' oratorical prowess may have represented an over-compensation for his stuttering. Louise Baker lost a leg in childhood but became a one-legged celebrity. In her autobiography (*Baker, 1946*), she indicates that but for the loss of her limb, she would not have achieved this fame. Glenn Cunningham burned his legs so severely as a child that his doctors predicted he would never be able to walk. In spite of this accident and the dire predictions—or because of them—Cunningham not only learned to walk, but became an Olympic runner. It is, of course, only conjecture that the superior achievements of these individuals represent over-compensations for their initial handicaps, but it is quite certain that many achievements are so motivated.

## Compensations in Kind

The instances listed above are all compensations in kind. The individuals reacted to personal deficiency or failure by increased effort presumably to make up for their initial defects. This increased effort results in excessive achievement in the area of the original deficiency. This type of compensation is simply the exaggeration or intensification of a direct and perfectly normal reaction to a difficulty. It may be considered a problem-solving or learning approach to a problematic situation. The only unique feature of direct compensation is the over-reaction and over-achievement deriving from the anxiety engendered by the threat aspect of the initial failures. Part of the motivation for the achievement derives from the original desire for affiliation or prestige that instigates the activity, but an additional sustaining motive arises from the threat of inferiority, which the individual feels compelled to deny and disprove. To put the same statement more positively, the person is motivated to prove his normality or superiority by over-achievement. The result of such motivation is an intensified effort to overcome a defect in a direct, straightforward way.

There are some disadvantages to direct compensation as a reaction to thwarting. Sometimes, despite the expenditure of tremendous time and effort, success is not possible. There are handicaps that are insurmountable; there are goals that are beyond the capacities of certain people to attain. When a person reacts to each failure by renewed effort, he may spend his life trying for the impossible. In such cases, reasonable attempts at overcoming one's limitations might be followed by some type of compromise solution. "Try, try again; and then try something else," may be a more intelligent approach to a problem than continuing to "beat one's head against a stone wall."

Another possible disadvantage of direct compensation as a response to failure is that it may result in a distorted conception of the relative importance of various fields of endeavor, and a one-sided development of the individual. When a person drives himself to achieve in areas where he is handicapped, and with the expenditure of tremendous time and effort does attain success, the goals achieved become the only important things in the world. His complete dedication to art, music, or athletics results in his exaggerating their importance and placing too much value on achievements in these particular areas, so that nothing is of value to him if it does not contribute to achievement in his chosen field. The achieving of his chosen goals may be at the expense or neglect of many other areas of life, and may result in the development of a one-sided person. In terms of a person's overall development, renunciation of one's original ambitions in favor of a more accessible goal might result in a more "normally developed" person.

## Vicarious Compensations

Compensation by means of *substitute achievement* is a common adjustment to frustration and failure. When one's deficiencies are extreme and irremediable, substitute achievements may be the only form of compensation either possible or practicable. The individual thwarted in one area of endeavor accepts achievement in a less desirable area as a substitute. In this type of compensation, the substitute achievement is always a "second choice." The physically weak but athletically ambitious boy may become a chess player, or an accomplished musician, artist, or actor. The disappointed actor may become a coach, playwright, or stagehand. The girl who is unsuccessful in love may renounce marriage in favor of a life as a teacher, governess, or nurse. Compensatory activities are characterized by their motivation rather than by the unique form they take.

Substitute or vicarious compensations serve two purposes. As substitute achievements, they reduce anxiety concerning one's inferiority. Demonstrated achievements, even in a substitute area, bolster one's self-concept, inflate one's ego, and may provide some positive satisfactions. They make a person feel less anxious, more adequate and secure. The compensatory achievements may also direct attention from personal defects or behavioral limitation in the area of one's original aspiration. The belief that positive achievements make one's defects less obvious also reduces anxiety and contributes to one's feeling of adequacy.

### SUBLIMATION

The reality of sublimation as an adjustment mechanism is questionable. Freud (1938) used the term to refer to the redirection of sexual energy (the libido) into nonsexual channels. The concept has since been expanded to refer to the indirect, socially acceptable expression of frustrated motives of all types. In the broader sense of using any substitute activity to gratify a motive, sublimation would include vicarious compensation and most, if not all, of the other defense mechanisms. All of these defensive reactions are substitute activities that occur when motives are frustrated. When the concept of sublimation is defined so broadly, it loses its original meaning and usefulness.

Most of the evidence indicates that drive originating in specific organic sources cannot be satisfied by substitute outlets. Kinsey *et al.* (1948) and Taylor (1928) found evidence of repression, but hardly any evidence of sublimation in the sex drive of males. The classical examples of sublimation concern the gratification of the unsatisfied sexual urge by channeling it into art, religion, music, or other aesthetic activities. Sports are often mentioned as an outlet for sublimated sexual desires. Similarly, social work, teaching, and nursing are said to operate as outlets for blocked sexual or maternal motives.

It seems that the concept of vicarious sexual outlets has resulted from the acceptance of a misleading physical analogy. When someone speaks of "sexual energy" or the "libido" as finding an "outlet" in substitute "channels," a hydraulic or gaseous system under pressure is suggested. The pressure in such a system exerts itself equally in all directions and can be relieved or reduced by means of its "normal" outlet or, if this outlet is blocked, by means of substitute channels. However, the organic sources of drive (hunger, thirst, sex) do not consist of energy under pressure that can be relieved by activity of various sorts. Stimuli from physiological hunger are reduced only by a limited number of things such as the ingestion of food, the intravenous injection of glucose, or injury to the neural mechanisms involved. Sexual activity does not take care of one's nutritional needs, nor does the ingestion of liquid satisfy hunger or sex. It is likewise doubtful that engaging in useful and even sexually related social and vocational activities actually serve as sexual outlets that quantitatively reduce the stimuli associated with hormonal and physical changes incident to sexual arousal. In the male, it is doubtful that anything short of ejaculation reduces the stimuli associated with sexual arousal. The physiological mechanism for reduction of sexual arousal in the female is less obvious, but it may possibly be the orgasm itself.

It must be recognized that eating, drinking, and sexual activity in humans come to represent much more than the relief of hunger, thirst, and sexual tension. What, how, where, and with whom one eats come to have affectional and prestige implications, so that eating and drinking satisfy personal and social motives as well as organic needs. Similarly, sexual activity and attractiveness may imply personal adequacy or inadequacy, social acceptability or rejection, personal strength or weakness, manliness or womanliness. When sexual activity has elements of personal and social as well as organic motivation, a substitute activity may reduce the total sexually related stimuli because the personal and social components, not the biological elements, are subject to other forms of gratification.

Unlike organic conditions, the social affiliation, prestige, and security motives do not require a specific type of object, goal, or activity for their satisfaction. The forms that affiliation, status, and security motives take and the symbols or indices of their satisfaction vary from culture to culture, from generation to generation, and, to some extent, from person to person. Thus, these motives may be satisfied by a great variety of experiences, all of which are interchangeable. If one's affectional advances are blocked by one person or group of people, one's affectional desires can still be satisfied by another person or persons. If a person fails to achieve prestige professionally, he may still attain a satisfactory social status by means of sports, music, or art as a vocation or community service activity.

When a man finds himself unacceptable to women and fails to marry, he may be deprived of a sexual outlet, but in addition he may feel personally inadequate, inferior, and lacking in normal attractiveness and power. If, as a result of his failure to marry, he becomes a professional strong man, a great out-of-doors man, or a mountain climber, these activities are not necessarily the manifestation of a blocked, repressed, and sublimated sex drive. They may instead be means of obtaining acceptance, affection, and status in a personal-social way. These activities are motivated by a desire to prove that he is really a masculine, competent, adequate, and powerful person.

Even sexual exhibitionism may be an attempt to demonstrate "sexual prowess" of a prestige rather than of a biological type. This is evidenced by the fact that many "exhibitionists" get satisfaction from exposing themselves only when the other person is greatly shocked or reacts violently. If the other person ignores, laughs at, or "makes fun" of the exhibitionist, he often feels disappointed and "cheated." In some cases exhibiting the genitals may be accompanied or followed by spontaneous or masturbatory ejaculation. This, of course, results in a reduction of the stimuli associated with sexual arousal. If, however, the exhibitionism has some strength-masculinity-sexual adequacy implications for the subject, a "completely satisfying" experience will include both a violent reaction on the part of the observer and ejaculation. The organic-sexual and the personal-social power motives will have both been either reduced or satisfied.

It is doubtful that physiological stimuli can be reduced by substitute activity. It is more likely that the motives satisfied by substitute activities (often labeled as sublimation), even when they are organic-drive-related, are of the personal-social type. Implications of personal failure and loss of self-esteem in one area of endeavor can be compensated for by achievement in some other area, but it is unlikely that the organic sources of drive and stimulation have substitute means of reduction. If our interpretation is correct, compensation as a means of obtaining satisfaction for the social motives by the substitution of one activity for another is very common, but sublimation as the redirection of sexual energy into nonsexual channels, as postulated by the psychoanalysts, probably does not occur.

### *REACTION-FORMATION*

Reaction-formation as a behavior pattern could just as logically be listed as a subclass of compensation as given a separate designation; however, it does have some distinguishing characteristics. Reaction-formation consists of the adoption of a behavior pattern that is directly the opposite of the reaction-tendency the person is trying to deny or refute. In other words, reaction-formation consists of the functioning of a pattern of behavior that is directly opposed to an anxiety-arousing impulse to act.

In compensation, the blocked behavior and the goals toward which the behavior is directed are typically personally and socially desirable. Anxiety is aroused by implications of personal inadequacy or inferiority because of failures in goal-attainment. Compensatory activity results in the attainment and "over-shooting" of either the original or a substitute goal. The motives involved and the goals attained are usually meritorious and are, therefore, not anxiety-arousing. In reaction-formation, the motive and goal are unworthy and therefore produce feelings of guilt or shame. The impulse to act in accordance with the motive is anxiety-arousing and the opposite type of activity is engaged in to keep the unacceptable behavior from occurring.

Some instances of reaction-formation are: (1) over-aggressive behavior as a reaction to fear; (2) over-sentimentality as a means of repressing or denying sadistic tendencies; (3) the over-solicitousness of the mother of a handicapped child as a reaction to either feelings of rejection or the presence of a death wish; (4) the over-precise and excessively polite treatment of a disliked person; (5) the frustrated spinster who covets other people's children but over-reacts by being "unable to stand" to have children about her; (6) the excessively prudish individual who is strongly tempted sexually; (7) the reformed drunkard who fights his own impulses to drink by becoming an ardent prohibitionist; (8) the daughter who really hates her mother but is over-solicitous of her health and comfort; (9) the father who is cruel to his daughter as a reaction to his incestuous love for her.

In these instances antisocial and personally unacceptable impulses, instead of finding an outlet in a related substitute activity (compensation), are kept either repressed or controlled (suppressed) by engaging in the opposite type of behavior. The psychoanalysts conceive of reaction-formation as being entirely unconscious; however, these same tendencies can operate on a conscious level. The reformed drunkard may still be aware of his desire to drink and may be using his public exhortations of others to bolster his own resolve. By making public pronouncements of his reformation, he enlists public approval of his behavior as insurance against a possible relapse.

The "bully," who is really afraid of others, acts "tough" to keep others from suspecting his weakness. He may be quite aware of his fear and the reasons for his belligerency. At the other extreme, reaction-formation can function on an unconscious level. A person may be unaware of his unacceptable, anxiety-arousing impulses and really believe that his true motives are the more socially acceptable ones.

### THE SIGNIFICANCE OF DEFENSIVE BEHAVIOR PATTERNS

The existence of reaction-formation as a behavior pattern points up a general problem involved in the inferring of motives from behavior.

Apparently, affectionate behavior can derive from either love or hate. Prudish behavior can be a manifestation of either high moral scruples or excessive preoccupation with sexual desires. Does it then follow that motives are never what they seem to be? Can motives ever be taken at their face value? Are appearances always deceptive? Is a person the victim of unconscious motives and impulses that control his behavior in a compulsive way? Is most of our conscious interpretation of our own behavior only a rational camouflage for the real motives, of which we are unaware?

Complete acceptance of the psychoanalytic interpretation of behavior seems to dictate an affirmative answer to these questions; however, the original psychoanalytic systematization and interpretation of the defense mechanisms were developed in a clinic with "mentally ill" people. The extension of this interpretation of the nature and manner of functioning of these "abnormal" behavior patterns to normal people was an extrapolation from the mentally ill. It seems likely that an emphasis on the irrational, unconscious, and compulsive nature of the defense mechanisms resulted from study of the more severely emotionally disturbed who, by definition, display those characteristics to an extreme degree.

A simplified statement of the traditional psychoanalytic conception of the dynamics of the defense mechanisms is as follows: Anxiety-laden, socially disapproved, and personally unacceptable thoughts and motives are "repressed into the unconscious." These tendencies to act persist as unconscious, dynamic, ideational, and behavioral trends and manifest themselves in indirect, camouflaged, and irrational ways. The defense mechanisms represent the devious ways in which the unconscious motives find expression in less ego-deflating and less anxiety-arousing activities. The repressed unconscious motives distort perception, warp thinking, and control behavior in a forced and compulsive way. The individual becomes a victim of his own unconscious impulses.

According to this conception, repression and unconscious motivation are the two basic mechanisms involved in producing the misperceptions, distorted thinking, and inappropriate emotional reactions of the defensive, neurotic, or psychotic individual. When a person feels personally inadequate and considers his motives, thoughts, and impulses socially unacceptable and personally repulsive, he experiences guilt and anxiety. To the degree that his behavioral trends are anxiety-arousing, the impulses to act are repressed and find less anxiety-laden outlets. When anxiety is not acute, the anxiety level may be reduced sufficiently by means of the various defense mechanisms such as rationalization, projection, compensation, and identification, so that the individual is able to tolerate any remaining anxiety. Such a person will experience misperceptions, distorted ideation, and irrational behavior of only a minor sort and can live a fairly adequate and socially useful life. The individual also will maintain a considerable amount of insight into himself, and most of his behavior will be socially appropriate.

The individual with greater feelings of personal inferiority and excessive guilt feelings experiences such a constantly high level of anxiety that he is threatened with complete behavioral disorganization and panic. With repression of the more powerful threatening impulses, more drastic forms of defense are required to prevent complete breakdown. In such cases, there occurs the dissociation of the unacceptable impulses and actions, conversion reactions, phobic reactions, and the compulsive-obsessive reactions that characterize the neuroses. In the neuroses, the misperceptions and distortions of thinking, feeling, and acting are more serious. The neurotic individual is, to a great extent, a victim of his repressed and unconsciously functioning impulses; however, the neurotic individual still maintains some degree of insight. For example, a person experiencing phobic or obsessive compulsive reactions recognizes the irrational nature of his fears, thoughts, and acts but is unable to either control them or understand why he has or does them. A considerable portion of his behavior may be socially inappropriate.

The psychotic person is the one who has experienced overwhelming anxiety, repressed completely the unacceptable, anxiety-laden impulses, and handled the unconscious repressed trends by the most extreme forms of perceptual, ideational, emotional, and behavioral distortions. Acute psychotics are characterized by a lack of personal insight. They perceive their own experiences and activities as rational, consistent, and appropriate even though other people do not share their beliefs.

If we accept the notion of the mildly defensive, the neurotic, and the psychotic behavioral syndromes as representing ranges on a scale representing varying degrees of perceptual-ideational distortion, inappropriate affect, and irrational behavior, and if we extrapolate in the opposite direction, we will come to a theoretical point at which these variables reach zero. There is no way of knowing whether this presumably ideal state is ever attained, but we can at least conceive of a wide range of either "normal" or "ideal" adjustment in which these "distortions" are minimal. In a negative way, we can think of this range of adjustment as resulting from motivational levels involving minimal anxiety (more a promise of positive reward than a fear of failure) and little, if any, repression, with a consequently low level of unconscious motivation. With little or no anxiety, minimum repression, and small amounts of unconscious motivation, there will occur little perceptual-ideational distortion and irrational social behavior. The individual will have fairly complete personal insight.

Those writers who have tried to define and describe personality

adjustment in terms of an "ideal" have included the above listed characteristics in a positive way as: (1) efficient perception of reality, (2) comfortable relations with reality, (3) acceptance of the "self" without real
concern, (4) spontaneousness and naturalness of behavior (the ability to
be oneself), (5) motivation of a positive-seeking type, (6) activity of a
problem-centered rather than a self-centered type, (7) flexibility of behavior, (8) an "open self." Movements toward, against or away from
others are not mutually exclusive for the well integrated person (*Maslow,
1956; Horney, 1945; Rogers, 1957*). Most of these characteristics are the
opposite of defensive, neurotic, or psychotic behavior patterns as described
above.

We now return to our original set of questions. To the degree that a
person is socially and personally adequate, to the extent that he has a
satisfactory self-concept and is free of anxiety, he will experience little
repression and minimal defensiveness, and his motivations will remain on
the conscious level. As a consequence, his perceptions will be reasonably
accurate, his thinking will be objective and problem-oriented, his emotions
will be freely and appropriately expressed, his overt behavior will be
rational and socially appropriate, and he will have good personal insight.
Of course, the possession of these characteristics is a matter of degree, but

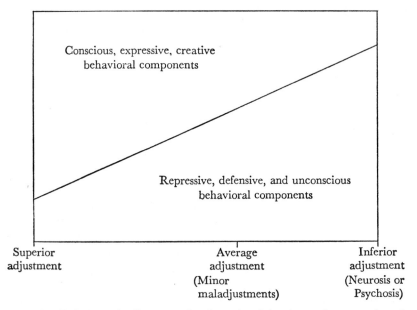

*Figure 4. Relation of adjustment level to the defensive and unconscious be-
havioral components.*

since, by definition, there are more "well adjusted" than "maladjusted" people, a given individual may be assumed to be insightful until he is proven otherwise. Motives can be taken at their face value until we have evidence to the contrary. To the extent that a given person is "normal" we can take his responses as reflecting his "true motives." To the degree that a person is defensive, neurotic, or psychotic, his true motives will be hidden, his perception and ideation distorted, and his socially relevant behavior irrational.

The psychoanalysts have described the motivation and defenses of "mentally sick" people. Their description needs to be supplemented by a recognition of the reasonably accurate perceptual-ideational processes and rational behavior of the "mentally healthy" individual (*Maslow, 1956; Allport, 1956, 1961; Kroeber, 1964*). Kroeber (*1964*) has attempted to extend the concepts of the defensive mechanisms to describe the behavior of effective persons. His extension of these concepts includes the efforts of people to cope effectively with their environment by essentially healthy means.

### SUMMARY

Not all aggression is defensive. Many cultures, subcultures, and families encourage and reward certain forms of aggressive behavior. Hostile and defensive aggression constitutes one class of adjustive behavior patterns. Hostile aggression is usually the result of frustrations. Frustrations originally consist of the hampering or restricting of bodily movement. As a result of learning, threats of physical restraints, verbal (symbolic) restraints, and threatened symbolic restraints come to function as thwarting agents. Responses to thwarting progress from the primitive diffuse anger outburst, to direct physical attack on the thwarting agent, to indirect physical attack, and finally to indirect symbolic (principally verbal) attack on the thwarting agent.

This developmental sequence may be supplemented by the appearance of displaced aggression (scapegoating) directed at a perfectly innocent person or thing. Delinquency may represent non-hostile aggression when it is culturally induced and supported. It may also represent aggressive retaliation for frustration.

Pathological aggression may be the result of encapsulated self-concepts and distorted social conceptions that are resistant to change and result in compulsive behavior of a self-defeating type.

Compensatory aggressive behavior may take the form of either vicarious compensations, in which the individual develops substitute aptitudes or activities in place of the ones in which he is deficient, or compensation in kind, in which by means of unusual drive and effort an initial handicap is overcome.

Sublimation is the redirection and satisfaction of a motive by way of substitute outlets. It is doubtful that sublimation of the organic needs is possible. Social motives have multiple outlets and one type of activity can substitute for another in their satisfaction.

Reaction-formation involves the exaggerated display of behavior that is the direct opposite of the reaction-tendency the person is trying to repress, control, or deny. To the extent that a person is personally and socially adequate, has a satisfactory self-concept, and is free of anxiety, his percepts and concepts are reasonably accurate and his motives can be taken at "face value." The personally inadequate, anxiety-ridden individual is likely to become defensive, neurotic, or psychotic, and his motives, percepts, and ideational processes suffer various degrees of distortion.

### *REFERENCES*

ALLPORT, GORDON W. The Trend in Motivational Theory. In Moustakas, Clark E. (ed.), *The Self*. New York: Harper & Brothers, 1956.

ALLPORT, GORDON W. *Pattern and Growth in Personality*. New York: Holt, Rinehart, and Winston, 1961.

BAKER, LOUISE. *Out on a Limb*. New York: Whittlesley House (McGraw-Hill Book Company), 1946.

BANDURA, A., and WALTERS, R. *Adolescent Aggression*. New York: The Ronald Press Company, 1959.

BERKOWITZ, LEONARD. The expression and reduction of hostility. *Psychol. Bull.*, 1958, **55**, 257–283.

BERKOWITZ, L. *Aggression: A Social Psychological Analysis*. New York: McGraw-Hill Book Company, 1962.

BETTELHEIM, B. *Love Is Not Enough*. Glencoe, Illinois: Free Press, 1950.

BOTHMAN, R. W., HARTINGER, W., and RICHARDSON, H. A comparison of two delinquency predicting instruments. *J. res. crime delinq.*, 1965, **2**, 45–48.

CLOWARD, R. A. and OHLIN, L. E. *Delinquency and Opportunity*. Glencoe, Illinois: Free Press, 1960.

DOLLARD, J., DOOB, L. W., MILLER, N. E., MOWRER, O. H., and SEARS, R. R. *Frustration and Aggression*. New Haven: Yale University Press, 1939.

FREUD, SIGMUND. A *General Introduction to Psychoanalysis*. Garden City, New York: Garden City Publishing Company, 1938.

GIBBONS, D. C. and GARRITY, D. L. Definition and analysis of certain criminal types. *J. crim. law criminol. police sci.*, 1962, **53**, 27–35.

GLUECK, S., and GLUECK, E. *Unravelling Juvenile Delinquency*. New York: Commonwealth Fund, 1950.

GOODENOUGH, F. L., *Anger in Young Children*. Minneapolis: University of Minnesota Press, 1931.

HATHAWAY, S. R., and MONACHESI, E. D. *Adolescent Personality and Behavior: MMPI Patterns of Normal, Delinquent, Dropout, and Other Outcomes.* Minneapolis: University of Minnesota Press, 1963.

HORNEY, KAREN. The Search for Glory. In Moustakas, Clark E. (ed.), *The Self.* New York: Harper & Brothers, 1956.

HORNEY, KAREN. *Our Inner Conflicts.* New York: W. W. Norton and Company, 1945.

KINSEY, A. C., POMEROY, W. B., MARTIN, C. E., and GEBBARD, P. H. *Sexual Behavior in the Human Male.* Philadelphia: W. B. Saunders Company, 1948.

KROEBER, T. C. Coping Functions of the Ego Mechanisms. In R. W. White (ed.), *The Study of Lives.* New York: Atherton Press, 1964.

MASLOW, A. H. Personality Problems and Personality Growth. In Moustakas, Clark E. (ed.), *The Self.* New York: Harper & Brothers, 1956.

MCCORD, W., MCCORD, J., and ZOLA, I. *Origins of Crime.* New York: Columbia University Press, 1959.

MCCORD, W., MCCORD, J. S., and HOWARD, A. Familial correlates of aggression in nondelinquent male children. *J. abnorm. soc. Psychol.*, 1961, **62**, 79–93.

REDL, F., and WINEMAN, D. *Children Who Hate: The Disorganization and Breakdown of Behavior Controls.* Glencoe, Illinois: Free Press, 1951.

REDL, F., and WINEMAN, D. *Controls from Within.* Glencoe, Illinois: Free Press, 1952.

RICHARDSON, H., and ROEBUCK, J. Minnesota Multiphasic Personality Inventory and California Psychological Inventory differences between delinquents and their nondelinquent siblings. *Proc. 73rd annual convention of Amer. Psychol. Assoc.*, 1965, 255–256.

ROGERS, C. R. The necessary and sufficient conditions of therapeutic personality change. *J. consult. Psychol.*, 1957, **21**, 95–103.

SEARS, R., MACCOBY, E., and LEVIN, H. *Patterns of Child Rearing.* Evanston, Illinois: Row, Peterson, 1957.

TAYLOR, W. S. A critique of sublimation in males. *Genet. psychol. monogr.*, 1928, **13**, 1–115.

WEISS, W., and FINE, B. The effects of induced aggressiveness on opinion change. *J. abnorm. soc. Psychol.*, 1956, **52**, 109–114.

*Part* II

*Basic*
*Psychological*
*Processes*

*Chapter 5*

# Learning:
# Some General
# Considerations

THE ACTIVITIES OF HUMANS that are of prime concern to the psychologist are those behaviors that are learned. Although a great number of human functions appear not to have been learned, they are of interest to the psychologist largely as they effect his learned behavior. Innate activities are no doubt basic to what is eventually learned, but the focus of psychological attention is on acquired or learned behavior. In order to understand the learned behavior of individuals, it is necessary to have some understanding of the foundation on which learned behavior is built. The structure, function, and organization of the human organism are of more than passing concern to psychologists who are interested in adaptive or social learning; however, a detailed study of anatomy, physiology, and neurology is not essential to the level of understanding of learning processes necessary to appreciate the important role played by learning in the acquisition of culturally relevant responses.

In considering the learned responses of human beings in a social situation we are dealing with a complex pattern of stimuli and responses. The human organism is constantly being bombarded by stimuli, both internally and externally. The organism is also constantly responding. It breathes, perspires, makes both gross and fine movements, senses, perceives, feels, and thinks. If the learning of this organism were to be studied in the usual environment where it functions, the complexity of both stimuli and responses would be so great that it would be extremely difficult, if not impossible, to isolate very many meaningful patterns or principles by which learning occurs. Therefore, learning is typically studied in situations that are more controlled. Learning under particular and known circumstances can be studied without so many of the confounding factors that are to be found in actual life situations. When human subjects are used in investigations of learning they are selected on some basis. The stimulation of the individual is placed under as much control as possible and the supposedly relevant responses are systematically observed. Even so, there are many factors in studying human learning that are difficult to control. For example, it is difficult or almost impossible to study the effects of fear on human learning in the laboratory. If the situation is made genuinely fear-inducing, the human being will remove himself from the situation and will no longer be available for study. Man, with his well developed nervous system, is a complex organism, and this complexity makes him difficult to study.

Many psychologists believe that the study of the behavior of lower animals in learning situations can be used to suggest hypotheses and formulate principles about learning in human beings. It is generally recognized that man is a more complex organism, but it is felt that the learning of lower animals may yield principles that are characteristic of learning as a phenomenon. These principles will be more readily discernible in the comparatively simple responses of laboratory animals. These responses, coupled with the greater latitude permitted in laboratory control, have made lower animals prime subjects in learning experiments. Principles developed or isolated in the animal laboratory, in many cases, can later be tested on human beings. Such procedures have been followed in many instances with confirmatory results.

### THE NATURE AND SCOPE OF LEARNING

Learning seems to be a universal phenomenon among the more highly organized forms of animal life. Whether or not the lowest forms of animal life learn is less certain. However, it has been shown that paramecia, with practice, will take less time to turn around in a capillary tube (*Day and*

*Bentley, 1911*). This is a change in behavior that does not result from simple development or maturation and is not the result of physically injuring the organism. It is a change in behavior resulting from experience. Although the effects of the experience seem to be short-lived, we are inclined to call it learning. The word "learning" is frequently used to designate the process by which an organism's response potentials are modified by experience. This does not imply that all changes in behavior are the result of learning. Some behavior changes may result from maturation or growth; or behavior may be altered by injury or a change in the organism. These developments are not considered the results of learning. Changes in behavior that cannot be accounted for by maturation, injury, or alteration of the organism, but result from experience, are usually designated as having been learned. Thus it can be seen that much of human behavior can be called learned behavior.

The importance of learning in the life of the individual varies tremendously from species to species. Only a small portion of the response repertoire of the lower animals can be said to be learned. The small amount of learning that does take place occurs very slowly and is not very important in the life of the animal. Protozoa are born as practically mature organisms. At birth, or shortly thereafter, most of the acts they will ever be able to perform are observable. They have a very short period of infancy, a low capacity for learning, a short period of retention, and the products of their learning play practically no part in their lives. Species-specific responses, which function quite adequately from birth, constitute most of the responses that they will ever use.

As the animal scale is ascended, the number and fixity of species-specific behaviors is reduced and the period of infancy, the capacity for learning, and the importance of learning in the life of the individual increase. Of all the animals, the greatest capacity for profiting from experience is to be found in man. He has a very long period of infancy and his acquired responses constitute the bulk of his response repertoire. Man's existence is a very complex one and he has a great deal to learn if he is to function adequately in society. His "built-in" responses are but few in relation to those that principally result from learning. Man starts to learn very early in his life. There is evidence that the fetus can be conditioned; however, prenatal environment is so uniform that learning before birth is probably not very extensive or very important in the life of the individual. From this early start, man continues to learn until his death. His rate of learning typically increases with age from infancy to maturity. The rate is fairly constant for the next ten or fifteen years after maturity is achieved; then there is a gradual decline (*McGeoch and Irion, 1952*).

Man learns to use his muscular system effectively. He learns manual skills, verbal skills, and graphic skills, and ways of utilizing them. Through learning he acquires knowledge, meanings, fears, attitudes, personality characteristics, ideals, frames of reference, prejudices, values, and "self" knowledge. These results of learning represent such a vast and imposing array of the characteristics of men as individuals that knowledge about learning and learning processes is vital to the understanding of man's behavior.

### CIRCUMSTANCES FOR LEARNING

There is disagreement among psychologists concerning whether or not there are different forms of learning. Some theorists contend that all learning involves basically the same process, but that the experimental conditions manipulated and controlled to produce learning vary, and as a consequence cause the experimenter to interpret differing responses as different forms of learning (*Hull, 1943*). Other theorists contend that there are several kinds of learning (*Mowrer, 1960; Tolman, 1949*). This disagreement is of little or no concern to the student taking a course in personal adjustment or mental hygiene. Without considering whether or not there are different kinds, varieties, or forms of learning, we will present several conditions under which learning does occur. The fact of the occurrence of learning (considered from whatever theoretical position) in specified circumstances is the imperative consideration for the elementary understanding of behavior.

In this chapter some of the conditions for learning will be presented. No single chapter or even book could purport to treat the general subject matter of learning because the field is too great and the complications are too numerous. Consideration will be given to those aspects of learning which are deemed the most imperative for understanding the socially relevant learning of people in general.

## Classical Conditioning

The work done in Pavlov's laboratory (*Pavlov, 1927*) on conditioning dogs to salivate to an auditory stimulus has become known to every student of general psychology. The essential feature of the procedure was the sounding of a tuning fork shortly before presenting food to the dog. After many such presentations the dog would salivate to the sounding of the tuning fork even if he wasn't given the food. Since the early reports of Pavlov's experiments, conditioning has been carried out using a great number of different organisms and a variety of stimuli. Conditioning of protozoa, worms, fish, reptiles, chickens, rats, sheep, dogs, monkeys, and men have been reported in the experimenal literature (*Hilgard and Marquis, 1940*).

Among the essentials of a classical conditioning procedure is a stimulus that reliably produces a given response. This stimulus is known as the *unconditioned stimulus* and the response that it produces is called the *unconditioned* response. Another stimulus (one that does *not* produce the unconditioned response) now needs to be introduced. This stimulus is presented either along with or shortly preceding the unconditioned stimulus; then the unconditioned response is allowed to occur. After repeated pairing of the two stimuli, the one that previously did not evoke the unconditioned response, the *conditioned stimulus,* becomes effective in producing a response that is similar to or identical with the unconditioned response. This response is called the *conditioned response.*

$$
\begin{aligned}
US &\ —————————→ UR \\
CS + US &\ —————————→ UR \\
CS + US \text{ repetitions} &\ ————→ UR \\
CS &\ —————————→ CR
\end{aligned}
$$

*Figure 5. Conditioning. Initially the unconditioned stimulus (US) elicits the unconditioned response (UR). The conditioned stimulus (CS) is then paired with the unconditioned stimulus and the UR is elicited. This pairing is repeated. Eventually the CS alone elicits a response highly similar to the UR. This response is called the conditioned response (CR).*

Carrying the classical conditioning procedures still further, it is possible to use the stimulus that was heretofore the conditioned stimulus and pair it with another conditioned stimulus to produce the response. The new stimulus that has never been directly connected with the original unconditioned stimulus will be effective in evoking the conditioned response. A report from Pavlov's laboratory (1927) describes such a procedure. A dog was conditioned to salivate to the sound of a metronome. Following this procedure a black square was held before the dog for a short period of time before the metronome was sounded. The dog, after nine such exposures started to salivate when the black square was placed before him. In a later experiment (*Finch and Culler, 1934*), a tone was used as a conditioned stimulus and paired with a shock in originally training a dog to withdraw its leg. When the tone became established as a sufficient stimulus to produce the leg withdrawal, it was paired with a squirt of water on the nose. Eventually, a bell and a fan were introduced as effective stimuli in evoking the conditioned response. Such procedures Pavlov called *higher order conditioning.*

Although higher order conditioned responses are usually difficult to establish in the laboratory, they appear to occur rather regularly in the course of living. If a child sees and feels an apple and subsequently eats the apple, the sight of the apple may become a conditioned stimulus for tasting and feeling it. If the word "apple" is said a number of times while the child is experiencing the apple, the word itself may come to be a conditioned stimulus for the responses heretofore associated with the actual object. Subsequently, if the printed word "apple" is displayed and pronounced, it, too, becomes a conditioned stimulus for the responses associated with an apple. Any number of synonyms for the word may be acquired by such procedures. As a child's repertoire of responses increases, higher order conditioning probably becomes more and more important in his learning. It may be particularly important in the acquisition of fears and anxieties, as well as in the expansion of verbal skills.

### STIMULUS GENERALIZATION

A concept used very frequently by learning theorists to account for certain observed phenomena is that of stimulus generalization. This concept is so vital to the understanding of much of human behavior that a great deal of research has been devoted to it. Enough empirical evidence has been compiled in a sufficiently great number of areas that the fact of stimulus generalization can hardly be denied. It is said to occur when a response has been learned to a particular stimulus but can later be elicited by a stimulus similar to the original one (*Mednick and Freedman, 1960*). The general manner for demonstrating stimulus generalization is relatively simple. An organism is conditioned to respond to a particular conditioned stimulus. The test for stimulus generalization is to present stimuli individually that vary in the degree of their similarity to the original conditioned stimulus. If these stimuli elicit the response, stimulus generalization is said to have occurred. The strength of the response to stimuli of varying degrees of similarity or closeness to the original conditioned stimulus is used as a measure of the gradient of stimulus generalization. The typical research findings have indicated that the degree of closeness or similarity between the original conditioned stimulus and the test stimuli is correlated with the response strength. The greater the discrepancy between the two stimuli, the less the strength of responding. Stimulus generalization has been demonstrated by stimulating areas of the body at varying distances from the original stimulus and measuring the response (*Bass and Hull, 1934*). It also has been demonstrated along a visual-spatial continuum (*Brown et al., 1951*). Training to respond to a particular pitch (*Hovland, 1937*), to intensity of light stimulus (*Bass, 1958*), to intensity of sound stimulus

(*Miller and Greene, 1954*), and to intensity of drive stimulus (*Yamaguchi, 1952*) have all demonstrated stimulus generalization; however, Johnsgard (*1957*) has indicated that absolute stimulus intensity may not be as important as the amount of stimulus-background contrast when studying the effectiveness of stimulus intensity. Mednick and Freedman (*1960*) have concluded that any condition that will increase drive state will increase stimulus generalization. Generalization has also been obtained using stimulus size as the variable (*Grice and Saltz, 1950*).

Stimulus generalization is apparent when a young child, who has learned to identify the family dog by the name "Spot," calls all dogs "Spot." He may generalize to include all four-legged animals and may call cows or horses "Spot" when he is taken for a ride in the country. With continuing experience, the stimulus generalization diminishes until only dogs of the same size and color elicit the response, and finally to the point where only the family dog will serve as the effective stimulus.

The concept of stimulus generalization is used in a variety of situations to help clarify what is happening. It will be used in later chapters to help understand the learning of certain psychotic and psychoneurotic responses. The important things to remember about stimulus generalizations are (1) that the effects of conditioning are not limited to the stimulus originally conditioned but go beyond it; (2) that the greater the dissimilarity or the distance from the original conditioned stimulus, the less the effectiveness of another stimulus in evoking the response; (3) that conditions that will increase the drive state may result in increased stimulus generalization.

Individual differences in stimulus generalization have been investigated, and significant differences have been reported. These variances, and those due to situational or experimental factors, make it difficult to describe the gradient of stimulus generalization in precise terms. Gradients are discernible, however, and they are regularly reported in the experimental literature (*Mednick and Freedman, 1960*).

## Instrumental Conditioning

A group of methods for establishing conditioned responses that have been used widely in laboratory experimentation have come to be known as *instrumental conditioning*. They are so called because the conditioned response is instrumental in doing something for the organism, typically in procuring a reward of some kind for the animal. This reward may be in the form of (1) reducing or escaping noxious stimulation, (2) avoiding some noxious stimulus, (3) securing a positive incentive such as food or water, or (4) some state of affairs that has previously been associated with either 1,

2, or 3. The consequences of the conditioned response are said to *reinforce* the response; thus, these consequences are called *reinforcers* and the obtaining of these consequences is called *reinforcement*. In the classical conditioning procedure previously described, meat powder on the dog's tongue was the reinforcement for the salivary response (*Pavlov, 1927*). The meat powder in this situation was also the unconditioned stimulus. In the classical conditioning situation the response is one that is well established and occurs regularly when the unconditioned stimulus is applied. This is not true in instrumental conditioning, where the response must become associated with the stimuli through learning. The unconditioned stimulus in the classical conditioning procedures is easily identifiable, whereas in the instrumental conditioning procedure it is often difficult to identify. Meat powder in the classical conditioning described was the unconditioned stimulus. In the instrumental conditioning situation the unconditioned stimuli may be a combination or a group of discrete stimuli; that is, food deprivation plus the experimental apparatus and various other internal and external stimuli may combine to form the effective stimulus for producing the unconditioned response.

In the form of training known as *escape* training, the organism is placed in a situation where it receives a noxious stimulus. This noxious stimulus is terminated if, for example, the animal runs off an electrically charged portion of a grid. Here the stimulus is the electric current. The unconditioned responses are increased body tension, jumping, etc. The animal soon learns to escape the noxious stimulus by running to the uncharged portion of the grid. His running is instrumental in procuring the reduction of electric stimulation. This reduction in pain is the reinforcer; running directly off the charged portion of the grid is the conditioned response.

A child soon learns to escape when placed in bath water that is too hot. Escape reactions to a variety of stimuli are learned. Adults have learned a great many ways of escape from physically, socially, or personally uncomfortable situations.

With experience in situations where there are cues that painful or distressing circumstances are imminent, people and other organisms learn to *avoid* the noxious situation. Avoidance training can be illustrated using the same electrically charged grid as in the discussion of escape training. If, before the grid is charged with electricity, an electric light comes on or some other distinctive stimulus occurs, the animal will learn to run off the charged portion of the grid before the current comes on; thus he avoids a noxious stimulus. Here the conditioned stimulus is the light, the unconditioned stimulus is the shock, the unconditioned response is running to escape shock, and the conditioned response is running to avoid shock. A tremendous number of avoidance responses are acquired in the course of living. We learn, for example, to avoid situations where embarrassment or physical injury will be encountered.

Many of our responses are learned as the result of being positively reinforced when they occur. If we approach another person and he smiles, converses with us, or otherwise indicates approval of us or our behavior, our social approach responses are reinforced and we continue to make them in comparable situations. This is illustrative of *positive reward* training.

If a hungry animal is placed in a box where there is a lever that must be pressed before food will be obtainable, he will learn to press the bar in order to obtain food. The unconditioned stimulus is rather complex. The stimuli are hunger and the experimental apparatus. The unconditioned responses are those of general high-level activity. Eventually the lever pressing response occurs and is reinforced (food becomes available). Lever pressing is the conditioned response. Reward training can be viewed in essentially the same way as escape training. If the food is consumed and the hunger contractions diminish, noxious stimulation is thereby being terminated; thus, the organism escapes noxious stimulation. These different interpretations may result from individual preferences for either positive or negative statements. A rat may press a lever in order to obtain food or in order to reduce noxious stimulation, depending upon what one chooses to identify as the goal.

The concept of fear can be introduced into the interpretation of these situations (*Mowrer, 1939*). Fear can be viewed as a response to aversive (painful) stimulation; thus, fear as a response can be conditioned to various stimuli. In the avoidance training procedure, it can be said that the animal responds with fear to the noxious stimulus and the fear response becomes conditioned to the conditioned stimulus in the situation. The light evokes a new response, which is terminated by running to the end of the cage that has come to mean safety from shocks. The reduction of fear is the reinforcement in such situations. That it may act as a reinforcement for learning has been rather well established (*Miller, 1948; Brown and Jacobs, 1949; Kalish, 1954*). The use of the concept of fear in interpreting the results of instrumental conditioning studies has been an exceedingly important development. That people learn to fear a variety of stimuli is quite obvious. If too many situations become fear-arousing for a given person, he can learn to avoid so many situations that he becomes shy, elusive, and both socially and personally ineffective. This concept will be further elaborated in subsequent sections of this book.

## Reinforcement

That the consequences of past behavior have an influence on future behavior is a doctrine of long standing. Deliberately rewarding children for the kinds of behavior approved or desired by the parents is a technique that is widely used in the practical control of learning. The effects of reward and punishment on behavior are commonly recognized. Thorndike (1911) formalized these observations in his "law of effect." Since that time, a great deal of research effort has been devoted to reward and punishment (*Logan and Wagner, 1965*). We shall not be concerned with the theoretical meaning of reinforcement or with the question of whether or not reinforcement is essential for learning. Without regard to how reinforcement operates, it can probably be said that controlling behavior in the learning situation can best be accomplished through reinforcement. It refers to a variety of ways in which the individual or his environment may be manipulated in order to influence the probability of response reoccurrence in a learning situation. A great number of things have thus been found to be either positively or negatively reinforcing. Food, water, companionship, electric shock, fear, and the reduction of fear are among those things having reinforcing properties. It can be argued that reinforcement is a performance vairable and not a learning variable, but for our purposes performance can be assumed as an indicator of learning.

### AMOUNT OF REINFORCEMENT

Amount of reward as a variable in performance really has more than one dimension. Amount can be treated as a quantitative variable. As such, the amount of reinforcement may be rather well controlled in the experimental situation. The physical magnitude of the reinforcement can be measured. Animals can be given so much food, or water, or electric shock as a reinforcement. When amount is conceived qualitatively rather than quantitatively, it is difficult to control. A dime to the hungry child who knows he can obtain an ice cream cone with it has more value than a dime to the child who is not hungry or who does not know that it can be used to procure an ice cream cone. Another dimension of amount is the positive-negative dimension.

In general, it has been found that quantitative increases (*Rock, 1935; Hutt, 1954*) and qualitative increases (*Hutt, 1954*) in amount of reinforcement have been followed by increases in performance. The same general condition would seem to prevail for amount of negative reinforcement (*Kimble, 1955; Marshall, 1965*). The effectiveness of punishment as a reinforcer appears to be rather undependable. However, Marshall (1965) indicates that discrepancies among the findings of earlier studies can be accounted for by significant weaknesses in experimental design. The use of punishment in the control of learning is a delicate matter, but investigations have attested to its utility when employed under controlled conditions (*Penney and Lupton, 1961; Logan and Wagner, 1965*).

In situations where reinforcement serves a primarily informational function, it would be expected that amount of reinforcement would not be an important variable. If the reinforcement merely acts as an indicator that the response was "right," it provides complete knowledge of the appropriateness of the response and will operate in an all-or-nothing fashion. The magnitude of the reinforcement would, then, be irrelevant as long as it served its informational function. Where the obtaining of the reinforcement is the dominant motivation for learning or performance, as in many instances of animal learning, it would be expected that the relationship between the amount of reinforcement and the performance level would be positive.

SCHEDULES OF REINFORCEMENT

The rate at which learning occurs and what is learned are functions of the schedule of reinforcements employed. The simplest and quickest way to establish a given response pattern is to reinforce it every time it occurs. It is possible to have learning occur very much as if every trial were being reinforced, by reinforcing every other trial or every third trial; it has been shown that learning may proceed in the rat when only 1/192 of the responses are reinforced (*Skinner, 1938*). It can be seen that learning under certain conditions can occur with but few and infrequent reinforcements.

Schedules of reinforcement have been investigated most thoroughly by Skinner and his associates (*Skinner, 1938; Ferster and Skinner, 1957*). They have indicated four basic varieties of reinforcement schedule. They are a *fixed interval, variable interval, fixed ratio,* and *variable ratio.*

In the *fixed interval* schedule, reinforcement is administered after an established time interval, without regard to the response rate of the organism. The person on a monthly salary can be said to be on a fixed interval schedule if money is conceived of as the reinforcement. School report cards are issued at fixed intervals, as are children's allowances. In many cases performance in fixed interval situations is characterized by an increase in level of performance shortly before the end of the interval.

In a *variable interval* schedule, the reinforcement is given on a time schedule, but at varying intervals. The intervals between reinforcements are on a time basis, but the times are indefinite. Sometimes the subject is reinforced a couple of times very close together, and sometimes a considerable amount of time may elapse between reinforcements. The rate of responding will be high or low depending on the size of the interval employed, but the steadiness of the rate of responding is most characteristic of organisms on this schedule (*Ferster and Skinner, 1957*). Teachers and parents tend to employ this schedule when they individually reinforce children's behavior verbally or otherwise on a rather random time basis. This is a fairly effective procedure, when it is considered that performance on such a schedule tends to be steady and may be at a high rate.

When reinforcement is administered after a predetermined number of responses it is referred to as a *fixed ratio* schedule. Employing this procedure, reinforcement may be given after every response, every third response, every tenth response, or on whatever schedule is desired. Using fixed ratio schedules it has been demonstrated that higher rates of responding occur than under fixed interval training. By starting at a low ratio of reinforcement (two or three responses before one is reinforced) and moving up by gradual increments, behavior can be established and maintained on very high ratios such as 500:1 or even 1,000:1 (*Ferster and Skinner, 1957*). Thus, it can be seen that habits may be maintained even though they are very infrequently reinforced.

When responses are randomly reinforced around some average ratio, the organism is said to be on a *variable ratio* schedule. Sometimes the reinforcement may come on two responses in a row and may vary in range up to a great number of responses before the next reinforcement. Such a procedure results in a steady rate of performance without breaks, and the rates of responding are typically very high (*Ferster and Skinner, 1957*). Variable ratio schedules are frequently employed by teachers and parents. This is done both intentionally and inadvertently, and results in a high level of performance and energy expenditure. The effectiveness of such schedules is probably best attested to by the persistence of gambling behavior on slot-machines. They employ a variable ratio schedule and are most effective in maintaining a persistent high rate of responding. Each of the schedules yields characteristic differences in responding, but all are effective in controlling performance. When reinforcement occurs at random intervals irrespective of what response is being made, learning is manifested by a reduction in the variability of behavior. The organism tends to repeat those responses that have immediately preceded the reinforcement (*Skinner, 1938*). Acquisition with partial reinforcement requires more trials, but fewer reinforcements, than acquisition with continuous reinforcement (*Kanfer, 1954*).

Although most of the work of Skinner and his associates has been on either white rats or pigeons, it has been shown that children's behavior under intermittent reinforcement closely resembles that of lower animals (*Long et al.*, 1959).

## DELAY OF REINFORCEMENT

In order to be most effective, reinforcements must be in close temporal proximity to the responses they are to perpetuate. It has been shown in experimental work with rats that if the effect of secondary reinforcement is controlled, the effectiveness of reinforcement diminishes very rapidly as the period of delay increases. Positive reinforcements have practically no effect on rats if the delay is more than ten seconds in length (*Spence, 1947; Grice, 1948*).

The number of studies concerned with a possible delay of punishment gradient is small. Kimble (1961) states that only three such investigations could be found. However, some interesting investigations of the effects of delay of punishment with children have been reported (*Walters and Demkow, 1963; Setterington and Walters, 1964; Walters et al., 1965*). These investigators have dealt with the relative effects of immediate and delayed punishment, but have not systematically varied the period of delay to determine the nature of a possible gradient. They have reported greater effectiveness for immediate than for delayed punishment. Kamin (1959) reports from his investigations on the delay of punishment that there is a gradient of the effectiveness of delayed punishment that has many of the same characteristics as the delay of positive reinforcement.

It is probable that delay of reinforcement decreases its effectiveness in humans as well as lower animals. Younger, less mature, or less intelligent humans would have to have the consequences of behavior follow their acts very closely in order for reinforcements to operate as practical controls or sustaining motivational influences. With older, more mature, or more intelligent people, reinforcements could be more remote and still be effective.

## SECONDARY REINFORCEMENT

Stimuli used to establish what Pavlov called higher order conditioning are said to acquire reinforcing values. They are generally called *secondary reinforcers* because they have never been directly associated with the originally effective stimulus but become effective in eliciting and maintaining a conditioned response. An example of secondary reinforcement in classical conditioning has already been presented in the work reported by Pavlov (1927) where a dog was conditioned to salivate in response to a black card as a stimulus even though the black card had never been paired with the initially effective stimulus for salivation.

Secondary reinforcement in instrumental conditioning is well demonstrated by Saltzman (1949). In his study, rats were trained to run down a straight alley to a goal box containing food. The goal box was either black or white. In initial training the goal box always contained food when it was black and never when it was white. The animals were then taught a simple maze in which they had to choose between two pathways, one leading to a black goal box and the other to a white one. The rats learned to go to the black goal box even though it never contained food. The black goal box became reinforcing because it had been previously paired with a primary reinforcement, food. The black goal box thus served as a secondary reinforcer.

The concept of secondary reinforcement is an important one because it accounts for learning in which there is no apparent primary reinforcement. It can be used, too, to account for the effectiveness of delayed reinforcement. When reinforcement is not immediate and learning still occurs, secondary reinforcement is probably active. It has been suggested that any delay between response and reinforcement is mediated by secondary reinforcement (Spence, 1947). Animals were run in a T-shaped maze with food in one of the arms and with doors just before the goal boxes so that the animals could be retained in the arms of the T before they were allowed to enter the goal boxes (Wolfe, 1934). The delay of reinforcement did little harm to the learning in this situation because the arm of the T that was a retention chamber became a specific secondary reinforcement.

## Extinction

If a conditioned stimulus is repeatedly presented to an animal that has been conditioned to respond to it and the conditioned stimulus is never reinforced by being paired with the unconditioned stimulus, the conditioned response gradually decreases. This progressive decrement in responding is called *extinction*. Extinction is not solely a function of the passage of time. Studies indicate that unless some extinction procedure is employed conditioned responses are well retained. Skinner (1950) found a pecking response in pigeons to be maintained for four years, and a conditioned eyelid reaction in man was retained for twenty weeks (Hilgard and Campbell, 1936). The massing of non-reinforced trials (extinction trials) has been found, in general, to be the most effective way of extinguishing conditioned responses (Kimble, 1961). This may be a fortunate occurrence in that it makes possible the comparatively rapid extinction of well established responses in a therapeutic situation.

CS — — — — — — → CR — — — — — — → Reinforcement
(well established)
CS — — — — — — → CR — — — — — — → Reinforcement
CS — — — — — — → CR
CS — — — — — — → CR
—
—
—
CS . . . . . . . . . No response

*Figure 6. Extinction. A conditioned stimulus (CS) elicits a conditioned response (CR) and is reinforced. This sequence is repeated and becomes well established. Then the reinforcement is withheld and the CR eventually is extinguished.*

The omission of reinforcement may result in inhibition or adaptation of the response mechanism, instigation of interfering responses, motivational level decreases, generalization decrement, and frustration (*Kimble, 1961*).

## Spontaneous Recovery

A response that has been extinguished may reoccur after some time has elapsed since the last extinction trial. Pavlov (*1927*) found spontaneous recovery after a series of extinction trials, when the dependent variable was the amount of salivation. He also reported an increase in latency of salivation responses under extinction conditions with a subsequent decrease after a period of time. Spontaneous recovery is highly characteristic of learned behavior after a series of extinction trials, and then a rest.

One interpretation of spontaneous recovery has to do with the concept of inhibition (*Hull, 1943*). Response inhibition is assumed to build up as a function of unreinforced conditioned responses and to dissipate with rest; thus, if the conditioned stimulus and any stimulus to which generalization may have occurred is not encountered for some time, the inhibition diminishes and the response may again occur on the presentation of the appropriate conditioned stimulus. The precise nature of spontaneous recovery is likely to depend upon the strength of the conditioned response, the number of extinction trials, the spacing of extinction trials, and the number of times extinction and reconditioning have already occurred.

Spontaneous recovery of old, well established habits can be observed in the behavior of children who are developing new habits. The older response may occur again if the new habit is not practiced regularly or if the stimuli for the responses are not encountered for some period of time. After having established dry nights with her youngster, a mother may find that he still wets even after some time if he consumes a large amount of liquid before retiring. He experiences an unusual amount of bladder pressure (which he probably has not experienced for some time), and will react with the old response of wetting his bed. Spontaneous recovery of established behavior patterns is to be expected in a variety of personal and social situations involving the learning of new responses.

1. CS – – – – – – – – CR – – – – – – – – Reinforcement
   (well established)
2. CS – – – – – – – – CR
3. CS – – – – – – – – CR
4. –
   –
   –
5. CS – – – – – – – – No response
6. –
   –
7. CS – – – – – – – – No response
8. (time lapse)
9. CS – – – – – – – – CR

Figure 7.  Spontaneous Recovery. *A conditioned response is well established (1) and then by failure to reinforce the response (1–4) it is extinguished (5–7). Some time is allowed to elapse (8) and the CR reoccurs to the CS (9).*

## Discrimination

Learning to make discriminations among stimuli is essential for learning to respond to particular stimulus situations. It has been indicated previously that generalization of stimuli occurs reliably in animals and men. Discrimination can be viewed as the process of breaking down or controlling generalizations. Discriminations of a very fine nature can be learned by arranging the learning situation so that responses to one stimulus are reinforced and responses to another are not reinforced and thus become extinguished. When the response is eventually made to one stimulus and not to the other, the organism has learned to discriminate.

Children must learn to make many discriminations. When a child first identifies the family dog as "Bow wow," he is likely to identify any other animal he may see as "Bow wow." If his verbalizations are consistently reinforced for dogs and not reinforced when he inappropriately labels cats, cows, or other four-legged animals, he will soon learn to discriminate most dogs from the rest of the animal kingdom. Discrimination among stimuli makes it possible to respond to discreet stimuli appropriately. Much of the "intelligent" behavior of man is dependent upon his ability to make discriminations.

## TRIAL-AND-ERROR LEARNING

In situations where the environment is less rigidly controlled than in laboratory demonstrations of learning, it is probably true that much of "incidental" learning is through either classical or instrumental conditioning. The manner of acquisition in a complex social situation is often not readily identifiable. The problem to be solved may be intricate and not observable, the stimulating situation may be ambiguous and confusing, and responses may be quite variable. When learning occurs in such situations it is frequently called "trial-and-error" learning. "Trial and error" is a purely descriptive term indicating that one aspect of learning may be a persistent variable attack on a problematic situation.

An analysis of trial-and-error learning reveals several elements: motivation, a problem, variable responding, chance success, elimination and selection, integration and co-ordination.

### MOTIVATION

Motivational levels of individuals may vary from being intense to being extremely low. Motivation may derive from being hungry or thirsty, or from pain or sexual deprivation as biological conditions. In addition to these "primary" conditions, motivation may be enhanced by various other conditions. One may be motivated by a desire for prestige, by desire for love and acceptance by others, by curiosity, or by the desire for security. Motivation is a complex problem that will be discussed in later chapters. The point to be made is that motivation to solve the problematic situation must be high enough so that activity is directed toward the problem.

### A PROBLEM

If no problem existed there would be no systematic behavior resulting in learning. If all of one's needs, wishes, wants, or desires could be fulfilled readily by automatic or species-specific behavior, there would be no need for learning to occur. When some obstacle to the fulfillment of motive is encountered there is a necessity for the employment of knowledge and skills in order to bring about a satisfying state of affairs. The satisfaction of motives is frequently not obtainable until some problem is solved or a barrier is removed.

VARIABLE RESPONDING

If the situation encountered is a new one, and if the problem encountered is beyond the level of comprehension of the individual, almost every response in the person's repertoire of responses may be tried. The attack on the problem is, thus, on an almost purely trial-and-error basis. If the person has previous learning that can be used in the situation, the ensuing behavior will not be as random in nature. The individual, without realizing that he is doing so, may respond as he has done in past situations that have something in common with the situation in which he now finds himself. On the other hand, he may survey and analyze the present situation deliberately, and recognize or think he recognizes familiar elements from past experience and organize a plan of attack accordingly. When this occurs the variability of response is reduced and, if the inferences he has made are correct, he has developed some "insight" into the situation. The degree of randomness in trial-and-error behavior may vary from individual to individual and from problem situation to problem situation.

The form of the variable attack on problematic situations may differ as much as the degree of randomness of attack. Presented with a problem situation, one individual may attack it aggressively with little or no attempt at analysis or understanding. His efforts may be disorganized, overt, and essentially emotional. Another person may approach the same problem quite differently. He may survey the situation, analyze it critically, attempt to determine accurately the nature of the difficulty, and relate his previous learning to the apparent demands of the present situation. He may set up tentative plans for solution (form hypotheses) and he may try out a number of such plans ideationally (vicarious trial and error). If the problem is not too difficult in terms of the experiential background of the person involved, most of his trial-and-error behavior will be of a vicarious or ideational nature. When learning occurs in such a fashion, skills and information developed in previous trial-and-error situations are transferred to the solution of the present problem. People differ greatly in what they learn about how to solve problems. The kinds of problems they have previously encountered, the nature of the problem solutions employed, and the reinforcement they have received for various behaviors in problem situations are all, no doubt, important variables in learning how to learn, how to resolve conflicts, and how to solve problems.

CHANCE SUCCESS

It is only in rare instances that problem solution is strictly a matter of "chance success." It is possible, of course, that solution may be obtained by random activities or responses, one of which may happen to be correct. In most situations the likelihood of "chance success" being the solution is altered because previous learning is brought to bear to reduce the randomness of behavior. Behavior that may appear to be random in nature may be quite systematic to the individual in the problematic situation. His previous experience with reinforcements in the form of success and failure in similar situations may not have been well understood by him, or it may not have been meaningful in that the reinforcement, from his frame of reference, may have seemed arbitrary and unpredictable.

The designation of problem solution as being correct may be quite an arbitrary business. Actually, as far as learning is concerned, the response that is reinforced most adequately is the "correct" one. This designation of what is appropriate or correct behavior may be contrary to what social convention dictates as "correct" or what moral or logical considerations might indicate as appropriate. Behavior in trial-and-error situations is controlled by reinforcement. The behaviors that are positively reinforced are the ones that are perpetuated.

Almost any response of which an organism is capable can be elicited on cue by reinforcing the response when it does occur, or by reinforcing approximations of the response until the appropriate response can be consistently reinforced. This is a common method for training animals. Through reinforcement of the more appropriate response until the precise response desired is obtained, animals can learn responses that are far removed from their original response repertoires.

It has been suggested that a child can be taught to cry for two hours for any desired object or privilege. To make the child cry for two hours for a piece of candy, all one has to do is show the child the candy and not give it to him until he cries. As soon as he cries he is given the candy. The next time the candy is displayed it is withheld until the child cries for one minute. On successive trials the length of time the child is required to cry before receiving the candy is gradually lengthened until the two-hour period of crying can be induced by simply showing the child the candy and withholding it. Although this example may seem quite farfetched, it is likely that many children learn socially inappropriate behaviors in much the same fashion. If a baby is picked up and fondled only when he cries, his crying is reinforced. If Junior receives extra attention and praise when he behaves riotously and becomes the center of attraction for guests in the home, this "cute" behavior is reinforced. This "cute" behavior for a three-year-old, perpetuated through reinforcement becomes much less "cute," of course, when Junior is 20 or 30 years of age. Examples of behavioral control through reinforcement are to be found in nearly every aspect of social existence.

ELIMINATION AND SELECTION

Those responses that are not reinforced tend to be eliminated (*extinction*). If all the responses that are made in a problematic situation are reinforced, these responses should be present to the degree that they are closely related in time or distance to the immediately reinforced response. If the behavior of children is always greeted with reinforcement in the form of adult praise, attention, or a favorable state of affairs, the child will have no way of determining which responses are favored and which are not. Through selectively reinforcing certain responses or certain patterns of response, desired behavior can be perpetuated.

In a social learning situation, those responses that are reinforced are "selected" from the total of social responses, and those that are not reinforced are eliminated. Refinements in behavior gradually come about through such selection and elimination until activities become more and more restricted and stereotyped. Those behaviors that are approved, or not strongly disapproved, by society become well established, whereas those that are not reinforced in one way or another tend to be eliminated from the response repertoire.

INTEGRATION AND CO-ORDINATION

Integration and co-ordination can be thought of as a further refinement of elimination and selection. The selected activities are organized into a smoothly operating, unified response pattern, which functions rapidly and with a minimum of further trial and error. When situations arise that require the responses so developed, the responses are used efficiently and are employed in many instances without the person's being fully aware of what he is doing or how he is doing it.

## Trial and Error in Social Learning

Social learning is extremely complex. The stimulating situation is complicated, responses are manifold, and reinforcement is sometimes obscure; but in much of social learning the elements of trial and error can be isolated.

If the behavior of a young child desiring companionship (*motive*) is observed, the trial-and-error nature of acquiring social responses becomes apparent. The child is motivated by his desire for companionship. If his behavior, designed to obtain companionship, is immediately unsuccessful or if he is rejected by the group on the playground (*problematic situation*), he must modify his behavior. He tries a number of responses to the situation (*variable attack*). He may pout or cry for a time, then try to force his way into the group. He may plead, coax, threaten, or try to buy his way into acceptance by the group. One of these various behaviors may be successful (*chance success*). In future comparable situations the successful behavior will be re-employed and become a conventional way of responding (*selection and elimination*). The ways of behaving found to be most successful become integrated with other reinforced behaviors, until a pattern of behavior develops that becomes characteristic of the person as a person and may be referred to as a personality trait (*integration*).

Trial-and-error behavior as observed in social learning grows out of previous learning; thus, social learning involves trial-and-error behavior that derives from previous learning. The randomness of behavior is reduced as a result of the previous experience.

### *LEARNING INVOLVING IMITATION*

The fact that people do imitate and that they sometimes appear to learn through imitation is indisputable. The important questions to be considered are how they learn to imitate and, once having learned, how imitation is involved in subsequent learning.

Historically, learning by vicarious experience has been generally labeled "imitation." More recently, psychological literature has referred to essentially the same phenomenon by a variety of other labels. "Vicarious learning," "observational learning," "social facilitation," "role playing," "identification," "contagion," "modeling," and "copying" are all labels for constructs that have been employed to designate essentially the same process. The diversity of constructs so employed probably reflects the great variety of conditions under which the process occurs and the nature of the responses involved. There is no need to invoke separate processes for the various constructs and no need to invoke unique associative processes to account for them collectively. They will be subsumed under the label "imitation" and examined within the framework of associative theory. Learning by imitation is said to have occurred when behavior is modified as the result of observation and without benefit of overt responding by the learner.

#### CONDITIONING AND IMITATION

Imitation may result from conditioning procedures. It is probable that much of imitation in lower animals is learned in this way. The tendency for cattle on the range to stampede may be the result of conditioning. A young calf, hearing a loud sound, becomes startled and runs. The calf's mother hears the same sound and runs at the same time. The sight and sound of the mother cow and other cattle running stimulates the young calf immediately following the occurrence of the loud sound. If this occurs a number of times, the sight and sound of other cattle running may come to serve as a conditioned stimulus, and the calf will learn to run in imitation of the others. The sound and sight of others running serves as a stimulus for further running, and the behavior is perpetuated.

This same sort of conditioning occurs with the young child. The baby in the mother's arms is startled by a sudden loud sound. The mother is similarly startled and shows alarm. The increased muscular tension felt by the baby when the mother starts, the sound of the catching of the breath, the outcry, and the frightened expression on the mother's face all may come to be conditioned stimuli to produce the startle or fear reaction in the child. In this way, the child comes to imitate the emotional responses of the mother or other adults. When other people become frightened we may become frightened; when they display anger we may become angry. On the basis of conditioning we may become imitative without really knowing that we are doing so.

### REINFORCEMENT AND IMITATION

If activities that are imitations of the activities of others are consistently reinforced, they will be perpetuated. Through the use of reinforcement, children are taught to imitate certain behaviors and individuals and not to copy others. If copying the behavior of superiors in age or grade is regularly rewarded, and imitating the behavior of an age or grade equal is not rewarded, a greater tendency to imitate age or grade superiors develops (*Miller and Dollard, 1941*).

The child's environment from birth consists of an intricate system of subtle (and sometimes not so subtle) social rewards and punishments. In some instances children are rewarded for doing as others do, and in other instances they are punished for doing as others do. The child learns to imitate certain behaviors and to avoid others. He comes to imitate those behaviors that are reinforced and to avoid those that are punished or not reinforced. More often than not, a child is rewarded for copying those activities in which he sees certain others engaging. He tries eating the things he sees others eating and finds them delicious. He finds that dancing, swimming, and skating are pleasant when he follows the behavior patterns of his friends in doing these things. Conversely, departure from certain social patterns brings reproof, rejection, and punishment sufficiently often that the child soon anticipates the unpleasant results. This anticipation soon takes the form of anxiety incidental to the child's discovery that he is simply different from others. The mere perception of difference may eventually constitute an anxiety-producing stimulus. When the child follows the approved social behavior patterns he gains acceptance, prestige, and a feeling of security. He may develop a tendency toward conformity. The average child soon discovers that a very efficient way to gain approval and acceptance is to observe others and follow the example of prestige-laden individuals. When being different produces anxiety and conforming reduces anxiety, there develops a tendency to copy the approved behavior patterns of others.

Imitation can be conceived as a learned response that is useful in the acquisition of other responses. We learn that we can shorten trial-and-error behavior, avoid certain failures, and expend less effort in problem solution if we imitate the behavior of individuals who have been successful. We develop a secondary tendency to imitate through repeatedly being reinforced for imitative behavior in a variety of situations (*Baer and Sherman, 1964*). Imitative behavior is learned. When the tendency to imitate has been developed it becomes very useful in the acquisition of social behavior.

CONTIGUITY AND SYMBOLIC RESPONSES IN IMITATION

A great deal of interest in the process of imitation and its role in social learning has been aroused by the extensive and systematic work of Bandura and his co-workers. Bandura and McDonald (1963) question the efficiency of reinforcement of successive approximations of behavior for learning in complex social situations. Bandura (1962) expresses doubt that many classes of social response would ever be acquired if social training proceeded solely by the method of differential reinforcement of emitted responses. He contends (1965a) that, in the social world of animals and man, if principles other than the shaping of behavior by reinforcing successive approximations of appropriate behavior did not occur, survival would be questionable.

Bandura does not deny the importance of reinforcement in the *performance* of imitative behavior, but emphasizes that there are differences between *acquisition* and *performance*. Acquisition is to be accounted for primarily on the basis of contiguity and associated symbolic processes (*Bandura, 1965b*). Verbal associations and images are treated as representational responses that become associated with observed stimuli by contiguity. Once these symbolic representations become established, they can serve as implicit responses that provide cues (stimuli) for directing and controlling instrumental responses in the same way as do environmental events (*Mowrer, 1960; Staats and Staats, 1963*).

Bandura (1965b) demonstrates imitative learning and the roles of contiguity and reinforcement in acquisition and performance in an interesting investigation. Children observed a film in which a model exhibited a sequence of novel physical and verbal aggressive responses. In one version of the film, the model was severely punished following the aggressive behavior; in the second, the model was generously rewarded with treats and praise; in the third version, there was no response consequence to the model. In a subsequent test of imitative behavior, children exposed to the model-rewarded and no-consequence version of the film spontaneously performed a greater variety of imitative responses than the children exposed to the punishment version. Boys reproduced more of the model's behavior than did the girls, particularly in the model-punished treatment.

Following the performance test, all children were offered highly attractive incentives for reproducing the model's responses. This was done in order to activate into *performance* what the children had *acquired* through observation. The introduction of positive incentives completely wiped out the previously observed performance differences. Testing under incentive reinforcement conditions revealed that the groups had learned equivalent amounts from their observations.

The results of this investigation serve to demonstrate the difference between performance (from which learning must be inferred) and acquisition. It is obvious that factors other than differences in learning by observation are needed to account for the differences in performance in the initial test situation. The groups had learned equivalent amounts but they did not display it equally (perform) without the use of positive reinforcers. This study has been cited in order to illustrate the efficacy of a contiguity principle in describing learning from observation. The results suggest that the role of reinforcement (except for vicarious reinforcements of anticipation, etc.) in observational learning may be limited to eliciting performance through which learning is inferred.

The imitation model has been extended to cover a variety of responses of a social nature and the effects of various influences on imitative learning have been explored. The interested reader will find the references in this section to be both informative and challenging.

LIMITATIONS OF IMITATION

Imitation cannot be used to produce new patterns of behavior appropriate to a novel situation, unless the necessary components have already been learned. The strict use of imitation to promote learning would reduce the variability of behavior so drastically that novel situations would present insurmountable obstacles. Imitation is simply one way of bringing about activities that are likely to result in successful problem solution. It is not an appropriate substitute for other forms of behavior in all learning situations. The social consequences of imitation tend toward extreme conservatism in that imitation places a premium on conformity. As the result of the unpleasant consequences of deviating too markedly from the group, being different comes to elicit anxiety, and being the same as others comes to reduce anxiety. The individual is often rewarded for conforming to group norms and for copying the activities of others; thus, a learned tendency to conform develops. Imitation promotes uniformity, which, at times, means mediocrity. It discourages uniqueness and originality, and works in favor of the perpetuation of the status quo.

### MORE ABOUT LEARNING

This chapter has dealt with the aspects of learning that seem to be of prime importance in the acquisition of personally and socially relevant behavior. There are other facets of learning that are valuable for understanding human adjustment. For discussions of some of these topics, the reader is referred to any of a variety of introductory psychology textbooks dealing with learning. A brief review of some of the textual material on insight, memory, forgetting, and transfer of training would serve as an excellent supplement to this chapter.

### SUMMARY

Most of the socially relevant behavior of man is learned. A great deal of research has been devoted to attempting to understand learning in both man and the lower animals. So much of human behavior that is of concern to psychologists and mental hygienists is learned that it is imperative that they have some understanding of the general principles of learning. Learning is a universal phenomenon among the higher organized forms of animal life.

Learning occurs in a variety of circumstances and can be described in a number of ways. Learning appears to occur in classical conditioning, instrumental conditioning, trial and error, and imitation. Some of the more important phenomena of learning are stimulus generalization, reinforcement, secondary reinforcement, discrimination, and extinction.

The literature of learning is extensive. Only some of those features of learning that have been considered to be most important in the learning of socially and personally relevant responses have been considered in this chapter. Further study of the nature of learning is recommended.

### REFERENCES

BAER, D. M., and SHERMAN, J. X. Reinforcement control of generalized imitation in young children. *J. exp. child Psychol.*, 1964, **1**, 37–49.

BANDURA, A. Social Learning through Imitation. In M. R. Jones (ed.), *Nebraska Symposium on Motivation: 1962.* Lincoln: University of Nebraska Press, 1962.

BANDURA, A. Vicarious Processes: a Case of No-Trial Learning. In L. Berkowitz (ed.), *Advances in Experimental Social Psychology.* Vol. II. New York: Academic Press, 1965a.

BANDURA, A. Influence of models' reinforcement contingencies on the acquisition of imitative responses. *J. pers. soc. Psychol.*, 1965b, **1**, 589–595.

BANDURA, A., and McDONALD, F. J. The influence of social reinforcement and the behavior of models in shaping children's moral judgments. *J. abnorm. soc. Psychol.*, 1963, **67**, 274–281.

BASS, M. J., and HULL, C. L. The irradiation of a tactile conditioned reflex in man. *J. comp. Psychol.*, 1934, **17**, 47–65.

BASS, B. Gradients in response percentages as indices of nonspacial generalization. *J. exp. Psychol.*, 1958, **56**, 278–281.

BROWN, J. S., BILODEAU, E. A., and BARON, M. R. Bidirectional gradients in the strength of a generalized voluntary response to stimuli on a visual spatial dimension. *J. exp. Psychol.*, 1951, **41**, 52–61.

BROWN, J. S., and JACOBS, A. The role of fear in the motivation and acquisition of responses, *J. exp. Psychol.*, 1949, **39**, 747–759.

DAY, L. M., and BENTLEY, M. A note on learning in paramecium. *J. animal Behav.*, 1911, **1**, 167.

FERSTER, C. B., and SKINNER, B. F. *Schedules of Reinforcement.* New York: Appleton-Century-Crofts, 1957.

FINCH, G., and CULLER, E. Higher order conditioning with constant motivation. *Amer. J. Psychol.*, 1934, **46**, 596–602.

GRICE, G. R. The relation of secondary reinforcement to delayed reward in visual discrimination learning. *J. exp. Psychol.*, 1948, **38**, 1–16.

GRICE, G. R., and SALTZ, E. The generalization of an instrumental response stimuli varying in the size dimension. *J. exp. Psychol.*, 1950, **40**, 702–708.

HILGARD, E. R., and CAMPBELL, A. A. The course of acquisition and retention of conditioned eyelid responses in man. *J. exp. Psychol.*, 1936, **19**, 227–247.

HILGARD, E. R., and MARQUIS, D. G. *Conditioning and Learning.* New York: D. Appleton-Century Company, 1940.

HOVLAND, C. I. The generalization of conditioned responses: I. The sensory generalization of conditioned responses with varying frequencies of tone. *J. gen. Psychol.*, 1937, **17**, 125–148.

HULL, C. L. *Principles of Behavior.* New York: Appleton-Century-Crofts, 1943, 78–79.

HUTT, P. J. Rate of bar pressing as a function of quality and quantity of food reward. *J. comp. physiol. Psychol.*, 1954, **47**, 235–239.

JOHNSGARD, K. W. The role of contrast in stimulus intensity dynamism (V). *J. exp. Psychol.*, 1957, **53**, 173–179.

KALISH, H. I. Strength of fear as a function of the number of acquisition and extinction trials. *J. exp. Psychol.*, 1954, **47**, 1–9.

Kamin, L. J. The delay of punishment gradient. *J. comp. physiol. Psychol.*, 1959, **52**, 434–437.

Kanfer, F. H. The effect of partial reinforcement on acquisition and extinction of a class of verbal responses. *J. exp. Psychol.*, 1954, **48**, 424–432.

Kimble, G. A. *Hilgard and Marquis' Conditioning and Learning*. New York: Appleton-Century-Crofts, 1961.

Kimble, G. A. Shock intensity and avoidance learning. *J. comp. physiol. Psychol.*, 1955, **48**, 281–284.

Logan, F. A., and Wagner, A. R. *Reward and Punishment*. Boston: Allyn and Bacon, Inc., 1965.

Long, E. R., Hammack, J. T., and Campbell, B. J. Intermittent reinforcement of operant behavior in children. *J. exp. anal. Behav.*, 1959, **1**, 315–339.

Marshall, H. H. The effect of punishment on children: a review of the literature and a suggested hypothesis. *J. gen. Psychol.*, 1965, **106**, 23–33.

McGeoch, J. A., and Irion, A. L. *The Psychology of Human Learning* (Rev. ed.). New York: Longmans, Green and Company, 1952, 536.

Mednick, S. A., and Freedman, J. L. Stimulus generalization. *Psychol. Bull.*, 1960, **57**, 169–200.

Miller, N. E. Studies of fear as an acquirable drive: I. Fear as motivation and fear-reduction as reinforcement in the learning of new responses. *J. exp. Psychol.*, 1948, **38**, 89–101.

Miller, N. E., and Dollard, J. *Social Learning and Imitation*. New Haven: Yale University Press, 1941.

Miller, W. C., and Greene, J. E. Generalization of an avoidance response to varying intensities of sound. *J. comp. physiol. Psychol.*, 1954, **47**, 136–139.

Mowrer, O. H. *Learning Theory and Behavior*. New York: John Wiley and Sons, Inc., 1960.

Mowrer, O. H. *Learning Theory and the Symbolic Processes*. New York: John Wiley and Sons, Inc., 1960.

Mowrer, O. H. A stimulus-response analysis of anxiety and its role as a reinforcing agent. *Psychol. Rev.*, 1939, **46**, 553–566.

Pavlov, I. P. *Conditioned Reflexes*. London: Oxford University Press, 1927.

Penney, P. K., and Lupton, A. A. Children's discrimination learning as a function of reward and puishment. *J. comp. physiol. Psychol.*, 1961, **54**, 449–451.

Rock, R. T., Jr. The influence upon learning of the quantitative variation of after-effects. *Teach. Coll. Contr. Educ.*, 1935, No. 650.

Saltzman, J. J. Maze learning in the absence of primary reinforcement: a study of secondary reinforcement. *J. comp. physiol. Psychol.*, 1949, **42**, 161–172.

Setterington, R. G., and Walters, R. H. Effects of concurrent delays of material rewards and punishments on problem-solving in children. *Child devel.*, 1964, **35**, 276–280.

Skinner, B. F. *The Behavior of Organisms*. New York: Appleton-Century-Crofts, 1938.

Skinner, B. F. Are theories of learning necessary? *Psychol. Rev.*, 1950, **57**, 193–216.

Spence, K. W. The role of secondary reinforcement in delayed reward learning. *Psychol. Rev.*, 1947, **54**, 1–8.

Staats, A. W., and Staats, C. K. *Complex Human Behavior*. New York: Holt, Rinehart and Winston, Inc., 1963.

Thorndike, E. L. *Animal Intelligence*. New York: The Macmillan Company, 1911.

TOLMAN, E. C. There is more than one kind of learning. *Psychol. Rev.*, 1949, **56**, 144–155.

WALTERS, R. H., and DEMKOW, L. Timing of punishment as a determinant of response inhibition. *Child devel.*, 1963, **34**, 207–214.

WALTERS, R. H., PARK, R. D., and CANE, V. Timing of punishment and the observation of consequences to others as determinants of response inhibition. *J. exp. child Psychol.*, 1965, **2**, 10–30.

WOLFE, J. B. The effect of delayed reward upon learning in the white rat. *J. comp. Psychol.*, 1934, **17**, 1–21.

YAMAGUCHI, H. B. Gradients of drive stimulus (Sd) intensity generalization. *J. exp. Psychol.*, 1952, **43**, 298–304.

*Chapter 6*

# Learning
# Personal-Social
# Behaviors

CERTAIN PERSONAL-SOCIAL behaviors have been deemed sufficiently important that society has developed institutional means for their systematic
development. Learning to read, write, and use numbers has been considered an absolute minimum for effective living. Because so much of
learning in these areas has become formalized in the school, there is a
tendency to assume that the word "learning" is really confined to the
formal acquisitions that result from attending institutions. Reading, writing, and deciphering are of great cultural concern because these skills are
essential for the kinds of future learning we expect of each other. The
learning of personal behavioral characteristics and patterns of social interaction have not been explored as systematically as academic learning.
Those behaviors that are acquired during the course of general experience
are of prime concern to psychologists because of their great personal and
social significance.

Personally and socially significant behaviors are difficult to study in the laboratory. When socially effective behavioral sequences are broken into smaller, more controllable units for laboratory study, they tend to lose their significance for understanding the complex nature of personal-social behavior. Laboratory studies of learning tend to deal with the acquisition of isolated bits of behavior. The acquisition of socially relevant behavior has been investigated much less thoroughly and systematically than the acquisition of isolated responses of various kinds. There are great difficulties involved in the controlled investigation of socially relevant behavior. Social stimuli are difficult to control, and social responses are elusive and difficult to measure.

The investigation of personal-social behavioral phenomena has been approached by two different procedures. One of these is to study the means by which learning occurs in rather simple situations where stimuli can be relatively well controlled and responses rather adequately observed and measured. The task of isolating principles by which learning occurs can then be explored in a variety of specific situations. Having learned what one can about learning in the laboratory, it then becomes necessary to apply these findings to the elaborate and complex social situation. This is indeed an imposing task, and the validity of interpretations of behavior is difficult to establish. Another way of investigating the acquisition of socially relevant behavior is to study the behavior as it occurs in the complex situation. In such studies, it is difficult to identify what the stimulating circumstance is for the individual, and his responses are elusive when it comes to their measurement. Studies of gross behavior in social situations are lacking in the control and precision that are desirable in scientific studies, but those observations that are made are more closely tied to the situation we are trying to understand.

Both of these methods have limitations. Well designed and controlled studies that are only tangential to the behavior we are trying to understand do yield more reliable findings from which to make predictions, but the predictions that are made in many cases seem to be rather far afield from the original study. On the other hand, the lack of precision of observation and measurement of the second method leaves us uncertain as to just what it is that has occurred.

Confronted with such a situation, the necessity for generalizing from some source, in order to treat the topic of social learning, becomes evident. In the treatment of the complex problem that follows, we shall rely both on theoretical formulations made from laboratory studies of learning and on observations of behavior made in social situations. It is the authors' opinion that the acquisition of social behavior has not been the focus of enough well designed studies to develop principles to account for social behavior independently of the principles that have been developed from the better controlled laboratory studies. It also appears that complex social behaviors are probably understandable by the same general principles that are employed in understanding more simple, discrete acquisitions. Both the simple and the complex are learned, and the principles of learning that have been developed are probably applicable in both situations.

## SOCIAL LEARNING IN CHILDHOOD

The problem of socialization of children has been solved in only a rough, crude fashion. The task of understanding the acquisition of social responsiveness in children is a large and complex one. Difficult discriminations must be learned, complex social response systems must be developed, and external restraints and controls must become internalized. These aspects of social behavior are, of course, in addition to the usual verbal and motor skills that must be learned.

## Complexity of the Infant's World

The infant has developed but a small repertoire of responses that are usable in avoiding the effects of painful stimulation. His responses are general and diffuse. He learns to cry when hungry, cold, thirsty, hurt, or uncomfortable. His crying sometimes brings relief from his distress and sometimes does not. He is relatively helpless and must depend upon the ministrations of others for his comfort. Infants cannot *understand* what is going on about them, and physically they are incapable of doing very much about it even if they could understand. They cry and thrash about in distress. Life must be confusing and unpredictable. An infant does not know if his distress is limited in time or if it is unrelievable. This kind of knowledge must await the neural-physical development that is to come. When development is such that language can be acquired, the child can learn that delays may be limited, that distress may be temporary, and that some order exists in his culture.

Viewed from an adult standpoint, the life of the infant may appear to be a period of transitory psychoses (*Dollard and Miller, 1950*). His world is confused, disoriented, sometimes painful, and always extremely complex. Primary sources of drive are operative, but means of satisfying them have not yet been acquired. He cannot avoid pain; he cannot speak, reason, plan, or control his activities. The complexity of changing from this condition to one in which he can avoid pain, speak, reason, plan, and control cannot be overemphasized. The change from chaos to understanding and predictability occurs gradually as the child develops and learns. The subtle reinforcements for behavior gradually become effective, and the child's world begins to assume some semblance of rationality.

## Learning Language

The learning of verbal language and the acquisition of skill in its use is an important part of learning in childhood. Not only does the use of oral language facilitate communication, but it makes it possible for the user to have vicarious experience and learn through and from the learning of others (*Mowrer, 1954*). The child, having learned to speak, can give himself directions. He can utter words that have been associated with various aspects of his behavior. In times of stress he can control himself by uttering words previously associated with consolation. The reinforcing value of such expressions as "good boy" or "good girl" become obvious when the child utters these phrases to himself. Many times children, having behaved inappropriately, will speak such phrases as "naughty boy" or "bad girl" to themselves. The labeling of various objects, behaviors, and situations by the child is certainly an aid to thinking about them and reacting toward them appropriately.

As soon as a child begins to talk, he is likely to find that speech is rewarded. Mother is pleased by his vocalizations and father is proud of his speech. He is rewarded in innumerable situations. If he says "cookie" he is rewarded with a cookie; if he says "drink" or "water" he is rewarded with water to drink; if he says "hurt" his injury is ministered to and the pain is reduced. In addition to these primary reinforcements, mother smiles or father pats his head or makes other signs of acceptance and approval. Such adult social responses have been demonstrated to be effective reinforcers for vocalization in infants (*Rheingold et al., 1959*). It would be strange indeed if under such circumstances the child did not enjoy developing the tendency to speak to himself and to others. The value of reinforcement in the development and use of language is being given increasing emphasis (*Staats and Staats, 1964*).

The child is rewarded for most of his learned responses. Quite naturally, he develops an interest in further learning. The more he learns the more he is rewarded. He asks questions in order to learn—he learns because of reinforcement. It is quite possible, from such an analysis, to observe that children become "curious." "Curiosity" may be the result of many sequences of behavior and reinforcement in a variety of learning situations.

Words develop meaning through having their use reinforced. A further element of meaning is derived from the manner in which words are spoken. Many words are emotionally toned, and children learn to recognize emotion-laden commands, requests, and threats from the inflection, speed, tone, and volume of their utterance.

Language is useful as a tool for the fulfillment of the wants, wishes, and desires of the child. As language skill develops, it becomes a more effective tool in this regard, and it also becomes an important tool in the establishment and maintenance of social relationships. Piaget (1926) reports from his studies of language in children that as they grow older, their speech becomes less egocentric and more sociocentric. As the child grows up in the culture, he learns that socially oriented speech is rewarded more consistently than egocentric speech. A diminution of self-centered speech and an expansion of socially oriented speech is thus a predictable phenomenon.

EARLY LANGUAGE DIFFICULTY

Hesitations and repetitions in speech appear to be common in the language development of the child. Children between the ages of two and five have been reported to repeat approximately one out of every four words (*Davis, 1940*), and 85 percent of children three to four years of age show hesitation in speech (*Martin and Stendler, 1953*). Speech difficulties can be regarded as normal during the pre-school years. Situational pressures of various kinds produce increases in speech hesitancies (*Davis, 1940*).

The vast majority of children who stutter in their early years tend to cease stuttering within a few months' time. Stuttering seems to be related rather closely to the emotional stress of the child. The alleviation of the emotional stress reduces the frequency of stuttering (*Siegal and Haregan, 1964*). Parental anxiety about stuttering at this age or high-pressure attempts to correct the child's speech may serve to aggravate the problem.

## Acquiring the Sex Role

The acquisition of behaviors appropriate to the sex of the child is an important area of social learning. In general, sex-appropriate behavior is reinforced in the family and behavior appropriate to the opposite sex is not. This comes about through complex and subtle systems of rewards and punishments for various behaviors.

From very shortly after birth, little boys are treated differently from little girls in our culture. Boys are dressed in a different manner and wear clothing of different colors from those of little girls. Little girls are given dolls and other "feminine" toys. Little boys are given teddy bears and "masculine" toys. Boys are more frequently rewarded for their rough and ready behavior than are little girls. The differential reinforcement of sex-appropriate and inappropriate behaviors typically produces the behavior considered culturally appropriate.

In the favorable family constellation little boys are rewarded for behaving like their fathers. They soon learn to model their behavior after that of their fathers. The parent is pleased by the emulation of his own characteristics, and mother, who loves father, enjoys seeing her son mature in his image. If a little boy tends to model his behavior after that of the mother he is not rewarded to the same extent as when he behaves in more masculine, father-like ways. He learns that the display of behavior more typical of his father is more satisfying for him. As his world expands he finds that behaviors modeled after those of his father are more characteristic of his playmates who, like him, are little boys. If he behaves in a manner more characteristic of mother he may find that he is called a "sissy" and that positive reinforcements for such behavior are not forthcoming.

In the home where parental discord rather than harmony prevails, the learning situation may be quite different. It is one thing to model one's behavior after a father loved by the mother; it is quite a different thing to model one's behavior after a father who is not liked by the mother. In the latter instance the child runs the risk of losing some of his mother's love by behaving as the father does. At the same time, if he copies the mother's behavior, the father does not approve. Parents who are antagonistic toward one another are unlikely to be pleased by the child's identifying with either parent. Mother is not pleased by the prospect of the son's being "a chip off the old block," and father doesn't want his son to grow up to be a "sissy." In such a disturbed situation the child has difficulty acquiring culturally appropriate sex role identifications. The system of rewards and punishments is so complex that it is almost impossible for him to learn which behaviors are appropriate and which are not.

The situation for the little girl is essentially the same as for the little boy. The task of learning the behavior appropriate to women rather than men is undertaken in the same general way. Her mother-like behaviors are rewarded more by both parents when the father loves and respects his wife.

## Aggressiveness

Children differ markedly in the extent to which they exhibit aggressive behavior. It seems highly doubtful that individual differences in children's aggressiveness can be accounted for without gross emphasis on social learning. The extent to which a child will express aggressive responses is probably more dependent upon his previous history of rewards and punishments for such responses than upon any other factor.

If a child finds that certain behaviors are rewarded, these behaviors tend to be perpetuated. If the rewarded behavior is aggressive in nature it should be expected that aggressive behavior will be common. Home environments differ a great deal in the extent of their elicitation and rewarding of aggressiveness. Some family structures are such that aggression in children is encouraged and rewarded, while in other families aggressiveness is punished and discouraged. On the basis of what is known about learning, it has been predicted that the child will inhibit his aggressive responses in settings where fear and anxiety have become associated with these responses through their punishment. This prediction has been experimentally confirmed by Hollenberg and Sperry (1950), who used nursery school children as subjects. They also concluded that a child, having learned to inhibit aggressive behavior in the home, may inhibit aggressive behavior in social situations that resemble the home setting closely, such as the nursery school, but may behave quite differently in a highly dissimilar situation, such as doll play. These findings fit in with what might be expected from the studies of stimulus generalization presented in the previous chapter. Similar results have been obtained by others in their studies of aggression (*Sears et al., 1953*).

The role of imitation in the acquisition of aggressive behavior has been thoroughly investigated by Bandura and his associates (*Bandura, 1965*). They demonstrated experimentally that children who had observed adult models behaving in a highly aggressive manner subsequently displayed approximately twice as much aggression as subjects who either witnessed inhibited adults or had no exposure to social cues (*Bandura et al., 1961; 1963*). Other investigators (*Mussen and Rutherford, 1961*) have shown that observation of models displaying aggressive behavior with no untoward consequences increased the incidence of aggressive responses in children. The acquisition and consequences of aggressive behavior have been the subject of a great deal of investigative effort. An interesting analysis of the topic of aggression has been undertaken by Berkowitz (*1958; 1962; 1964*).

## Generalization of Early Social Responses

Social responses of children are likely to be reinforced directly from very early childhood. In democratic, freedom-giving, calm, happy homes, socially oriented responses are regularly encouraged. Through reinforcement, being a member of a social group acquires reward value early in the life of the child. Group contacts come to be regarded as satisfying and desirable. By the age of three years most children should be socially outgoing and interested in relationships with other children.

If a child has found social interaction to be associated with frustration and painful experience, his responses are not likely to be strongly socially oriented. A rejecting mother may be so severe in the treatment of her child that he learns to avoid her and, by generalization, to withdraw and avoid social relationships in general. Most children try to apply the social techniques they have learned at home with parents, brothers, and sisters to their interactions with others, including peers.

Evidence that children transfer social responses learned in the home to other social situations has been provided by Bishop (1951). From her observations of 34 children interacting first with their mothers and later with neutral adults, she concluded that such transfers do take place. The children reacted to the neutral adult in roughly the same manner in which they had reacted to their mothers with respect to aggressive stimulation, inhibited and reluctant co-operation, non-co-operation and resistance. The findings of this study are clearly consistent with the hypothesis that responses learned at home are likely to be carried over to other social situations. The study serves to emphasize the importance of responses learned in the home as far as social behavior outside the home is concerned. The child's social behavior can be understood only if we know the conditions for learning that exist in his family. Knowledge of the variety and consistency of positive and negative reinforcements of social responses in the home is imperative to an understanding of other social behaviors of children.

Parents are representatives of the child's culture. A child's learning of social responses at home helps him to acquire his role in society. The members of his family provide the reinforcements for social learning. He models his behavior after them, identifies with them, and imitates them. He learns familial patterns of humor, fun, pleasure, fear, aversion, and suspicion. These patterns of responding and ways of thinking become internalized and become his own. He learns the ideals, values, and morals of his family and these, too, become his. As his social world expands to include peers, teachers, movie stars and T.V. heroes, he acquires a portion of the values and ideals that they represent. Eventually behavioral modes and standards learned from social interaction outside the home blend with those acquired within the home to form the basis for rather broad general patterns of behavior. These broad patterns of thinking, feeling, and behaving constitute a large portion of his personality. In that the personality is derived from so many sources, it is a complex and unique organization (Sappenfield, 1954).

Each home provides a different learning situation for the children who live in it. Thus, the children learn to behave in a variety of fashions. An interesting study of the relationships of "democracy" and "control" in the home and children's behavior in nursery school has been reported (Bald-

*win*, 1948). In this study democratic homes are characterized by general permissiveness, avoidance of arbitrary decisions, and a high level of verbal contact between parent and child. Controlled homes emphasize clear-cut restrictions on behavior and, consequently, friction over disciplinary procedures is low. As would be predicted from the total learning situation provided by the home atmospheres, children from "democratic homes" were generally active, competitive, and outgoing. Children from homes rated high in "control" showed relatively little quarrelsomeness, negativism, disobedience, aggression, planfulness, tenacity, or fearlessness. This study well illustrates the generality of social behavior acquired in the home.

### LEARNING MALADAPTIVE BEHAVIOR

It is relatively easy for most people to accept the fact that the characteristics of ordinary and usual social behavior are acquired via learning processes. So much of the usual behavior of children does reflect rather directly the behaviors, attitudes, and values of the family that it appears self-evident that these aspects of adjustive behavior are learned. When children behave in ways that are not socially acceptable, or display manners that are not considered adaptive, the use of learning principles to explain these behaviors is less common. When the child's behavior is not *directly* reflective of intentional and obvious teachings in the home, he is frequently considered odd, strong-willed, or maladjusted. Little attention is given to the learning situation that has been instrumental in producing these maladaptive behaviors.

## Early Acquisition of Fears

Children's fears are many and varied. It is difficult to predict the number or variety of fears that will be learned. It is certain that every child learns to be fearful in a variety of situations. If children learn to be frightened in too many situations or under too many conditions, their fear responses are rather constant and interfere with the development of more stable and effective behaviors. The child who rather consistently makes responses of crying, trembling, appealing for help, or clinging to the parent for protection can hardly be said to be making the most acceptable of responses; however, these are typically the responses of fearful children. If more effective behaviors are to evolve, these socially unacceptable fear responses must be replaced by responses more typical of the mature individual.

An extensive study of the fears of children indicates that the frequency and intensity of children's fears decrease with age (*Jersild and*

*Holmes, 1935*). The same study indicates that new fears tend to grow out of the older ones. A child, frightened by a mouse running through his room, begins to fear all scratching sounds at night. Fear responses to stimuli that did not previously elicit fear become apparent. This can occur in at least two different ways. The fear of the child who is afraid of all scratching noises in the night could probably be accounted for quite adequately through *stimulus generalization*. If the child subsequently begins to fear his room or the dark because of the previous frightening experiences, this can be understood as the product of *classical conditioning*. Through *stimulus generalization* and *higher order conditioning*, theoretically any number of fears could be acquired.

Most fears are learned, and since the young child spends most of his time in the home, it seems likely that this is the place where he learns them. If a mother is frightened by animals, the child may notice the change of expression on her face, the quickening of her step, the tenseness of her grip, and the general manner of her behavior, which he has learned to associate with previous frightening situations. With several such encounters, the child learns to respond with fear at the sight of an animal without the cues previously supplied by the mother. In a very real sense he learns to fear animals from his mother. She has been a very effective teacher and because *she* is frightened there is little she can do about it. Subsequently, when the child encounters an animal he is frightened and withdraws from the situation, thus reducing the fear provoked by the stimulus and at the same time preventing any new, more effective responses from becoming conditioned to the stimulus. Research findings have indicated a distinct tendency for a child to have the same fears as his mother (*Hagman, 1932*). When children have learned to fear the same things as their mothers they become mutually reinforcing. The mother's reactions reinforce the fears of the child and the child's fear reinforces the fear and subsequent avoidance responses of the mother. The elimination of the fears in children involves the same processes as the elimination of other conditioned responses. *Extinction* procedures can be instituted by presenting the feared stimulus when the child is distracted or when he is experiencing other, pleasant stimuli at the same time. When the fear is reduced new responses can be attached to the previously fear-arousing stimuli (*Lang, 1964*).

## Effect of Parental Attitudes and Behaviors

Homes characterized by friction and internal tensions tend to produce children with more adjustment problems than homes characterized as relaxed and easygoing (*Baruch, 1937*). Distraught, dissatisfied, and unhappy parents have difficulty providing an atmosphere wherein children can learn that interpersonal relationships are rewarding. They have tense, unpleasant interactions with each other and provide an inadequate model for children to pattern their behaviors after. They are also likely to have unpleasant, harried, and difficult social interactions with the children. A child in such a situation can learn to feel unworthy and unwanted and develop a concept of himself that prevents him from developing effective social relationships outside the home. Few desirable social skills are acquired in such a home, and initial social relations outside the home are dependent upon such skills.

Studies of maternal over-protection have indicated that the behaviors acquired under conditions of maternal indulgence generalize from the maternal relationship to relationships with peers. Indulged children who are disobedient, impudent, excessively demanding, and tyrannical at home tend to be aggressive and bossy with their peers. When maternal domination and excessive discipline and control are the means of over-protection the children are shy, submissive, and withdrawn both with their mothers and with neighborhood children (*Levy, 1943*). Tense, anxious parents tend to engender more behavior problems in their children than do relaxed parents. Research results strongly indicate that children who have large numbers of adaptive problems during the pre-school period tend to have a relatively large number of emotional problems as they grow into adulthood (*Macfarlane et al., 1954*).

## LEARNING RESPONSE TENDENCIES OR PREDISPOSITIONS

It can be observed that people are inclined to respond in various ways to the complex stimuli provided by the social environment. Some people have a tendency to respond to many situations in an aggressive fashion; others respond to the same situations with timidity and withdrawal. Some are challenged by the competitive situations in our environment and become fierce competitors; others avoid situations in which competition is a strong element. Some people are anxious to co-operate and participate in social processes and others tend to avoid participation and group endeavor. The lives of some people seem to be dedicated to affectional and generous behavior and in others these responses seem to be of little value.

The extremes of response predispositions have been mentioned. It is not intended that a dichotomy of behavioral tendencies be established. Indeed, the gradations of responses from one extreme to the other are numerous. The extremes have been mentioned in order to point out the tremendous range of acquired predispositions to respond. The response tendencies of people can be more adequately described as forming a continuum of responses than as forming an all-or-none type of distribution. Combinations of various acquired response predispositions constitute much of what is ordinarily referred to as a "personality."

## Learning Aggression and Timidity

The acquisition of behaviors in specific instances is more readily understood then the acquisition of predispositions to respond in a particular way. However, it is from learning to respond to discrete stimuli that general trends in responding develop.

In some family constellations, it has previously been observed, aggressive behavior is not only accepted and expected but actually encouraged. The correlation between the socio-economic status of the family and its tolerance for aggression has been noted. Families provide the social stimuli for early social learning, and they also largely control the reinforcements for the responses elicited.

If a child is "teased" until he cries and then the teasing is terminated, the termination of the teasing reinforces the most recently occurring response, crying. Children can thus be taught to cry on cue. If a child is teased or annoyed by a stimulus situation and this annoyance continues until the child strikes out or moves aggressively toward the annoyance, his aggressive behavior is reinforced by the cessation of the annoyance. If this occurs a number of times, the child soon learns to be aggressive toward the annoying stimulus situation. Through stimulus generalization he learns to respond to other stimuli that resemble the initially effective one in the same aggressive manner. Eventually he may acquire a tendency to respond to annoyances in general with aggression and, finding these responses effective, adopt a general attitude of aggressiveness toward the social environment. Thought processes can be conceived of as responses, and aggressive patterns of thought and action come to be characteristic of the individual.

Stern parental disapproval of aggressive behavior can produce behavior that is characterized by timidity. In this kind of setting, if a child strikes out or is verbally aggressive toward the source of annoying stimulation he is likely to find that the annoying stimuli are compounded. He is spanked or otherwise painfully punished, and his aggressive act has done nothing to relieve his discomfort but, indeed, has increased it. Parents who punish minor aggressions are likely, too, to provide reinforcement for timidity or withdrawal. If a child is punished for aggressive behavior he must find some other effective way of reducing the annoying stimuli. He can do this by vocal pleas to the parent for help. If his pleas result in the diminution of the annoyance, he may learn to depend upon the intervention of others for the alleviation of his distress.

Another way to terminate noxious stimuli is to escape. Children can acquire habits of escape, when fleeing from the annoyance is rewarded by termination of the aversive stimuli. The over-protective parent may reinforce such behavior by such admonitions as: "If the others bother you, come tell mother," "If the boys are not behaving themselves, come home," "If there is trouble, get out of the way," "If you can't play without fighting, you'll have to play by yourself." When the child reports that "they were fighting so I left," the parent further reinforces the behavior by verbal reassurance that he did the "right" thing and was a "good boy" to do it.

Aggressiveness is sometimes punished with such severity that that kind of behavior is studiously avoided. Not only is the child physically punished, but social sanctions in the form of reproof and reprimand are involved. The child then comes to fear being aggressive and may feel guilty and unworthy even when thinking about aggression. The most effective tools he has for coping with his environment, he has learned, are those of appeal for help or sympathy, withdrawal or escape, and avoiding the situations that are anxiety-arousing. These responses generalize to include many social situations; timidity and avoidance become well established, generalized response tendencies. They are sufficiently over-learned responses that they can be thought of as "unconsciously motivated." No thought or deliberation is required, new situations are avoided systematically, and the individual is not "aware" of the origins of his response tendencies.

## Rebelliousness and Docility

Rebelliousness and docility are components of aggression and timidity. Modern society attempts to make children meek and obedient in the home and aggressive and competitive outside the home. The problem of establishing the culturally appropriate training in rebelliousness and docility is an imposing one.

If aggression in the home is strongly reinforced, the aggressive patterns of behavior so acquired may generalize to the rest of the social world. If this aggressiveness is sometimes reinforced and sometimes punished in the home and the pattern of its reinforcement is relatively unpredictable as far as the child is concerned, he may learn to rebel against parental authority and resent and be suspicious of those outside the home who represent authority. Chronic rebellion against authority and authority figures may be the end result of the frustration provided by the inconsistent and unpredictable reinforcement of aggressive behavior.

Training in docility in the home likewise can be so strong that the child can never learn to hold his own in the world outside the family. Where breaches of discipline are consistently harshly and repressively punished, there is little opportunity for the practice of rebellion or aggressiveness and its reinforcement. In such instances meekness and submissiveness become characteristic of the individual both in the home and in the rest of the social world. These are the only effective tools he has had an opportunity to learn to use. The old expression "the worm will turn" is true only if the worm has had some reinforced experiences with turning. Without consistent help from outside it is improbable that sufficient aggressive behavior will develop in such an individual to enable him to contend with a competitive and aggressive culture. This discussion of defiance and docility is indicative of the delicate nature of the task of learning culturally important behavior patterns. Unfortunately, the guide lines for training in such behaviors have been only partially and tentatively drawn. The complexity of the task is such that only the crudest of guiding principles are available to parents who themselves are less than perfect in their applications of recommended procedures. Confusion in the learning of the appropriate times, places, and manners for aggression and timidity is a predictable phenomenon. Conflicts and uncertainty are logically to be expected in such a situation.

## Learning to Compete and to Co-operate

Our culture is an extremely competitive one and most children learn very early in life to compete in various situations. Parents in our culture have acquired the competitive characteristics common to much of our society. Parental attitudes toward competition and competitive situations is such that siblings who do "better" than their brothers or sisters are singled out for extra praise, attention, and affection. In family situations where this is true, competition for the affection and attention of parents can develop to a rather extreme degree. The child in such a home soon learns that, if he is to receive the praise and the affection of his parents, he must achieve at a higher level than his brothers or sisters in some area where achievement is revered by the parent. He must do better than some other person. He must win in order to receive acclaim. If he makes the team it is because he is better than the person who did not. To win is better than to come in second and either is superior to being the loser.

Approval for excelling extends beyond the confines of parental influence. In the community there is more virtue attached to competition for the winner than for the loser. Being first, being the leader, and being triumphant are rewarded by the culture with praise, increased attention, and a high regard for the person. The social distinction attached to winning in competitive situations is a prominent aspect of our culture. Scholarship winners, athletic champions, social leaders, election winners, and others are given tremendous social and affectional reinforcement for their victories. The loser, the "also ran," and the second best are not given equal acclaim for their gallant efforts.

Competitive success is so frequently rewarded that many children develop a general tendency to be attracted by competitive situations; great importance is attached to winning and to symbols of victory. Trophies, awards, and emblems bestowed for competitive success are valued and treasured. Competition becomes a way of life. All contests are entered for the purpose of winning, and competition gives life and verve to activities that might otherwise be quite uninteresting.

Co-operative effort frequently does not receive the same reinforcement that is given to competitive success. In most families, children must learn to co-operate and to be helpful. But although co-operative behavior is reinforced by parental approval within the family, it is frequently frowned upon in the school. Children are expected to do their own work independently and are not expected to be helpful or to co-operate when taking an examination. The child must learn the circumstances under which co-operation is approved and those under which it is disapproved, as he must learn when to compete and when not to compete. The emphasis placed on success in competitive situations is such that many children learn that it is *better never to have tried at all than to have tried and failed.*

Co-operative behavior is encouraged by parental approval when co-operation is evident, and by threats when it is not forthcoming. The child attempts to behave in conformity with the wishes of parents whose affection and esteem he has learned are valuable. If reinforcements for co-operative and helpful efforts are regularly forthcoming, the child learns that co-operation and helpfulness are rewarded virtues, and he may acquire a general "style of life" characterized by efforts to co-operate with and be of assistance to others.

Training in both co-operative and competitive behaviors can be overdone. The child must learn which situations are competitive and which are to be looked upon as calling for co-operative effort. Those who have unfortunate experiences with competitive situations may develop feelings of inadequacy and inferiority that prohibit their success in many ways. Our emphasis on the virtues of co-operative behavior may result in behavior that prohibits success in an essentially competitive society. Patterns of co-operation and competition learned in the home tend to transfer to the social world outside the home and to become established means of dealing with social situations.

## Learning Affectional Responses

Children soon learn that the making of affectional responses is reinforced by parents. The little boy is called "daddy's boy" and the little girl, "mama's girl." Such terms are frequently accompanied by other words and acts of endearment. The child is rewarded by approval for giving daddy a "big hug" or giving mommy a kiss. He is told to kiss the poor dolly that has bumped its head or been dropped. Empathy is encouraged by teaching the child to say "poor dolly" and other sympathetic remarks. He soon learns that the bestowal of affection on dolly, mother or father, the family pet, and other members of the household is an approved behavior. The affectional responses acquired toward members of the family transfer to people who are encountered in the general social environment outside the home. Kindliness and generosity are encouraged through the reinforcement of kind and generous behavior. Thus children growing up in homes where this kind of behavior is reinforced by the verbal and overt behavioral responses of parents and other members of the household learn to be affectionate, empathetic, kindly, and generous in their relations with others.

If the pattern of affectional relationships in the home is a relatively stable one where father loves mother and both love the children, the parental attitudes toward each other and their affection and consideration for each other serve as models for the children to emulate. If the people who love the child and whom the child loves demonstrate affection for each other they become a source of satisfaction to the child. He learns to imitate the behavior of the parents and may show affection in the same general way in which the parents do. These childhood affectional response tendencies tend to be carried into adulthood, and the ensuing adult behavior is likely to be friendly, considerate, and kindly.

In some homes the learning situation is such that love or affectional responses are quite difficult to acquire. Where children are resented and unwelcome, or where the adults themselves have not learned to bestow affection, the patterns of personal interaction may be extremely constricted. Constant quarreling and disagreement between parents, and distant affectional relationships of either parent to the child, provide a poor atmosphere in which to learn to love others or to be loved by others. Sometimes the child is greeted affectionately, sometimes he is ignored, at other times he is used as an affectional weapon by one parent against the other. In such situations a genuine distrust of others may develop; affectional relationships are not satisfying but are sources of future discouragement and pain. Affectional relationships are to be avoided rather than sought if those one has learned to love become sources of frustration.

Homes that are broken by divorce, separation, or death frequently have a profound influence on the development of affectional behavior in the child. If the death of a loved parent produces great sorrow and loneliness the person can learn not to form deep-seated relationships because such relationships have previously been disrupted and anxiety-arousing. Interpersonal relationships then become characterized by aloofness and indifference. The refusal of some people who have "loved and lost" to seek out new friends and establish new affectional contacts is a learned means of protecting themselves from further distress.

## Response Tendencies Are Numerous

The number of general social response tendencies that are acquired through learning is not limited to those we have just considered. They are but illustrative of the many predispositions characteristic of a given person. Social behavior could be broken down into many component parts and each of these could be analyzed to demonstrate the manner of their acquisition. This would serve only to further emphasize the importance of learning in the development of patterns of social interaction. It is important to consider that behavior acquired in a limited social situation may generalize to other social situations and after continued use may become a general predisposition to respond to all social stimuli in a particular fashion.

### THE LEARNING OF SYMPTOMS

When the stimulus situation is relatively clear and the responses to the stimuli are apparent, there is little difficulty in understanding the learned nature of behavior. Certain behaviors of people are sufficiently unusual and different that they have been labeled deviant or neurotic. Neurotic behavior is still behavior, and its acquisition must be accounted for in some way. It is well established that social behavior is learned. The learning of unusual social responses should be accounted for by the same principles that are used to account for "normal" behavior. There are various theoretical ways of doing this. Some writers have treated neurotic behavior as resulting from qualitatively different learning than normal behavior. Others have insisted that the difference between neurotic behavior and normal or usual behavior is to be understood as quantitatively different but of the same general nature. Although learning in social situations is complex, and stimuli and responses are difficult to isolate, it would seem to be economical to account for as much novel behavior as possible by means of the principles appropriate for the acquisition of usual behavior.

## Anxiety

Human fears, anxieties, and feelings of insecurity have been widely recognized as having important effects upon behavior. Freudian (1936) theory assigns anxiety and feelings of guilt a major role in the interpretation of normal behavior. Other theorists have given equal prominence to fear or anxiety as an important variable in behavior. These feelings are believed to constitute the basis for the development of the bizarre behaviors of the neurotic and the psychotic.

In the course of a child's growth in a culture there are innumerable opportunities for him to acquire fears of certain stimuli in specific situations. All too little is known about how these anxieties are learned, but it seems reasonable to believe that they are acquired in essentially the same way that other responses of the organism are learned. It has been adequately demonstrated with both animals and humans that fears are learnable. Moreover, it has been demonstrated that reduction in fear or anxiety is sufficient reinforcement for the learning of new responses (Miller, 1948).

Anxiety is basic to all neurotic behavior. It is so prominent in certain behaviors that they have been labeled anxiety disorders or anxiety neuroses. Under conditions of high anxiety, responding becomes ineffectual and discriminations tend to be difficult. Anxiety appears to be cumulative. As it mounts, effectiveness in dealing with new situations is impaired. This leads to new sources of anxiety and the number of conditions that give rise to anxiety continue to multiply. High anxiety becomes a chronic condition and interferes with achievement. So many stimuli have become anxiety-arousing that anxiety cannot be avoided. There eventually develops the condition where the person's behavior has become so impoverished that he becomes ineffective in carrying out the ordinary affairs of living. He feels exhausted, helpless, and excited. He cannot identify the stimuli that provoke his feelings and actions because the sources for his anxiety are multiple and obscure. If other symptoms of disorder develop, reduce the anxiety, and become well established through their reinforcement, the disorder is labeled according to the nature of the symptomatic behavior. If the anxiety persists and no means of coping with it is acquired, the person is called an anxiety neurotic.

## Phobias

Phobias are *apparently* irrational fears. It is relatively easy to see how ordinary fears are acquired through conditioning. A child is burned by a match and fears matches. A young man nearly loses his life while swimming and learns to fear the water. A person has a severe automobile accident and thereafter fears riding in automobiles. When the "reasons" for the fear are obscure, that is, when we cannot readily determine the cause of the fear, and it is rather extreme and persistent, it is called a phobia. The individual suffering from a phobia does not "know" how his fear developed but it is very real and may be incapacitating. There is nothing particularly bizarre about his not knowing the source of his fear when one considers the possibilities of stimulus generalization from the originally effective stimulus (*Miller, 1951*), or when one considers the many possibilities for higher order conditioning to occur, causing the fear to become attached to stimuli that were never *directly* associated with the original stimulus.

A person suffering from fear of closed places presents a baffling behavioral situation if one does not examine the background from which the fear initially arose. If it is discerned that the person was in an automobile accident in which he was injured and encapsulated in the wrecked auto for many hours, it is not quite so baffling. While the person was isolated in the small space of the wrecked automobile, he was fearful that he would not be discovered in time to prevent his death. Fear became associated with the closed space to which he was confined. Anxiety was aroused when he later thought about his narrow escape and his distress while unable to escape from the wreck. Through stimulus generalization anxiety and fear came to be evoked by a variety of stimuli. Each time anxiety was aroused by thoughts of confinement, he quickly thought of something else and his avoidance of thinking about confinement was reinforced by the reduction in anxiety associated with thoughts of closed places. If he felt anxious in a closed room or an elevator he escaped and his avoidance of the closed places was further reinforced through the reduction of his fear. His escapes from the fear-inducing stimuli were performed without further exploration of the stimuli so that new and nonfearful responses could not become conditioned to the fear-evoking stimuli.

When the background of phobic reactions is systematically explored, the behavior loses much of its "irrational" character. The principles of learning seem to be applicable to the acquisition of such behavior as readily as to the acquisition of the more usual fears.

## Compulsions and Obsessions

Compulsions and obsessions differ from each other in that the responses in compulsive behavior are readily observable, whereas those in obsession are not (*Lundin, 1961*). Both involve the repetition of some response that often appears to be unnecessary and futile. A compulsion is the repetition of simple acts or series of acts. Obsessions are more implicit in nature, involving the recurrence of thoughts that one cannot dispel. Both appear to involve avoidance behavior. The anxiety level becomes high and the anxiety is reduced by the compulsive behavior; thus, the behavior is reinforced by the anxiety reduction and persists as the result of the reinforcement (*Fenichel, 1945; Dollard and Miller, 1950; Lundin, 1961*). As long as a person commits some compulsive act such as hand washing, simple repetitive responding, or maintaining things in an excessively orderly fashion, he feels better. The reinforcement for such behavior comes from the alleviation of the aversive stimuli and from the reduction of anxiety aroused by the stimuli. The compulsive behavior, once committed, is maintained through reinforcement.

The maintenance of the behavior is more clearly understandable than are the conditions for the establishment of the behavior in the first place. That these are learned responses seems to be quite clear, but the exact manner of their acquisition is camouflaged by the complexity that is common to most social learning phenomena. The establishment of compulsive responses probably derives from the conditioning history of the individual involved. A person, having been excessively conditioned to avoid dirt and contamination, avoids contaminated things because of the anxiety aroused by them. To avoid exposure to these anxiety-arousing stimuli, he develops habits of extreme orderliness, cleanliness, or hand washing. When he is exposed to these aversive stimuli he engages in behaviors designed to reduce the stimuli and alleviate the anxiety associated with them.

Psychologists have frequently found that the anxiety of people engaging in compulsive behavior is of a moral nature. When this is so it is called *guilt*. The compulsively clean individual may have been excessively punished for dirtiness and may have had a variety of stimuli labeled as dirty. Sex organs and sex functioning may have been associated with being dirty or "nasty." Masturbation or other sexually oriented behavior may have aroused feelings of guilt (anxiety about moral behavior) that were also associated with being dirty; cleanliness responses were initiated to dispel the anxiety. The compulsive act reduces the intensity of the conditioned aversive stimuli only temporarily. The effects of the act are short lived because as soon as it is concluded the aversive stimuli return (i.e. the person is back among the stimuli that generate anxiety or is thinking of the aversive stimuli). As long as he continually performs his compulsive acts the aversive stimuli and their consequences are avoided.

## Hysterical Symptoms

Hysterical symptoms (tics, tremors, paralysis, anesthesias, cramps, dual personality) develop in people who suffer from a high level of anxiety. The anxiety may derive from a single, intense, traumatic experience or may develop from experiences extending over the lifetime of the individual. The hysterical symptoms develop as an avoidance reaction and operate to reduce or avoid the anxiety-arousing stimuli. Hysterical symptoms are frequently closely enough related to the initially anxiety-arousing events that their utility value is unmistakably apparent. Aviators have been reported to develop hysterical disturbances in depth perception and night vision under the stress of combat, whereas paratroopers were more likely to develop paralyzed legs (*Grinker and Spiegel, 1945*). Writers develop writer's cramp; students develop headaches that prevent study; and athletes develop symptoms that interfere with their performance.

An example of hysterical adjustment may serve to illustrate how these symptoms develop. A young man graduated from high school after considerable difficulty. He was not a good student and had to exert himself to get passing grades. His father was eager for the boy to get a job and start earning some money as soon as possible. He was able to get the son a job in the poultry processing industry. The job consisted of hanging the birds up by the feet and sticking them so that the blood would drain. This was the boy's first real experience with physical labor. He found the job not only physically fatiguing but highly distasteful as well. He wanted to quit his job and go to school to learn a trade, but paternal pressure to earn money kept him on the job. Lifting the birds up by the feet and placing them on the racks was tiring. By the end of the day the boy's arms would ache and tremble.

He shortly developed a severe tremor in his right arm. It was so severe that he could not return to work. He was examined by a physician and no organic damage was found. Because of the tremor he stayed home and did no work for two or three weeks. The tremor began to subside following a discussion with his father about going to school to learn a trade. Within a short time the arm was back to normal and the boy was sent to a business school. His progress in the school was not good; he had as much difficulty in business school as he had had in high school. He learned to operate the typewriter, but not very well. He was anxious that he was going to fail in school. The tremor in his arm returned and persisted for some time.

This case can illustrate several things. The fatigue from the physical strain of his work caused his arms to tremble when lifting. This probably served as a cue for the symptoms that later developed. Obviously a person with a severe tremor in his preferred arm could not be expected to do the work required on the job. He found the job highly distasteful and this was an adequate excuse for avoiding the noxious stimuli. His incapacity was a socially acceptable excuse for not working. It served to avoid the aversive stimuli and to reduce the anxiety caused by parental pressure to "get a job and earn some money." When the tremor became less useful (when it was arranged for him to go to school) it disappeared. When failure at school became imminent the tremor returned. It, again, was a socially acceptable excuse for failure to perform, reduced his anxiety about failing out of school, and reduced parental pressure to secure employment.

In the development of hysteria, it can be observed that an individual has a high level of anxiety. He engages in a great variety of behaviors that do not seem to reduce the anxiety. By trial and error he eventually finds some response that is, at least, partially successful. This response is repeated and the consequent anxiety reduction serves to reinforce the behavior. The factors determining the nature of the particular hysterical response are not always very clear, but the reinforcing value of the symptom is usually apparent. The response is typically a personally useful one in avoiding some circumstance. It is a socially useful response in that it constitutes an adequate excuse for failure to perform in the expected or prescribed manners.

## The Use of Alcohol

There is ample evidence to indicate that alcohol consumption reduces fear. If it does reduce fear or anxiety, and anxiety reduction is an effective reinforcer, the consistent use of alcohol would seem to result from its indirect reinforcing effects. The results of several experimental investigations confirm the hypothesis that alcohol is fear-reducing. Animals trained to fear a food delivery apparatus to the point where they consistently refused to approach it, would approach and manipulate the apparatus under the influence of alcohol (*Masserman and Yum, 1946*). Animals trained to fear (avoid) a goal box containing food were injected with either water or alcohol. Five minutes following the injections, the animals that were injected with water would not approach the fear-conditioned goal. The animals injected with alcohol solution ran freely toward the previously feared goal (*Conger, 1949*).

If drinking alcohol reduces fear, it would be expected that alcohol consumption would be reinforced under frightening circumstances. This finding has been confirmed by Masserman and Yum (1946). Cats normally preferred plain milk to milk containing five percent alcohol; however, after they had been frightened, and then forced to drink milk with alcohol in it, thus relieving their fear, they developed a preference for the milk containing five percent alcohol. Subsequently, when the animals had been conditioned not to be frightened in the situation, the preference for alcohol disappeared.

Among human beings alcohol no doubt serves to reduce fear or anxiety, but it has acquired certain social values as well. Being intoxicated or under the influence of alcohol is an acceptable excuse for inappropriate social behavior. "He would not have done it had he not been drinking" is a frequently used rationalization in our culture. Intoxication can be used as an excuse for inadequate performance and as an excuse for the avoidance of social and personal responsibilities. Personal accountability is successfully avoided in many situations through alcohol consumption. The reinforcement value for the use of alcohol in human beings stems partially from the direct reduction of anxiety and partially from the cultural-social attitudes toward the levels of performance in various situations of those who drink.

### SEVERE DISORDERS

Certain response patterns of people are less tolerated by the culture than others. In some cultures, hallucinations (nonverifiable sensory experiences) are not only expected and tolerated but are encouraged and rewarded. Visions and communications from spirits enhance the social prestige of the individual reporting them. This is not the case in our culture, where hallucinations and delusional behavior are looked upon as symptomatic of severe disturbance.

## Delusions

In a discussion of rationalization and projection in a previous chapter, it was indicated that we live in a society that attaches a great deal of importance to *rational* behavior. It was indicated that as a result of this emphasis we learn to rationalize—to give acceptable and plausible reasons for our behavior. One *rational* way to explain behavior is to project, or blame others for occurrences that would be embarrassing if we admitted our personal responsibility for them. If an honest explanation for our behavior would provoke anxiety, guilt, and feelings of inadequacy, there develops a tendency to blame others for our misfortunes and for our own shortcomings. We are in the position of having to find some explanation for our behavior but avoiding the true one. When we chance on some rationalization that is acceptable, it is reinforced by a reduction in anxiety.

It has been contended that a delusion (a belief that is grossly false) is only quantitatively different from rationalization (*Dollard and Miller, 1950*). According to this position the problem of finding a socially acceptable explanation is more difficult, and much stronger anxiety or guilt is involved. The reduction of the strong drive is a powerful reinforcement for the delusional utterances. The reinforcement value of the delusion is greater than the negative reinforcing value of social or self-criticism. Because the reinforcement value of the delusion is higher than that of other competing responses, the delusion is repeated and reinforced, and becomes "fixed" in nature.

## Hallucinations

Thinking is probably the most complex of human responses. This complex mode of responding probably goes on during most of one's waking hours. Images and perceptions are internal responses that have a cue or stimulus function. These images and perceptions should, then, be governed by the same principles that govern the occurrence of external responses. As stimuli they should be subject to the same phenomena as other stimuli. Stimulus generalization should be as applicable to these internal stimuli as it is to externally identifiable stimuli. If the principles of behavior applicable in other areas are also applicable here, we would expect that as drive increases, imagery and perceptual responses in general should become stronger and generalized to cover a wider range of sensory cues. One source of hallucinations may be an exceedingly wide effective stimulus generalization under conditions of high drive or high levels of anxiety.

Children are trained to differentiate between perceptual reality and imaginary experiences. They are more consistently reinforced for responses that are tied to the physical environment. If fanciful tales and outlandish imaginings are reported they are not likely to be favorably received. However, if children are consistently thwarted in their attempts to deal effectively with reality, they may find that their imaginary world holds more possibilities for positive reinforcement than the real one. The "building of air castles" can be an extremely satisfying business. In the imaginary situation there are no annoyances, no frustrations, and no worries. The child learns that anxiety aroused by the frustrations encountered in the social world can be dissipated by imagined happenings. His world of personal perceptions, images, and occurrences holds greater satisfaction for him than reality. Having learned to imagine and to perceive, he now uses these methods of responding to reduce anxiety and provide the satisfactions that have not been forthcoming from the external environment; thus the child learns to hallucinate, and his hallucinating is reinforced by the anxiety reduction it affords.

## Psychotic Behavior

Behavior that is typically disorganized, disconnected, and bizarre is frequently designated as *psychotic*. Principles of learning should be applicable to the acquisition of such behavior. Mednick (1958), using the processes of conditioning and stimulus generalization, has presented an interesting analysis of schizophrenia.

Although schizophrenics are often described as emotionally "flat," it would appear that this "emotional flatness" is more descriptive of chronic schizophrenics than it is of those in the acute or early stages. Experimental studies have shown that the acute patient is a victim of very high anxiety (*Malmo and Shagass, 1949*). His consequent high level of drive produces an abnormal amount of stimulus and associative generalization (*Mednick, 1957*). The number of stimuli to which the individual learns to respond with fear and anxiety is thus expanded. Some people learn to avoid potential anxiety-producing situations, and they maintain a relatively high level of anxiety throughout their lives because the anxiety is never extinguished.

If an event or series of events occurs which serves to increase the anxiety level and heighten drive, the individual responds with increased stimulus generalization, and a large number of new stimuli become anxiety-arousing. Situations that previously made him bearably anxious now tax his ability to control himself because of the already high anxiety state present. His high drive level will keep thoughts running through his mind. As the spiral of anxiety and generalization mounts, his ability to make discriminations is almost totally overcome by his generalization tendencies. Unusual associations based on stimulus response generalizations begin to appear. Bodily positions associated with any slight reduction of anxiety will tend to be maintained. He rationalizes his behavior and uses previously learned projective responses to the point where he may be classified as paranoid.

When he finds means (however drastic) of reducing his anxiety, these responses are perpetuated. If the responses he acquires are very successful he will begin to appear as a nonanxious, emotionally flat, chronic patient. His pre-psychotic fears have not been extinguished, but they have been hidden. If the protective associations developed by the psychotic are disturbed he again becomes an overtly highly anxious person.

Lundin (1965) has employed well established psychological principles and emphasized the role of reinforcement in his extensive study of psychopathology. The same principles are used in explaining the development of bizarre behavior that are used in describing normal or usual behavior. The application of principles of learning to the development and treatment of severe disorders is receiving a great deal of investigative attention (*Krasner and Ullmann, 1965; Ullmann and Krasner, 1965*).

## A GLANCE FORWARD

Personal adjustment and personality as problems in learning theory have been recognized for a long time (*Guthrie, 1938*). However, those interested in learning as an area of investigation have not been vitally concerned with personality, and those involved in the study of personality have not been particularly interested in learning. This has been an unfortunate circumstance. Interest in the problems of social learning has been generated by the work of Dollard and Miller (*1950*), Mowrer (*1960*), Lundin (*1961*), Bandura and Walters (*1963*), and Bandura (*1965*). The learning of adaptive and adjustive responses is coming under the closer scrutiny of psychologists interested in adjustment and personality as well as those psychologists who have concerned themselves with learning and perception. Further research in this area should serve to shed light on a lot of personal-social learning phenomena that have been explored only vaguely and tentatively up to the present time.

## SUMMARY

The study of social learning has been more indirect than the study of other forms of learned behavior. Generalizations have to be made from laboratory studies in controlled situations or from general observations made in the complex social environment. The direct study of social learning in controlled situations has not been adequately explored.

Children begin to learn social responses and formulate means of dealing with their social environments very early in life. Socialization is a long and involved process. One of the features of childhood learning that opens up new learning possibilities is language. Children must acquire patterns of responding appropriately to either sex, learn when and how to be aggressive and submissive, and acquire the subtle meanings of social interaction.

Maladaptive behavior is acquired by the same general principles as adaptive behavior. Children learn to fear objects and to make responses appropriate to the fearful stimulation. Parental attitudes and behaviors serve as guides for various behavioral acquisitions. General patterns of responding develop from the learning of great numbers of specific responses to specific stimuli. Through stimulus generalization and higher order conditioning a general predisposition to respond in particular ways evolves.

The last part of this chapter has been devoted to applying the general principles of learning to the acquisition of symptoms of disorder. Various neurotic and psychotic behaviors can be accounted for using existent principles and theories of learning. Further research in the area of learning as it relates to adjustment and personality development is needed, and interest in this area seems to be increasing.

## *REFERENCES*

BALDWIN, A. L. Socialization and the parent-child relationship. *Child Develpm.*, 1948, **19**, 127–136.

BANDURA, A. Vicarious Processes: A Case of No-Trial Learning. In L. Berkowitz (ed.), *Advances in Experimental Social Psychology*. Vol. II. New York: Academic Press, 1965.

BANDURA, A., ROSS, D., and ROSS, S. A. Transmisson of aggression through imitation of aggressive models. *J. abnorm. soc. Psychol.*, **63**, 575–582.

BANDURA, A., ROSS, D., and ROSS, S. A. Imitation of film-mediated aggressive models. *J. abnorm. soc. Psychol.*, 1963, **66**, 3–11.

BANDURA, A., and WALTERS, R. H. *Social Learning and Personality Development*. New York: Holt, Rinehart and Winston, Inc., 1963.

BARUCH, D. W. A study of reported tension in interparental relationships as coexistent with behavior adjustment in children. *J. exp. Educ.*, 1937, 6, 187–204.

BERKOWITZ, L. The expression and reduction of hostility. *Psychol. Bull.*, 1958, **55**, 257–283.

BERKOWITZ, L. *Aggression: a Social Psychological Analysis*. New York: McGraw-Hill Book Company, 1962.

BERKOWITZ, L. Aggressive cues in aggressive behavior and hostility catharsis. *Psychol. Rev.*, 1964, **71**, 104–122.

BISHOP, B. M. Mother-child interactions and the social behavior of children. *Psychol. Monogr.*, 1951, **65**, No. 328.

CONGER, J. J. *An analysis of the effect of alcohol upon conflict behavior in the albino rat*. Ph.D. dissertation. New Haven: Yale University, 1949.

DAVIS, I. M. The relation of repetitions in the speech of young children to certain measures of language maturity and situational factors. Part III. *J. speech Dis.*, 1940, **5**, 242–246.

DOLLARD, J., and MILLER, N. E. *Personality and Psychotherapy*. New York: McGraw-Hill Book Company, 1950.

FENICHEL, O. *The Psychoanalytic Theory of Neurosis*. New York: W. W. Norton and Company, 1945.

FREUD, S. *The Problem of Anxiety.* New York: W. W. Norton and Company, 1936.

GOLDMAN, R., and SHAMES, G. H. Comparisons of the goals that parents of stutterers and parents of non-stutterers set for their children. *J. Speech and Hearing Disord.,* 1964, **29**, 381–389.

GRINKER, R. R., and SPIEGEL, J. P. *Men Under Stress.* Philadelphia: The Blakiston Company, 1945.

GUTHRIE, E. R. *The Psychology of Human Conflict.* New York: Harper & Brothers, 1938.

HAGMAN, R. R. A study of fears of children of pre-school age. *J. exp. Educ.,* 1932, **1**, 110–130.

HOLLENBERG, E., and SPERRY, M. Some antecedents of aggression and effects of frustration on doll play. *Personality,* 1950, **1**, 32–43.

JERSILD, A. T., and HOLMES, F. B. Children's Fears. *Child Develpm. Monogr., 1935,* No. 20.

KRASNER, L., and ULLMANN, L. P. *Case Studies in Behavior Modification.* New York: Holt, Rinehart and Winston, Inc., 1965.

LANG, P. J. Experimental Studies of Desensitization Psychotherapy. In Wolpe, I., Salter, A., and Reyna, L. J. (eds.), *The Conditioning Therapies.* New York: Holt, Rinehart and Winston, Inc., 1964.

LEVY, D. M. *Maternal Over-protection.* New York: Columbia University Press, 1943.

LUNDIN, R. W. *Personality.* New York: The Macmillan Company, 1961.

LUNDIN, R. W. *Principles of Psychopathology.* Columbus, Ohio: Charles E. Merrill Books, Inc., 1965.

MACFARLANE, J. W., ALLEN, L., and HORZIK, M. P. A developmental study of the behavior problems of normal children between twenty-one months and fourteen years. *Univ. of Calif. Publications in Child Develpm.,* 1954.

MALMO, R. B., and SHACASS, C. Physiologic studies of reaction to stress in anxiety and early schizophrenia. *Psychosom. Med.,* 1949, **11**, 9–24.

MARTIN, W. E., and STENDLER, C. B. *Child Development: The Process of Growing up in Society.* New York: Harcourt, Brace and Company, 1953.

MASSERMAN, J. H., and YUM, K. S. An analysis of the influence of alcohol on experimental neurosis in cats. *Psychosom. Med.,* 1946, **8**, 36–52.

MEDNICK, S. A. Generalization as a function of manifest anxiety and adaptation to psychological experiments. *J. consult. Psychol.,* 1957, **21**, 491–494.

MEDNICK, S. A. A learning theory approach to research in schizophrenia. *Psychol. Bull.,* 1958, **55**, 316–327.

MILLER, N. E. Studies of fear as an acquirable drive: I. Fear as motivation and fear-reduction as reinforcement in the learning of new responses. *J. exp. Psychol.,* 1948, **38**, 89–101.

MILLER, N. E. Learnable Drives and Rewards. In Stevens, S. (ed.), *Handbook of Experimental Psychology.* New York: John Wiley and Sons, Inc., 1951.

MOWRER, O. H. *Learning Theory and Behavior.* New York: John Wiley and Sons, Inc., 1960.

MOWRER, O. H. The psychologist looks at language. *Amer. Psychol.,* 1954, **9**, 660–694.

MUSSEN, P. H., and RUTHERFORD, E. Effects of aggressive cartoons on children's aggressive play. *J. abnorm. soc. Psychol.,* 1961, **62**, 461–464.

PIAGET, J. *The Language and Thought of the Child,* trans. by M. Warden. New York: Harcourt, Brace and Company, 1926.

RHEINGOLD, H. L., GEWIRTZ, J. L., and Ross, H. W. Social conditioning of vocalization in the infant. *J. comp. physiol. Psychol.*, 1959, **52**, 68–73.

SAPPENFIELD, B. R. *Personality Dynamics.* New York: Alfred A. Knopf, Inc., 1954.

SEARS, R. R., WHITING, J. W., NOWLIS, V., and SEARS, P. S. Some childrearing antecedents of aggression and dependency in young children. *Genet. psychol. Monogr.*, 1953, **47**, 135–234.

SIEGEL, O. M., and HAREGEN, D. Audience size and variations in stuttering behavior. *J. Speech and Hearing res.*, 1964, **7**, 381–388.

STAATS, A. W., and STAATS, C. K. *Complex Human Behavior.* New York: Holt, Rinehart and Winston, Inc., 1964.

ULLMAN, L. P., and KRASNER, L. *Research in Behavior Modification.* New York: Holt, Rinehart and Winston, Inc., 1965.

*Chapter 7*

# Motivation:
# Nature
# and Sources

MOTIVATION IS A MUCH DISCUSSED FACET of human behavior. It is undoubtedly of great significance in the understanding of man's personal and social behavior. There is some disagreement as to the exact meaning of motivation. However, there is enough agreement as to what constitutes motivational phenomena that some general level of understanding can be established. Motivational phenomena are those behaviors that seem to be guided by the biological functioning of the organism, such as the need for food, water, pain avoidance, and, indirectly, sex; they are also those behaviors that appear to result from acquired wants, wishes, desires, aversions, purposes, interests, affections, fear, anger, love, and a host of other related concepts. It would seem that such a list of "sources" for behavior is so comprehensive as to include everything that man does, and indeed it is thought by some psychologists that all behavior is motivated. Whether or not this is true, it appears certain that motives constitute the dynamic aspects of behavior.

Two general questions arise under the topic heading of motivation. The first of these is, "Why is the organism active?" This will be given primary consideration in this chapter. The second question is, "Why is the organism active in a particular way?" This topic will be treated primarily in Chapter Eight. One might ask, "Why not accept the organism as an active organism and just deal with the second question?" The answer to this is that frequently the direction that behavior takes cannot be adequately understood without considering the nature of the instigation to activity.

Before attempting to deal with either of these questions, a brief look at some of the ways that men have dealt with the topic of motivation may help clarify the nature of the problem.

## HISTORICAL CONSIDERATIONS

Motivation could hardly have existed as a problem for primitive man. His belief systems were such that motivation was readily "accounted for" and thus could not constitute a problem. For primitive man, behavior resulted from special "forces." These special forces were spirits or demons that possessed the individual and caused him to behave in particular ways. If he was possessed by a good spirit he behaved in socially acceptable ways. If he was possessed by an evil spirit or demon he would behave in ways that were not socially acceptable. The proof of the nature of the spirit was in behavior, and the spirit exhibited its nature through the behavior of the individual. This reasoning was circular in nature, and because of its circularity the results could have appeared as self-evident truths. The names by which these forces were identified changed, but the concept remained the same. It made little difference whether the concept was called a spirit, a demon, a soul, or a mind.

An early conception of man was that he was really composed of two "selves." The first of these was a physical self. It could be seen and felt and had physical dimensions. The second was an immaterial self. It could detach itself from the body, as in dreams. Death represented a permanent separation of the two. When the immaterial self abandoned the material self, the material self lost most of its functions; therefore the immaterial came to be considered the real animating force. Behavior, then, was the result of "a man within a man" who directed the physical being. As long as this "animistic" notion prevailed, motivation constituted no particular problem; this "entity" or "man within a man" was responsible. It was a handy way of dealing with the problem by refusing to recognize it; however, it did not prove to be very satisfactory. As a hypothetical concept such postulations were neither useful nor fruitful. They did not explain or describe but simply labeled. Explaining an event by claiming that an immaterial entity was responsible made scientific inquiry impossible, and inevitably led to postulating still further entities to explain those already proposed. The end result was a group of postulated entities that were supposed to explain each other. The problem would still be there, but attention was then diverted to understanding the operation of the immaterial entities.

The German educator Herbart thought that motivational forces were inherent in ideas themselves. He conceived of ideas as dynamic entities that resolved themselves into patterns of action. Carrying this position to the extreme, mere knowledge of what constitutes socially acceptable behavior in any situation should result in socially acceptable behavior in that situation. All that need be done in order to produce an ethical generation of college graduates would be to require knowledge of the appropriate ethics of the culture, or just to require a course in ethics. Knowledge was thought to carry its own dynamic drive, so that knowledge of what constitutes appropriate behavior should result in appropriate behavior.

We no longer accept the Herbartian idea of motivation, but we frequently behave as if we, too, believed that knowledge in and of itself had motivational properties. Perhaps every adult has been criticized and in turn has criticized others for their behavior on the grounds that they "certainly know better than to do a thing like that." A professor of philosophy known to the authors expressed considerable disappointment when a student stole an advance copy of his final examination in ethics. He implied that if this had happened in any other course he would not have felt so badly.

The French philosopher Descartes explored the possibilities of answering questions about motivation without reference to a "soul." He considered animals as machines, and postulated fluid spirits rushing through the nerves as the dynamic or driving agents that moved the complex machines. He had some difficulty in applying this theory to the behavior of human beings, but maintained that many human acts were mechanistic in nature and could be accounted for by the theory. He resorted to the soul concept, however, to account for "rational acts," such as judgments, choice, and will. The practice of interpreting animal behavior in terms of one set of concepts and human behavior in terms of radically different concepts was not discarded until Darwin's influence became widespread.

In 1873, Darwin discussed the anatomical and physiological continuity between animal and human species and implied that there was also a corresponding continuity in their behavior. From this time on, the study of animal behavior gradually came to be regarded as providing clues to the more complex, but essentially similar, behavior of human beings.

## Instincts

The concept of "soul" gradually was replaced by "instincts" as the dynamic agents for moving organisms to different kinds of activity. Instinct as a concept has been a part of intellectual thought for centuries (*Beach, 1955*). With its biological implications, it was formally introduced into psychological theorizing by McDougall (*1908*). McDougall postulated that instincts were the fundamental "motives" that moved organisms toward particular goals or purposes. For him an instinct was an innate biological process. It was an emotional impulse or striving that predisposed the organism to notice particular stimuli and to make either approach or avoidance movements in response to them. Thus a pugnacity instinct was an emotional impulse to fight that manifested itself in fighting when the stimuli were appropriate. The instinct to escape referred to a fear impulse and a tendency to move away from a threatening situation. McDougall first accounted for all behavior with twelve instincts. He later had to revise his list by adding to it. His list (*McDougall, 1923*) eventually included eighteen native propensities. Among these were food seeking, disgust, sex, fear, curiosity, gregariousness, submission, anger, laughter, migratory propensity, and a cluster of specific body needs such as coughing, sneezing, and elimination. To account for the varieties and complexities of observed behavior, he suggested ways in which these "instincts" or innate propensities could be modified, compounded, and integrated into more complex functional units.

Theories of instincts became popular in psychology and related fields. The concept was used extensively in explaining various aspects of animal and human behavior (*Dewey, 1917; Thorndike, 1913; Watson, 1914; Woodworth, 1918*), but its uncritical use in psychology was short lived. Criticisms of instinct began to appear in the literature following a general attack on the doctrine by Dunlap (*1919*). It was argued that there was no way to observe directly processes called instincts, and that it was an easy substitute for true explanations of observed behavior. To say that an animal fights because of the instinct of pugnacity is merely to give a redundant description of the observed activity. The description would be complete if one stated merely that the animal fights or runs away (*Watson, 1925*). It was argued that instinct was not explanatory, and that an attempt to determine in each specific instance the relative roles of learning and innate factors should be made.

As a result of the criticisms of the instinct doctrine, psychologists started analyzing activities that were attributed to instincts. Experimental analysis of migration, nest building, maternal behavior, sexual responses, and many other complex patterns of behavior was accomplished. These studies revealed some very interesting hormonal, perceptual, and experiential factors as the basis of the complex activities that had been labeled instinctive (*Morgan, 1943; Beach, 1951*). It was shown that nest building in rats was related to the mechanisms of temperature control and that migration in birds was related to gonadal development. Obstacle avoidance in bats, which had long been a mysterious phenomena, was shown to be related to the echoes of sounds they produced in flight. Much of the mystery of some of the complex activities that had been attributed to instinct was removed. It became obvious that, though there were probably innate components in these complex activities, the concept of instinct was too broad to be used as an adequate basis for explaining them. The notion that such activities could be explained in terms of instincts has been widely discarded by psychologists. "Instinctive" may still be used as descriptive of certain classes of behavior, but it is becoming increasingly popular to refer to these behaviors as being "species-specific"; thus, the explanatory connotations of the word "instinct" are avoided and a more accurate label is applied.

The analysis of instinctive behavior always reached a point where it became necessary to postulate some other more basic or primary innate forces or agents. Even if it could be demonstrated that complex activities that were called instinctive resulted from the integration of many simpler component acts, the origin of the simple component acts still needed to be explained. The use of the concept of drive was an attempt to do this by postulating the existence of some simpler, innate agents. These simpler or more fundamental agents were called primary drives. Hunger, thirst, sex, and pain as more elementary sources of behavior were gradually introduced. The use of such elementary concepts as the basis for activity allowed sufficient latitude to attribute individual and cultural differences in behaviors that had been previously designated as instinctive to learning. It seemed appealing and logical that complex behavior patterns were acquired from elementary processes rather than that complex behaviors themselves were unitary and not meaningfully analyzed by component parts. Drives, as the primary dynamic agents of behavior, gradually replaced instincts and have played an important part in the development of modern day psychological theorizing.

## Drive Theory

The reduction of sources of behavior to more fundamental biological functions has not resulted in unanimity regarding the nature or function of these basic processes. The task of explaining how complex behaviors can be built from such elementary desires as hunger, thirst, sex, and pain avoid-ance has been an imposing one. The further task of demonstrating that complex activities not only *can be* built from such a fundamental basis but *are* built from such a basis looms still larger. There is a great difference between demonstrating that a theory *can* account for observed behavior and proving that it *does* account for the behavior. If it can be demon-strated that a theory in fact does account for the observations, then it is no longer a theory but a body of facts. Drive theorists have been able to demonstrate that complex behaviors can be built from more fundamental ones. The tasks of proving that a theory does account for the observed behavior is common to all theories of behavior. As long as no such proof is available, competing theories will thrive.

The tremendous amount of research done within the general frame-work of drive theory makes it an appealing one. The lack of agreement among drive theorists indicates that the concepts involved should be closely examined.

### THE NATURE OF DRIVE

Drive is an intervening variable. It is a construct used as a logical connec-tion between those conditions that establish it and the effect of those conditions on behavior. It is assumed that drive is produced by certain conditions and is reflected in the consequent behavior.

The desirability of invoking drive or some drive-like construct in attempting to understand human behavior stands out rather clearly in several instances. Weak stimuli sometimes evoke vigorous responses. An example of this would be the slight stirring of a sick infant (stimulus) and the consequent vigorous behavior by the distraught mother (response). The mother is, no doubt, being stimulated from a variety of sources, but the addition of this one slight stimulus causes the appropriate reaction to be made with vigor and alacrity. This can be conceived of as a threshold effect. As long as the stimulus events are below a certain level they produce no particular behavior, but when the threshold has been reached the appropriate reaction occurs. In such instances, it may be desirable to view the stimulus as controlling a source of energy that is released in the response.

Another behavioral phenomenon that causes psychologists to invoke some intervening variable is the variation in response from time to time when the stimulating conditions are constant. When food is presented to an animal, sometimes it eats and sometimes it does not; when food is presented to two identical animals, one may eat and the other may not.

Such basic phenomena give rise to the concept of drive according to Skinner (1938). If hunger is viewed as a drive or as a source of drive, it can be said that food deprivation establishes drive and the resultant behavior effects the state of deprivation.

The motivation of behavior comes about through the existence of drive-establishing conditions that release energy that comes from the metabolic processes of the organism. Drive is originally blind. The energy released by drive is directionless and may serve any variety of behaviors. The apparent directionality of motivated behavior derives from learning associated with the arousing stimulus (drive stimulus). For example, a dog aroused to activity by food deprivation learns appropriate acts to reduce the stimuli that produce hunger. He may go to a place where food is customarily obtained, he may seek out the person who usually feeds him, he may bark and tug at his leash, or he may cast about in search of food. The behavior elicited by the release of energy and the stimuli associated with hunger can be as varied as the capacity of the animal to learn and the conditions for learning that prevail. Any behavior of which the animal is capable can probably be learned as the consequence of association with drive-producing stimuli.

The apparent directionality of drive derives from learning associated with drive stimulus. That animals can make discriminations between drive stimuli was demonstrated in an early study by Hull (1933). He used a simple maze in which rats were run while hungry on some days and thirsty on others. On the days the rats were run while hungry, a turn in one direction in the maze was rewarded by food; on the days the rats were run while thirsty, the opposite turn was rewarded with water. The animals eventually learned to make the appropriate turn for the particular condition of deprivation. Technical problems of the maze made it difficult for the animals to learn. Bolles and Petrinovich (1954) refined the procedure and apparatus, and demonstrated that rats could readily learn to go to one arm of a T-maze when thirsty and to its other arm when hungry.

It has been further demonstrated that animals can discriminate between different intensities of the same drive-producing stimulus (*Jenkins and Henratty*, 1949). Rats were taught to go to one arm of a T-maze after a short period of water deprivation and to the other arm after a longer period of water deprivation. Stimulus generalization from both levels of drive stimulus was also obtained.

## Drive or Drives?

It is common practice to speak of various "drives." The implication readily follows that drive exercises a directional control of behavior. Hunger drive, it is implied, directs the organism toward the attainment of food, thirst drive toward water procurement, sex drive toward sexually satisfying activity. It has been indicated that drive is directionless. If drive is to be understood as an energizer or activator and not as a direction indicator, the use of the plural form of the word becomes confusing. If drive is to be treated as directionless, wherein lies the logic of referring to drives? If they all operate alike when functioning as motivators of behavior, then they must share common processes; all drives become one as far as the activating function is concerned. One might suppose that all drives are alike, except that each results from a different motivational variable. If this is the case, there are not different drives as behavior determinants, but rather *different* sources of drive (*Brown, 1961*). In referring to the stimulus events that serve to arouse behavior, it then seems logical to refer to these as *primary sources of drive* rather than as *primary drives*. Primary drives have been designated as those that have a primary biological effect. The usual primary drives have been hunger drive, thirst drive, pain-avoidance drive, and sex drive. Hereafter these functions will be referred to as primary sources of drive.

It may be of some help to the reader to conceptualize drive as a degree of arousal. The living organism is constantly activated to some extent. In addition to accepting the organism as a living one that is active, further sources of drive, arousal, or activation are designated as either primary or secondary. Secondary sources will be given consideration later in this chapter and in Chapter Eight. Primary sources of drive serve to increase the extent of arousal or activation directly. Hunger contributes a portion of the total, as do thirst, pain, and sex. A person possesses drive in a rough positive relationship to the amount of deprivation or discomfort experienced. Although he is constantly motivated to some extent, his drive level will fluctuate with the activation of primary sources of drive. The hungry person will possess more drive than the sated one, and the person who is both hungry and thirsty will have more drive than the one who is only hungry. The reduction of drive stimulus, whch results in learning, can come about by reducing the stimulus from any of the primary sources of drive. It is doubtful that all of the primary sources of drive are simultaneously inactivated except in the comatose individual; thus, the person who is not completely sated in terms of his physiological functions is probably being stimulated from a variety of primary sources. The urgency of drive reduction probably does not arise until one or more of the primary sources of drive become sufficiently active to cause a marked increase in total drive. At this time the individual becomes active. The direction of activity will be determined by the inherent equipment and organization of the organism, and by the learning that has occurred. The apparent directionality of the behavior derives largely from the associations of the drive stimulus with behaviors that the individual has learned will reduce the drive stimulus. Drive stimulus, thus, has two separate aspects. One is that of drive as an activator or energizer, and the other is that of providing a stimulus or cue that can become associated with behavior that reduces it. This cue function is an important one in the behavior of humans because it is the drive stimulus that can then become associated with appropriate behavior.

The conception of drive as a unitary rather than a multiple construct and as an activator rather than a director is consistent with the position taken by Hull (1943). This position was logically derived from the then existing behavioral evidence. The two most important determiners of behavior for Hull were *drive* (D) and *habit strength* (H). Drive in this theory was a broadly acting, nondirective factor that functioned to facilitate both learned and unlearned associative tendencies. Its capacity to facilitate behavior was independent of the stimulus condition from which it derived. Drive due to hunger was indistinguishable from drive due to any intense stimulation as far as activation was concerned. The directionality of motivated behavior was determined, for Hull, by associative tendencies functioning in combination with both internal and external stimuli. These associative tendencies could be either learned ones or tendencies that were an inherent part of the structure and function of the organism. An animal could move away from or toward an object depending upon the nature of its learned associative predispositions. Drive, being only an activator and not a director, could facilitate whatever behavioral predisposition was dominant at the moment.

## SOME PHYSIOLOGICAL CONSIDERATIONS

More recent evidence of a physiological nature has given support to the unitary nature of drive. The role of the brainstem reticular formation in the activation of behavior has received a great deal of attention. The reticular formation is a dense network of neurons extending from the medulla of the lower brainstem to the thalamus in the diencephalon (*Lindsley, 1957*).

The reticular formation serves a two-way function. Fibers pass downward from the reticular formation into the spinal cord, carrying impulses that may either inhibit or facilitate certain complex postural and muscular reactions. Other fiber systems pass upward to basal ganglia, thalamus, hypothalamus, hyppocampus, and cortex. The diffuse nature of the ascending reticular formation allows impulses from lower segments of the formation to bring about widespread changes in cortical activity. The wave-form pattern of electrical potentials recorded from the brain differs markedly between sleep and waking states. Stimulation from the ascending reticular formation has an "activation effect." This effect is widespread in that it can be observed at numerous points on the cortical surface. Electrical stimulation in the area of the reticular formation has been found to change the cortical brain-wave pattern from that of "sleep" to one of a "waking" or "excited" nature (*Moruzzi and Magoun, 1949*). Stimulation of this area results in activation or arousal. These nonspecific activating or arousal effects of the ascending reticular system appear to be consistent with the construct of a general purpose drive.

Though Lindsley (*1951*) had observed the broad importance of reticular system activity for problems of emotion and motivation, Hebb (*1955*) first commented on the diffuse bombardment of the cortex as being synonymous with a general drive state. He further observed that the concept of drive could now assume anatomical and physiological identity. The reticular system is thought to be affected primarily by signals diverted via collaterals from the primary sensory pathways. It is also thought to be affected by impulses descending from the cortex. It has been pointed out (*Lindsley, 1957*) that the activity level of the reticular formation can thus be modified by stimulation peripheral to the organism or from within the organism. Ideational impulses from the higher cortical centers may then serve to increase reticular activity and effect drive.

Cofer and Appley (*1964*), in an extensive treatment of motivation, abandoned the conventional concept of drive and, in effect, substituted *arousal*. This may be more of a semantic manipulation than a conceptual one when drive is conceived as a unitary activator and not as a director of activity.

Nonspecific drive can be seen to be effected by both internal and external stimuli. Drive, if it is subject to ideational effects, can be altered in various ways by verbal instructions as well as by self-induced ideations and directions. This would seem to be an important source of drive regulation among human beings. If arousal or activation became too intense the bombardment of the cortex by the ascending reticular system would become excessive and decrements in performance would result. In this way, the decrements in performance of the "overly motivated" person might be better understood, as might the reverse situation, where the person is not sufficiently activated to perform adequately. Optimal arousal or activation, then, becomes imperative for optimal performance.

Olds and Milner (*1954*) demonstrated that electrical stimulation of the brain can function as a reinforcer for the performance of instrumental acts. They implanted electrodes in the brains of rats and administered an electrical stimulus of controlled strength and duration to the animals whenever they pressed a lever in an experimental box. With no reward other than electrical stimuli, rats would press the lever for long periods of time at high rates. The reinforcing effects of brain stimulation have been found not only in rats but in cats (*Roberts, 1958*) and in monkeys (*Bursten and Delgado, 1958*); thus, the phenomenon of stimulation of the brain (limbic system) acting as a reinforcer for instrumental behavior is rather well established.

It is difficult to determine why subcortical electrical stimulation acts as a reinforcer in view of the fact that the same intensity of stimulation may be either reinforcing or inhibiting (*Roberts, 1958*). Whether stimulation will be reinforcing or inhibiting is dependent upon the training procedures, stimulation duration, and testing environment. Brown (*1961*) has pointed out that behavioral effects quite similar to those produced by brain stimulation have been reported with externally administered shock and other strong stimuli. He cites Masserman's (*1946*) studies of "experimental masochism" in cats. In these studies, cats were trained to operate levers in order to get a blast of air in their faces. The air blast ordinarily elicits violent avoidance behavior in untrained animals. It has also been found that by introducing mild electric shock in the middle of an alley leading to food, and then gradually increasing the shock intensity, rats can be trained to tolerate shock intensities that would otherwise cause them to cease running (*Farber, 1948*). Before any conclusive statement can be made about how central brain stimulation serves as reinforcement, further research in this area must be forthcoming.

### GENERAL ACTIVITY

Evidence for the lack of specificity of drive can be garnered indirectly from a great number of sources. The early work of Bridges (*1932*) on emotional development indicates that the first emotional behavior of the infant is a diffuse, undifferentiated, elementary form of excitement. Reactions to stimuli by the newborn are not at all specific. A specific reflex such as sucking is normally elicited by stimulation of the lips of the infant, but when the infant is hungry a number of different stimuli can produce the sucking response. Stimulation of the cheeks or the eyes or changes in temperature can be effective in producing the sucking reflex because the response is high in the response hierarchy (well established) of the infant. Any increase in drive is likely to elicit the sucking response.

Although the human infant is equipped with a number of specific reflexive patterns, the gross behavior of the neonate is uncoordinated, diffuse, and general. The first emotional response of the infant, according to Bridges, is a general agitation or excitement produced by a great variety of stimulating conditions. This lack of specificity of behavior can be interpreted as evidence for the existence of drive, without the infant having had experiences from which to learn the specific behaviors essential to its reduction. The responses, then, must be random, diffuse, and general in nature until maturation and learning make the acquisition of directed behavior possible. Probably any response high in the response repertoire of the infant can be elicited by any stimulus resulting in an increase in drive.

Duffy (1934, 1957, 1962) insists that a clear distinction should be made between factors that determine the *intensity* of behavior and those that determine the *direction* of behavior. She uses such terms as "behavioral arousal" and "activation" when referring to the intensity of behavior. Degree of behavioral arousal or activation is a determinant of the intensity of responding but not of the direction of response. Duffy maintains, too, that the concept of activation helps to further obliterate the unnecessary distinction between "drives" and "emotions." Activation encompasses the functions of both drives and emotions in that both have to do with the arousal of the organism. The importance of general activity in the analysis of behavior is emphasized by Bindra (1961). He points out that directed activities, or those related to specific goals, tend to be "isolated, infrequent events in the life of an animal," and that "general activity" usually takes up a major portion of an animal's waking hours. Knowledge of the factors that determine the occurrence of the components of general activity is essential for the precise formulation of principles of behavior. Bindra suggests that components of general activity may play an important part in the execution of many normal and directed activities of animals.

General activity, comprised of many specific activities, may not only serve as a basis from which analysis of behavior should proceed, as Bindra indicates, but its diversity and intensity may also serve as a measure of drive and an indicator of various sources of drive. If certain aspects of "general activity" can be linked to certain directed behaviors or bodily states, it may become possible with precise observation of components of general activity to get some estimate not only of the amount of drive but the nature of the sources of drive at the time the animal is under observation. Systematic and detailed observations of the nature of general activity may yield information leading to the eventual better understanding of drive as well as the nature of learning.

### PRIMARY SOURCES OF DRIVE

There is probably a great number of primary or physiological sources of drive. Deviations from optimal temperature and humidity levels in the environment, pressures of accumulating bodily wastes, pressures from the wearing of clothing, and a host of other stimulus factors in addition to hunger, thirst, and sex may serve as primary motivational variables by causing an increase in arousal or an increase in drive. Any event that produces variation in drive is said to be a motivational variable. Those that exert their influence in a direct physiological or biological way are primary motivational variables.

## Need

The concept of need has been a much used one in psychological theorizing. Need and drive have been used interchangeably as have drive and motive. These words have been used without adequate definition in many instances. As a result, the use of need as a psychologically serviceable word has been impaired.

Need can certainly be used effectively to designate those organic conditions essential for the organism's survival. Such absolute necessities for survival as food, moisture, and certain aspects of pain avoidance can readily be related to organic needs. Sexual deprivation is a bit more remote, but sexual activity can be viewed as a necessity for the survival of the species; however, the immediacy of sexual demands can hardly be accounted for in this way. The removal of food or water from the organism results in its death. Uncontrolled severe temperature also destroys the organism, as does the absence of an appropriate combination of gases for breathing. Subjecting the individual to extreme pain in the form of tissue destruction cannot be tolerated for long by the individual. There is no evidence that sexual abstinence is destructive of the individual in any such imperative way, but the necessity for sexual activity for reproduction may be adequate to include sex as a need.

The use of the word "need" to designate motives of one kind or another probably stems from the making of value judgments about effective living. It has become popular to speak of a need for love, a need for acceptance, a need for self-expression, a need to understand, and a need to master. These designations seem to be more psychological than physical in nature and do not refer to the biological survival of the organism. They refer instead to apparent motives that must be fulfilled in order for a person to live happily and effectively in his environment. As such, the list can be extended to include almost any behavior of which the organism is capable. When employed in such a sense the meaning of "need" becomes vague, indefinite, variable, and lacking in the precision required for effective scientific communication.

When need is used as a basis for drive, the biological meaning of the word is employed. It is assumed that these necessities for existence have accompanying biological mechanisms that operate to increase the probability that the organism's necessities for survival will be procured. Absence of food gives rise to hunger as a stimulus (stomach contractions, low blood sugar level), increases activity level, and increases the probabilities of food procurement. Absence of moisture gives rise to thirst as a stimulus (dryness of throat and mouth), increases activity level, and enhances the probability of obtaining water. Noxious or painful stimulation increases the activity of the organism and increases the chances of pain avoidance or termination. Sexual stimulation heightens the activity of the individual and produces sexual responses that act as stimuli that increase the possibilities for reproductive behavior.

Need can thus be employed as a basis for drive; the need for nourishment producing hunger, the need for moisture producing thirst, noxious stimulation or tissue destruction producing pain, and the necessity for reproduction producing sexual arousal. The *stimuli* produced by need deficit seem more imperative to the concept of drive than the needs themselves. Stimuli or changes in stimulation other than those associated with need conditions may have inherent motivational properties. This subject will be explored later in this chapter.

Vitamin deficiency in the diet results in vitamin deficiency for the organism, but the affected animals do not demonstrate any increase in activity as the need for vitamins increases over time. If activity level is taken as a measure of drive, the covariance of need and drive in this instance is not very great; it seems clear that the two concepts should not be identified as one. Further, as an exclusive basis for drive, need would seem to be rather inadequate.

## Homeostasis

*Homeostasis* is a term used by Cannon (*1923, 1929*) to designate the constant *states* maintained by the body. The concept is essentially a physiological one. In physiology, *homeostatic processes* are those processes involved in the maintenance of certain rather constant conditions of the body. The mechanisms for the control of body temperature and salt content of the body fluids are examples of homeostatically functioning mechanisms. When the concept of homeostasis is applied to motivation, it is implied that appropriate activity will result in the restoration of equilibrium.

The concept of homeostasis has been a most useful one in terms of productivity of physiological and psychological research. Lewin's (*1936*) field theory, Festinger's (*1957*) cognitive dissonance, Helson's (*1959*) adaptation level, and cybernetics (*Wiener, 1948; Ashby, 1960*) all can be said to be basically homeostatic models.

The maintenance of constancy in the life of the organism has come to be referred to as homeostasis. In using homeostasis in this way, it can be said that any physiological or psychological tension acts to increase activity and could be considered a source of drive. The tendency to maintain states of physiological constancy in the organism has been expanded to include psychological phenomena. Thus any regulatory or compensatory behavior on the part of the individual can be viewed as homeostatic in nature. If viewed from a physiological standpoint, certain behaviors are difficult to interpret within a homeostatic frame of reference. Beach (*1956*) has indicated that it is difficult to place copulation into a homeostatic interpretation. It is also difficult to interpret all of behavior in terms of homeostasis and still have the concept retain enough of its physiological meaning to be useful. If the term is stretched to mean too many things, we are as well off saying simply that an organism does thus and so, as in saying that he is in a state of disequilibrium and does thus and so. The proof of the disequilibrium is in the individual's behavior, and he behaves as he does because of the disequilibrium. This circularity of reasoning is difficult to avoid and the level of understanding deriving from it is limited.

## Stimulation

It is a commonplace observation that stimulation of certain kinds evokes activity on the part of an animal. A pin prick incites the human infant to activity that is vigorous; sudden noises produce increased activity; food deprivation results in hunger as a stimulus serving to increase drive; irritations of various kinds serve to increase drive as reflected in increased activity. Some of the stimulus conditions that may act as motivational variables are well recognized. Others have been discounted or ignored. Intense stimulation as a source of drive has a moderate acceptance, but stimulation that is not intense or persistent has received but little attention. There is good reason for this. Stimuli that are not intense are difficult to measure, and the effects of nonintense stimuli would, of course, be elusive.

Some stimuli that are well demonstrated to have motivational consequences will be considered as well as some stimuli that may have motivational consequences.

### HUNGER AND THIRST

Hunger and thirst have been manipulated in physiological and psychological experimentation in order to produce variations in motivation. It is an ordinary observation that the hungry child seeks food and that the thirsty child seeks water. The precise manner by which hunger (food deprivation) or thirst (water deprivation) come to act as motivational variables and as directors of activity is not so obvious.

This problem can, perhaps, be better understood if hunger and thirst are both thought of as complex stimulus events. They may have their bases in the physiological needs of the organism and be responses to the biochemical changes occurring within the organism. If they are responses to some such condition, they must have stimulus value to the organism. The hungry individual learns to identify the stimulus conditions as conditions that are relieved by food ingestion; the thirsty individual learns to identify the stimulus conditions of thirst as those that are relieved by drinking water. The directionality of the behavior can be understood as having been learned. The stimuli of hunger or thirst, thus, serve two purposes, one being that of an identifiable cue or physical stimulus with which appropriate behavior can become associated, and the other, that of increasing the drive or arousal of the organism. If stimuli are understood as serving such a dual function, the directionality of behavior then becomes a topic for consideration within the general framework of "learning," and the arousal or drive aspects of stimuli remain as problems essentially in the area of motivation.

Changes in the general activity level of the organism deprived of food for various lengths of time have been investigated. It has been demonstrated that general activity increases are roughly proportional to the degree of food or water deprivation up to a given point (*Finger and Reid, 1952*). If food deprivation is extended beyond 72 hours for the rat, his activity level tends to go down. Increases in activity level occur not only when the animal is completely deprived for a long period of time, but also when it is moved from a free to a restricted feeding schedule (*Hall et al., 1953*). Morgan and Stellar (*1950*), after reviewing the literature on the relation between activity level and nutritional deficiencies, concluded that nutritional conditions that produce a decrement in general activity are those that tend to weaken the animal physically. Prolonged deprivation has a weakening effect and consequently produces a decrement in general level of activity.

The periodic nature of spontaneous activity has been investigated by Richter (*1927*). From these extensive investigations, he reports two-hour rhythms of activities in both animals and man and relates these activities to food ingestion and digestion. These activity rhythms in the white rat do not appear until about the tenth day, and are well established by the sixteenth day. It should be noted that in certain lower animals, activity rhythms are present from birth. Other factors than food ingestion and digestion may be involved in the establishment of cycles of activity, but the presence of other causal factors does not negate the effect of these vegetative processes.

Richter reports on the periodic nature of many physiological functions, including eating, drinking, urination, and defecation. The influence of water deprivation on the rate of water consumption has been demonstrated in a rather well controlled experiment (*Siegel, 1947*). In this study rats were placed in environments where temperature and humidity were thermostatically regulated and other experimental variables well controlled. Animals were tested after various periods of water deprivation to determine the amount of water they would consume in five minutes' time. It was found that the longer the deprivation up to 48 hours, the greater the amount of water consumption in the five-minute period. Findings relative to food consumption after controlled deprivation essentially parallel the results obtained in the study of water deprivation (*Horenstein, 1951*).

Deprivation has an influence not only directly on eating and drinking behavior but on the performance of instrumental responses in the obtaining of food or water (*Bass, 1958; Fredenburg, 1956*). After reviewing the literature relative to deprivation and level of activity, Brown (*1961*) tentatively concluded that consummatory activities (eating, drinking) and the speed of acquisition and resistance to extinction of responses instrumental to consummation tend to be enhanced by deprivation.

Hunger and thirst as primary sources of drive or as primary sources of variation in drive may exert their influence via several different physiological channels (*Grossman, 1955*). The dryness of the mouth and throat induced by water deprivation, and the impulses arising from vigorous contractions of the empty stomach when hungry, serve as one way in which hunger and thirst may become distinctive stimuli (*Cannon, 1929*). The stimulation of sensory receptors in the mouth and throat produced by the presence of food or water in the mouth, and the stimulation resulting from the subsequent swallowing, have an effect on the cessation of eating or drinking (*Miller et al., 1957*). Grossman (*1955*) has demonstrated that stomach distention, in addition to the stimulation of head receptors from food in the mouth, chewing, and swallowing, plays an important role in the control of eating. Circulating nutrients in the blood and stored nutrients in the tissues are also of importance relative to the control of eating and drinking. Neural impulses from various places in the body (mouth, throat, stomach, intestines, and possibly other tissues) may have central nervous system consequences that exert a controlling influence over consummatory behavior. Appropriate stimulation of the brain results in eating and gnawing in rats (*Smith, 1956*); injections of hypertonic saline solution into the hypothalamus of cats increases water consumption (*Miller, 1958*). The effects of various changes in the organism are reflected in the brain in such a manner that the brain itself becomes an integral portion of the mechanism of hunger- and thirst-produced activity.

NOXIOUS STIMULATION

Ordinary observation leads one to conclude that various noxious stimuli have a motivational effect. It can be observed that general activity increases or decreases with extreme changes in temperature. Loud noises, bright lights, and strong odors bring about changes in the vigor of response and behaviors appropriate to the avoidance or escape from these stimuli. The unconditioned stimulus in a classical conditioning situation can be an aversive one. Air puffs delivered to the eye have been used in eye-wink conditioning with human subjects. The intensity of the puff of air has been found to be positively related to the frequency of conditioned eyelid responses (*Passey, 1948; Spence, 1958; Spence and Platt, 1966*). Few studies of the effects of aversive stimuli on drive in human beings are available. Air puffs to the eye as unconditioned stimuli have been more systematically investigated than other aversive stimuli.

Electric shock has been widely used in laboratory situations as an aversive stimulus. This is probably because it can be readily administered under a variety of circumstances. Overt behavior produced by electric shock may not be a very good measure of its motivational effects because the behavior may vary not only with the intensity of the shock, but with its duration and temporal relationship to the behavior being observed. Mild shocks have been shown to effectively facilitate learning when such shocks follow the correct responses in a maze (*Tolman et al., 1932*). In such cases the mild shock may have very little or no motivational value and may serve only an associative function. As to results, the shock serves an informational function. Hall (*1961*) proposes that so-called weak punishment or shock is not really punishment at all and serves only as a stimulus that directs the organism's attention to certain stimuli. Electric shock, depending upon such experimental variables as temporal relationships, opportunities to escape, intensity, and duration, may serve to increase drive level or to evoke competing responses, and thus reduce response efficiency. If an animal is given a shock to his feet in order to get him to run down an alley, the response of jumping or leaping may compete with the running response and serve to decrease the efficiency with which the running response is executed.

In laboratory research on the motivational effects of noxious stimuli, the experimental arrangement is typically such that the subject, by performing a previously established response or by learning a new response, can escape, avoid, or terminate the noxious stimulus. Performance measures are then taken for different intensities or durations of the noxious stimulus. Increasing intensities of electric shock, in general, have yielded increased performance measures (*Campbell and Kraeling, 1953*). If the intensity of the shock does not become too great, performance on easy discriminations has been found to improve progressively with shock intensity. On difficult problems performance is poorer with either weak or strong shocks than with shocks of a moderate intensity (*Yerkes and Dodson, 1908*). The optimal motivational level for problem solving appears to decrease as the difficulty of the problem increases.

In a study using air deprivation as the noxious stimulus, Broadhurst (*1957*) found that the speed with which rats swam under water in a straight alley increased as the period of air deprivation previous to their being released, increased. In that the rats were experienced under-water swimmers, the changes in performance level could reasonably be attributed to the noxious stimulus of air deprivation.

SEX

Sexual arousal appears to have both internal and external controls (*Beach, 1951*). The internal nature of sexual arousal is indicated by the role of sex hormones in the blood stream. The external nature is illustrated by the variety of stimulus events that may contribute to excitability. Glandular, sensory, and experiential factors combine to determine the ease and extent of arousal. The female rat is more active during cycles of sexual receptivity than when she is not sexually receptive. Removal of the sex glands (gonadectomy) has a profound influence upon the activity level of rats (*Richter, 1933*). This suggests strongly that sex makes a contribution to general drive level. Sexually aroused males of various mammalian species demonstrate increases in general activity level as well as increased sensitivity to sexual stimuli.

The important role of experiential factors in human sexual behavior is well illustrated by the great variety of events to which sexual significance is attached. The role of sex in the motivation of social behavior will be more adequately explored in the following chapter.

## Possible Additional Primary Sources of Drive

It is likely that there are other primary sources of drive besides those of hunger, thirst, pain avoidance, and sex. It is difficult to evaluate many of the possible primary sources of drive because, although they may inherently contribute to drive level, the contribution may be rather small or the source may be difficult to manipulate experimentally. Any stimulus event, besides having cue value that is imperative for learning, may have the potential capacity to increase the arousal of the organism. Thus any change in stimulation may provide at least a temporary increase in drive. According to Hebb (*1949*), the disruption of cerebral processes is emotional disturbance. One source of this disruption is a discrepancy between present receptor inputs and the residues of previous sensory experiences of a similar nature. According to this position any change in receptor input (novelty) should increase affective arousal. One kind of discrepancy is absence of accustomed stimulation. Exceptions to this would seem to be in the case of the absence of aversive but accustomed stimulation (*Meier et al., 1960; Hunt and Quay, 1961*). Hunt and Quay (*1961*), after reviewing evidence for innate reinforcement values, indicate that these values deserve serious investigative consideration. Some colors, tastes, and odors appear to have greater attractiveness for human infants than others. Fiske and Maddi (*1961*) have indicated that variation in stimulation is an important source of arousal.

Opportunities to explore and to manipulate have been found to be adequate reinforcement for learning (*Montgomery, 1954; Butler and Harlow, 1954; Fowler, 1965*). It has been suggested (*Harlow, 1953*) that there is a drive to explore, and that the drive is reduced by exploration. The postulation of this special purpose drive may not be essential to understanding the behaviors involved, but the fact that opportunities to explore and manipulate are reinforcing is well established.

Primary sources of drive, indeed, may be rather numerous. It is difficult to distinguish those sources of drive in which learning is involved and those that are relatively independent from learning. Until such distinctions can be more readily drawn, the question of the number of sources of primary drive can have no definitive answer. It is possible that learning itself may have some motivational properties that are distinct from the motivational properties of what is learned. Acquired sources of drive will be treated in Chapter Eight.

### SUMMARY

Motivation did not constitute a problem for primitive man. Behavior for him resulted from special forces in the form of spirits or demons. The animistic conception of man dominated for a long period of time. Entities postulated as animating forces were the responsible agents. As long as this "man-within-a-man" notion prevailed, no particular motivational problem existed. Explaining an event by postulating an entity as responsible made scientific inquiry impossible.

Herbart conceived of ideas as dynamic entities that resolved themselves into action patterns. Knowledge was thought to carry with it its own dynamic drive. Descartes explored the possibilities of answering questions about motivation without reference to a "soul." He was only partially successful. Darwin's influence in stressing the anatomical continuity between animal and human species laid the groundwork for the study of behavioral continuity.

The concept of "soul" gradually disappeared as a motivational one, and was replaced by the instinct doctrine. Instincts became very popular in psychological circles. The list of instincts grew to great lengths and was finally abandoned in favor of the "drive" concept. Drives were more elemental than instincts had been. Hunger, thirst, sex, and pain as more elementary sources of behavior gradually were introduced. It seemed appealing and logical that complex behavior patterns that had heretofore been labeled instinctive should be built up from more elementary processes and not be considered as unitary. Drives became the primary dynamic agents of behavior. The task of explaining how complex behaviors evolved from such elementary desires as hunger, thirst, sex, and pain avoidance became the task of drive theorists.

Drive is an intervening variable. It provides a logical connection between the conditions that establish it and the effect of those conditions on behavior. The motivation of behavior comes about through the existence of drive-establishing conditions that release energy that comes from the metabolic processes of the organism.

Drive was treated in the chapter as an activator or energizer, and not as a director of activity. Drive was treated as a multidimensional unitary concept; that is, drive was conceived as a unitary, directionless energizer of behavior. Need and homeostasis as bases for drive were discussed, and hunger, thirst, pain avoidance, sex, and some sensory events were considered as primary sources of drive.

## REFERENCES

Ashby, W. R. *Design for a Brain* (2d ed.). New York: John Wiley and Sons, Inc., 1960.

Bass, B. *The Effect of Drive Variations within and between Subjects on Conditioning Performance.* Unpublished Ph.D. dissertation. Iowa City: State University of Iowa, 1958.

Beach, F. A. Instinctive Behavior: Reproductive Activities. In Stevens, S. (ed.), *Handbook of Experimental Psychology.* New York: John Wiley and Sons, Inc., 1951.

Beach, F. A. The descent of instinct. *Psychol. Rev.*, 1955, **62**, 401–410.

BEACH, F. A. Characteristics of Masculine Sex Drive. In Jones, M. R. (ed.), *Nebraska Symposium of Motivation*. Lincoln: University of Nebraska Press, 1956.

BINDRA, D. Components of general activity and the analysis of behavior. *Psychol. Rev.*, 1961, **68**, 205–215.

BOLLES, R., and PETRINOVICH, L. A technique for obtaining rapid drive discrimination in the rat. *J. comp. physiol. Psychol.*, 1954, **47**, 378–380.

BRIDGES, K. M. B. Emotional development in early infancy. *Child Develpm.*, 1932, **3**, 324–341.

BROADHURST, P. L. Emotionality and the Yerkes-Dodson law. *J. exp. Psychol.*, 1957, **54**, 345–352.

BROWN, J. S. *The Motivation of Behavior*. New York: McGraw-Hill Book Company, 1961.

BURSTEN, B., and DELGADO, J. M. R. Positive reinforcement induced by intracerebral stimulation in the monkey. *J. comp. Physiol. Psychol.*, 1958, **51**, 6–10.

BUTLER, R. A., and HARLOW, H. F. Persistence of visual exploration in monkeys. *J. comp. physiol. Psychol.*, 1954, **47**, 258–263.

CAMPBELL, B. A., and KRAELING, D. Response strength as a function of drive level and amount of drive reduction. *J. exp. Psychol.*, 1953, **45**, 97–101.

CANNON, W. B. *Bodily Changes in Pain, Hunger, Fear, and Rage* (2d ed.). New York: Appleton-Century-Crofts, 1929.

CANNON, W. B. *The Wisdom of the Body*. New York: W. W. Norton and Company, 1923 (2d ed., 1939).

COFER, C. N. and APPLEY, M. H. *Motivation: Theory and Research*. New York: John Wiley and Sons, Inc., 1964.

DARWIN, C. *The Expression of the Emotion in Man and Animals*. New York: D. Appleton-Century, 1873.

DEWEY, J. The need for social psychology. *Psychol. Rev.*, 1917, **24**, 266–277.

DUFFY, E. Emotion: an example of the need for reorientation in psychology. *Psychol. Rev.*, 1934, **41**, 184–198.

DUFFY, E. The psychological significance of "arousal" or "activation." *Psychol. Rev.*, 1957, **64**, 265–275.

DUFFY, E. *Activation and Behavior*. New York: John Wiley and Sons, Inc., 1962.

DUNLAP, K. Are there any instincts? *J. abnorm. Psychol.*, 1919–20, **14**, 307–311.

FARBER, I. E. Response fixation under anxiety and nonanxiety conditions. *J. exp. Psychol.*, 1948, **38**, 111–131.

FESTINGER, L. *A Theory of Cognitive Dissonance*. Evanston, Illinois: Row, Peterson, 1957.

FINGER, F. W., and REID, L. S. The effect of water deprivation and subsequent satiation upon general activity in the rat. *J. comp. physiol. Psychol.*, 1952, **45**, 368–372.

FISKE, P. W., and MADDI, S. R. *Functions of Varied Experience*. Homewood, Illinois: Dorsey Press, Inc., 1961.

FOWLER, H. *Curiosity and Exploratory Behavior*. New York: The Macmillan Company, 1965.

FREDENBURG, N. C. *Response Strength as a Function of Alley Length and Time of Deprivation*. Unpublished master's thesis. Iowa City: State University of Iowa, 1956.

GROSSMAN, M. I. Integration of Current Views on the Regulation of Hunger and Appetite. In Miner, R. W. (ed.), *The Regulation of Hunger and Appetite*. Ann. N.Y. Acad. Sci., 63, Art. 1. New York: Academy of Sciences, 1955.

HALL, J. F. *Psychology of Motivation*. Chicago: Lippincott Company, 1961.

HALL, J. F., SMITH, K., SCHMITZE, S. B., and HANFORD, P. V. Elevation of activity level in the rat following transition from ad libitum to restricted feeding. *J. comp. psysiol. Psychol.*, 1953, **46**, 429–433.

HARLOW, H. F. Motivation as a Factor in the Acquisition of New Responses. In Jones, M. R. (ed.), *Current Theory and Research in Motivation: A Symposium*. Lincoln: University of Nebraska Press, 1953.

HEBB, D. O. Drives and the c.n.s. (conceptual nervous system). *Psychol. Rev.*, 1955, **62**, 243–254.

HEBB, D. O. *The Organization of Behavior*. New York: John Wiley and Sons, Inc., 1949.

HELSON, H. Adaptation Level Theory. In Koch, S. (ed.), *Psychology: A Study of a Science, Vol. II*. New York: McGraw-Hill Book Company, 1959.

HORENSTEIN, B. R. Performance of conditioned responses as a function of strength of hunger drive. *J. comp. physiol. Psychol.*, 1951, **44**, 210–224.

HULL, C. L. Differential habituation to internal stimuli in the albino rat. *J. comp. Psychol.*, 1933, **16**, 225–273.

HULL, C. L. *Principles of Behavior*. New York: Appleton-Century-Crofts, 1943.

HUNT, J. McV., and QUAY, H. C. Early vibratory experience and the question of innate reinforcement value of vibration and other stimuli. *Psychol. Rev.*, 1961, **68**, 149–156.

JENKINS, J. J., and HENRATTY, J. A. Drive intensity discrimination in the albino rat. *J. comp. physiol. Psychol.*, 1949, **42**, 228–232.

LEWIN, K. *Principles of Topological Psychology*. New York: McGraw-Hill Book Company, 1936.

LINDSLEY, D. B. Emotion. In Stevens, S. (ed.), *Handbook of Experimental Psychology*. New York: John Wiley and Sons, Inc., 1951.

LINDSLEY, D. B. Psychophysiology and Motivation. In Jones, M. R. (ed.), *Nebraska Symposium on Motivation*. Lincoln: University of Nebraska Press, 1957.

MASSERMAN, J. H. *Principles of Dynamic Psychiatry*. Philadelphia: W. B. Saunders Company, 1946.

McDOUGALL, W. *An Introduction to Social Psychology*. London: Methuen, 1908.

McDOUGALL, W. *Outline of Psychology*. New York: Charles Scribner's Sons, 1923.

MEIER, G. W., FOSHEE, D. P., WITTRIG, J. J., PEELER, D. F., and HUFF, F. W. Helson's residual factor versus innate S-R relations. *Psychol. Rev.*, 1960, **6**, 61–62.

MILLER, N. E. Central stimulation and other new approaches to motivation and reward. *Amer. Psychologist*, 1958, **13**, 100–108.

MILLER, N. E., SAMPLINER, R. I., and WOODROW, P. Thirst reducing effects of water by stomach fistula vs. water by mouth, measured by both a consummatory and an instrumental response. *J. comp. physiol. Psychol.*, 1957, **50**, 1–5.

MONTGOMERY, K. C. The role of exploratory drive in learning. *J. comp. physiol. Psychol.*, 1954, **47**, 60–64.

MORGAN, C. T. *Physiological Psychology*. New York: McGraw-Hill Book Company, 1943.

MORGAN, C. T., and STELLAR, E. *Physiological Psychology* (2d ed.). New York: McGraw-Hill Book Company, 1950.

MORUZZI, G., and MAGOUN, H. W. Brain stem reticular formation and activation of the EEG. *EEG clin. Neurophysiol.*, 1949, **1**, 455–473.

OLDS, J., and MILNER, P. Positive reinforcement produced by electrical stimulation of septal area and other regions of the rat brain. *J. comp. physiol. Psychol.*, 1954, **47**, 419–427.

PASSEY, G. E. The influence of intensity of unconditioned stimulus upon acquisition of a conditioned response. *J. exp. Psychol.*, 1948, **38**, 420–428.

RICHTER, C. P. Animal behavior and internal drives. *Quat. Rev. Biol.*, 1927, **2**, No. 3, 307–343.

RICHTER, C. P. The effect of early gonadectomy on the gross bodily activity of rats. *Endocrinology*, 1933, **17**, 445–450.

ROBERTS, W. W. Both rewarding and punishing effects from stimulation of posterior hypothalamus of cat with same electrode at same intensity. *J. comp. physiol. Psychol.*, 1958, **51**, 400–407.

SIEGEL, P. S. The relationship between voluntary water intake, body weight loss, and number of hours of water deprivation in the rat. *J. comp. physiol. Psychol.*, 1947, **40**, 231–238.

SKINNER, B. F. *The Behavior of Organisms*. New York: D. Appleton-Century, 1938.

SMITH, O. A. Stimulation of lateral and medial hypothalamus and food intake in the rat. *Anat. Rev.*, 1956, **124**, 363–364.

SPENCE, K. W. A theory of emotionally based drive (D), and its relation to performance in simple learning situations. *Amer. Psychologist*, 1958, **13**, 131–141.

SPENCE, J. W., and PLATT, J. R. UCS intensity and performance in eyelid conditioning. *Psychol. Bull.*, 1966, **65**, 1–10.

THORNDIKE, E. L. *Educational Psychology*. (Vol. II, *The Original Nature of Man.*) New York: Teachers College, Columbia University, 1913.

TOLMAN, E. C., HALL, C. S., and BRETNALL E. P. A disproof of the laws of effect and a substitution of the laws of emphasis, motivation, and disruption. *J. exp. Psychol.*, 1932, **15**, 601–614.

WATSON, J. B. *Behavior: An Introduction to Comparative Psychology*. New York: Henry Holt and Company, 1914.

WATSON, J. B. *Behaviorism*. New York: W. W. Norton and Company, 1925.

WIENER, N. *Cybernetics*. New York: John Wiley and Sons, Inc., 1948.

WOODWORTH, R. S. *Dynamic Psychology*. New York: Columbia University Press, 1918.

YERKES, R. M., and DODSON, J. D. The relation of strength of stimulus to rapidity of habit formation. *J. comp. Neurol.*, 1908, **18**, 459–482.

# Chapter 8

# Motivation:
# Acquired Sources
# of Drive

IN THE PREVIOUS CHAPTER the discussion of motivation was centered around the concept of drive. Some of the more basic considerations concerning the sources of drive were presented. In this chapter some of the sources that are considered to be less basically physiological in nature will be treated. The significance of acquired or learned sources of drive in humans can hardly be over-estimated because of the pervasive nature of human learning. People learn to attach importance to a great variety of stimulus objects and events, almost any of which may contribute to drive. Because it is essential for learning to occur before significance can be attached to many of these occurrences, they will be referred to as learned sources of drive. The complexity of human learning makes it impossible to explore all of the possible learned sources of drive. The focus of attention will be on those that seem the most relevant in adaptive and adjustive behavior.

Many of the observable behavioral tendencies of people appear to have been learned. People are not born with a desire for social status or with a built-in desire for money or for other things that appear to be sought after in our culture. Specific stimulus events produce different behaviors in people of varying cultural backgrounds as well as in individuals from within the same general culture. The events that produce anger in one person do not necessarily do so in another; those occasions that are frightening for one person are not necessarily frightening for another; and the occurrences that produce joy or happiness are variable from person to person. People learn to make responses like anger, fear, and joy to specific stimuli or, through stimulus generalization, to classes of stimuli. These affective responses have stimulus value for the individual and as stimuli add an increment to drive. It is not contended that these stimulating responses are the exclusive sources of drive; rather, it is maintained that they add to the already existing drive level deriving from primary and secondary or acquired sources.

Both learning and motivation are involved in acquiring drive. Though responses like fear and anger are complex and may be either inherent or resultant of development, the capacity for many stimuli to produce these responses is acquired through the course of experience. For an event to serve as a stimulus for these complex responses, learning must occur. To acquire a motive, an organism must learn to respond, and when this response is evoked the organism's behavior must be affected motivationally (drive must be altered). Learned responses or acquired predispositions to respond can serve as secondary sources of drive. They can be interpreted to include not only overt, physically observable responses but also implicit responses like wishes, wants, attitudes, opinions, expectancies, fears, and similar conditions. As such, they serve as motivational variables and on the occasion of their occurrence become secondary sources of drive. The number of stimuli that can evoke these responses, which have strong stimulus value by themselves, is tremendous and is dependent to a considerable degree upon the learning that has occurred.

People tend to live together and from their social experiences acquire patterns of behavior that are common to the community. Thus one would expect that within a given culture or community there would be a number of stimuli that would acquire the capacity for producing responses that have motivational value for most of its members. People with common social experiences will learn to make fear responses to the same or similar situations and to form attitudes or predisposition to respond to various aspects of the collective environment. Each individual's unique experiences with various aspects of his environment plus his inherent predispositions will allow for his individuality in learning to respond to the environment.

### FEAR AS A LEARNED SOURCE OF DRIVE

Although fear may be an innate reaction to pain, it does not follow that it cannot be learned as a response to a previously nonpainful cue or stimulus. On the contrary, fear can be very readily learned in a variety of circumstances. Not only can it be learned as a response, but it can be effectively used as a motivator for performance in essentially the same way as hunger or thirst.

The motivational effects of fear or anxiety upon other responses has long been a common sense notion. The writings of Cannon (1929) and Freud (1936) focused psychological attention on this phenomenon, and Mowrer (1939) formulated the notion of conditioned fear as a motivational variable with sufficient conciseness to make it an experimental variable in psychological research. According to Mowrer, fear or anxiety is a learned emotional reaction to stimuli that denotes the advent of either pain or noxious stimuli. The reaction is acquired via classical conditioning. Fear seems to operate as a general energizer, and its reduction may serve to reinforce the learning of a new response.

Investigations have been conducted on fear as an energizer and on fear reduction as a reinforcer of behavior. Both of these functions are of importance in considering fear or anxiety as a learned source of drive. We turn our attention first to fear as an activator or energizer.

## The Energizing Function of Fear

The energizing function of fear has long been popularly accepted. It is well illustrated in tales of the increased vigor of responding under conditions of fear. Stories of tremendous feats of running, lifting, or climbing while frightened have become a part of the literature of our culture. References to these feats are common and no doubt have been encountered by every college student. Observations of the physiological consequences of fear led Cannon (1929) to treat it as an emergency reaction involving mobilization of energy for use in expediting the responses evoked by the fearful situation.

An interesting series of studies dealing with the increase in intensity of responding as a result of fear has been reported. Assuming that fear as a learned source of drive should increase existing reaction tendencies, Brown, Kalish and Farber (1951) chose to investigate the startle response as it is altered by fear. The startle response was chosen because it had been observed that anxious people showed an exaggeration of this response.

They reasoned that if a loud noise, which induced the startle response in rats, was presented during the time a conditioned stimulus for fear was being presented, that the startle response would be greater than if the loud sound were presented when the animal was not receiving a fear-conditioned stimulus. They further reasoned that, as fear increased, increased startle reactions to loud noises would be exhibited, and that as fear decreased during extinction, the startle response would show diminution as well as spontaneous recovery during periods of rest following extinction trials.

The fear conditioning was carried out by pairing the presentation of a buzzer and a light (conditioned stimuli) with an electric shock (unconditioned stimulus) for seven trials on each of four successive days. Measures of the startle reactions of the animals were obtained by means of a confinement box with a grid floor in which the animals were contained while being trained and tested. The animals' movements were reflected by the movements of the confinement box, which were automatically recorded. This apparatus was known as a *stabilimeter*. Three test trials per day, during which time the conditioned stimuli were presented without the electric shock but with the sound of a toy pistol, were also given. A control group was treated in the same way except that the conditioned stimuli-unconditioned stimulus pairings were so temporally arranged as to prevent the conditioning of fear to the conditioned stimuli.

The results obtained indicated that the magnitude of the startle responses evoked by the pistol shot in the presence of the conditioned stimuli increased progressively during the four days of conditioning for the experimental animals. No such increase was obtained for the animals in the control group. During a subsequent period of extinction training, fear apparently diminished as did the amplitude of the startle response. The startle response of the experimental animals showed an increase in strength following a day's rest (spontaneous recovery). It was concluded that the conditioned stimulus aroused more fear in the experimental than in the control animals and that fear functioned as a drive to increase unlearned startle responses. Extinction and spontaneous recovery followed the usual pattern expected from classical conditioning procedures.

A study designed to determine whether a primary source of drive (food deprivation) would increase sound-induced startle responses in rats, and whether hunger and conditioned fear together would produce greater increases in startle response than either alone, was conducted by Meryman (1952). The apparatus used in this study was essentially the same as that used by Brown, Kalish, and Farber (1951). Meryman used four groups of animals. The experimental procedures were arranged so that one group was fearful and 46 hours food-deprived; another was fearful and one hour food-deprived; a third group was nonfearful but 46 hours food-deprived; and a fourth group was nonfearful but one hour food-deprived. Animals were individually placed in the confinement box and the amplitude of their startle responses to the sound of a toy pistol was recorded for two trials daily for ten days. On the third trial of each day the fearful groups were administered an electric shock in place of the sound of a pistol. This was designed to produce fear associated with the stabilimeter confinement box. The stabilimeter confinement box, thus, served as the conditioned stimulus for fear. The nonfearful animals were given a third trial daily but were not shocked at any time. Before the animals had had any shock, the four groups were approximately equal in their reactions to the shot.

The results of the ten days of training and testing indicated that the responses of the two fearful (shocked) groups increased markedly from their initial levels. The response of the fearful-nonhungry group increased in amplitude as compared with the nonfearful-nonhungry group. The fearful-hungry animals showed a decided rise in their responses as compared with the nonfearful-hungry rats. Fear was found to be more effective

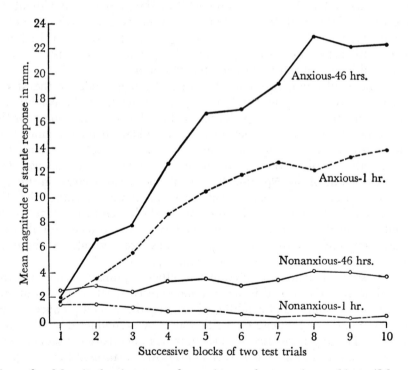

*Figure 8. Magnitude of response by anxious and nonanxious subjects (Meryman, 1952).*

than hunger in enhancing the startle response, and fear and hunger combined were more effective than either one alone. This study clearly supports the view that fear may serve as a learned source of drive.

Meryman (1953) has also demonstrated that the amplitude of the galvanic skin response in humans is enhanced by conditioned fear. Galvanic skin response (GSR) is a measure of change in electrical conductivity of the skin. The conductivity is a function of sweat gland activity. The GSR has been used as a measure of emotional involvement. Meryman's subjects were conditioned to fear a visual stimulus (a light), which was followed by a mildly painful shock. When, in testing, a click replaced the shock, it was observed that there was a significant increase in the galvanic skin response. The click was never paired with the shock so that it would be difficult to argue that the click itself was becoming a conditioned stimulus for fear. Meryman concluded that fear intensified an unlearned tendency to respond to a weak click.

These experiments rather clearly demonstrate that fear causes an increase in both the startle response and in the galvanic skin response. Both of these responses may be taken as indicators of arousal or of increases in drive.

### Fear-Reduction as a Reinforcer

Fear, as a response, can be learned under a wide variety of stimulus conditions. The fear response has stimulus properties that have been demonstrated to increase drive (*Brown et al., 1951; Meryman, 1952, 1953*). The same factors that reduce other responses should, then, serve to reduce the fear response and thus reduce the stimuli produced by the response. If this is true, the reduction of fear should act as a reinforcer for the learning of new responses. Experimental results have indicated that fear-reduction does indeed act as a reinforcer for the acquisition of new responses.

A frequently cited study by Miller (1948) illustrates the reinforcing properties of fear-reduction. Miller gave rats electric shock in a white compartment of an experimental box and the animals learned to escape from the white compartment through a door into a black compartment. After this response was learned, he used the fear created by the stimuli of the white compartment to teach his animals to turn a wheel located by the door in order to open it and escape from the white to the black compartment. The animals were not given electric shock in order to motivate the wheel turning. They learned this response from the previously neutral cues in the white box that had subsequently become fearful. Escape from the white to the black compartment had acquired the functional properties of reward. The wheel turning response of the animals was later extinguished by being reinforced through escape, and the animals learned to press a lever without further shock in order to escape to the black compartment. Escape from the white compartment served as a reward for the acquisition and maintenance of a new habit. Brown and Jacobs (1949) further demonstrated that tension, created by conflict and frustration produced by the door that prevented the animals from escaping in the usual manner, was not responsible for the drive that Miller had attributed to fear. Further support was thus added to the hypothesis that fear-reduction functions as a reinforcer of behavior.

## Intense Fear

It has been demonstrated that fear is related to the number of acquisition and extinction trials (*Kalish, 1954; Sawrey and Sawrey, 1964*); the reinforcing effect of fear reduction has been demonstrated in various other studies (*Mowrer and Lamoreaux, 1942; Gwinn, 1951*).

Intense fear may produce response inhibition (*Estes and Skinner, 1941; Amsel, 1950*); animals may "freeze" and "crouch" when they are exposed to intense fear-producing stimuli. These apparent negative effects at first glance appear to conflict with the notion of fear as a motivator. Amsel (1950) has interpreted such behavior as resulting from the simultaneous activation of competing responses. On such a view, the hypothesis that fear acts as a source of drive is not impaired. It is possible, too, that intense fear may produce such neurological disorganization that acquired response tendencies are delayed in their emission. Not enough is known about intense fear and its inhibitory effects to make anything but the most cautious of generalizations.

## Effects on Human Behavior

Our treatment of the topic of motivation has been largely involved with laboratory studies of motivational variables. It is extremely difficult and hazardous to experimentally manipulate stimulus conditions that will provoke responses of fear in human beings, although this can be done with relative ease in animals. The question of translating laboratory results with animals to human behavior is always an imposing one. However, it is commonly observed that human fears do affect behavior. Many of the factors eliciting fear and many of the consequences of fear, which have been discovered largely in animal studies, are probably very similar to those which exist in human beings.

Feelings of guilt, anxiety, insecurity, and fear occupy important positions in the interpretations of normal and abnormal behavior (*Freud,* 1936; *Mowrer,* 1960); there is reason to believe that these reactions are acquired and function in human beings in much the same way that they are acquired and function in animals.

### FEAR OR ANXIETY: ITS ACQUISITION AND INTENSITY

Pain is one of the stimuli that are considered to produce fear innately (*Miller,* 1951). Although distinctions have been drawn between fear and anxiety (*Goldstein,* 1940; *Jersild,* 1954), the two responses have sufficient elements in common to be treated as one insofar as motivational phenomena are concerned. The most important distinctions made are relative to either the immediacy or the identifiability of the stimulus conditions. Anxiety can probably be adequately conceptualized as fear with a future referent.

If fear is considered an inherent reaction to pain, it is not difficult to see how any number of situations can become fearful ones to the infant or young child. Infants often experience pain in the ordinary process of their dependent existence. The most careful of mothers cannot prevent her child from experiencing it. Hunger pangs as painful stimuli are experienced by every child. Children get stuck by pins, receive bumps and bruises, are gripped too roughly in handling, are placed in bath water that is too hot, and have colic. The number of painful events in the life of the infant are probably rather great in number. If this is so, then, the opportunity to acquire fears through conditioning are many.

If an infant is resented by older brothers or sisters he is likely to experience pain in their presence. If he is frequently pinched or bitten by his brother or sister, and can see the tormentor at the same time, he will soon learn to respond with fear at the sight of him. The infant, previous to these experiences, responded with fear to the stimulation of *pain;* he now responds with fear to the stimulus of *seeing* his older brother or sister. Through stimulus generalization the infant may not only respond with fear to the sibling who has inflicted pain upon him, but may respond similarly to other children of the same general age and stature. If he is physically hurt by a sibling only when the parent is not present, the absence of the parent may serve as a sufficient cue to provoke a fear response. Thus the child can come to fear the absence of the parent.

If an infant experiences pain and discomfort in his crib as the result of soiled diapers, the stimuli associated with being in the crib may come to evoke anxiety. If mother expresses alarm or concern immediately before pain is experienced by the child the expressions of alarm may come to evoke fear. Verbal expressions of parents as well as their manner may come to serve as stimuli for fear. If a child hears the word "hot" or "burn" before experiencing the pain resulting from his explorations, he can come to respond to the spoken words with fear without the primary stimulus of pain. The conditioning of fear to verbal cues is important in providing the child with protective fears. The parent can arouse his anxiety by verbal means in situations where he has had no previous experience. Innumerable examples of acquired fears could be cited from everyday experiences. The point to be made here is that fear or anxiety may be more pervasive in nature than would appear from a first quick appraisal.

## The Persistence of Fears Once Acquired

It has been established that avoidance responses are highly resistant to extinction. Avoidance responses can be thought of as responses elicited by fear conditioned to a previously ineffective stimulus. Animals conditioned to avoid electric shock have maintained the response over long periods of time without apparent reinforcement (*Solomon and Wynne, 1954*). Specific fears acquired early in life are alleged to persist and have motivational effects in adulthood. The persistence of acquired fears has produced speculation that fear conditioning is partially irrevocable. It has been suggested, too, that fear is relatively resistant to extinction; when the fear-evoking stimulus is encountered, avoidance behavior is quickly instituted and fear does not become sufficiently aroused for extinction to occur. It is also possible that when fear-provoking stimuli are encountered, fear is experienced and avoidance behavior, which reduces the fear, is elicited; thus, the stimulus situation is not further explored and counterconditioning cannot take place.

It has been hypothesized that both fear and overt responses become conditioned to the CS in a fear conditioning situation and that there is a reciprocal relationship between fear and overt responding. This reciprocal relationship tends to maintain both the fear and the overt responding at a high level (*Sawrey and Sawrey, 1966*).

Whatever the theoretical reasons for the persistence of acquired fears, the fact remains that they are apparently long lived and can act as learned sources of drive and as a basis for the development of further fears, which can in turn act as sources of drive.

## Relatively Constant Anxiety

Considering fear or anxiety as a source of drive, it follows that those persons who maintain high levels of constant anxiety should also operate at higher levels of drive than those who maintain lower levels of constant anxiety. Anxiety maintained without a specific referent as to what it is that the person is anxious about has been called "free-floating anxiety" by some psychologists. Taylor (1951) has referred to such anxiety as manifest and has developed a scale for its measurement. The scale has been called the Manifest Anxiety Scale (MAS). Scores on the scale reflect differences in a chronic emotional state, so that individuals scoring higher on the scale possess more anxiety and a consequent higher drive level than persons scoring lower on the scale (Taylor, 1956). The test was devised solely to select subjects differing in general drive level, and was not designed as a clinically useful tool for the diagnosis of anxiety. The items on the scale were selected by clinicians as referring to manifest anxiety as it is described psychiatrically. This test has been employed in a number of studies attempting to determine the relationship between drive level and performance in learning situations. Theoretically, anxious subjects perform at a higher level than nonanxious subjects in a classical conditioning situation.

The results of studies of eyelid conditioning, using groups with high and low scores on the MAS, have demonstrated that anxious subjects show a greater number of conditioned responses than do nonanxious subjects (Spence et al., 1954; Taylor, 1951). Greater stimulus generalization for anxious groups has been reported (Wenar, 1954). In maze learning it has been found that the greater number of errors and trials are made by anxious subjects (Taylor and Spence, 1952; Matarazzo et al., 1955). This is in line with the predictions of the performance of anxious subjects in complex situations. In such situations errors may be largely the result of interfering response tendencies. The number of errors for anxious subjects is positively related to the difficulty of the choice point at which they are made. In verbal learning studies, anxious groups have been found to differ from nonanxious groups in the learning of lists of syllables differing in amount of intra-list similarity (Montague, 1953). Anxious subjects were significantly superior in performance on the list for which similarity was low and association value high. Nonanxious subjects were significantly superior in learning a list of high similarity and low association value. When investigators attempted to minimize the presence of competing response tendencies, the superior performance of anxious subjects was demonstrated (Taylor and Chapman, 1955), and when an attempt was made to maximize the number of competing tendencies by increasing the similarity among stimuli, anxious subjects were inferior in performance (Spence, 1953). That there is an interaction between anxiety level and task complexity is fairly well substantiated by experimental evidence.

## *HUMAN BEHAVIOR UNDER STRESSFUL CONDITIONS*

The experimental evidence relative to performance and anxiety levels fits the general observations of human behavior under stressful conditions. If stress and consequent anxiety are not too high, performance increments are noted. If anxiety level is too high, performance breaks down and irrelevant and nonadaptive responses are observed. It is frequently noted that an individual is not doing well at a given task because he is trying too hard (motivation or drive level is too high). This is not infrequently encountered in the taking of examinations or in intelligence testing. Gordon and Berlyne (1954), using a verbal learning task, found that, after he had informed anxious subjects that the task was a measure of intelligence and that their performance was below average, their errors increased more than those of a comparable nonanxious group on a similar list of words.

It is not uncommon among amateur athletes to find that in a given contest, because they want very badly to win (anxiety and drive are high), they perform less well than they ordinarily would. In basketball and other games requiring a good deal of coordination, it can be observed that the vigorousness of execution may increase to the detriment of over-all performance.

Increments of anxiety in those who are already chronically high in anxiety level leads to increased drive resulting in disorganization and performance decrement. Increments of anxiety in those who are relatively low in chronic anxiety may result in an increased drive level that is more appropriate to the task. In such cases performance should improve.

It is no doubt true that all people experience anxiety rather constantly. The sources for this are many and varied. They may range from vague fears about the future to immediate concern for what is happening. The lives of people are filled with situations that can contribute to anxiety. When individuals are relatively free from uncertainty, conflict, and frustration they are less anxious than when their lives and futures are uncertain and unpredictable, and their frustrations and conflicts are many. The degrees of anxiety that are constant vary tremendously from individual to individual. Variations in drive can be expected to result from the differences in levels of basic anxiety as well as from changes due to immediate concerns.

## Language as a Learned Source of Drive

One of the most important differences between man and the lower animals is man's amazing ability to express himself through language. This faculty is accompanied by a high level of ability to communicate through written language, facial expressions, and gestures. Man's language facility makes it possible for him to learn a great number of things without first-hand contact with them. Not only does language expand the horizons of learning but it serves as an instrument for modifying man's general drive level as well.

## DRIVE PROPERTIES OF LANGUAGE

It has been indicated that many of the protective fears of children can be acquired through association with language. The child's fear or anxiety can be aroused by the spoken word "hot" or "hurt" after he has previously associated these words with painful stimuli. Thus he can learn to avoid objects that are so labeled without directly experiencing the pain these stimuli would evoke. The words "hot" and "hurt" become anxiety-arousing in and of themselves. The reduction of drive through reducing anxiety by moving away from the harmful stimulus reinforces the avoidance behavior.

Words become associated with events in the world of the child, and he can be aroused by them. If he has a painful or frightening experience with an object in his environment that is labeled "dog" or "puppy," the spoken word may come to have a fear-arousing effect. If an adult utters the word "dog," the child may respond to the word with the same degree of fear that would be elicited if the dog were actually present. Furthermore, if the child, upon seeing a dog and reacting with fear, now utters the word "dog" to himself, he has a double stimulus—the animal itself and his own spoken word.

If the child is riding his tricycle and is told not to go too "fast" or he will get "hurt," and subsequently does lose control of his vehicle and gets hurt, mother or father may say, "you were going too 'fast.' " If this occurs a number of times or in a variety of situations, the word "fast" may come to elicit a fear reaction similar to that caused by the accident. When the word "fast" is heard or used, the child responds with moderate anxiety, which acts as a source of drive. He may consequently learn to respond with fear to other objects or situations that are associated with speed.

The word "naughty" or "bad" and the expression "naughty boy" or "bad girl" are frequently encountered by the child at the same time that pain in the form of punishment is inflicted. Through the association of these words with painful stimuli, the words themselves become anxiety-arousing and add increments to drive when they are heard or used.

The word "fire" for the adult may indicate a dangerous situation, and as such, can bring about an increase in level of anxiety that adds an increment to drive. In the world of golf the word "fore" is used as a warning signal, and people respond with an increase in general anxiety upon hearing it. Almost any word in the language may come to evoke a small amount of anxiety in the individual in much the same way as in the illustrations above.

### EXHORTATION

It is well known that language becomes an effective tool in arousing people to greater efforts. Exhortation is used by coaches in athletic contests to get the players *up* for the game. The indignity of failing to put forth one's best effort and the consequences of failure to win the contest are stressed. Sometimes coaches will deliberately try to induce anger or hostility in their men so that they will exert their best efforts. A football coach known to the authors kept a very good player on the bench at the start of each game. The avowed purpose for doing this was to make the player anxious to get into the game and do well, if for no other reason than to demonstrate the poor judgment of the coach in not placing him on the starting team. This technique was employed for most of the season with observably favorable consequences.

Parents verbally instruct their children to "be good," to "try hard," "do the best you can," and in some cases to "win," "be the best," and "get an 'A.' " Such exhortations create anxiety in children for not doing what their parents demand or request. When exhortations are modest in nature they probably serve to enhance the drive state to the point where more adequate performance is forthcoming; however, when exhortations are vigorous and impelling and the anxiety level and consequent level of drive are already very high, the performance of the child may deteriorate. The level of drive may be so high that performance will be hindered by interfering responses, and behavior will become disorganized and ineffective.

In sales meetings, salesmen are encouraged to "make a favorable impression for the company," "create a friendly atmosphere," "increase sales," "be there at the most opportune time," "know your product," and "know the territory." The avowed purpose of sales meetings is to increase sales through greater effort and efficiency on the part of the sales force. "Pep" talks as well as educational meetings are integral parts of the sales convention. These meetings subtly arouse the anxieties of the salesmen should they fail to increase sales; the level of drive and subsequent effort are enhanced.

Exhortation in both subtle and obvious forms is employed throughout our culture. It is used in schools to encourage achievement, in industry to increase productivity, by parents to achieve appropriate behavior, and among many other groups to increase the energy level and enthusiasm with which various problems and situations are approached.

Certain words may have drive-augmenting properties because they serve as conditioned stimuli to arouse learned responses that have motivating effects upon other responses. Words can be used, then, as fear-arousing conditioned stimuli. It is probable that in order for words to have significant drive-augmenting effects, they must designate concepts that are applicable to wide varieties of human functioning. Specific directions or commands such as "shut the door" have a specific goal as a referent and probably do not have over-all drive-increasing properties unless the manner of their utterance is such as to create emotional or motivational consequences.

Verbal instructions such as "hurry up," "pay attention," and "be careful" tend to facilitate behavior in a variety of situations. No matter what the child is doing at the time such instructions are given to him, his behavior may be facilitated. Brown (1961) has pointed out that such commands can be given in a relatively soft voice and still be motivationally effective. The manner of their expression or the volume with which they are uttered cannot entirely account for their motivational effects. Words such as "hurry" or "pay attention" may facilitate whatever behavior is going on at the moment. The motivational property of these words may arise because of the specific nature of the expression itself or because these commands have been given under a sufficient variety of conditions so that the meaning has become generalized in nature. It may be, as Brown (1961) suggests, that in order for verbal commands to serve as learned motivating agents, they must be essentially devoid of specific content.

SELF-INSTRUCTION

Having acquired skill with the use of language, people tend to instruct themselves in what to do and how to do it. Brown (1961) has suggested that self-administered instructions may act as an acquired source of drive in much the same way as verbal instruction from others. Self-administered verbal commands, through a process of conditioning, may acquire the power to affect overt reactions motivationally.

When specific directions are self-administered, they are probably mostly connotative in nature and have more of a directional than an arousal influence on behavior. Such self-administered commands as "I must read the morning paper" may have slight motivational consequences, but are more likely to act as behavior directors without adding much of an increment to drive.

Self-administered commands of a more general nature are probably much more motivational. During times of stress, people give themselves miniature "pep" talks by using such instructions as "try hard," and "hurry." These commands evoke learned responses that increase bodily tension and facilitate performance of both motor and ideational tasks (*Courts, 1942*).

Self-administered instructions may also evoke anxiety when they are of the try-hard variety. "I must study hard for this examination or I will flunk out of school" is definitely an anxiety-arousing type of instruction (*Brown, 1961*). This anxiety-arousal adds to drive so that the response of studying is facilitated.

Actual overt verbalization may not be essential to self-instruction. Instructions can probably be given ideationally; that is, the person merely has to think about hurrying or failing in order for increments in drive to occur. Such ideational functioning is a common phenomenon and can provide an almost limitless source of stimulation for the individual. It is difficult, of course, to demonstrate experimentally that it does result in increased arousal or enhancement of drive. Everyone is aware that thinking about certain things is sufficiently anxiety-arousing to interfere with going to sleep. The proper "frame of mind" is considered essential for both relaxation and effective, vigorous energy expenditure.

## Thought Processes as Acquired Sources of Drive

Certain thoughts may be sufficient to arouse anxiety and increase drive. Thoughts relative to sex and sexual functioning may lead not only to increases in general drive but to responses that are sexual in nature. They can serve not only a drive function but a "cue" function as well. They have the properties of other drive-stimuli in that they add increments to drive and serve as stimuli to which responses become attached through learning.

Some ideas that are anxiety-arousing in the extreme may be avoided by a person. In certain social circles and in particular situations, politics or religion are systematically avoided as topics of conversation. For example, a hostess may implore her husband not to mention politics while some friends are visiting because they become very emotional about political discussions. The topic becomes "taboo." Anxiety is evoked over the possibility of disturbing the guests; even thinking about politics evokes feelings of anxiety stemming from possible losses of friendship or esteem. The topic becomes sufficiently anxiety-arousing to cause the avoidance of thoughts as well as discussions.

That thinking about certain topics leads to increases in anxiety is attested to by such expressions as "I don't want to think about it," or "Let's not think about it," or "I'll think about that when the time comes." When a great number of thoughts become sufficiently anxiety-arousing to be systematically avoided and intellectual functioning becomes limited, conversations center around such innocous topics as the weather, hobbies, and minor social events.

## AN EXPECTANCY MECHANISM $(r_g - s_g)$

A persistent problem in dealing with motivation as a topic has been that of accounting for the apparent drive-arousing effects of stimuli that are nonaversive. The increased activity of the child upon observing an object with which he has had previous pleasant experiences, the running of a rat through a maze when he has previously been rewarded in the goal box, and the apparent attractiveness of certain goals are phenomena that are difficult to put into an avoidance of the aversive "frame of reference."

Several ways of handling this problem of expectancy have been proposed. One of these $(r_g - s_g)$ has been described by Hull (1937). According to this position, when an organism is rewarded and makes consummatory responses, such as eating, associations are formed through classical conditioning between eating and the stimuli associated with the reinforcement. The stimuli are many and varied: the smell, sight, and taste of the food, the distinctive stimuli of the physical environment, the internal stimuli produced by the need for food. The consummatory goal reaction $(R_G)$ thus becomes conditioned to the stimuli that are present. Some of these stimuli (hunger, stimuli of the physical environment) are present throughout all phases of the response leading to the goal as well as during the actual consumption of the food. There is a tendency for the stimuli that occur before the onset of the consummatory reaction to become conditioned to the consummatory reaction. The reaction itself (eating) cannot be engaged in before the food is reached. However, portions of the reaction can be engaged in without the physical presence of food. Salivating, smacking of the lips, and swallowing can be performed as portions of $R_G$ and are elicited by the conditioned stimuli present. These responses produce distinctive internal stimuli. These *fractional anticipatory goal reactions* have been designated by the symbol $r_g$ and their resulting internal stimuli as $s_g$. The internal stimuli $(s_g)$ serve as stimuli to which a variety of responses become conditioned. Spence (1956) has pointed out that this $r_g - s_g$ mechanism might have applications in the area of motivation as well as in the area of learning for which it was devised. The stimuli $(s_g)$ resulting from the learned fractional anticipatory goal reactions $(r_g)$ act as other internal stimuli do to enhance the drive state.

Miller and Dollard (1941) believe that any strong stimulus has drive value and that the stimuli produced by learned responses are the basis for all acquired drives. In dealing with responses toward positive goal objects,

# Anticipatory Goal Reactions
## $(r_g - s_g)$

### A. Bar-pressing by the rat

| | *Stimuli* | | *Responses* | |
|---|---|---|---|---|
| Initial Behavior | Hunger (Principal stimulus) ($S_G$) | Behavioral arousal | Bar Pressing | Obtaining food and eating ($R_G$) Smacking lips and salivating as possible fractional goal reactions. ($r_gS$) |
| Later Behavior | Hunger ($S_G$) Salivation ($s_g$) Smacking lips ($s_g$) (Anticipation of food) | Behavioral arousal | Bar Pressing | (various $r_g - s_g$ sequences) |
| Still Later Behavior | Smacking lips ($s_g$) Salivation ($s_g$) (Anticipation of food) | Behavioral arousal | Bar Pressing | |

### B. Anticipation of father's home-coming by a baby

| | *Stimuli* | | *Responses* | |
|---|---|---|---|---|
| Initial Behavior | Father arriving home at 6:00 P.M. (Principal stimulus) ($S_G$) | | Being picked up, eating and playing with ($R_GS$) Anticipation of father's arrival $r_gs$ such as looking for toys, standing up, reaching for bib, etc.) | Stiffening body, reaching, salivation, increased activity. ($r_gS$) |
| Later Behavior | Sight and sound of father's arrival ($S_G$) Salivation ($s_g$) Increased activity ($s_g$) Other incidental Ss | | Anticipation of father's arrival | |
| Still Later Behavior | Salivation and increased activity ($s_gS$) or/and Time of day Characteristic sounds (incidental stimuli) Thought of father (ideation) Self-instruction | | Anticipation of father's arrival (Various ($r_g - s_g$) sequences) | |

such as food, it is reasoned that the sight of food may elicit a learned appetitive response, the stimuli from which will serve as a drive to impel food-seeking and other behavior. This analysis is not unlike the $r_g - s_g$ analysis of such behavior.

Other theories attempting to account for positive goal-oriented behavior can be interpreted within the $r_g - s_g$ paradigm. McClelland *et al.* (*1953*), in their treatment of motive, postulate a positive affective arousal that can be readily fitted to such a model. Mowrer (*1960*) has used "fear" as a mediating response that has motivational properties in aversive situations. His emotion of "hope" as a mediational response that is aroused in positive affective situations is very much like McClelland's positive affective arousal and could equally well employ the $r_g - s_g$ mechanism.

An example of how this mechanism is proposed to operate might serve to clarify this concept. A child, upon seeing an ice cream cone, moves toward it. He is not particularly hungry, but he has previously eaten ice cream cones when he was hungry. The sight of the cone now serves as a stimulus to which $r_g$'s have been conditioned. The $r_g$'s (salivating, licking) have stimulus consequences $(s_g)$ to which approach responses have become conditioned and that serve to increase drive. The child makes fractional anticipatory goal reactions, which arouse stimuli to which responses have become attached that will result in his obtaining and consuming $(R_G)$ the ice cream. Such a mechanism can be called an "expectancy" mechanism. It is possible that thoughts related to ice cream may come to serve the same purpose as the sight of the ice cream cone itself. Through stimulus generalization a variety of stimuli may come to be effective in evoking $r_g$'s; it may not be possible to identify the particular stimuli that are effective in complex social situations.

### FRUSTRATION AND CONFLICT

Frustration and conflict will be treated as phenomena in a subsequent chapter. People are frustrated by a variety of situations when their directed activities are interrupted. Frustration produces responses that have stimulus consequences that may act to increase drive in the same way that other internal stimuli do. Experimental evidence that frustration and conflict do have drive consequences is available (*Wagner, 1959; Hollenberg and Sperry, 1951*) but will not be reviewed at this time.

The increased vigor of responding when frustration is encountered by both children and adults serves as testimony to its drive effects. The multiplicity of events that produce frustration in varying degrees indicates that frustration and conflict may be rather important sources of drive among humans.

## MOTIVES AND THEIR DRIVE FUNCTIONS

Drive-enhancing stimuli typically serve an additional function that derives from the distinctive nature of the stimuli and can be called a "cue" function. It is this cue function that is involved in learning. It is the aspect of the stimulus to which responses become conditioned. When responses have been conditioned to distinctive drive stimuli, these stimuli result in behavior that appears to be goal-oriented or purposive in nature. Thus the food-deprived person is stimulated by hunger stimuli, which results in an increment in drive *and* provides a stimulus-cue that can result in learning when it is reduced.

The person stimulated by hunger learns responses that reduce this drive stimulus. When such conditions prevail in the future, he actively seeks food. It can be seen, here, that food deprivation results in distinctive stimuli that enhance drive and provide cues to which responses become conditioned. The food seeking and subsequent consummatory responses have become conditioned to the drive stimuli. Such a complex of stimulation, increased drive, and learned responses is called a *motive*. The number of motives that can be acquired is limited only by the learning ability and the opportunities for learning to occur. A person can thus acquire motives for almost any object, event, or circumstance available in the environment. Motives for food, money, sex, friendship, achievement, prestige, esteem, security, and a host of more specific motives are typically acquired in the course of social living. Desires, wants, wishes, and interests are words used to refer to motives. Motives have a specific goal orientation or direction and are numerous. Drive, on the other hand, is unitary and nondirectional.

Once acquired, these motives may themselves have motivational or drive-enhancing properties. Having developed a food-seeking motive or a motive for money, one can learn to feel anxious when these objects are not available. The anxiety is drive-enhancing. It is possible, too, that the sight, sound, smell, or feel of an object may produce fractional anticipatory goal responses $(r_g)$ that have stimulus consequences $(s_g)$ that are drive-enhancing. Frustration resulting from conflict of two or more motives may also have motivational effects.

Various theorists and authors of textbooks have attempted to classify motives in some meaningful way. As a result of these attempts, there has developed a body of literature that uses behavioral classifications to delineate motives. Much of human behavior must be encompassed in such classificatory systems. The classifications of motives are rather arbitrary and are derived chiefly from opinion. It appears to the authors of this textbook that attempts to classify all or nearly all of the acquired responses of people in an effort to clarify the study of motives may have resulted in more confusion than clarification. There is much overlap among classifications, and no classification can be considered as a discrete category. They all deal with complex learned responses in various circumstances. If motives are treated as having been learned, there is no more reason to classify them than there is to attempt to classify responses when one is studying learning.

### COMPLEX ACQUIRED BEHAVIORS

Some illustrations of the acquisition and function of motives in the determination of behavior will be presented here. Certain motives are used in these illustrations because they are well known and popular. They are but a few of the illustrations that could be used, and are not intended as classificatory but as illustrations of complex human behavior as it is reflected by "motives." It can be observed that men strive to attain goals or purposes. This apparent goal-directed aspect of behavior has long been considered within the area of motivation, although it is probably more an associative or learning function than it is a motivational one.

## Money Seeking

That man in our culture does learn to strive for the acquisition of money is rather obvious. It has been demonstrated that chimpanzees can be taught to perform tasks for a token reward (poker chips) that can be exchanged for food (*Wolfe, 1936; Cowles, 1937*). In these studies, the poker chips are interpreted as having acquired *secondary reinforcing* value through their association with the obtaining and consuming of food. This explanation is a plausible one, and the same general explanation may account for man's acquired tendency to work for money.

Brown (1953) has suggested an additional explanation that would not negate the value of the secondary reinforcement principle, but would provide an additional explanatory mechanism that could operate along with that of secondary reinforcement. Brown has postulated that the individual, having learned that money can be used to obtain desired items and that the lack of it means that certain things must be foregone, becomes concerned and behaves in such a way as to appear anxious. The individual comes to feel anxious when money is not present or when indicators or cues denoting the absence of money are present. The obtaining of money reduces the anxiety associated with the cues denoting its absence. Money-seeking responses, while the person is anxious, are reinforced by the reduction of anxiety when money is obtained.

The money-seeking behaviors in which people engage are many and varied. People learn to perform a great number of tasks, jobs, occupations, and professions, in part at least, in order to obtain money. The variety of behaviors that they acquire in order to obtain money defy enumeration, but the same general principles are, no doubt, operative in most cases. That they become anxious when cues denoting the absence of money are present is a commonplace observation. Children are told, "It is too expensive, we cannot afford it"; "If we had enough money we could do thus and so." Such expressions are often accompanied by tones of voice and facial expressions associated with anxiety. Through such language media as well as through direct experience, anxiety comes to be aroused with indicants of the absence of funds. The total absence of funds is not necessary in order to create anxiety over their insufficiency. Anxiety in some people may be aroused by the fact that they have only a meager amount to "get by" on until the next pay check, while in others anxiety may be aroused when they are about to lose one of their many millions of dollars. The anticipation of the consequences of insufficient money may create anxiety that can be reduced by opening and maintaining savings accounts.

In considering the adjustive functions of men, it should not be overlooked that responses other than those of vigorous money-seeking behavior can be acquired as the result of anxiety associated with its absence or insufficiency. It has been indicated in previous chapters that a variety of responses can be learned in order to reduce anxiety. A person can escape anxiety-arousing stimuli by going to sleep, getting drunk, or seeking various diversions. These reactions produce a temporary reduction of anxiety and can be acquired in the same way that positive money-seeking behavior is acquired.

## Affectional Responses

The social phases of the infant's environment soon become his most potent sources of stimulation. His needs are constantly ministered to by others. People are the warmth providers, the food and moisture providers, and the removers of irritants. This constant association of people with drive-stimulus reduction provides an excellent conditioning situation. People are constantly associated as a CS with the reduction of the US of hunger, thirst, pain, or discomfort. They soon come to evoke the same general responses that have been associated directly with drive stimulus reduction. The child can come to like people, to enjoy being with them, and co-operate with them. Thus, he becomes gregarious. He feels lonely (anxious) when deprived of human fellowship, and strives to establish and maintain affectional relationships.

Having developed affectional responses toward others, the child can become anxious in the presence of cues denoting an absence of affection, and can acquire behaviors that insure or maximize probabilities that affectional relationships will be obtained. This probably happens in much the same way that the absence of money becomes anxiety-arousing. Children soon learn that when mother or father behave in nonaffectional ways (they get angry and they punish) life is not very pleasant. It is not likely that small children can understand the expression, "this is for your own good," or "this hurts me worse than it does you."

Punishment, especially painful physical punishment, is often interpreted by the child as an indication that he is not loved. This assumption may be a fairly accurate one! If punishment is associated with the absence of affection, and occurs following behavior that is disapproved, absence of affection can become synonymous with punishment and be anxiety-arousing in the extreme. Engaging in behaviors that one has learned are approved by others reduces anxiety associated with cues indicating a lack of affection. We learn to behave courteously and with regard for our affectional relationship with others in order to reduce anxiety over cues indicating the absence of affection.

Certain environmental cues, when not accompanied by sights and sounds of the mother, may arouse fear in the young child. The child's seeking and approaching the mother is reinforced by the reduction in fear provided by her presence (*Dollard and Miller, 1950*).

While gregariousness, co-operation, and affection are revered in our culture, these characteristics can be developed to a personally disabling degree. The individual becomes so anxious over loss of affection or possible loss of affection that he behaves in ways inappropriate to the establishment and maintenance of these relationships. The person who is afraid to express an opinion is over-solicitous of the welfare of others, and overly apprehensive lest he offend someone. He becomes so innocuous as to be uninteresting or even boring to others.

## Sex-Oriented Behavior

That certain objects in the environment have acquired sexual significance for certain individuals is rather apparent. The sight of a pretty girl is attractive to men, and they engage in behavior designed to maximize their contacts with her. These apparent attractions are probably developed in the same general way (secondary reinforcement and anxiety reduction) as are tendencies to seek money. If pretty girls have become associated with reduction in drive stimulation related to sex, the mere presence of a pretty girl may come to have drive-arousing functions; thus pretty girls are sought after and their company cherished. Anxiety engendered by fear that one is unattractive to members of the opposite sex can be diminished by friendly association with them.

It is possible, of course, for previously neutral stimulus objects to develop sexual significance for the individual because of their association with the reduction of stimuli associated with sexual arousal. That certain objects have symbolic sexual value by their very nature is doubtful. Stimulus generalization may account for a modicum of objects that are attributed with having universal or near universal sexual significance, but the concept can hardly account for the vast array of objects involved. The attributing of sexual significance to objects that have some of the same general characteristics as the male sex organ seems to have derived from the fact that someone, somewhere, somehow did attach sexual significance to that particular object or to one not too dissimilar to it. Considering the amazing ability of the human to learn, if one followed such a criterion for sexual symbolism, it might be possible to attach sexually symbolic meanings to objects of all kinds, shapes, and varieties.

## Prestige-Oriented Behavior

A great deal of attention has been paid to behavior that is said to enhance one's prestige or esteem. Motives to attain a given status or to maintain a certain level of prestige have been invoked as descriptive of a great variety of behaviors.

A child soon learns that if he is thought well of, if he is regarded highly, he will not be subjected to punishment and embarrassment. He observes that those who are highly regarded by others are treated with affection and have attributes that can be emulated. He learns to behave in ways that will bring him affection and regard. The rewards and punishments associated with growing up in the culture provide adequate direction for the adoption of values. Children learn that many of life's sweetest satisfactions are associated with the elevation or maintenance of prestige and that there are few absolutes in their world. No one is big or small, bad or good, strong or weak, sinful or virtuous, except by comparison to others. They learn to excel in order to be highly regarded.

Once having learned that prestige and esteem are of value, the child can strive to do those things that will insure or enhance his status. Situations that are threatening or even potentially threatening to his status in the eyes of others will create anxiety. Engaging in those behaviors that are approved by the culture will reduce the anxiety aroused by the threatened loss of stature. One can acquire a tendency to maintain or enhance his prestige through secondary reinforcement (as in the acquisition of money or possessions that are associated with prestige) or through anxiety arising from the consequences of the absence of appropriate esteem or the potential loss of prestige. Ours is a vigorous and competitive culture, and the possible ramification of prestige motives could be made as endless as the list of potential sex symbols.

It would be interesting for us to recall the number of social contacts we have made within the last 30 days, and make a list of those wherein idle social conversation degenerated into a duel for supremacy between the participants. If a funny story is told, someone will try to top it; if a frightful experience is related, someone is certain to relate a more frightful one. It is proverbial in such situations that the first man doesn't have a chance. The person who relates the funnier or more startling story is telling a better story. The story is his and his prestige is enhanced by association with it.

Prestige and affection are probably closely related and interdependent. To be liked is to be regarded well. Behaviors that result in prestige and esteem for the individual, in general, are the same ones that enhance the probability of affection and affectional relationships.

### A WORD OF CAUTION

The motivation of behavior is a complex matter and one that is not completely understood. Any simple system for describing or explaining the motivation of human behavior will probably be quite inadequate. A great many theories can be constructed to account for human behavior, and illustrations to fit the theories can be numerous. The *ad hoc* nature of such theories renders one as improbable as the other unless the predictions made can be verified without resorting back to the theory for the verification. Human beings have a tremendous capacity for learning, and the variety of behaviors they will display is almost infinite. Caution should be observed in any attempt to fit these behaviors into a motivational theory. Theories that rely entirely upon *ad hoc* observations for their validity hold little promise for increasing the understanding of human behavior.

### SUMMARY

In dealing with the problem of acquired sources of drive, it has been emphasized that learning and motivation are both involved. People tend to live together and acquire patterns of behavior common to the community. Within a given culture a number of stimuli acquire the capacity to elicit responses that have motivational value for most people.

People learn to respond with fear to a number of stimuli. Fear responses have stimulus counterparts that serve an energizing function. A number of experiments have demonstrated the energizing function of fear and fear-reduction. Fear was found to be a potent reinforcer of behavior. Fear and anxiety have sufficient elements in common that they are treated as synonymous as far as motivation is concerned. As motivators of behavior they can be rather persistent because of the persistent nature of fear itself.

Individuals experience anxiety rather constantly. Attempts to measure this anxiety in human subjects have been made. Manifest anxiety is found to be a relatively good measure of drive. Human behavior under conditions of stress indicates that stress results in anxiety, which has an effect on general drive.

The possibilities of language, self-instruction, thought processes, expectancy, frustration and conflict, and motives themselves, operating as learned sources of drive, have been considered and some typical motives have been discussed.

## REFERENCES

AMSEL, A. The effect upon level of consummatory response of the addition of anxiety to a motivational complex. *J. exp. Psychol.,* 1950 ,**40**, 709–715.

BROWN, J. S. Problems Presented by the Concept of Acquired Drives. In *Current Theory and Research in Motivation: A Symposium.* Lincoln: University of Nebraska Press, 1953.

BROWN, J. S. *The Motivation of Behavior.* New York: McGraw-Hill Book Company, 1961.

BROWN, J. S., and JACOBS, A. The role of fear in the motivation and acquisition of responses. *J. exp. Psychol.,* 1949, **39**, 747–759.

BROWN, J. S., KALISH, H. I., and FARBER, I. E. Conditioned fear as revealed by magnitude of startle response to an auditory stimulus. *J. exp. Psychol.,* 1951, **41**, 317–328.

CANNON, W. B. *Bodily Changes in Pain, Hunger, Fear, and Rage* (2d ed.). New York: Appleton-Century-Crofts, 1929.

COURTS, F. A. Relations between muscular tension and performance. *Psychol. Bull.,* 1942, **39**, 347–367.

COWLES, J. T. Food tokens as incentives for learning by chimpanzees. *Comp. psychol. Monogr.,* 1937, **14**, No. 5.

DOLLARD, J., and MILLER, N. E. *Personality and Psychotherapy.* New York: McGraw-Hill Book Company, 1950.

ESTES, W. K., and SKINNER, B. F. Some quantitative properties of anxiety. *J. exp. Psychol.,* 1941, **29**, 390–400.

FREUD, S. *The Problem of Anxiety*. New York: W. W. Norton and Company, 1936.

GOLDSTEIN, K. *Human Nature in the Light of Psychopathology*. Cambridge: Harvard University Press, 1940.

GORDON, W. M., and BERLYNE, D. E. Drive level and flexibility in paired associate nonsense-syllable learning. *Quart. J. exp. Psychol.*, 1954, **6**, 181–185.

GWINN, G. T. Resistance to extinction of learned fear drives. *J. exp. Psychol.*, 1951, **42**, 6–12.

HOLLENBERG, E., and SPERRY, M. Some antecedents of aggression and effects of frustration in doll play. *Personality: topical symposia*, 1951, **1**, 32–43.

HULL, C. L. Mind, mechanism, and adaptive behavior. *Psychol. Rev.*, 1937, **44**, 1–32.

JERSILD, S. T. Emotional Development. In Carmichael, L. (ed.), *Manual of Child Psychology*. New York: John Wiley and Sons, Inc., 1954.

KALISH, H. I. Strength of fear as a function of the number of acquisition and extinction trials. *J. exp. Psychol.*, 1954, **47**, 1–9.

MATARAZZO, J. D., ULETT, G. A., and SASLOW, G. Human maze performance as a function of increasing levels of anxiety. *J. genet. Psychol.*, 1955, **53**, 79–96.

MCCLELLAND, D. C., ATKINSON, J. W., CLARK, R. A., and LOWELL, E. L. *The Achievement Motive*. New York: Appleton-Century-Crofts, 1953.

MERYMAN, J. J. *Magnitude of Startle Response as a Function of Hunger and Fear*. Unpublished master's thesis. Iowa City: State University of Iowa, 1952.

MERYMAN, J. J. *The Magnitude of an Unconditioned G.S.R. as a Function of Fear Conditioned at a Long C.S.-U.C.S. Interval*. Unpublished doctoral dissertation. Iowa City: State University of Iowa, 1953.

MILLER, N. E. Studies of fear as an acquirable drive: I. Fear as motivation and fear reduction as reinforcement in the learning of new responses. *J. exp. Psychol.*, 1948, **38**, 89–101.

MILLER, N. E. Learnable Drives and Rewards. In Stevens, S. S. (ed.), *Handbook of Experimental Psychology*. New York: John Wiley and Sons, Inc., 1951.

MILLER, N. E., and DOLLARD, J. *Social Learning and Imitation*. New Haven: Yale University Press, 1941.

MONTAGUE, E. K. The role of anxiety in serial rote learning. *J. exp. Psychol.*, 1953, **45**, 91–96.

MOWRER, O. H. A stimulus-response analysis of anxiety and its role as a reinforcing agent. *Psychol. Rev.*, 1939, **46**, 553–565.

MOWRER, O. H. *Learning Theory and Behavior*. New York: John Wiley and Sons, Inc., 1960.

MOWRER, O. H. *Learning Theory and the Symbolic Processes*. New York: John Wiley and Sons, Inc., 1960.

MOWRER, O. H., and LAMOREAUX, R. R. Avoidance conditioning and signal duration— a study of secondary motivation and reward. *Psychol. Monogr.*, 1942, **54**, No. 5.

SAWREY, W. L. and SAWREY, J. M. Conditioned fear and restraint in ulceration. *J. comp. physiol. Psychol.*, 1964, **57**, 150–151.

SAWREY, W. L. and SAWREY, J. M. Research proposal, USPHS. Washington, D.C., 1966.

SOLOMON, R. L., and WYNNE, L. C. Traumatic avoidance learning: the principle of anxiety conservation and partial irreversibility. *Psychol. Rev.*, 1954, **61**, 353–385.

SPENCE, K. W. Current interpretations of learning data and some recent developments in stimulus-response theory. In *Learning Theory, Personality Theory, and Clinical Research: the Kentucky Symposium*. New York: John Wiley and Sons, Inc., 1953.

SPENCE, K. W. *Behavior Theory and Conditioning*. New Haven: Yale University Press, 1956.

SPENCE, K. W., TAYLOR, E., and FARBER, I. E. The relation of electric shock and anxiety to level of performance in eyelid conditioning. *J. exp. Psychol.*, 1954, **48**, 404–408.

TAYLOR, J. A. The relationship of anxiety to the conditioned eyelid response. *J. exp. Psychol.*, 1951, **41**, 81–92.

TAYLOR, J. A. Drive theory and manifest anxiety. *Psychol. Bull.*, 1956, **53**, 303–320.

TAYLOR, J. A., and CHAPMAN, J. Paired-associate learning as related to anxiety. *Amer. J. Psychol.*, 1955, **68**, 671.

TAYLOR, J. A., and SPENCE, K. W. The relationship of anxiety level to performance in serial learning. *J. exp. Psychol.*, 1952, **44**, 61–64.

WAGNER, A. R. The role of reinforcement and nonreinforcement in an "apparent frustration effect." *J. exp. Psychol.*, 1959, **57**, 130–136.

WENAR, C. Reaction time as a function of manifest anxiety and stimulus intensity. *J. abnorm. soc. Psychol.*, 1954, **49**, 335–340.

WOLFE, J. B. Effectiveness of token rewards for chimpanzees. *Comp. psychol. Monogr.*, 1936, **12**, No. 5.

# Chapter 9

# Frustration and Conflict

FRUSTRATION IS EXPERIENCED by people and lower organisms as a part of daily existence. Ordinarily a person experiences frustration when the satisfaction of important motives is thwarted. The hungry person who must await the preparation of a meal is frustrated by his inability to satisfy his hunger. Obtaining a college education or entering a career may be delayed because of compulsory military service. Economic factors may thwart ambitions and desires. Limitations in physical strength, attractiveness, or skill may act to thwart the individual and produce frustration. One cannot immediately and directly satisfy all of his wants, wishes, and desires. As a consequence frustration is inevitable.

Because frustration stems from the thwarting of some motive, and because the motives of men vary from individual to individual, it is difficult, if not impossible, to itemize those situations that result in frustration. Frustration is observed to result from the interruption of a behavior being carried on to fulfill some motive. When behavior is deviant (different from the behavior of the nonthwarted) as the result of thwarting, it is called *frustrated behavior*. Thus frustration is a logical construct inferred from the behavior of organisms. It can be treated as a *response* that has stimulus properties. It can become attached to a number of stimuli through conditioning and *learning*. Because it is a response that has stimulus properties it may have effects on *drive*. It can be seen that frustration as a topic can be considered a logical extension of *motive*, which is also composed of elements of *drive* and *learning*.

Stimulus conditions that result in frustration as a response can be referred to as stressful. Stress is a kind of class name for a variety of barriers, blockings, and thwartings. The response of frustration is a complex one that is not thoroughly understood. The stimulus effects of frustration as a response lead to a variety of behaviors, some of which have been discussed previously in this book under the headings of *defensive behavior, avoidance and withdrawal,* and *aggressive behavior.* The biochemical, neural, and physical nature of the response itself is not completely known. Selye (1956) has published extensively on the nature of stress and has emphasized the role of hormonal factors. His use of the word "stress" is roughly comparable to our use of the word "frustration."

Although the number of situations that can result in frustration defy enumeration, it is possible to discuss some *general* factors that are involved in its elicitation. The consequences of frustration are also numerous and they will be discussed in terms of the general nature of responses to the stimulation provided by frustration.

### ELICITING FRUSTRATION

The variety of circumstances in which people exhibit frustrated behavior indicates that there is more than one procedure by which frustration can be elicited. The means of producing frustration can be divided into three varieties for purposes of study. These classes can be called *frustration by delay, frustration by thwarting,* and *frustration by conflict.* Frustration by conflict has some components that differ from frustration by delay or by thwarting. Conflict will be given somewhat more extensive treatment than either of the others and will be considered in a later section of this chapter.

## Frustration by Delay

Frustration by delay is accomplished by withholding from an organism the reinforcement that it has previously learned follows a given sequence of behavior. When a response has regularly been reinforced and then the reinforcement is delayed or is not available, the consequences are frequently those of frustration. The period of delay may be momentary or involve an indefinite period of time. If it is momentary there is only a slight break in the behavior of the organism. This slight delay in receiving reinforcement frequently precipitates frustration. The reactions are emotional and the ensuing behavior is effected.

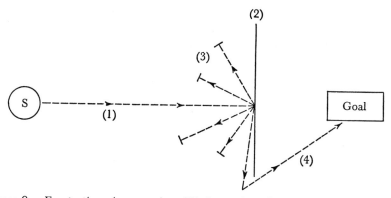

*Figure 9. Frustration. An organism (S) is motivated to approach (1) a goal. It encounters a barrier (2), is thwarted, and tries various responses (3). Successful solution is depicted (4).*

Frustration by delay is an everyday occurrence in most of our lives. We wait for a bus or taxi when they are not on time; the keys to the car cannot be found and we are in a hurry to go some place; the door is locked when we try to enter the house or office in a hurry; a friend is late for an appointment or for a date; the check-out line in the supermarket is long and we must wait; dinner is not ready and we are hungry; we have something vital to say and we must wait until someone else finishes talking. These and many others are instances of frustration by momentary delay. They are the little frustrations that most people adapt to very readily. They are not typically the occasions for violent reactions because we have learned from previous experience that the delays are short lived and that our motivated behavior can soon be resumed. However, it cannot be denied that frustration results from such trivia.

Small delays apparently are more frustrating for children and young adults than they are for older persons. The reactions of the hungry child when the customary stimuli for eating are present and he must wait are much more vigorous than are those of the average adult. The infant is in a pretty helpless condition. He has no way of knowing that the delay is unavoidable or that it is only temporary. His reactions are emphatic. If his feeding schedule is determined by time, he must wait until sufficient time has elapsed before he can eat. As he grows older, he finds he must wait until he is five before he can start kindergarten. This delay may seem interminable to him. Waiting for a holiday or for a birthday before he can celebrate appropriately can be frustrating. The delay between the time the child is informed that the family is going to visit the grandparents and the time of the actual visit can be most aggravating.

As the child matures, he encounters different frustrations. Most people reading this book can probably recall the expression, "wait until you are old enough." A friend of one of the authors reported that his daughter experienced extreme frustration because she could not wear lipstick until she was in the seventh grade. She still had a whole year to go and wondered if she could live through it. Her father wondered if he would be able to tolerate her behavior for another year.

Frustration resulting from delay in achieving sexual reinforcement is prominent among adolescents in our culture. Autosexual behavior is frowned upon in our society and other sexual contacts are forbidden. The adolescent must wait until a certain age when marriage is permissible to engage in heterosexual activities. Stimulation for sexual activity is strong and its expression must be delayed. Sexual frustration as a source of later personality problems has received a great deal of attention from clinical and personality theorists. Clinical evidence indicates that these frustrations have important dynamic influences on personality.

The frustrating effects of delay of reinforcement have been demonstrated in the experimental laboratory using both animals and humans as subjects. Amsel (1958) has presented documentation for the frustrating effects of nonreward, and has indicated that a learned form of frustration develops through classical conditioning and operates as an inhibiting factor in nonreward. This learned form is called *fractional anticipatory frustration* $(r_f - s_f)$. It develops in essentially the same way that other fractional anticipatory goal responses $(r_g - s_g)$ develop. The organism, having learned that certain stimuli are followed by reward, makes fractional anticipatory goal responses $(r_g)$ that produce effective stimuli $(s_g)$. After this learning and performance is well established, the reward is delayed or is given only intermittently. The organism responds by frustration (F) when reward is not present. In subsequent trials, fractional anticipatory frustration responses $r_f$ and their stimulus components $s_f$ are elicited and act as inhibitory factors in performance because they are now in competition with fractional anticipatory approach reactions. This mechanism $(r_f - s_f)$ will be used later in the chapter when considering responses to frustration.

When an animal has been conditioned to receive a reward in a certain situation and the reward is withheld (delayed), this procedure is called *extinction*. Increases in response strength following the first few extinction trials in classical conditioning have been reported (*Hilgard and Marquis, 1935; Hovland, 1936*), and inreased activity and response intensification after periods of enforced waiting (delay) have been reported (*Skinner, 1932; Brown and Gentry, 1948*). Intensity of responding has been reported to increase following nonreward in situations where reward previously had been obtained consistently (*Finch, 1942*). Experimental evidence indicates that delays lead to the weakening of pre-delay responses (*Cooper, 1938; Holder, 1951; Renner, 1964*).

An interesting experiment designed to induce frustration in human beings by delaying reinforcement has been reported by Sears *et al.* (*1940*). The experimenters kept a group of college students awake all night; that is, they withheld or delayed sleep as a reinforcement. The purported reason for this was to study the effects of fatigue. Other sources of frustration in this situation were many. The subjects were prohibited from smoking; food and entertainment, which had been promised, were not given; and conversations were broken up. The students responded with behavior that indicated their frustration. They were aggressive, made derogatory remarks about the experimenters, and belittled the experiment.

## Frustration by Thwarting

Interference with motivated behavior in almost any fashion can be considered thwarting. Any prevention of a response from occurring or interference with the occurrence of motivated behavior results in frustration. In the learning situation presented by a hungry rat in a maze, there are barriers between the animal and food. Frustration of a minor sort probably occurs as the result of such obstructions. Minor frustrations are an inevitable part of a learning situation. The thwarting in the usual learning situation usually is temporary and can be overcome by appropriate behavior. The thwarting that produces frustration of a more serious nature is typically more intense or more prolonged than the frustration resulting from interference with the satisfaction of motives through having to learn some skill or acquire some knowledge.

Physical restraint of the infant results in responses that are indicative of frustration. When an infant's movements are restrained, he struggles and responds emotionally (*Watson, 1926*). It is probable that the restriction of infant mobility by clothes that are clumsy or ill-fitting and the confinement of his feet in shoes produce frustrations to which he adjusts rather rapidly. The frustrations produced by confining a child to the playpen or by limiting his activity to the back yard can be more severe. Children must learn to eat in a particular way and with particular instruments. They must learn that certain attractive objects are not to be touched or played with. They must learn to control their elimination, and to evacuate bowels and bladder only at certain times and in certain places.

Many rules, regulations, and restrictions in behavior are placed on the child. The setting of unattainable standards by parents is a child-frustrating procedure (*Jost, 1941*). Some thwarting of infants and children is inevitable, but it can safely be said that much of adult thwarting of children is unnecessary for the welfare and protection of the child. The unnecessary thwarting of children's activities probably stems from the thwarting experienced by the parents and their own consequent frustrations.

## THWARTING BY PERSONAL CHARACTERISTICS

Some obstacles to performance that produce frustration may be physical characteristics of the person. The short college athlete can be frustrated when trying to engage in the tall man's sport, basketball. The physically small person is prevented by his stature from playing the big man's game, football. The physically clumsy or inept cannot do well in games calling for physical agility. The fat boy is prevented by his obesity from gaining proficiency in running and jumping. The person who is physically ill cannot engage in physically strenuous activity. The physically handicapped can be severely frustrated by their disabilities.

Other physical characteristics of individuals may serve as thwarting agents, not because of actual physical restriction but by the personal or social value placed on the possession of the characteristics (*Telford and Sawrey, 1967*). It is more frustrating for a girl or woman to be physically unattractive than it is for a man because of the social evaluation of characteristics of beauty in the female. Complexion difficulties and skin blemishes, because of their social or personal evaluation, may act as thwarting agents and prevent the establishment or the maintenance of satisfactory social relationships. Although physical characteristics of unattractiveness may be a deterrent to effective social interaction, it is probably true that it is the person's own *evaluation of himself as a person* possessing these characteristics that operates as the more effective barrier to socialization. One's own personality characteristics or his own self-concept may act as a barrier to achievement in particular ways. Lack of self-confidence that leads to anxiety over personal failure can be a thwarting agent.

## SOCIAL SOURCES OF THWARTING

The source of much frustration is *social* in nature. A person may want to become a member of a particular group, club, or society and be prevented from doing so by religion, race, or economic status. Attending college may be interrupted or prevented by economic or social barriers. Legal restrictions may operate as social barriers when they prevent the satisfaction of motives in particular ways. A person cannot drive his car as fast as he would like when he is in a hurry; or he cannot marry as young as he would like.

The thwarting of our motivated behavior is frequently accomplished by other people. Others do not always behave in the way that is most conducive to the satisfaction of our motives. Other peoples' behavior is designed to satisfy their own motives rather than ours and the resultant behavior may constitute a barrier to the satisfaction of our own motives. The frustration of adolescents by the behavior of their parents has received a good deal of attention in our culture. Adolescents also frustrate their parents in many instances. Girl friends thwart their boy friends. Brothers and sisters can be sources of frustration to each other. Teachers frustrate students and students frustrate teachers. The listing of persons who act as thwarting agents for other persons could be extended almost indefinitely.

## Further Sources of Frustration

Frustration by one circumstance or another is a life-long process. Some of the sources of frustration for children and young people have been mentioned. The frustrations of adults include many of those common to younger people in addition to some that are characteristic of adult living in our culture. The desire to be independent and free from the restraint of living with one's parents results in frustration when independence is unattainable because of lack of employment, immaturity, or other reasons. Many people would like to travel and see the world but are thwarted by economic considerations, social circumstance, or emotional involvements. People are frustrated when they want to get a job and employment is unavailable or they do not possess the necessary training or experience. A young man wants to buy a car but he cannot afford it, or the automobile that he would really like is beyond his means for one reason or another. The desire to get a college education may be thwarted by a number of factors—admission requirements, economic status, or social circumstances. The wish to marry can be thwarted by a host of factors, including age, financial insecurity, emotional insecurity, inability to establish affectional relationships, and physical illness. Married couples are thwarted by an inability to procure the kind of home they want in the location that is most suitable. Vacations from work cannot be arranged for the most convenient time, or the activities that can be arranged for the vacation are not those that are really desired. The furnishing or refurnishing of the home must be carried out within the restrictions imposed by budgetary and space considerations as well as those imposed by convention. As life moves along a person may want to retire but cannot because of personal responsibility and social obligation, or he may want to work behond retirement age but find employment impossible because of legal restriction or physical infirmity.

Frustration through *physical prevention* occurs when one cannot get into a room because of a locked door or when one is prevented from going some place by a storm, flood, or fire. Imprisonment of men provides a form of physical restraint that is frustrating in the extreme. Distance and physical disability may act as barriers that are essentially physical in nature. The inability of certain married couples to have children acts as a source of frustration for them. The death of one's husband or wife places a great deal of stress on the survivor and results in a number of frustrations. Examples of frustration by the prevention of responses can be derived from the experience of every individual.

## Frustration in the Experimental Laboratory

Methods of producing frustration that closely parallel the frustrations of real life situations have been devised and used in the experimental laboratory. Hungry infants have been allowed various amounts of milk and then the bottle was removed (*Marquis, 1943; Sears and Sears, 1940*). The infant's behavior as a consequence of this frustration was observed and related to the amount of food he had ingested previous to the thwarting. In this situation the infant was prevented from making the responses that would satisfy his motives. The analogy between this procedure and "taking candy from a baby" seems obvious. Using the same general principle in another experiment (*Barker et al., 1941*), children were allowed to play with some interesting toys for a few minutes and then the toys were taken away and placed at the other end of the room. A wire-mesh screen was used as a barrier to prevent the children from reaching the toys, but they could still be seen. Reactions to the consequent frustration were observed.

In animal experimentation the prevention of responding has been used successfully as a frustrating device in a number of instances (*Skinner, 1932; Haslerud, 1938*) besides those previously mentioned in connection with frustration by delay. Studies by Masserman (*1943*) are illustrative of the methods employed. He placed cats in a glass cage wherein they were trained to open a food box and eat upon the presentation of a light and buzzer. They were then frustrated by having the food box locked after they had learned to eat from it. The reactions of the animals to this thwarting were vigorous. Another procedure was that of confining animals to a small box and administering small amounts of electric shock in either a predictable or nonpredictable fashion. Rats that were administered shock following a conditioned stimulus (predictable) did not ulcerate as readily as those that received the same amount of shock unassociated with any conditioned stimuli (nopredictable) (*Sawrey, 1961*). Berkowitz (*1960*), using human subjects, found frustration resulting from nonpredictable frustrating situations to be more severe than that resulting from predictable frustrating situations. An almost total restriction of overt responding has been accomplished by immobilization of rats through binding (*Weininger, 1956; Ader et al., 1960; Sawrey and Sawrey, 1964*). Ulceration occurs rather rapidly using such a technique.

At the adult level several procedures have been used to produce frustration experimentally. In these studies the experimenter typically sets a difficult or impossible task for the subject and emphasizes that the task must be done with speed and accuracy (*Adams, 1940*). Falsifying scores on experimental tasks (*Sears, 1937*) and condemning the subject for his inferior performance (*McClelland and Apicella, 1945*) have been used as *frustrating devices*.

The frustration of adults by the use of physical barriers is difficult to accomplish in an experimental situation. However, an experiment has been reported using this technique (*French, 1944*). Groups of subjects were placed in an attic room and the exit door was locked without their knowing it. It was then arranged for a fire to break out. The reactions of the subjects were observed through a one-way screen in the roof of the building. This was probably the nearest thing to a panic situation that has been established with human subjects for experimental purposes in the laboratory.

### FRUSTRATION BY CONFLICT

Conflict has been indicated as one of the means by which frustration is produced. In the first two general methods of producing frustration something occurs or is used to delay or thwart motivated behavior. Conflict is one of the ways by which motivated behavior can be prohibited. In conflict, the delay or thwarting is caused by the interfering response tendencies of the organism. The basic conflictual situation involves the presence of simultaneous stimuli for two incompatible responses in a situation where, if present alone, each would yield a response (*Verplank, 1957*).

Decisions must be made in the ordinary processes of living. Whenever a choice among alternatives has to be made, some element of conflict is introduced. Conflict is an inevitable consequence of life. It cannot be avoided completely, even in the best organized and regulated of cultures.

## Varieties of Conflict Situation

Just as frustration can be produced by different methods, there are means of producing conflicts that result in frustration. Basically, there are three varieties of situations that produce conflict (*Lewin, 1933*) and a fourth variety that takes into account the complex situations in which there are more than two response tendencies competing simultaneously (*Hovland and Sears, 1938*). Response tendencies can be directed toward either a stimulus or incentive (*approach responses*), or they can be directed away from a stimulus that is noxious (*avoidance responses*). Incompatible or competing responses produce conflict in a situation in which approach responses to two different stimuli are evoked simultaneously. This is called *approach-approach* conflict. A second situation, in which two stimuli evoking avoidance responses are present, produces *avoidance-avoidance* conflict. Another situation, in which there are two distinct stimuli, one of which evokes approach and the other evokes avoidance responses, sets the stage for *approach-avoidance* conflict. In the fourth variety there are many stimulus elements evoking both approach and avoidance in the situation. This is called *double-approach-avoidance* conflict.

### APPROACH-APPROACH CONFLICT

The girl who has two extremely attractive suitors whom she must decide between is in this kind of conflict situation. A hungry child given a choice between two well liked foods is also in an approach-approach conflict situation. The frustration of this situation was recently illustrated while one of the authors was visiting friends who have a small child. The child was fretful while preparations were being made for a picnic. One of the guests took charge of the child so that the parents could get ready. In a few moments both parents emerged from the kitchen, each with a bottle for the youngster. They laughed and said they would give him a choice. The mother took both bottles and presented them to the child. The child grasped one, then let it go and grasped the other; then he reached for the first again. Within moments the child was crying and thrashing his arms wildly. When he was calmed down and then presented with one bottle, he took it and nursed eagerly.

Many students have difficulty deciding between two majors in college. Each major has great attraction for them and they have difficulty making a decision as to which one offers the greater satisfactions. Two job offers of equal or near equal description, salary, and opportunity for promotion present a common conflict for the college graduate seeking employment. Minor approach-approach conflicts are involved in deciding which theatre to attend, what to order from a menu in a café, which refreshment to accept, which motel to stop at, which suit or which dress to wear, and a host of other decisions of an essentially social nature. Whenever a person is asked whether he would rather have X or Y and he feels like saying "yes," he is in an approach-approach conflict situation. Frequently in such situations as the X or Y choice, the response of, "either one would be fine" is made. The decision can thus be avoided with a minimum of conflict.

In the experimental laboratory, animals are given food or water with equal frequency at both ends of a straight-alley maze. When testing for conflict, the animals when both hungry and thirsty are placed midway between the two ends of the maze.

Two equal goal objects can be offered to children who are allowed to have but one of them, or two different objects of equal or near equal value can be presented (*Godbeer, 1949*). There is some evidence that when goal objects differ in kind, but are equal in attractiveness, the amount of conflict is greater than if the two are of the same kind (*Underwood, 1949*).

In a study of conflict (*Hovland and Sears, 1938*), subjects were seated at a table on which there was a six-inch square piece of paper, framed by brass strips. At the corners of the paper away from the subjects were two green lights. The subjects were instructed to place a pencil at the bottom of the paper and draw a diagonal line as quickly as they could directly to whatever light was flashed on. Each subject was given 20 practice trials. Conflict was produced by flashing on both lights at the same time. Nine percent of the group tested were unable to respond to the conflict test. Twelve percent drew a line halfway between the two lights, and twenty-one percent drew a line to one light and then across to the other. Over one half (fifty-eight percent) of the subjects drew a line to one or the other of the lights. This study illustrates some of the possible behaviors when faced with a conflict situation involving two positively reinforcing stimuli. The subject may *make a decision* (go to one light or the other), try to "have his cake and eat it too" (go to both lights), or *make a compromise* (go between the two lights). Those who were unable to respond to the test or "blocked," represent those who do not make up their minds readily when faced with conflict. Their behavior is comparable to that of the infant who was offered two bottles of milk at the same time.

Approach-approach conflicts appear to be rather readily resolved in the laboratory. The girl with two equally attractive suitors between whom she must choose may not find her conflict so readily resolved, but it is probable that a perfect approach-approach balance rarely is achieved outside the laboratory (*Miller, 1944*). In most cases, some factor of distance, chance, or temporary condition usually occurs that permits or forces a decision to be made. The girl with two suitors should find the particular suitor closest at hand to be extremely attractive and make a decision in his favor. The closer we come to either of two attractive goal objects, the stronger our behavior toward that goal becomes, and the weaker the behavior toward the other. The tendency for approach behavior to become stronger as the goal is approached is called the *approach gradient*. In view of the approach

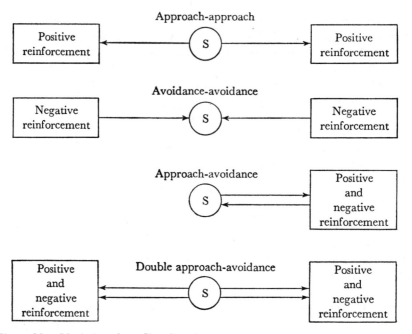

Figure 10. *Varieties of conflict situations.*

gradient, the old adage "absence makes the heart grow fonder" would seem to be a rather inappropriate observation, and our young lady's two suitors should take heed and "stick around for the decision."

### AVOIDANCE-AVOIDANCE CONFLICT

Conflicts of the avoidance-avoidance variety occur with regularity in our lives. They occur whenever a person is *simultaneously stimulated by two aversive stimuli in a situation where movement away from either stimulus results in approaching the other aversive stimulus.* The avoidance-avoidance conflict places the individual in a dilemma. Whichever of the two available means of responding he uses, he is bound to lose. He is in a situation where he cannot really win.

The college student who doesn't like to study but does not want to fail either is in an avoidance-avoidance conflict. He wants to avoid both study and failure but he cannot avoid both. Other examples of avoidance-avoidance conflict in life situations are plentiful. The child must perform his assigned tasks or lose his allowance. He doesn't want to do either. The youngster in school may be exposed to a tyrannical teacher. He must tolerate this situation or run the risk of failure. Children in the home are frequently given a choice of two disliked tasks to perform. They must choose either to wash the dishes or to dust the living room, or must either mow the lawn or straighten up the garage.

A young woman may be faced with the prospect of marrying an unloved man or becoming a spinster. A young man may face temporary distasteful employment or be without a job. The conflict experienced by deciding whether to take sick leave from one's job for a day when one is not really ill is of a slightly different nature. The person does not want to go to work that day and neither does he want to tell the necessary falsehood that would allow him to stay home. If he goes to work he will not enjoy it and if he doesn't he will feel guilty and inadequate. He is "between the devil and the deep blue sea." Whichever choice he makes he will be uncomfortable.

Avoidance-avoidance conflicts are thought to be the basis for the development of much pathological behavior. The situation is a difficult one when comparing it to the approach-approach conflict. It will be recalled that in the latter situation, the nearer a person approached a stimulus the more attractive it became. In the avoidance-avoidance situation the gradient is reversed. *As an aversive stimulus is approached the avoidance behavior becomes stronger.* Decisions are very difficult and vacillation is common. As a stimulus is approached its aversive nature becomes more apparent and avoidance responses occur. As this stimulus is avoided, the other aversive stimulus is approached. Attempts at escape from such situations are common, and depression and withdrawal may result.

In the experimental laboratory an avoidance-avoidance situation can be arranged with animals. One technique is that of forcing animals to make difficult discriminations (*Maier et al., 1940*). Rats are placed on a stand in front of two doors. They are then taught to jump a short distance from their stand to the door in order to obtain food. If they miss they fall in a net and are returned to the stand. After they have learned to jump across the open space, one of the doors is distinctively marked with a square figure and the other with a round figure. They are taught to jump to the square and never to the circle by keeping the door with the circle locked. When the animal has learned always to jump to the square, the figures are changed so that the discrimination becomes increasingly difficult. Eventually the animal will no longer jump. The situation is made an avoidance-avoidance one by administering an electric shock to the animal if he does not jump within a few seconds. The animal is in a conflict involving not wanting to jump and fall and not wanting to get shocked.

Using human subjects Hovland and Sears (1938) required subjects to draw a line from the bottom of a paper to the top corner of the paper opposite the one on which a light flashed. Conflict was introduced by then flashing the light on both top corners. When the same general procedure was used in approach-approach conflict only 9 percent of subjects "blocked" or failed to respond. In this avoidance-avoidance situation, 46 percent of the subjects failed to make a response.

### APPROACH-AVOIDANCE CONFLICT

A commonly encountered conflict situation is one *in which two stimuli are presented at the same time and in the same location and one of the stimuli elicits approach responses and the other avoidance responses.*

Children can be observed to be in conflict when they want to pet the dog and are at the same time frightened by it. Nearly everyone has observed the vacillation of the child's behavior in such a circumstance. Partial approach responses are made and these are quickly followed by avoidance responses before approach responses are again instigated. A child may want a cookie that is on a plate being offered by a person strange to him. His conflict is evidenced by his withdrawal and his later procuring of the cookie when the strange person leaves it and departs.

In order to be accepted in a new school a youngster must make some socially aggressive responses. He wants desperately to be accepted but is afraid to make the socially appropriate responses for fear that he will be rejected. His desire for acceptance and his fear of rejection produce conflict. A student may want to be a successful student but fears failure so badly that he will not make the attempts necessary to insure success. On the playground, a boy or girl may really want to play and take part in the activities but at the same time be afraid to try for fear of being clumsy, inept, or rejected by peers.

A young lady wants very much to receive the attention and affection of a particular young man. He finally asks her for a date. She does not want to reject his offer and close the door on her chances with the young man, but at the same time she is afraid that she will not make a favorable impression on him because she regards herself as socially inept. A young man may have similar conflicts in trying to decide whether or not to call a particular young lady for a date. He anticipates the pleasantness of being with her but also fears that she will not accept his invitation. He finally works up enough courage to call. He goes to the telephone and picks up the receiver. As he reaches for the dial he thinks about being rejected and replaces the receiver. His behavior vacillates between approaching the phone and avoiding possible rejection. If he does not call he will condemn himself later on for not having done so. A case of a young man who sat in a telephone booth for an hour in such a conflict situation has been reported (*Cameron, 1947*). After an hour the young man left without calling, feeling dejected and hopeless.

A young man may want to marry and at the same time not want to give up the liberties of being a bachelor. A young woman may want to marry but be frightened of losing her independence.

Approach-avoidance conflicts are encountered throughout life. Mature adults want to buy homes but the prospect of making high monthly payments is not welcome. Retirement frequently represents conflict of this kind. The person wants to retire but at the same time is concerned about what will happen when he quits work and must live on a reduced income.

Laboratory situations designed to produce approach-avoidance conflict have been devised in great number. A few of the representative procedures will be described briefly.

An early method of producing approach-avoidance conflict was employed by Pavlov (1927). In one of his experiments using conditioning procedures, dogs were trained to salivate to a luminous circle presented on a screen. When this response was well established, a luminous ellipse was projected on the screen but was not followed by the usual meat powder on the tongue. Subsequently the circle was always followed by meat powder while the ellipse was not. The dog learned to respond to the circle and not to the ellipse. When the ellipse was gradually changed in shape the animal continued responding appropriately until the ellipse became so much like a circle that he could not discriminate between the two. After several weeks of alternate presentation of the circle and the ellipse that could not be adequately discriminated by the animal, he "broke down." This method of making discriminations between two stimuli (one of which elicits approach responses and the other avoidance responses) increasingly difficult has been used by a number of investigators in attempting to produce experimental neurosis in animals.

A straight-alley maze in which rats were trained to run to procure food when a light was turned on has been used to produce approach-avoidance conflict (*Miller et al., 1944*). In this procedure the rats wore little harnesses to which a cord was attached so that the strength of pull of the animal toward or away from a goal could be measured. After the animals had learned to run the length of the alley to get food on signal they were given various intensities of shock while eating. After this, animals started at the far end of the alley, would approach part way and stop. The point at which they stopped was found to be a function of the strength of shock and amount of food deprivation.

Approach-avoidance conflict was produced by Sawrey and Weisz (1956) by placing rats in a rectangular box with a brass rod grid floor with food at one end and water at the other. The animals lived in these boxes. The floor was divided electrically into three equal parts. The two sections immediately adjacent to the food and water were kept charged with electricity. As the animals became hungry or thirsty and attempted to approach food or water they had to cross the electrically charged portion of the grid floor. In this way a strong and chronic approach-avoidance conflict was maintained. "Conflict boxes" in investigating the consequences of prolonged conflict on rats have been extensively employed (*Sawrey et al., 1956; Sawrey and Sawrey, 1964, 1966*).

Masserman (*1942*), in studying approach-avoidance conflict, trained cats to lift the lid on a box in order to get food. After this was learned, an air blast was delivered just as the cat opened the box. The blast of air was an aversive stimulus; thus, the animal had to receive the aversive stimulus of the air blast in order to obtain the food. The conflict in response was between approaching the food box and avoiding the blast of air.

### DOUBLE APPROACH-AVOIDANCE CONFLICT

Double approach-avoidance conflict situations involve two stimuli, each of which is complex. That is, each of the two stimuli elicit both approach responses and avoidance responses. If the choices are multiple rather than between only two complex stimulus situations, the conflict would be more appropriately designated as multiple approach-avoidance; however, it is conventional to refer to all of these complex situations as double approach-avoidance.

Conflict situations that develop in the course of living are frequently of a complex nature. Actually, the illustration of the young lady with two attractive suitors between whom she must choose is more illustrative of double approach-avoidance than it is of approach-approach conflict. It is likely that, though both men are extremely attractive to her, one is more talkative than the other, one is more economically secure, one is interested in one form of athletics and the other in another, one is taller, one has a better sense of humor, or one is more aggressive than the other. When the conflict is described in this manner it becomes apparent that, although the over-all picture is one of approach-approach conflict, the situation is really a double approach-avoidance conflict. The young woman can choose to remain single or she can seek still another prospective mate.

The factory worker who has an option of whether to take his two weeks' vacation and go on a trip, or work and get double pay for the period of time during which he could have taken his vacation, is in a complex conflict situation. Either choice has both positive and negative aspects.

Double approach-avoidance situations have not been used experimentally very extensively. The previously discussed experiment of Hovland and Sears (1938), using a conflict board with lights on the top edge of the board and the starting position at the bottom, can be arranged to illustrate all four varieties of conflictual situation. It will be recalled that the subject places his pencil at the bottom of the board halfway between the two sets of lights. When a red light comes on he is to draw a line from the start position to the opposite corner of the board from the light. When the

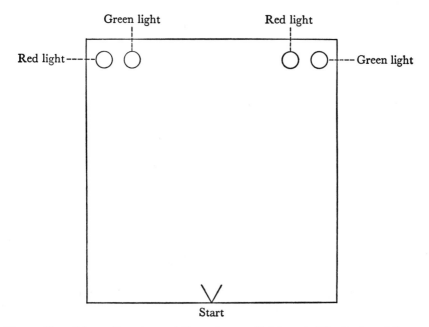

*Figure 11.* *Schematic representation of a conflict board (Hovland and Sears, 1938).*

green light is flashed he is to draw a line directly to it. After a considerable number of trials under these instructions, all four lights can be flashed on at the same time. In this manner a double approach-avoidance conflict is achieved.

## Some Sources of Conflict

Some sources of conflict that may have particular significance in the development of personal-social behavior patterns are to be found by examining the social conditions in which we live and learn.

### THE FAMILY

Children growing up together in a family may experience conflict in a number of ways. They learn to like their brothers or sisters and at the same time are often forced to compete with them in areas of achievement considered important either by the parents or by the child. In such instances a conflict develops between the empathy felt for the sibling and the desire to obtain the rewards that are contingent upon being better than he is in some way. Parents may be insensitive to this as a source of conflict for their children and allow too many situations of this variety to develop.

Resentment of siblings and parents can stem from such a situation. Severe competition within the family, unwittingly fostered by parents, can generate conflicts that may have tremendous importance in personality development and in the later happiness of both parents and children.

Methods of discipline that involve punishment can create disturbances of a conflictural nature for children. Parents are in a position of responsibility relative to the rearing of their child. Parents are in a unique position to foster the development of conflicting emotions and subsequent conflictual behavior in their children. Most of the child's satisfactions stem either directly or indirectly from the ministrations of his parents. As a consequence, the child develops strong attractions for his parents and makes approach responses to them. The parent is also the source of frustration for the child when his behavior is interrupted by the parent. Parents correct their children. They prevent them from doing some things and force them to do others. If the child is punished or disciplined in a manner that for him is inconsistent and unpredictable, he learns to fear his parents and make avoidance responses. An approach-avoidance conflict is thus generated. At the level of how the child feels, he may be entertaining feelings of love and hate at the same time. If he has learned that children are supposed to love their parents and he now finds himself disliking them, he may entertain feelings of guilt, unworthiness, and inadequacy.

As children grow older and as their experiences with the culture expand, they develop a great deal of cultural sophistication. By the age of sixteen or seventeen many children are more conversant with contemporary culture than their parents. This is understandable when consideration is given to the rapid cultural changes that have come about in the past fifteen years. Many a teen-age son knows more about automobiles than his father does. His father grew up in a culture that was quite different from that in which his son is maturing. Conflicts may develop within the family due to the increased sophistication of children and to the "lag" in parental appreciation of maturity. It is sometimes difficult for parents to realize that their children are, in reality, more adult than children. As a consequence many a young man or young lady is treated as if he or she were five to ten years less mature than they really are. Conflicts develop for the adolescent over whether he is a child or an adult. In some matters he is expected to behave as an adult; at other times he is treated like a child. He sometimes feels very adult and at other times feels much like a child.

In extreme instances we may find a 35-year-old offspring still being harbored and protected in the familial home. The 35-year-old experiences conflict about becoming independent and about leaving the protected environment. The parent feels conflict over the loss of the offspring from the home and wanting his "child" to be independent and responsible.

CONFLICTING VALUES

As children mature in their homes they learn the acceptable and valued ways of behaving. They form ideas about what behavior is good and what is bad. These things they learn from their parents. Frequently there are discrepancies between the advocated behavior of the parent and his actual behavior. Father and mother teach their children that honesty is virtuous. Father, at the same time, revels in the "shrewd" business deal he has made, which has strong elements of dishonesty about it. He also exaggerates his donations and business expenses when filing his income tax returns. Mother insists that she is most unhappy with an annoying and gossiping neighbor and maintains that if she never sees the person again it will be too soon. Still, the next day when the neighbor calls, mother says how glad she is that the neighbor dropped in. Children in such a situation can experience conflict about what values are important. It is possible that this kind of inconsistent value orientation fosters the development of "psychopaths."

When values or standards of behavior learned in the family are in marked contrast to those in the community, considerable conflict may be generated. The conflict for the youngster growing up in such a situation is whether to behave according to the standards of the community and thereby gain acceptance from the community, or to accept the values and standards of his home as his own and thereby insure acceptance in the home. Such conflicts frequently develop between the values and standards for behavior of the family and the peer group of the adolescent. The pressures to conform to both are strong, and the consequent conflict is rather severe for many people.

A person learns from his family and his community that certain values are revered and he comes to accept these values as his own. He evaluates them as right and good. Not infrequently he finds that behavior in accordance with these values is extremely difficult. When he behaves in ways that are contrary to what he himself believes to be right he experiences considerable conflict. He firmly resolves to behave more in accordance with what he has learned are acceptable values, but finds that he cannot do so. Conflicts of this nature are chronic and may lead to serious problems of adjustment.

A source of conflict for a number of people exists when they are motivated to engage in behaviors that previously have been associated with negative values. Such is the instance with a number of young people who have been taught that sex and sexual functioning is immoral, dirty, or sinful. Boys who masturbate are frequently plagued with such conflicts. Many a young woman has acquired such negative attitudes toward sex before she is married that it is extremely difficult for her to learn to enjoy sexual relations. Here again there is a conflict between behavior, on the one hand, and long established values, on the other.

Conflicts arise between what a person thinks he should do and what he actually has the opportunity to do. There are strong temptations for many people to do what they firmly believe to be wrong because it will result in their gaining financially or socially. If they do the thing that will cause them to profit but that they know is wrong, they may experience strong feelings of guilt and inadequacy. That thousands of dollars of "conscience money" is anonymously paid to the federal government by people who have previously falsified their income tax returns is testimony to the severity of the conflict experienced by many people. If they pass up the opportunity to profit from some inappropriate behavior, they must forego the pleasures that would be provided through the gain in social stature, acceptance, or financial ability.

There are many sources of conflict in our culture, and it is likely that no two people experience exactly the same frustrating situation. Only a few sources of conflict have been mentioned in this discussion. These are intended to be illustrative of the many possible sources and not as an exclusive listing of them.

### CONSEQUENCES OF FRUSTRATION

The behavioral consequences of frustration have been given extensive description in earlier chapters of this book. Some additional consideration of the results of frustration may serve to increase the understanding of the role of frustration and conflict in the genesis of problems of adjustment.

### Frustration and Motivation

Many of the consequences of frustration can be understood by using well established principles of learning without resorting to motivational variables. However, motivational consequences of frustration have received a good deal of attention from behavior theorists, and experimental investigations have been undertaken to explore the motivational consequences of frustration.

Brown and Farber (1951) have formulated a frustration theory that allows for changes in motivation as well as associative changes. According to this position, frustration is regarded as having two primary effects on the organism. It results in an increment in general drive and it provides

distinctive internal stimuli. The increments in drive attributable to frustration are assumed to have no functions not common to increments in drive
from any other source. The frustration-generated stimuli are treated as any
other stimuli; that is, unlearned tendencies to react to the frustration
stimuli may exist from birth, and/or new habits can be established to these
internal stimuli by conditioning.

Amsel's (1958) theory of frustration assumes that the major source
of frustration is nonreward in a situation where the organism has learned
to expect reward. Frustration would seem to be the reaction to nonreward
when reward is expected. Frustration is assumed to lead to an increment in
general drive and to frustration-specific internal stimuli. Amsel assumes
that frustration as a response can be conditioned and that, after a series of
nonrewarded trials, it can come to be anticipated by the organism. The
mechanism for this anticipation is essentially the same as Hull's $r_g - s_g$
mechanism. On trials following nonreward, fractional anticipatory frustration responses are elicited $(r_f)$ that produce characteristic internal stimuli
$(s_f)$. The $r_f - s_f$ mechanism operates much as the $r_g - s_g$ mechanism. It
is assumed that frustration is inherently aversive, and that tendencies to
avoid a nonrewarding goal box become associated with the frustration-
produced stimuli. Partial avoidance responses as well as approach responses
are elicited by stimuli associated with nonreward when such stimuli have
been associated with reward previously. Increments are added to drive by
frustration and, because frustration is aversive, decrements in task performance are produced by fractional anticipatory frustration responses competing with approach responses.

The Brown and Farber (1951) formulation and the Amsel (1958)
formulation are closely related. Both are worthy of serious consideration, and experimental evidence in their support has been offered.

Frustration as a source of drive and consequent increased emotional
responding have been reported from the observations of a number of early
investigators who were not specifically investigating this phenomena. Reports of increased response vigor or increased "emotional" responding as a
consequence of frustration have come from Thorndike (1898), Hamilton
(1916), Skinner (1932), Brown and Gentry (1948), and others.

Brown (1961) reports on a systematic experimental investigation of
frustration drive by Marzocco (1951). Marzocco hypothesized that frustration resulting from thwarting would function as an irrelevant drive to raise
the organism's total effective drive level. This increased drive level would
operate to increase the amplitude of any response during thwarting. He
also predicted that frustration would increase with degree of hunger and
with amount of practice in making the frustrated response.

Rats were trained to press a bar in a modified Skinner box in order to test the hypotheses. Measures were taken of the increased vigor of bar-pressing following frustration by nonreward. The results clearly indicated increased response vigor following frustration. Frustration effects were positively related to hours of food deprivation and to the number of reinforced trials before frustration. Brown (1961) points out that the data of this study provide clear evidence for increased response vigor following frustration, but that associative interpretations as well as motivational ones are possible, and, therefore, that the results do not *prove* that thwarting leads to an increment in drive. The animals may have learned to exert increased effort to overcome resistance to the completion of a response in a variety of pre-experimental situations. If this were true the increased response vigor demonstrated in the experiment could be the result of transfer of training rather than increased drive. Doubt is cast on this interpretation, however, because the number of reinforcements should have been more clearly related to the frustration effect if this had been the instance.

Experiments by Amsel and Roussel (1952) and by Wagner (1959), using animals as subjects, have given further support to the hypothesis that frustration affects drive. Experimental investigations of the drive effects of motivation on human subjects have yielded confirmatory results. An investigation demonstrating increased plunger-pressing vigor by children following thwarting (*Haner and Brown, 1955*) is interesting, because the plunger-pressing response of children and the bar-pressing response of rats in the previous studies are closely related. In this study the probability of response transfer was drastically reduced and increased response vigor due to frustration was reported.

Evaluation of the experimental evidence in support of frustration as a general energizer lends considerable support to the early observations that drive was enhanced by frustration. Reductions in response strength that have been reported to result from frustration (*Holder et al., 1957*) can be explained either as due to the growth of anticipatory frustration reactions (*Amsel, 1958*) or as a consequence of the conditioning of avoidance responses to the noxious cues accompanying frustration (*Brown and Farber, 1951*). The energizing effects of frustration seem to be rather well established. Reductions in frustration should, then, be usable as reinforcements for learning. Reinforcement for learning may be provided by reduction in frustration in some situations where the reinforcement for learning has been difficult to identify.

## Aggression

It was early hypothesized that frustration invariably results in aggressive behavior (*Dollard et al., 1939*). This statement that aggression is always the consequence of frustration was revised a short time later to allow for other types of response as well as aggression (*Miller, 1941*). The treatment of aggression as an inevitable consequence of frustration in a text entitled *Frustration and Aggression* (*Dollard et al., 1939*) created a great deal of interest in the field. Though admitting that frustration frequently does result in aggressive behavior, many workers in the field attacked the assumption that frustration always causes aggression. Numerous exceptions to this hypothesis can be reported from the experience of most individuals. It was indicated earlier that the aggression elicited by frustration could be directed at the frustrating agent as well as at an innocent bystander. The aggression could be vigorous and undisguised, or it could be subtle and indirect. Operationally, of course, one can define aggression as the response to frustration. This would do considerable injustice to the concept as we usually understand it, because the reactions to frustration appear to be many (*Stamford and Hsu, 1948; Kaufmann, 1965*). Zander (*1944*) was able to classify the behavior of fifth- and sixth-grade children, who were experimentally frustrated, into categories of aggression, withdrawal, and nonadjustive behavior. Scott (*1948*), working with pairs of hungry goats, produced frustration by placing grain in a bucket that was only large enough to allow the animals to eat one at a time. The results of this study indicated that only the dominant animals became aggressive when they were thwarted by being prevented from eating.

Aggression, as a behavioral phenomenon, has been extensively investigated (*Bandura, 1965; Berkowitz, 1964*), and the results of these investigations indicate that aggressive behavior may stem from learned habits of responding as well as from excessive frustration. The hypothesis that aggressive behavior is cathartic in nature has been seriously challenged by empirical research findings. It is no doubt true that aggression may result from frustration. Many instances of apparent frustration-induced aggression can be cited. However, it would appear that other responses to frustration besides aggression are made, and that aggression does not invariably result from frustration.

## Regression

Regressive behavior has been discussed in a previous chapter of this text. A brief discussion of the topic and some of the experiments relative to regression may serve to clarify the dynamics of such behavior.

A controversy surrounds the characteristics of regressive behavior. As a consequence the methods of investigating the phenomenon are not well standardized. Lewin (*1937*) has stated that people under stress "regress" to a more "primitive" level. He indicates that this is a regression to a more primitive level of responding (*primitivization*). Primitivization takes place, according to this position, not because of habits learned previously while the person was younger, but because frustration tends to destructure the personality. His hypothesis, then, is that regressive behavior is not behavior that has been previously learned.

One of the famous studies of regressive behavior in human beings was that of Barker, Dembo, and Lewin (*1941*). They used children between the ages of two and five as the subjects in the experiment. The children were frustrated by being separated by a wire screen from toys that they previously had played with and enjoyed. Less attractive toys were left for the children to play with while they could still see the forbidden ones. Behavior descriptions and ratings indicated a mean regression in constructiveness of play, from the level of pre-frustration play to about twenty-two months at the four and one-half-year level and five months at the two and one-half-year level. The amount of regression was related to the strength of frustration.

Animals were trained (*Hull, 1934*) to run a 20-foot runway in order to receive food, and then the alley was lengthened to 40 feet. The animals, when first confronted with the extended runway, tended to stop at about the 20-foot mark, but with further training they continued to run steadily down the full extended length. When extinction trials were started (frustration), the animals again tended to stop at about the 20-foot mark. A previously learned and abandoned habit reappeared.

Mowrer (*1940*) placed experimental animals in a box in which electric shock was built up gradually from zero to a maximum intensity, where it was maintained for fifteen minutes. The rats discovered that if they sat quietly on their hind legs and held their forepaws up off the grid floor, they received comparatively little shock. The animals quickly adopted this posture when shock was subsequently turned on. They were then placed in an experimental box in which a pedal had been placed. Pressing down on the pedal would immediately turn off the shock. With some difficulty the animals learned to press the pedal and turn off the shock. When the pedal-pressing response had become well established, the animals were placed in the box with the pedal but the pressing of it caused the animal to receive a slight shock. In this situation four out of five animals "regressed" to their earlier posture response. Control animals that had not learned the posture response, but had learned the pedal-pressing response, continued to press the pedal in this new circumstance.

Most of the laboratory studies of regression have dealt with return or regression to a response that had previously been *learned* by the organism in the laboratory. A difficulty involved in not using such behavior as a basis for determining regression is that, unless some such procedure as this is instituted, the experimenter can never really know whether or not earlier behavior patterns are actually being elicited. It is extremely difficult, if not impossible, to have a complete learning history of even the simplest organism.

## Fixation

As a consequence of frustration, it has been hypothesized, stereotyping of responses develops (*Maier, 1949; 1956*). Maier has used stereotypy to designate extremely persistent behavior. The persistency of behavior appears to be much greater in frustration than in usual learning situations, and Maier contends that the behavior cannot be explained by using learning principles. In his text, *Frustration: The Study of Behavior Without a Goal*, he makes it clear that he regards frustration-instigated behavior as behavior with no goal orientation. The behavior is a terminal response and not a means to an end.

The procedures that Maier has used to produce frustration and elicit fixation responses are not complicated. An experimental animal is placed on a small stand and is trained to jump a short distance at one of two stimulus cards. If he chooses correctly, the card falls over and the animal lands on a feeding platform; if he chooses the incorrect card he bumps his head on the stationary card and falls down into a net. Neither cue is consistently rewarded or punished. After a while the animal refuses to jump. When this happens he is given an electric shock, a blast of air, or is prodded with a stick, and jumping is resumed. Animals may develop fixation or stereotyped responses to this situation. Maier reports that most of the time the fixated response is related to position; that is, the animal always jumps to the stimulus on the right or always to the one on the left. He further reports that an animal may make the fixated response without variation for hundreds of trials without once attempting to jump at the other card.

The permanent nature of "abnormal" fixations has been demonstrated in the laboratory (*Maier and Klee, 1941*). Ten animals that had fixated position responses were subjected to a variety of experiences, and for a four-month period no tests were given. Seven of the ten animals retained their fixated-position responses during this period.

A number of investigators have analyzed the acquisition and retention of these responses within the general framework of learning theory (*Mowrer, 1950*). That the fixated behavior persisted despite the fact that it was punished half of the time becomes more readily understandable when it is recalled that the fixated behavior was also positively reinforced half of the time. Fifty percent reinforcement is quite adequate to maintain behavior. When an "incorrect" response was made, the rat was in an avoidance-avoidance conflict situation. He really had a choice between the blast of air and a bump on the nose followed by a falling into a net. The stimuli received while on the jumping stand were more aversive than jumping and falling, or the animal would not have jumped. The animal was being reinforced by escape from the more aversive of two stimuli. It appears that the animals made the most adaptive responses possible for them in this situation (*Lundin, 1961*). Mowrer (*1940*) considers fixated responses simply well conditioned responses. Responses that are highly resistant to extinction can be conditioned by using irregular schedules of reinforcement in establishing them. Responses that are extremely resistant to extinction can be interpreted as *fixated*.

It is obvious that certain human habits persist in spite of their apparently nonadaptive nature. It is difficult to arrange experimental conditions in the laboratory to produce fixated behavior. Even the usually docile experimental animal known as the college sophomore would become aroused by the severity of the procedures necessary to produce fixation in the laboratory.

## Withdrawal and Escape

People who are severely frustrated in a given situation may try to escape or withdraw from that situation. It should be noted that such withdrawal or escape has been classified as either physical or psychological. It is not our intention to create a physical-psychological dichotomy here. What is intended is that the actual physical behavior may be more or less open, observable, and direct in its withdrawal or escape implications. There is probably no actual physical withdrawal without psychological components and no psychological withdrawal without physical implication. The organism makes withdrawal responses, and so-called physical and psychological processes are involved in varying degrees. An example of escape or withdrawal behavior resulting from a common avoidance-avoidance conflict situation may illustrate this point.

A college student has not been studying at regular intervals and is now confronted with the prospects of an examination at the next class meeting. He is in an avoidance-avoidance conflict situation. He wants to avoid failure in this course. The only way that he can do it is to study but he wants to avoid studying this uninteresting material. He firmly resolves that he will spend the evening in preparation for the examination. After dinner he goes to his room and makes elaborate preparations for study. He sharpens a couple of pencils and locates a pen with which to make notes. He arranges the reading lamp just right and the study table is made neat and orderly. He gets all the things that he will need including cigarettes, ash tray, extra paper, lecture notes, textbook, and references. He sits down to the table and ponders the situation. Should he look at the notes first or read the text? He notices a copy of a current picture magazine, picks it up and thumbs through it casually. He tries to study and finds that his attention is wandering. About that time a friend comes into the room. This friend does not have a test the next day. They visit a few minutes and the friend suggests that they go to a movie. Our scholar protests, but in a few minutes he has been persuaded to go along with his friend. He has escaped the situation, both physically and psychologically, at least temporarily.

Some other aspects of behavior under frustration were also demonstrated by this conflict situation. The elaborate preparations can be interpreted as a temporary means of avoiding study, and the ease with which the student was distracted from the aversive task of studying by a magazine and by his friend are evidence of the general distractibility of people in conflict. These distractions serve as temporary escapes. The response of going to the movie will lead to further distraction through fantasy. Temporary escape may be fairly complete. When the student was not faced with the study table but was pondering the possibilities of failure, he resolved to study. When contemplating failure, failure was more imminent than study. When faced with the immediate study situation, the disliked study was more imminent than failure. He could withdraw from study by accompanying his friend. He was, thus, immediately avoiding the aversive stimulus that was psychologically closest. *Psychological distance* may have been involved in the resolution to study when the task was not at hand and in later going to the movie when study was imminent. Avoidance responses tended to increase as aversive stimuli were approached and failure wouldn't occur until sometime in the future.

Factors determining conflict reactions in difficult discrimination situations have been investigated in rats (*Brown, 1942*). Avoidance-avoidance conflict was found to produce greater amounts of withdrawal than other conflict situations. This finding is in support of the general notion of the severity of avoidance-avoidance conflicts and with the results of research using humans as subjects.

## Physiological Responses

The effects on various body tissues of frustration and conflict have been the focus of much research. Chronic conflict is deleterious to physical health. Organic changes that are the result of psychologically induced frustration and conflict can be observed in many different ways. Physical symptoms deriving from psychological factors include ulcers, high blood pressure, asthma, skin eruptions, and others of a less severe or less common nature. Much of the research in psychosomatics has not been very successful in relating specific psychological conflicts to specific psychosomatic disorders. This may be because of various learned ways of responding to frustration, physical differences among individuals, differences in the vulnerability of various organs and systems within a given person, or various other factors.

Chronic frustration can lead to a great number of organic difficulties. One of these is the development of ulcers. Mahl (1949) has shown that under chronic stress, increased amounts of hydrochloric acid are secreted in the stomach. Sawrey and Weisz (1956) developed a means of giving rats ulcers, and a subsequent investigation (Sawrey et al., 1956) demonstrated that conflict played a significant role in the production of ulcers.

Sawrey et al. (1956) placed rats one at a time in experimental boxes with brass rod grid floors. A food platform was placed at one end of the rectangular box and a water bottle at the other end. The grid floor was divided electrically into three equal sections, and the two sections immediately adjacent to the food and water were kept charged with electricity for 23 out of every 24 hours. The center portion of the grid was not charged. Animals were placed in these boxes and lived in them with the charged portions of the grid being turned off to permit eating and drinking for one hour per day. At other times when the animals approached either food or water they were shocked; thus, a chronic approach-avoidance conflict was maintained.

Control animals were placed in boxes identical with those of the experimental animals and maintained on a 23-hour deprivation schedule. The control box was wired in series with the experimental box so that each time an experimental animal received a shock a control animal was also shocked an equal amount. The difference between the experimental and

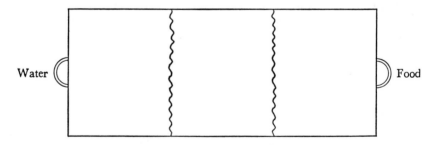

Figure 12. Conflict Box (Sawrey and Weisz, 1956). The conflict box has a brass rod grid floor divided electrically into three parts as indicated by the wavy lines. The parts nearest food and water are electrically charged. The rat is placed in the middle section (safe zone) and must cross the electrically charged sections of the grid floor to obtain either food or water.

control animal was that the experimental animal was in a conflict situation whereas the control animal was not. Both control and experimental animals received identical electric shock and were maintained on identical deprivation schedules. The animals in the conflict situation developed a significantly greater number of ulcers than the control animals.

Individual differences in susceptibility to ulceration in the conflict situation are found. Some animals tend to be much more resistant than others. Sawrey and Long (1962), using rats as subjects, found significant sex differences and strain differences in susceptibility to ulcers in the conflict situation designed to produce ulcers.

Ulcers have been produced experimentally in monkeys by Brady (1958), using a situation comparable to the one used by Sawrey *et al.* (1956). A monkey was placed in an apparatus where it could avoid electric shock which came at 20-second intervals if he pressed a lever at appropriate times. A control animal was placed in a comparable box with a lever that could be manipulated but controlled nothing. If the first monkey (which was designated the "executive") did not press the lever at the appropriate time, both animals received shock. The "executive" monkey developed ulcers and the control animal did not.

It will be recalled that, in some experiments involving difficult discrimination, a jumping stand was used. An air blast was used in a study in order to produce jumping when the discrimination became difficult (*Maier*, 1939). The avoidance-avoidance conflict created, appeared to produce convulsive behavior. Actually, it was not the conflict situation per se that produced the convulsive behavior. A primary cause appears to have been the high frequency sound waves created by the air blast. Some rats, when exposed to high frequency sounds, are highly susceptible to convulsive behavior, called *audiogenic seizures*. The threshold for audiogenic seizures can be lowered significantly by placing animals in an avoidance-avoidance conflict situation (*Maier and Longhorst*, 1947). Using an air blast intensity that was below the seizure threshold for most rats, it was found that over three times as many animals in the conflict situation exhibited audiogenic seizures than comparable animals in the situation without conflict.

## CLASSIFICATION OF REACTIONS TO FRUSTRATION

An attempt to make a gross classification of conscious reaction to frustration has been made by Rosenzweig (1944). According to his classification system, responses to frustration can be designated as *extrapunitive, intropunitive,* and *impunitive.*

In the "extrapunitive" type of conscious reaction to frustration the individual directs his reactions outward toward others. He expresses his anger toward other people and blames them for his misfortunes. Elements of the external world are the targets for his aggression and projection is frequently exercised without regard to the objective situation.

The "intropunitive" reaction is involved when the individual experiences humiliation and guilt. He holds himself responsible. This reaction to frustration is directed toward oneself. The person may conceive of himself as inferior and unworthy and feel helpless or depressed.

The "impunitive" reaction to frustration is involved when the person experiences embarrassment and shame. The emphasis is not on blame of either the person involved or some other person or event. The situation is condoned or dismissed as being of little consequence. The situation that developed was bound to occur and it couldn't be prevented.

These three types of reaction to frustration have been used by some workers in the field of adjustment as descriptive labels to apply to particular behaviors. As such, they may serve to facilitate communication. Others have used these types of reaction to describe persons rather than responses and by implication have classified personalities within this framework. This would imply that a particular person uses one variety of reaction to the exclusion of others. Rosenzweig (1944) has cautioned against the classification of persons according to this system because a person may behave one way in one circumstance and another way in a different situation, in spite of the fact that he may have some over-all predisposition to respond in one of the three ways he has described.

### DETERMINANTS OF THE NATURE OF BEHAVIOR FOLLOWING FRUSTRATION

It is obvious that a variety of behaviors are instigated in part, at least, by frustration. One of the factors involved in reactions to frustration is probably a motivational one. Evidence has been cited in support of the general energizing function of frustration. Other factors than increased drive are necessary if one is to understand the conglomeration of behavior, both in humans and animals, that is elicited by thwarting in one way or another.

#### MOTIVE STRENGTH

Strength of the motive thwarted is, no doubt, one of the determinants of the ensuing behavior. If the organism is at a high level of drive when thwarting occurs, the responses would be expected to be more vigorous than if a low drive state existed. Severity of the conflict of motivated behavior is no doubt a factor.

## PREVIOUS LEARNING

The previous learning history or gross experiential background of the frustrated organism must be considered. If the person has had previous experience with being frustrated in a particular way he may have learned quite satisfactory ways of responding to the thwarting, or he may have learned that the thwarting situation was a particularly aversive one and developed violent reactions to it. Previous experience with the components of the situation should be a variable in that adaptation could take place and the subsequent behavior would be modified.

## THE SPECIFIC SITUATION

The specific situation involved is no doubt a factor in determining the behavior that follows. Different degrees of interference with motivated behavior or degrees of conflict produced by the situation will produce different behaviors. If the chances of escape or avoidance are great, the frustrated behavior will be grossly different from behavior in a situation in which escape or avoidance is impossible. Length of time in the conflict situation or number of interferences with motivated behavior are variables that must be considered in trying to predict the behavior of frustrated individuals.

## FRUSTRATION TOLERANCE

Individual differences in behavior in frustrating situations are readily observable. Some people show marked behavioral disorganization in a frustrating situation; others are able to perform adequately under stress for long periods of time. The concept of frustration tolerance has been employed to cover these individual differences in performance. A great deal is yet to be learned about the causes of these individual differences that have given rise to the concept of frustration tolerance. Constitutional factors, in addition to those already discussed as determinants of the nature of behavior following frustration are, no doubt, involved.

Many adult behavior patterns that are maladaptive in nature are not the results of adult thwarting but stem from thwarting during childhood and infancy (*Freud*, 1936). Experimental evidence tending to support this observation has been supplied by a number of investigators. Hunt (1941) and McKelvey and Marx (1951) have shown that food deprivation for a time shortly after weaning rats resulted in the deprived animals exhibiting hoarding behavior in adulthood in excess of the hoarding behavior of nondeprived animals. Dogs raised in extremely restricted environments (confined to opaque cages for seven to ten months after weaning) exhibit higher levels of general activity several years later than do normally reared animals (*Thompson and Heron, 1954*), and make less adaptive emotional responses one year following restriction (*Melzack, 1954*). The restricted animals were dominated by normally reared animals when they were placed in competition for a bone. This was true even when the restricted animals were placed in competition with normally reared animals that were considerably younger (*Thompson and Melzack, 1956*). The learning of avoidance responses of various kinds by the dogs reared in isolation was severely retarded suggesting that, if an organism does not learn appropriate avoidance responses in infancy, he may never acquire the appropriate avoidance behavior of the normal adult (*Melzack and Scott, 1957*).

In order for frustration tolerance to develop adequately, it would appear that experience with thwarting is essential (*Sawrey and Sawrey, 1963*). Too much thwarting in the developmental years, however, does not permit the organism to develop adequate reaction to frustration. If frustration and conflict are introduced gradually they can be more adequately handled by developing appropriate reactions. Children can be trained to tolerate increasingly difficult tasks through gradual exposure to problems of increasing difficulty (*Keister and Updegraff, 1937*).

The experimental investigations of frustration tolerance have usually dealt with a specific frustrating situation and rather specific responses to that situation. Variations in tolerance to a situation as the result of exposure to it are dependent, of course, on many conditions. Some of these conditions are the severity of the situation, length of exposure to the situation, age at exposure to the situation, and avoidance possibilities. Whether or not a general over-all tolerance of frustration can be established by exposure to a limited number of frustrating circumstances, is not really known. It is possible that general frustration tolerance would be overshadowed by the specific tolerances to any thwartings that might be used to test for the development of a general frustration tolerance.

## SUMMARY

Frustration is an evitable consequence of living. As a response, frustration can become conditioned to any number of stimuli. It is produced by interfering with or blocking the motivated behavior of an organism. The means by which frustration can be produced are designated as frustration by *delay, thwarting,* and *conflict.* The frustrating effects of delay and thwarting are common and there is experimental evidence in support of their producing frustration. Sources of frustration for children and adults were discussed and examples of situations that are thwarting were mentioned. Thwarting can be accomplished by physical restraint, by personal characteristics, social circumstance, and other situations.

Conflict as a source of frustration was developed more extensively than were delay and thwarting. The varieties of conflict situations can be described as *approach-approach, avoidance-avoidance, approach-avoidance* and *double approach-avoidance*. Resolution of conflict of the approach-approach variety appears to be more readily accomplished than conflict of the other varieties. Avoidance-avoidance conflicts can be extremely frustrating and result in deviant behavior. There has been a good deal of laboratory experimentation on the general topic of conflict with both humans and lower animals. Conflictual situations are to be found in great number in the lives of children and adults. When conflicts are between values or are essentially moral in nature, they are called *inner conflicts*.

Frustration may have motivational consequences and produce changes in drive. Frustration may result in responses of aggression, regression, withdrawal and escape, and fixation, in addition to others. Organisms can learn responses to frustration, and reduction in frustration may serve as reinforcement for learning in certain situations. Physiological reactions to thwarting include many of the so-called "psychosomatic" illnesses. Ulceration and seizures have both been produced in the experimental laboratory by placing the organism in chronic conflict.

There are a number of factors that can be considered determinants of the nature of behavior following frustration. Among these are constitutional characteristics, strength of motive, experiential background, and the specific frustrating circumstance. Tolerance to frustration is a function of all of these factors, and changes in frustration tolerance can be produced by training.

### REFERENCES

ADAMS, C. R. Individual differences in behavior resulting from experimentally induced frustration. *J. Psychol.*, 1940, **10**, 157–176.

ADER, R., BEELS, C. C., and TATUM, R. Blood pepsinogen and gastric erosions in the rat. *Psychosom. Med.*, 1960, **22**, 1–12.

AMSEL, A. The role of frustrative nonreward in noncontinuous reward situations. *Psychol. Bull.*, 1958, **55**, 102–119.

AMSEL, A., and ROUSSEL, J. Motivational properties of frustration: I. Effect on a running response of the addition of frustration to the motivational complex. *J. exp. Psychol.*, 1952, **43**, 363–368.

BANDURA, A. Vicarious Processes: A Case of No-Trial Learning. In Berkowitz, L. (ed.), *Advances in Experimental Social Psychology*. New York: Academic Press, 1965.

BARKER, R. G., DEMBO, TAMARA, and LEWIN, K. Frustration and regression. An experiment with young children. *Univ. Ia. Stud. Child Welf.*, 1941, **18**, No. 386.

BERKOWITZ, L. Repeated frustrations and expectations in hostility arousal. *J. abnorm. soc. Psychol.*, 1960, **60**, 422–429.

BERKOWITZ, L. Aggressive cues in aggressive behavior and hostility catharsis. *Psychol. Rev.*, 1964, **71**, 104–122.

BRADY, J. V. Ulcers in "executive" monkeys. *Scient. Mon.*, 1958, October, 89–95.

BROWN, J. S. Factors determining conflict reactions in difficult situations. *J. exp. Psychol.*, 1942, **31**, 272–292.

BROWN, J. S. *The Motivation of Behavior*. New York: McGraw-Hill Book Company, 1961.

BROWN, J. S., and FARBER, I. E. Emotions conceptualized as intervening variables— with suggestions toward a theory of frustration. *Psychol. Bull.*, 1951, **48**, 465– 495.

BROWN, W. L., and GENTRY, G. The effects of intra-maze delay: II. Various intervals of delay. *J. comp. physiol. Psychol.*, 1948, **41**, 403–407.

CAMERON, N. *The Psychology of Behavior Disorders*. Boston: Houghton Mifflin Company, 1947.

COOPER, J. B. The effect upon performance of introduction of a delay within a maze. *J. comp. Psychol.*, 1938, **25**, 457–462.

DOLLARD, J., DOOB, L. W., MILLER, N. E., MOWRER, O. H., and SEARS, R. R. *Frustration and Aggression*. New Haven: Yale University Press, 1939.

FINCH, G. Chimpanzee frustration responses. *Psychosom. Med.*, 1942, **4**, 233–251.

FRENCH, J. R. P. Authority and frustration. Studies in topological and vector psychology: III: Organized and unorganized groups under fear and frustration. *Univ. Ia. Stud. Child Welf.*, 1944, **20**, 231–308.

FREUD, S. *The Problem of Anxiety*. New York: Psychoanalytic Quarterly Press, 1936.

GODBEER, E. Factors Introducing Conflict in the Choice Behavior of Children. Master's thesis, Yale University, 1940. Cited in Underwood, B. J. *Experimental Psychology*. New York: Appleton-Century-Crofts, 1949.

HAMILTON, G. V. A study of perseverance reactions in primates and rodents. *Behav. Monogr.*, 1916, **3**, No. 2 (whole No. 13).

HANER, C. F., and BROWN, P. A. Clarification of the instigation to action concept in the frustration-aggression hypothesis. *J. abnorm. soc. Psychol.*, 1955, **51**, 204– 206.

HASLERUD, G. M. Frustration as an experimental problem: III. Some interrelations of behavioral measures of frustration in chimpanzees. *Charact. & Pers.*, 1938, **7**, 136–139.

HILGARD, E. R., and MARQUIS, D. G. Acquisition, extinction, and retention of conditioned lid responses to light in dogs. *J. comp. Psychol.*, 1935, **19**, 29–58.

HOLDER, E. Response strength as a function of changes in the length of the delay interval. Unpublished master's thesis, New Mexico State College, 1951. Cited in Holder, W. B., Marx, M. H., Holder, E. E., and Collier, G. Response strength as a function of delay of reward in a runway. *J. exp. Psychol.*, 1957, **53**, 316–323.

Hovland, C. I. "Inhibition of reinforcement" and phenomena of experimental extinction. *Proc. Nat. Acad. Sci., Wash.*, 1936, **22**, 430–433.

Hovland, C. I., and Sears, R. R. Experiments on motor conflict: I. Types of conflict and their modes of resolution. *J. exp. Psychol.*, 1938, **23**, 477–493.

Hull, C. L. The rat's speed of locomotion gradient in the approach to food. *J. comp. Psychol.*, 1934, **17**, 393–422.

Hunt, J. McV. The effects of infant feeding frustration upon adult hoarding in the albino rat. *J. abnorm. soc. Psychol.*, 1941, **36**, 338–360.

Jost, H. Some physiological changes during frustration. *Child Develpm.*, 1941, **12**, 9–15.

Kaufmann, H. Definitions and methodology in the study of aggression. *Psychol. Bull.*, 1965, **64**, 351–364.

Keister, M. E., and Updegraff, R. A study of children's reactions to failure and an experimental attempt to modify them. *Child Develpm.*, 1937, **8**, 241–248.

Lewin, K. Environmental Forces. In Murchison, C. (ed.), *A Handbook of Child Psychology*. Worcester, Mass.: Clark University Press, 1933.

Lewin, K. Psychoanalytic and topological psychology. *Bull. Menninger Clin.*, 1937, No. 1, 202–211.

Lundin, R. W. *Personality: An Experimental Approach.* New York: The Macmillan Company, 1961.

Mahl, G. F. Anxiety, HCL secretion and peptic ulcer etiology. *Psychosom. Med.*, 1949, **11**, 33–44.

Maier, N. R. F. *Studies of Abnormal Behavior in the Rat.* New York: Harper & Brothers, 1939.

Maier, N. R. F. *Frustration: The Study of Behavior without a Goal.* New York: McGraw-Hill Book Company, 1949.

Maier, N. R. F. Frustration theory: restatement and extension. *Psychol. Rev.*, 1956, **63**, 370–388.

Maier, N. R. F., Glazer, N. M., and Klee, J. B. Studies of abnormal behavior in the rat: III. The development of behavior fixations through frustration. *J. exp. Psychol.*, 1940, **26**, 521–546.

Maier, N. R. F., and Klee, J. B. Studies of abnormal behavior in the rat: VII. The permanent nature of abnormal fixations and their relation to convulsive tendencies. *J. exp. Psychol.*, 1941, **29**, 380–389.

Maier, N. R. F., and Longhorst, J. U. Studies of abnormal behavior in the rat: XXI. Conflict and "audiogenic" seizures. *J. comp. physiol. Psychol.*, 1947, **40**, 397–412.

Marquis, D. P. A study of frustration in newborn infants. *J. exp. Psychol.*, 1943, **32**, 123–138.

Marzocco, F. N. *Frustration Effect as a Function of Drive Level, Habit Strength, and Distribution of Trials During Extinction.* Unpublished doctoral dissertation. Iowa City: State University of Iowa, 1951.

Masserman, J. H. Psychobiologic dynamism in behavior. *Psychiatry*, 1942, **5**, 341–347.

Masserman, J. H. *Behavior and Neurosis.* Chicago: University of Chicago Press, 1943.

McClelland, D. C., and Apicella, F. S. A functional classification of verbal reactions to experimentally induced failure. *J. abnorm. soc. Psychol.*, 1945, **40**, 376–390.

McKelvey, R. K., and Marx, M. H. Effects of infantile food and water deprivation on adult hoarding in the rat. *J. comp. physiol. Psychol.*, 1951, **44**, 423–430.

MELZACK, R. The genesis of emotional behavior: an experimental study of the dog. *J. comp. physiol. Psychol.*, 1954, **47**, 166–168.

MELZACK, R., and SCOTT, T. H. The effect of early experience on the response to pain. *J. comp. physiol. Psychol.*, 1957, **50**, 155–161.

MILLER, N. E. The frustration-aggression hypothesis. *Psychol. Rev.*, 1941, **38**, 337–342.

MILLER, N. E. Experimental Studies of Conflict. In Hunt, J. McV. (ed.), *Personality and the Behavior Disorders*. New York: The Ronald Press Company, 1944.

MILLER, N. E., BROWN, J. S., and LIPOFSKY, H. A Theoretical and Experimental Analysis of Conflict Behavior: III. Approach-Avoidance Conflict as a Function of Drive. Reported by N. E. Miller in Hunt, J. McV. (ed.), *Personality and Behavior Disorders*. New York: The Ronald Press Company, 1944.

MOWRER, O. H. An experimental analogue of "regression" with incidental observations on "reaction formation." *J. abnorm. soc. Psychol.*, 1940, **35**, 56–87.

MOWRER, O. H. *Learning Theory and Personality Dynamics*. New York: The Ronald Press Company, 1950.

PAVLOV, I. P. *Conditioned Reflexes*. Trans. by Anrep, G. V. London: Oxford University Press, 1927.

RENNER, K. E. Delay of reinforcement: a historical review. *Psychol. Bull.*, 1964, **61**, 341–361.

ROSENZWEIG, S. An Outline of Frustration Theory. In Hunt, J. McV. (ed.), *Personality and the Behavior Disorders*. New York: The Ronald Press Company, 1944.

SAWREY, J. M. and SAWREY, W. L. Ulcer production with response and conflict. *J. comp. physiol. Psychol.*, 1964, **57**, 307–309.

SAWREY, J. M. and SAWREY, W. L. Age, weight, and social effects on ulceration rate in rats. *J. comp. physiol. Psychol.*, 1966, **61**, 464–466.

SAWREY, W. L. Conditioned responses of fear in relationship to ulceration. *J. comp. physiol. Psychol.*, 1961, **54**, 347–348.

SAWREY, W. L., CONGER, J. J., and TURREL, E. S. An experimental investigation of the role of psychological factors in the production of gastric ulcers in rats. *J. comp. physiol. Psychol.*, 1956, **49**, 457–461.

SAWREY, W. L., and LONG, D. H. Strain and sex differences in ulceration in the rat. *J. comp. physiol. Psychol.*, 1962, **55**, 603–605.

SAWREY, W. L., and SAWREY, J. M. Fear conditioning and resistance to ulceration. *J. comp. physiol. Psychol.*, 1963, **56**, 821–823.

SAWREY, W. L. and SAWREY, J. M. Conditioned fear and restraint in ulceration. *J. comp. physiol. Psychol.*, 1964, **57**, 150–151.

SAWREY, W. L., and WEISZ, J. D. An experimental method of producing gastric ulcers. *J. comp. physiol. Psychol.*, 1956, **49**, 269–270.

SCOTT, J. P. Dominance and the frustration-aggression hypothesis. *Physiol. Zool.*, 1948, **21**, 31–39.

SEARS, R. R. Initiation of the repression sequence by experienced failure. *J. exp. Psychol.*, 1937, **20**, 570–580.

SEARS, R. R., HOVLAND, C. I., and MILLER, N. E. Minor studies of aggression: I. Measurement of aggressive behavior. *J. Psychol.*, 1940, **9**, 275–295.

SEARS, R. R., and SEARS, P. S. Minor studies of aggression: V. Strength of frustration reaction as a function of strength of drive. *J. Psychol.*, 1940, **9**, 297–300.

SELYE, H. *The Stress of Life*. New York: McGraw-Hill Book Company, 1956.

SKINNER, B. F. Drive and reflex strength. *J. gen. Psychol.*, 1932, **6**, 22–37.

STAMFORD, J. W., and HSU, E. H. Experimental frustration in human adults. *J. clin. Psychol.*, 1948, **4**, 269–276.

TELFORD, C. W., and SAWREY, J. M. *The Exceptional Individual: Psychological and Educational Aspects.* Englewood Cliffs, N.J.: Prentice-Hall, 1967.

THOMPSON, W. R., and HERON, W. The effects of early restriction of activity in dogs. *J. comp. physiol. Psychol.*, 1954, **47**, 77–92.

THOMPSON, W. R., and MELZACK, R. Early environment. *Scient. Amer.*, 1956, **194**, No. 1, 38–42.

THORNDIKE, E. L. Animal intelligence; an experimental study of the associative processes in animals. *Psychol. rev. monogr. suppl.*, 1898, **2**, No. 4 (whole No. 8).

UNDERWOOD, B. J. *Experimental Psychology.* New York: Appleton-Century-Crofts, 1949.

VERPLANK, W. S. A glossary of some terms used in the objective science of behavior. *Psychol. Rev.* (supp.), 1957, **8**, No. 6, Pt. 2, 1–42.

WAGNER, A. R. The role of reinforcement and nonreinforcement in an apparent frustration effect. *J. exp. Psychol.*, 1959, **57**, 130–136.

WATSON, J. B. Experimental Studies on the Growth of Emotions. In *Psychologies of 1925.* Worcester, Mass.: Clark University Press, 1926.

WENINGER, O. The effects of early experience on behavior and growth characteristics. *J. comp. physiol. Psychol.*, 1956, **49**, 1–9.

ZANDER, A. F. A study of experimental frustration. *Psychol. Monogr.*, 1944, **56**, No. 256.

*Part* III

*Higher Levels of
Personality Organization*

# Chapter 10

# Attitudes, Ideals, Values, and the Self

A DISCUSSION OF THE ORIGIN AND NATURE of ideals and character must include a consideration of values. The term "value," as used here, refers to the abstract concept of desirability in a moral or ethical sense. It has reference to a person's implicit evaluation of either means or ends as desirable or undesirable, good or bad, right or wrong. Although values are often preceived as inherent in the objects or acts themselves, they are really functions of the valuing individual. Valuing is a component or accompaniment of the process of reacting to objects, acts, or goals. A value system is a more or less coherent set of values that tends to guide a person's conduct, often without his being aware that they do so. One's value system is often reified as moral character, as conscience, or as a superego—an inner voice that tells the individual what is right and wrong.

It is possible to distinguish four different conceptions of the nature and origin of "conscience," or one's value system. The first of these is the historical-theological conception, which is still accepted by the "man on-the-street" as "common sense." According to this conception, man is born with a conscience—an innate sense of right and wrong. The strength and explicitness of conscience, which operates as an inner voice, may vary from person to person, but everyone is born with at least a rudimentary sense of right and wrong. This inner guide to conduct is God-given as a part of man's inherent nature. When man lives in keeping with this internal guide he feels right and he is good. When he violates the dictates of the inner voice, he has pangs of conscience and feels guilty. Conscience, or at least the rudiments of conscience, are universal and absolute and are a part of divinity.

The next two conceptions both assume that conscience has a social origin. One of these, the psychoanalytic, considers conscience (the super-ego) the complete "introjection" or internalization of the pattern of parental prohibitions and punishments or threats. The other social origin conception of conscience is a "social learning" interpretation. This, like the psychoanalytic concept, holds that conscience represents the internalization of social patterns of reinforcement. The social learning theorists, however, consider conscience more diverse in its social origins and more subject to modification throughout life. The social learning conception considers conscience the internalization of patterns of reinforcements (rewards and punishment, social approvals and disapprovals) of one's entire cultural heritage. The social learning theorists conceive of conscience roughly as we have earlier defined a value system—as a more or less coherent set of acquired evaluative tendencies or standards that have behavioral, feeling, and ideational components. In other words, conscience is a tendency to feel, act, and believe in certain ways with reference to situations, acts, and ends perceived within a desirable-undesirable frame of reference. The social learning theorists consider conscience more modifiable and more variable than do either the classical theologicians or the Freudians. They also consider conscience to involve approving and confirming as well as inhibiting and guilt-producing mechanisms. The social learning interpretation also provides room for a more humanistic-rationalistic conscience than do the theological and psychoanalytic concepts. It holds that approvals and disapprovals, instead of being evoked automatically in a programmed sort of way, consist partially of moral principles derived from a reflective and rational consideration of value systems and their relevance to the unique circumstance under consideration.

A fourth conception of the origin and nature of one's value system or conscience is the humanistic one. The people who subscribe to this point of view attempt to derive a universal morality from the inherent nature of man. Dissatisfied with the relativism of the social learning and psychoanalytic conceptions, they, like the classical theologicians, assume that the basis of conscience and morality is inborn. According to the humanistic conception, man is born with certain capacities and potentials. In addition, he has the one overriding *drive* to actualize his capacities—to fulfill his potential. The development of one's potential consists of growth from within rather than an acquisition from without. The *good* is anything that contributes to the unfolding and development of this inherent potential as it is actuated by the drive for self-realization. Anything that frustrates or inhibits, or twists man's inherent nature or the directions that it normally takes, is *bad*. Psychopathology represents the consequences of the frustration or distortion of man's potentialities and their self-actualization. Psychotherapy helps restore the individual to the path of self-actualization and permits his development along the lines that his inner nature dictates.

Since man's potential is genetically based and is characteristic of the entire human species, and the unfolding and developing of this potential to its maximum is always good, this provides the basis for a universal morality, devoid of the supernatural overtones of the classical theological conceptions. The present-day humanistic moralists are primarily individual-centered, and have considerable difficulty relating self-actualization to the demands and expectancies of diverse cultures. People who subscribe to this point of view seem to assume that the relatively unfettered natural unfolding of one's potential as impelled by the self-actualizing drive not only represents the individual's personal good but also leads to maximum social welfare. The *best* society is the one that is most permissive of man's personal self-realization. Such a conception seems to assume a relationship between man's innate nature and the necessities of social life. It seems to require a return to the notion of social instincts—an inborn set of socially appropriate reaction tendencies. Some humanistic moralists are claiming as much (*McCall, 1963; White, 1959; Rogers, 1963*).

In the introduction we indicated our commitment to a social learning point of view. We propose to deal with the topics of values, conscience, and moral character primarily from this point of view. We find the social learning interpretation to be most consistent with the available evidence, to have the broadest explanatory scope, and to minimize the temptation to reify processes, to postulate special agencies and forces, and to substitute names for explanations. While we believe that the humanistic point of view has much to recommend it, we feel that the facts of self-actualization can be handled more satisfactorily within a social learning frame of reference. We consider the goals and directions of self-realization to be socially derived. The motivational component of self-actualization results from the self-reinforcement that occurs whenever the individual performs certain classes of responses or perceives himself as moving toward goals that he has come to value as indices of personal worth. In other words, reducing the distance between where one is and where he aspires to be and diminishing the discrepancy between what one is (his present self) and what he would like to be (his ideal self) operate as rewards and motivate continued progress toward these goals. We shall develop this topic more fully in a later chapter.

In the following discussions attitudes, ideals, values, and moral character are assumed to be the products of social learning.

## *ATTITUDES*

### Nature

An attitude is a relatively persistent, acquired tendency to respond in a consistent way toward a given class of people, objects, or concepts. The attitudinal response tendency includes overt (motor), ideational (belief), and affective (emotional) components. In other words, an attitude is a relatively permanent acquired predisposition to act, believe, and feel in a somewhat uniform way toward certain perceptual or conceptual objects.

Attitudes are not observed directly. They are inferred from the consistency of behavior that an individual displays toward a group of similar situations or objects. Attitudes are postulated to account for certain persistent and consistent behavioral trends. For example, when a person consistently avoids contact with the members of a given race, when he displays signs of disgust and displeasure in their presence or whenever someone mentions them, and when he repeatedly makes derogatory remarks about the members of that race, we infer that he possesses negative attitudes toward that racial group. The inferred negative attitude (prejudice) is then used to account for the observed behavior.

The three components of an attitude previously mentioned consist of the following: (1) The overt response tendency. An attitude represents a tendency to act in certain ways (toward or away from) with reference to a given class of persons, things, or ideas. (2) The ideational component. An attitude typically includes a belief or set of beliefs (that a given class or race of people are deceitful or honest, inferior or superior). (3) The affective component. The person, possessing an attitude, has definite feelings about the related people, objects, or ideas. He likes or dislikes them. He has pleasant or unpleasant feelings whenever he sees, or hears, or thinks about them. An attitude represents a fusion of behavioral, ideational, and affective elements.

### Origin

When we identify attitudes as *acquired* predispositions to act, think, and feel in certain ways, we indicate that they are learned; however, most attitudes are not acquired formally and consciously. Instead, they are acquired incidentally from our social environment. Most of our attitudes are absorbed from those about us without our being aware of the fact.

Experiments have demonstrated that attitudes can be learned by ordinary associative means without the subject's awareness. For example, if a given name is frequently associated with a consistent evaluative meaning (as good or bad), the name will come to be liked or disliked without the subject being aware of the reason for his preference (*Staats and Staats, 1958; Tach and Cantril, 1957; Rhine and Silun, 1958*). A color preference for yellow was established in children by consistently rewarding (reinforcing) the choice of a given class of objects (rectangular blocks) of this color. It was then found that these children showed an increased preference for yellow eggs, toy cars, or shoes as compared to the pre-training condition. Thus, a color preference (positive attitude) developed in one situation with one class of objects generalized to quite different situations and objects (*Eisman, 1955*). This is an example of stimulus generalization.

A person is born into a given culture, subculture, community, and family, and unconsciously acquires the prevailing attitudes of these groups. He acquires them unknowingly and therefore accepts them uncritically. The prevailing attitudes and beliefs of his group seem self-evident and not in need of proof. When a person finds himself with certain attitudes, the origins of which he is unaware and that are shared by all, or most, of his acquaintances, he assumes that they are innate or at least are universally accepted, self-evident truths.

The affective components or accompaniments of attitudes contribute to the apparent self-evident nature of attitudes. The prevailing cultural attitudes are not only the correct ones, they are the "good" ones, the desirable ones. We feel that our culturally transmitted, ready-made attitudes are good and right—they are pleasantly affectively toned. This affective element makes the attitudes seem inherently correct.

## Relation to Ideals, Value Systems, and the Self

Just as attitudes represent a higher level of personality organization as compared with the more specific defense mechanisms, so ideals, value systems, and the self constitute still higher levels of personality integration as compared with attitudes. These levels are "higher" in the sense that they are more complex and more general in their nature. For example, a person may, on the lowest level, *rationalize* his emotionally motivated behavior to prove to others and to himself that he is not an impulsive, irrational person. On a higher level, he may develop a prejudice against impulsive, emotional people and a preference for orderly, predictable, logical individuals. On a still higher organizational level, he may internalize an ideal of rationality. Rational people are "good" people; he approves of rationality in himself and in others. He strives to reduce any observed discrepancy between his own behavior and his ideal of rationality. On a somewhat more complex level, his ideal of rationality may become part of a value system that puts a high premium on orderliness, dependability, rationality, and predictability in general. On the highest level of personality organization is the "self," which, in turn, is superordinate to the more specific and simpler behavior systems already listed. On this level, the person may eventually become an orderly, systematic, predictable, rational person and rate himself very highly in terms of his value system. He sees very little discrepancy between his ideal of rationality, his value system of orderliness, and his ideal self, on the one hand, and his own behavior, on the other. His self-concept requires that he rationalize his own behavior, like rational people, value rationality, and be an all-round orderly and predictable person.

## *IDEALS*

### Nature

Ideals differ from attitudes in that they are more general in nature. They refer to a larger group of situations or actions. Ideals represent a relatively high level of conceptual organization and exert a unifying and integrating influence on a person's behavior. An ideal is the personal level of conduct toward which one strives. It is a standard of behavior that a person uses to evaluate his own acts. Ideals constitute one of the enduring and more general aspects of an individual's nature.

Ideals always have an evaluative component. They represent the desirable levels of action. The evaluative element is more prominent in ideals than it is in attitudes; ideals are evaluative concepts.

### Origin

Ideals develop in the same way as nonevaluative concepts. Their evaluative dimension is acquired from the social environment. They also develop in the same way as attitudes. They differ from attitudes only in their higher level of abstraction and their greater prominence of the evaluative component.

The basic pattern of the conceptual abstraction and the development of the evaluative dimensions of attitudes, ideals, and values is fairly simple. However, the ramifications of the outcomes of the process of concept

formation are infinite. The ideational conceptual component often represents a hierarchy of meanings that are abstracted in the same way that a
hierarchy of concepts relating to quantity develop. The number concepts
of "oneness" and "twoness" develop at one conceptual level. At a higher
level of abstraction a concept of "number" evolves, and at a still higher
level the idea of "quantity" may be abstracted. Similarly the concepts of
dog and cat, quadrupeds and mammals, animals, and living things come to
be abstracted as different levels in a hierarchy. In a similar way particular
instances of correspondence between the "facts" as known and one's
statements regarding these "facts" come to be abstracted as "truth telling"
as contrasted with "lying"; obtaining property by purchase, barter, or as
gifts becomes a legitimate way of getting things as contrasted with "stealing"; observing the codified and uncodified social mores in dealing with
other people becomes "fairness" as contrasted with "deceitfulness." Being
truthful in one's statements and fair in dealing with others and obtaining
property in approved ways are, in turn, conceptualized on a still higher
hierarchical level as "being honest" as contrasted with "being dishonest."

The essential difference between the development of the purely
cognitive numerical and animal concepts, on the one hand, and the
honesty concept, on the other, is the greater affective-evaluative component of the latter. The specific acts that are abstracted at one level as
truthfulness and fairness are not only "correct" or "appropriate" cogni-

Individual acts or statements | Intermediate level of abstraction | Level of ideals

Saying "I did it," "I don't know," "I took it," when these statements are true. → Truth telling

Abiding by the rules of the game. Being impartial in dealing with others. → Being straightforward → Being honest

Earning money to buy things, Receiving things as gifts, Obtaining goods by barter, (In contrast to stealing.) → Being fair and obtaining goods legitimately

*Figure 13. The development of ideals.*

tively; they are also "good" as a consequence of the consistent social approval associated with them and the social disapproval associated with the opposites—lying, cheating, and stealing. With consistent positive social reinforcement (rewarding) of "good" acts and negative reinforcement (punishment) of the opposite "bad" responses, an evaluative dimension is added to the purely intellectual (meaning) component of the concept. The diagrams of Figure 13 may help clarify this process.

It is probably an over-simplification to consider attitudes, ideals, value systems, and the self-concept as various conceptual levels in a hierarchy but, to some extent, they are.

## Function

Attitudes, ideals, value systems, and even the self-concept are considered to be social products. They are products of experience that serve to condition and control further activity and experience. Although they are products of social learning, they are internalized and then become autonomous and function relatively independently of external circumstances. As internal, partially autonomous determiners of behavior, they serve both as anchoring points in integrating social perceptions and as predispositions to act in consistent ways toward classes of objects, persons, and situations. In this way they contribute to the consistency and continuity of one's perception and behavior, and even to one's sense of being.

A person's attitudes, ideals, value systems, and self-concept are also important motivationally, as was shown more fully in earlier chapters. He "feels right" when he acts consistently with these internalized systems and he feels uneasy or anxious or suffers "pangs of conscience" when he acts in ways that conflict with them. He therefore has a general tendency to behave consistently with these predispositions. He also does what he can to bolster and maintain them. These predispositions are partially responsible for the persistent and consistent behavior toward families of related persons, situations, and objects.

### VALUE SYSTEMS

Value systems have much the same characteristics as do attitudes and ideals, but they have a more explicit evaluative judgmental component. They represent a superordinate level of personality integration. A person's value systems represent a more or less coherent, integrated set of ideals having common elements that regulate his conduct and experience. They are abstract concepts of "worth" that typically function without the individual's awareness. Value systems, like attitudes and ideals, are not the products of the individual's own original judgments. They are social products that have been accepted and used as the person's own criteria of worth.

## THE "SELF"

It will be necessary to differentiate three aspects of the self. These are the physical self, the social self, and the self-concept. The self begins as the physical self, the boundaries of which must be discovered by the infant. The self, defined in terms of its physical limits, its organic sensations, and its limited contacts with its immediate environment, is of relatively short duration.

As the child becomes aware of the social as contrasted with the nonsocial aspects of his environment, he comes to act differentially to them. He develops ways of responding to the presence of other people that differ from his behavior when he is alone. He acquires a set of social habits—a social self. To the degree that he learns to act differently in the presence of different groups of people, he becomes a multiple social self.

While the individual is discovering his physical self and developing a social self, he is also acquiring a "self-portrait" of the kind of person he is. He is developing a "self-concept."

A person's physical self is "given" to him; he only discovers it. His organic make-up sets limits to his competences. His size, strength, physique, and sensory make-up may enlarge or restrict the range of his possible acquisitions. Because of the social evaluations of his physical make-up, his physical characteristics may indirectly influence both his social self and his self-concept. The period of life during which the self is purely a physical self is normally very short. However, the mentally deficient person who has such a limited capacity for learning that he lives his life as a "vegetative idiot" probably never progresses beyond the stage of the physical self.

The average child very early in life progresses from a condition of simple awareness of his physical self to the level of social awareness and differential social responsiveness. Whereas the child is born a physical self, he *acquires* a social self. The person's integrated set of socially relevant response tendencies develops as the result of his inevitable social interaction with other people. His physical characteristics may impede or facilitate social acceptance. They may be important determiners of other people's treatment of him, which in turn influences his own social behavior. Thus, although a person's physical self soon becomes relatively unimportant in itself, it may be a significant determiner of other people's evaluation of him which, in turn, may greatly influence his social self.

As soon as the child becomes socially sensitive, he begins to develop a "self-concept." The child very early in life accepts as valid other people's judgments of him and his characteristics. As the result of other people's treatment of him, he comes to have a general idea of the kind of a person he is and begins to act in accordance with his "self-concept."

An individual's "self-concept" eventually becomes a more important determiner of behavior than either his physical potential—his physical self—or his social competences—his social self. In other words, a person is more likely to act according to what he thinks he is and believes he can do than according to what he actually is or is physically capable of doing.

The "social self" constitutes the highest level of personality organization. It represents a superordinate integration of the more specific behavior patterns, attitudes, ideals, and value systems. The social self is not a thing. It is an individual's current level of personality organization and has many lower-order systems within it. People differ markedly in the degree of permanence and stability with which the self is organized. The self of some

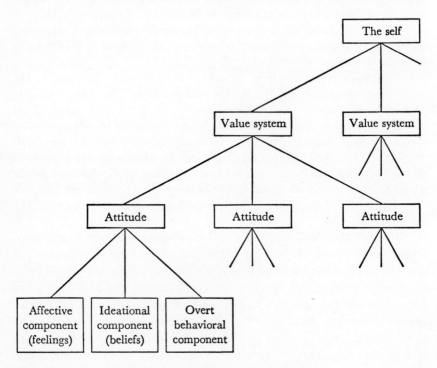

Figure 14. A hierarchy of levels of personality integration.

individuals is a very loosely organized pattern of different selves with a small core of elements common to all of them. Each of these selves may be quite distinct and may operate with considerable autonomy. Such cases are typified by the classical dual or multiple personalities, of which some ten or twelve have been described in the literature of psychology.

For other poorly integrated individuals, the "self" consists of the various "roles" that the individual characteristically plays in life. These roles are evoked by the social group with which he is placed. With such individuals the self is situationally determined. Lacking the stabilizing influence of a well integrated self and a stable self-concept, these people display differing characteristics with different groups of people (other-directed people).

Most individuals are neither purely self-directed nor other-directed. They are, to some extent, both. They act somewhat differently and show different characteristics according to their face-to-face relationships with other groups and individuals. They develop and play various roles in life, and may even conceive of themselves as quite different people in their various roles; however, there is a large core of personal characteristics and behavior traits that are constant factors in their lives. The individual internalizes his roles to some degree and may come to "be" these roles that were originally situationally induced.

### EMERGENCE OF THE SELF-CONCEPT

The emergence of the "self-concept" goes on concomitantly with the development of the "social self." The "self-concept" refers to the individual as known to himself. His self-concept is his conception of the kind of a person he is.

As already indicated, the self-concept is more important than the "real self" in determining behavior. In other words, what I do or try to do, what I achieve or try to achieve, how I relate to other people, how anxious or relaxed I am, or how neurotic or psychotic I become may be more closely related to my self-concept and various factors relating to it than they are to my "real self." Certainly what a person believes may be a more important determiner of his behavior than the "facts" that he does not believe. If he believes that I am his enemy he will act in accordance with this belief irrespective of my true feelings toward him. If he believes himself to be dependent, inadequate, and inferior, this belief will dictate his actions and, to some degree, his probabilities of success. The emergence of the social self and the self-concept are coincident with each other.

The listing of steps always suggests a chronological sequence of events. To some extent the steps indicating the development of the self and the self-concept do occur in a given order, but the steps overlap in time. For example, a person continues to differentiate between people and groups of people all his life.

## Differentiation Between Physical Self and Environment

The child originally does not differentiate himself from the rest of the world. He does not recognize the boundaries of his own body. He learns to make this distinction as the result of the differential effects of contact with his own body as compared with other things. When the child touches the bed, the bedclothes, or other people, he has an experience of contact from his own body part (hand) making the contact; however, when he touches his own body he has a double experience. He has an experience from both of the parts of the body in contact with each other. If he pinches the bedclothes he has a cutaneous-kinesthetic experience from the hand, but when he pinches his own nose, he experiences contact, pain, and restriction of respiration in addition to finger pressure. The sensory consequences of exploring his own physical self are quite different from his exploration of the other objects in his environment. As the result of a succession of such experiences, the child learns the limits of his physical self; he learns to differentiate between himself and the rest of the world.

Although the infant learns this distinction early in life, any marked change in the sensory feedback from a body part may modify the person's conception of that part. An adult suffering from a paralysis and anesthesia of one side of the body may experience the affected part as something foreign to him, or he may feel as if the paralyzed side of the body were missing. Some patients regard their paralyzed limbs as strange, ugly, disfigured, or shortened (*Fisher and Cleveland, 1958*).

## Differentiation Between Persons and Things

The typical infant of a few months begins to distinguish between the human and nonhuman parts of his environment. At least, at two to four months of age, the child begins to show differential responses to the human voice as contrasted with nonhuman sounds (*Munn, 1961*).

The distinction between persons and things is based on the relative stability and predictability of persons as contrasted with objects, and on their differential responsiveness to the child's activities. People are constantly moving about; they appear and disappear. They change their appearance periodically. As contrasted with people, the bed, bedclothes, walls, and doors remain quite stable as stimuli. Things do nothing when the child is hungry, thirsty, cold, or in pain; however, when he squirms, twists, and cries, people move about. They minister to his needs. They are the food and warmth providers and the irritant removers. They are also sources of pleasureable experiences in the form of holding, patting, and rocking. Inanimate objects do none of these things. Thus, the child come to differentiate two classes of environmental stimuli—people and objects— that stand for quite different groups of experience. If this distinction begins as early as two to four months, it overlaps in time the child's learning to differentiate between himself and the rest of the world.

## Differentiation Between Categories of People

After people have been differentiated from things, the next distinction to be learned is among groups or categories of people. This distinction probably precedes the child's coming to differentiate between individuals. Women as typified by mother or nurse are recognized as different from men as represented by father. This differentiation depends upon two things: (1) the difference in appearance of the two groups and (2) their differential responsiveness to the child's needs. Certain classes of people (women) are more regularly present. They respond more readily and uniformly to the child's responses (crying). They provide food, warmth, and other positive satisfactions more regularly than men do. Thus, women come to be more significant patterns of stimulation than men.

Another finer distinction for the child is between smiling and scowling faces, caressing and scolding tones, and inviting and threatening gestures (*Spitz, 1946; Munn, 1961*). The infant comes to differentiate among classes of people and categories of human responses. Of course, the continuous differentiation of groups of people on the basis of differential appearance, activity, and origins never ceases. The child learns to recognize not only categories of people and classes of responses (smiling, frowning); he also comes to differentiate characteristically organized acts or roles. Some groups of people and some roles become much more important to the child than others.

## Differentiation Among Individuals

The pattern of differentiation among individuals proceeds along exactly the same lines as does the differentiation of groups of people or classes of response. Some people stand out as potent sources of pain or pleasure. They become particularly significant individuals whose favor is courted. These significant people and groups play an important part in the development of the child's self-concept.

## Development of the Social Self

Because people, early in the child's life, become important sources of pleasure and pain, they constitute prepotent stimuli for him. People become more important than other objects because they respond to the child's responses whereas things do not. The child also learns that people treat him somewhat according to what he does. Consequently he learns to act in certain ways in the presence of others and these may differ considerably from his ways of acting when he is alone. He develops a set of social habits that characteristically function only when he is in the presence of other people. These social habits become integrated into a "social self."

While people differ considerably in their social sensitivity and responsiveness, every individual develops a social self that is somewhat different from his nonsocial self. The following common experience demonstrates this fact. A person enters a room and remains there for some time believing that he is alone, only to discover that someone else has been in the room all the time. His first reaction is to give a start and then think back over everything that he has done since entering the room to see if he has acted as he should when others are present. If his retrospective survey is satisfactory, he feels relieved; if it is not, he is a bit chagrined. Everyone develops a social self that, to some extent, differs from his nonsocial self.

The development of the social self is the outcome of a person's attempts to elicit favorable responses from other people. One way of doing this is to get people to think favorably of him; they then expect him to act in certain "good" ways. He, in turn, tries to behave consistently with his conception of what others think of him and expect him to do.

## Extensions of the Self

The child is not very old before he makes various extensions of his "self." These extensions occur because of other people's evaluation of him in terms of things other than the physical self and its acts. The child discovers that his value in the eyes of others is partly a result of his competences and his behavior (earned prestige), but is also the result of certain assigned values that accrue to him from things extraneous to himself and his acts. Such things are his clothes, his toys and other possessions; his family, their possessions and reputation; his racial, religious, club, and social class affiliations; his clique, gang, community, city, state, and national groups all contribute to the self as perceived by others as well as to his own self-concept. The extensions of the self also come to include his ideas, beliefs, attitudes, ideals, and value systems. These all come to be considered a part of the individual's self. When these things are valued highly by others, the individual experiences an expansion of the self and an increment of personal value and prestige. When these extensions of the self are downgraded, the individual feels personally belittled. A person comes to react to remarks and events relating to these extensions of the self much as though these same things were similarly related to his physical or social self.

The form and extent of ego-involvement in these various extensions of the self vary from person to person. The miser has a strong identification with his money; the farmer feels that his land is a part of him; the owner and builder of a company sees the organization as an extension of himself; the leader of a religious, social, or political movement may see the growth of his following as the prolongation of his own shadow.

For some people, the self remains closely identified with the physical body. The model, the movie star, the physical culture enthusiast, and the wrestler may remain largely on the physical level in their self-concepts. As they become more beautiful, stronger, or more physically attractive, their egos expand and their self-concepts are inflated. Likewise their feeling of worth diminishes as their physical attractiveness and strength decreases. Their selves remains closely tied to their physiques.

Physical characteristics are always evaluated within a cultural context. Except for the more extreme deviations, what constitutes a physical asset or liability is a matter of social judgment. Every culture has its own standards of physical attractiveness. Our cultural folklore, our fiction, and our movies reflect and stereotype the cultural ideal so far as desirable physical characteristics are concerned.

In the United States people spend billions of dollars each year to bring themselves closer to the culturally defined physical ideal. The self-concepts of many people are either inflated or deflated as they approach or depart from this ideal.

The very young child's self-evaluation is largely a reflection of his evaluation of his physical self. This is partially a result of the stage in his development of his self-concept, but it is also partly a reflection of the frame of reference within which other people evaluate him. Originally the child is judged within a physical framework. He is big or small, shapely or deformed, pretty or ugly. He has a turned-up nose, pretty blue eyes, and mouse-colored hair. He is strong and mature enough to creep, stand, and walk at an early or a late age. Insofar as the child becomes sensitive to social evaluation of himself, this is the framework within which he is judged, and it forms the basis for his early self-evaluation. His self-concept is organically oriented.

As the child matures and expands his world, his self-evaluative frame of reference enlarges and differentiates. If he lives in a musical subculture in which individual worth and status are evaluated in terms of musicianship, and he internalizes these values, his self-concept will be tied up with his musical successes. Physique, as such, becomes relatively unimportant except as it influences musicianship. Size of fingers and hands and strength of arms are significant only if they affect his musical performance. The individual growing up in an intellectual subculture conceives of himself as superior or inferior in terms of his intellectual prowess, while athletic and artistic achievements make only minor contributions to his total self-concept. Corresponding changes in the evaluative framework occur for the individual who develops financial, political, humanitarian, or scientific ambitions.

## Social Class Differences

There seem to be important differences in the extensions of the self related to social class in America. The loyalties and identifications of typical lower-class citizens are largely limited to the members of their own immediate family and friends. The self-involvement of these people is rather circumscribed both in time and place, and is on a personal rather than on a group basis. Their identification with the community, church, school, or other institutions or groups is minimal (*Havighurst and Taba, 1949*). The time orientation of the lower-class individual is characteristically short. His identification with his ancestors is slight, and his projected plans for the future are in terms of immediate rather than long-term goals.

The extensions of the self are considerably broadened for the average middle-class individual. Members of this social class devote much time to community, church, school, and social club affairs, and are typically very loyal to these organizations. They make relatively long-range plans for themselves and their children. Middle-class parents expand their own selves via the accomplishments of their children.

The members of the upper social classes in America constitute a heterogeneous group, but many of them owe their superior social status to family tradition and name. Such individuals identify excessively with family line and name. Genealogy, "blood line," and the accomplishments of past generations are important. Many such individuals perceive of themselves as the repositories of the superior characteristics and accomplishments of their ancestors. They feel an obligation to transmit this inheritance to future generations. Their self-identifications have a long time orientation.

## CULTURAL DIFFERENCES

Cross-cultural studies disclose differences in the areas of ego-involvement for different national groups. The "ancestor worship" of the older Chinese culture was characterized by a long time orientation on the part of its adherents. Authority and veneration were the prerogatives of age. The oldest male family member was the patriarch of the group and outranked all others in reputed wisdom and virtue and acknowledged authority. Such authority did not originate with the individual himself, but derived from the accomplishments and good name of numerous forebears reaching back many centuries. The patriarch served as the ancestors' agent and was the repository of the ancestral virtues, accomplishments, and good name. Each family member can contribute to or subtract from his ancestral inheritance by his personal achievements; thus ambition functions within such an ancestral tradition, and meritorious achievements are important more because they enhance the ancestral name and tradition than because they increase the status of the individual. Achievement and merit belong more to parents, family, and ancestors than to the individual (*Hsu, 1953*). In such a culture the self has a very extended temporal frame of reference.

## DEVELOPMENT OF THE SELF-CONCEPT

While the child is learning to differentiate among the various components of his social environment, he is also learning who he is and what he is. At the same time that he is learning the limits of his physical self, the difference between people and things, and the significance of certain individuals in his life, he is also becoming aware of the kind of person he is. He is developing a "self-concept."

This self-concept is largely a social product. It seems doubtful that a Robinson Crusoe, devoid of previous human contacts and without a man Friday, would have a self-concept that would extend beyond the physical self. He would discriminate between himself and the rest of the world, but the various "extensions" of his self would depend upon the reflected evaluations of other people. An isolated person can develop some notion of his own competences. He can lift a given stone but not another; he can control some but not all animals. He can climb certain mountains but not others. He can swim some but not all rivers. However, whether he is strong or weak, big or small, ugly or beautiful, sinful or virtuous requires standards, comparisons, and evaluations in terms of other people.

The child raised in a normal social environment does not objectively compare his own competences with those of others and then develop a notion of the kind of a person he is as a result of a series of such self-comparisons. Rather, he is born into a given culture with criteria and standards of worth already defined and established. From the moment of birth, the child is subject to a set of built-in reinforcements (rewards or punishments) for being or failing to be a certain type of person and for doing or not doing certain things. He comes to evaluate himself and his worthiness as an individual in terms of these social reinforcements, which consist largely of the reflected appraisals of other people.

Originally the child appraises himself and develops his self-concept in terms of what the parents and others close to him manifest by means of physical punishment and rewards, facial expressions, gestures, and words. A six-year-old boy, when asked if he was good, thought for a moment and then said, "My mother says I am, so I guess I am."

The child also gains a larger frame of reference for self-evaluation when he observes how others are treated in comparison with himself. If an only child is constantly praised and rewarded, he may come to conceive of himself as "good" in a kind of absolute way. However, when he has opportunities to compete with others for attention, affection, and status he becomes strong or weak, ugly or beautiful, superior or inferior in comparison. He, in time, comes to conceive of himself in much the same way that he thinks others perceive him. If other people, particularly the most important people in his world, display respecting, approving, and loving attitudes toward him, he comes to view himself in a favorable light. If they are derogatory or hateful toward him, he develops a low self-concept. The child, and, to a large degree, the adult, has no other measure of his own value than the recognition he receives or has received from others.

The individual eventually comes to accept as valid the judgments of other people concerning his worth. When he finds that other people consider him to be a given type of person and expect him to act in certain ways he tends to accept the roles assigned to him and act in accordance with these expectancies.

The expectations of others that come to be accepted dictate an individual's behavior and finally become internalized and incorporated into his self-concept. When this happens, he thinks of himself as having the characteristics that others have ascribed to him and he expects himself to behave in ways that are congruent with these characteristics. His own role expectations are built up on the basis of his perception of others' evaluations of him. In other words, my self-concept is largely my idea of "my neighbor's" idea of me (Cooley, 1907). In both fact and fiction, people who have been erroneously reported missing, declared dead, and duly mourned have been reluctant to disclose their identities and upset everyone by "coming to life." This has formed the theme for many works of fiction.

Conformity to social group expectancies may be either temporary or relatively permanent. Most people have had the experience of formally or informally, intentionally or accidentally, participating as a member of a group for some time. A person discovers that the members of the group hold views, condone certain acts, and behave in ways that are not in keeping with his own beliefs and practices. Such an individual is often reluctant to disclose his divergence from the group. The longer he lets the misconception go uncorrected, the greater is his reluctance to correct it. If his convictions are not very strong, and if he is strongly influenced by the others' conceptions of him, he may go along with the group rather than declare his own divergent views. What starts out as acquiescence may first develop into passive acceptance, then be followed by half-hearted participation, and finally become a genuine acceptance and active participation as a member of the group.

Many people have had the experience of being strongly suspected of either committing a crime or performing some unworthy act. If the evidence is so overwhelming that one thinks his friends are convinced of his guilt, he is often so disturbed that he begins to act in a "guilty manner" and even experiences vague feelings of guilt.

An ex-convict finds it very difficult to play the part of a respectable, law-abiding citizen among people who know of his past. Having lived as a guilty man among people who take guilt for granted and treat him as a convict—an outcast from society—he has come to live the role, thinks of himself in this way, and finds it very difficult to develop a new self and a new self-concept. It is much easier for him to start a new life among strangers who are ignorant of his past delinquencies. Among strangers, he is free of the influence of expectant attitudes of other people and free of his feeling that others think of him as a criminal and expect him to act like one.

The tendency to conform to one's conception of other people's expectations may be reciprocal and result in the prolongation of the enactment of a role which is mutually distasteful. Many personal quarrels and family feuds have been greatly prolonged merely because each person felt that the other expected him to act like an enemy. Each person assumes that his social "role" is reciprocated. Teachers and parents require students and offspring as complements to their roles. Personal dependency assumes a counterpart. Of course, dependent social relationships can be mutual, just as enemies are. One person has a hard time acting as an enemy if the other person refuses to act similarly. When a former enemy acts in a friendly way, there is a strong tendency for one to respond to the implied expectancy and behave similarly.

Whether we recognize it or not, we are very much "our brother's keeper." As societies' representative, we convince him that he is what we say he is. To some extent, we force him to maintain and either actually live or play the role to which we have assigned him. These commands are no less commands because they are disguised as social expectations. When we label a person a sissy, a liar, a thief, a juvenile delinquent, a cripple, a "dago," "wop," or "nigger," we may be indicating a social stereotype—a role-expectancy—that the individual may accept. He may act in accordance with this role-expectancy.

## Cultural Values as Determiners

We are seldom aware of the norms of our own culture. They tend to be accepted as the natural design of the universe. However, one's worth as an individual is unconsciously measured in terms of these norms. Contemporary American culture tends to be highly competitive, and one's value is indicated largely to the degree to which he succeeds in comparison with others.

The American child is permitted a good deal of freedom and may receive a great deal of attention, affection, and approval, but much of it is conditioned on competitive success. If the child is unsuccessful in competitive situations in play, at school, and in sports, approval, attention, and even affection may not be forthcoming. The approval given to the "also ran" for "playing a good game" or "being a good sport" is a poor consolation prize compared with the recognition and admiration afforded to the winner. Lack of success and failure to win may mean loss of admiration and love.

Strength, knowledge, and skill are not important in themselves. They become important for what they mean in competitive situations with others. Parents and teachers may recognize effort and progress toward a goal, but the real test is the individual's standing in comparison with his peers. As a consequence of these differential cultural reinforcements, the child learns to struggle for position and power. This conditional reinforcement makes him try to outdo and displace his rivals.

The child's self-concept is conditioned by his competitive success. The person who always fails may build up defenses against the implications of his failures, but he can hardly develop a satisfactory self-concept without achieving success in some significant areas of endeavor.

Social class is always culturally defined. Higher social classes are defined as those rating high in culturally defined values. Individual members of differing social classes would be expected to have differing self-concepts deriving either from membership in these classes or from the social evaluation of the characteristics that place them in these classes. Research studies support this expectancy. We find different modal self-concepts among members of different socio-economic classes. Members of the same socio-economic groupings have more homogeneous self-concepts than do random samplings of the same population (*Klausner, 1953*).

### THE IDEAL SELF

As the result of the internalization of socially approved attitudes, ideals, and values, each individual develops a concept of an ideal self against which his own self-concept is evaluated. The ideal self represents the composite of those traits, characteristics, and values that the individual would like to possess. It is a conception of the kind of a person he would like to be—the ideal individual.

## Discrepancies Between Self-Concept and Ideal Self

Discrepancies between a person's self-concept and his conception of the ideal self are sources of dissatisfaction and anxiety. Research studies have consistently indicated that a reasonable congruity of a self-concept and a concept of the ideal self is one of the most important conditions for personal happiness and for satisfaction in specific life areas (*Brophy, 1959*). Indices of "general satisfaction" are found to be negatively related to discrepancy between self-concept and ideal self; vocational satisfaction correlates negatively with discrepancies between self-concept and occupational role, and between ideal occupational role and imposed occupational role (*Brophy, 1959*).

Marked discrepancies between the ideal self and the conceived self can be anxiety-arousing, which in turn may result in the various defenses already described. As suggested in an earlier chapter, the neurotic and psychotic reaction patterns are often considered to be reactions to prolonged and overwhelming threat. There is evidence indicating that, as compared with neurosis, psychosis constitutes a more complete resolution of an ideal-self-self-concept discrepancy.

Neurotics characteristically report greater discrepancies between their self- and ideal-self concepts than psychotics. Research on this topic regularly discloses that neurotics have a greater self-ideal discrepancy than either psychotics or normal individuals. Schizophrenic psychotic individuals rate themselves as just as effective in their need-satisfaction patterns as the normals. The neurotics are lowest in this respect (*Hillson and Worchel, 1957*). The psychotic typically has a lower level of aspiration than the normal, whereas the neurotic's aspiration level is unrealistically high. The neurotic groups also make significantly poorer self-evaluations (have lower self-concepts) than either normals or psychotics. Normals and psychotics make practically similar self-evaluations (*Hillson and Worchel, 1957*).

The psychotic's lowering of the ideal self, combined with distortion (unrealistic elevation) of the self-concept, results in a small discrepancy between the ideal and self-concept. This enhancement of himself relative to his ideal avoids the anxiety resulting from any marked discrepancy between the two. The psychotic with highly developed defenses experiences little incongruity between the self- and ideal-self concepts. On the other hand, the neurotic sees himself as markedly inferior to the average person (he has a low self-concept), whereas his ideal self is practically the same as that of the normal. This gives the neurotic a large self-ideal-concept discrepancy, with considerable resulting anxiety. Research studies have quite consistently shown that defensiveness is more a function of discrepancies between the self-concept and the self-ideal rather than of the "facts of objective reality" or the person's insight into the objective reality (*Wylie, 1957*).

### STABILITY OF THE SELF-CONCEPT

It has been indicated that the self-concept is largely the product of the reflected appraisals of the significant individuals and groups making up a person's social environment. Once established, the self-concept tends to remain relatively stable; at least the individual resists efforts to modify it, particularly when the modification would constitute a lowering of his conception of himself. The stability of the self-concept is maintained in the following ways (*Secord and Backman, 1961*):[1]

[1] While we are indebted to Secord and Backman's illuminating article for most of the points developed in this section, we have done considerable violence to their principal contention. Whereas we have conceived of the self-concept as the anchoring point in the maintenance of stability, Secord and Backman insist that behavioral stability (and change) derives from the interpersonal matrix consisting of (a) the individual's self-concept or some aspect of it, (b) the person's interpretation of those elements of his behavior that relate either to his self-concept or the pertinent aspects of his self-concept, and (c) the person's perception of the related aspects and behavior of the person with whom he is interacting. These authors interpret most of the behavior patterns that we have treated as defending and supporting one's self-concept, as attempts to achieve and maintain maximum congruence among the three components of the matrix. Interested readers are referred to the original article.

Some additional concepts dealing with essentially these same behavioral characteristics are Osgood and Tannenbaum's (1955) term "congruence," Cartwright and Harary's (1956) "structural balance," Festinger's (1957) "cognitive dissonance," and Heider's (1958) theory of "balance."

(1) A person tends to repeat and prolong those interpersonal relationships that confirm his own self-concept. For example, the "dependent" individual will prefer to associate with people who assist and support him, since such behavior is congruent with his own picture of himself as a dependent person. The person who is independent will elect to associate with those who recognize and defer to his independence. If such a person is able to mingle with others who are equally independent and value this characteristic so that independence is mutually permissible and rewarded, he will continue to associate with other independent people. On the other hand, if a person who conceives of himself as independent finds that other independent people expect him to play a dependent role, he will prefer to associate with more dependent or inferior individuals so that he can be perceived as independent by contrast. Very dependent and independent individuals often find social relationships mutually satisfying because each one's role reciprocates and confirms the other's self-concept. A dependent person may need an independent person for support. The independent person willingly supplies this support and thus, each has the dependent or independent component of his self-concept confirmed.

(2) When a person finds himself in a situation that threatens the validity of his self-concept, he will try to modify the situation in such a way as to maintain the stability of the picture he has of himself. For example, an individual who perceives himself as intelligent and finds that he is unable to play the part when the topics under discussion are foreign to him may try to introduce into the discussion topics on which his intelligence will be obvious.

(3) People who mutually support and confirm each other's self-concepts develop reciprocal affectionate relationships (they come to like each other), and strive to perpetuate their social interactions. This mechanism is operative in many "mutual admiration societies" wherein the members' activities are congruent with each other's roles.

(4) Each individual establishes social relationships that will maximize the number of his congruent relationships with other people. He will expand his social relationships to the degree that he is able to contact others who behave in such a way as to confirm his own self-concept. If an individual finds relatively few people who act congruently with his self-concept, he may elect to confine his relationships to those people who will behave in this way. In other words, an individual selects and interacts predominantly with those people whose behavior requires a minimum modification of his own self-concept.

For example, when a "dominant" individual finds that the average person reacts to his dominating behavior by "putting him in his place," he finds his self-concept challenged. Such a challenge threatens his conception of himself. A person thus threatened may protect his self-concept by confining his contacts to submissive people who permit him to act in a dominant manner without threatening his notion of the type of individual he is.

(5) People support and increase the esteem of their own self-concepts by their selective evaluation of others. An individual not only likes, but also values highly, those individuals who behave consistently with his own role. The athlete who enjoys mutually congruent and ego-inflating relationships with other athletes will put a high value on such individuals and do what he can to get others to over-value athletic prowess and athletic people.

Conversely, a person will tend to devalue those who, by their behavior toward him, either fail to support or actively challenge his self-concept. The artist whose artistic achievements are questioned sees his detractors as insensitive, ignorant, malicious, or jealous. If his critics can be perceived as jealous, his self-concept as a superior artist is confirmed and the superiority of his achievements is indicated.

(6) The stability of a person's self-concept is protected by selective comparison of himself with those with whom he interacts. An individual selectively attends to and perceives those acts of others that he sees as consistent with or supportive of his self-concept. Out of all that other people say and do, the listener selectively notices, perceives, and remembers those things that support his self-concept. Thus, two people listening to the same lecture come away with quite different interpretations of what was said. One cause of these differing interpretations is the tendency to hear what one wishes to hear (autistic perception), for everyone wishes to hear his own self-concept confirmed.

Conversely, an individual selectively ignores those activities that threaten his self-concept. This perceptive selectivity may amount to an actual misperception of other's activities. This misperception operates to produce a maximum congruency between the perceived behavior of others and one's self-concept. The individual who perceives himself as a "lady killer" perceives women as more interested in him than they really are. The person who perceives himself as inferior sees others as continually belittling him.

In order to maintain the stability of one's self-concept, selectivity of contacts extends to ideas as well as to people. People protect their own beliefs and attitudes by avoiding exposure to contrary points of view (*Papageorgis and McGuire, 1961; Festinger, 1957*). It has also been found that forced exposure to counterarguments may actually produce increased resistance to subsequent very strong, but different, forms of counterarguments. Pre-exposure to arguments that threaten his beliefs motivates the individual to develop supporting arguments and other protective devices that make his beliefs still more resistant to counterarguments encountered later (*Papageorgis and McGuire, 1961*).

(7) A person may develop social techniques for evoking congruent responses from other people. The "clinging vine" acts in such a way as to evoke "protecting" behavior in others. The "good" housewife may "fish" for compliments from others concerning her housekeeping activities. Self-deprecation may be a device for calling attention to and confirming one's superior status and achievements.

(8) The individual acts selectively according to the behavior of others in order to maintain a maximum consistency between his self-concept and the activities of others. Everyone plays varying roles in different situations and with different people or groups of people. No one is entirely consistent in those aspects of himself or in the particular role that he displays in social situations. A person is inclined to play the role and behave in such a way as to produce maximum congruence between his perception of the other person and that component of his self-concept manifesting itself in his behavior. In other words, the person tends to behave so as to maximize congruency between his perception of others and his own self-concept. He will "match" his behavior to that of others in order to minimize his conflict with them and do the least damage to his self-concept. Thus, we may have a person boasting to another person of having done something that he would be ashamed to admit to a third person. We conceive of each person as approving of certain activities and disapproving of other activities, and tend to display to a person those components of our selves of which we think he will approve. To the teacher, the student displays the studious component of himself; to his peers he may show his fun-loving aspects; to his sweetheart he shows those components of himself that will be most congruent with his loved one's expectancies and desires. A person will feel most comfortable in and prefer to play that role which produces maximum consistency among his self-concept, his perception of his own behavior, and his interpretation of the behavior of other people with whom he interacts.

(9) Misinterpretation of a person's own behavior is one means of maximizing congruency between his self-concept and activities that may be inconsistent with his over-all conception of himself. Many of the defense mechanisms discussed in earlier chapters operate in this way. For example, the person who perceives himself as a logical and reasonable person "rationalizes" his impulsive behavior in such a way as to make his behavior congruent with his self-concept. He then perceives his impulsive and irrational behavior as consistent with his concept of himself as a rational person.

## Changes in the Self-Concept

We have stressed the relative stability of the self-concept and have indicated various ways in which people resist changes in their own conceptions of themselves. The self, once established, tends, to some degree, to become autonomous. However, the self-concept does change. To some extent it is constantly changing.

The self-concept is changed in essentially the same ways that it is formed. We have already indicated that the self-concept is largely a function of how the individual is treated by other people. Even though the already established self tends to resist change, it is not impervious to social influences. When his social environment suddenly undergoes drastic and persistent modification, the person's concept of himself is likely to change. When those about him, particularly the significant people whose opinions he values, uniformly behave toward him in new ways, he first questions and then revises his conception of himself. In his own eyes, he becomes a changed person.

The ease with which one's self-concept shifts in accordance with others' evaluations of him, or in accordance with his interpretation of others' evaluation of him, depends upon the rigidity of one's self-concept, the degree and consistency of the modified behavior of others, the effectiveness of one's defenses, and the degree of one's social sensitivity. Early in life, when the self-concept is less clearly defined, inconsistencies between one's notion of himself and others' behavior will be reconciled by changing the self-concept. Older people with well encapsulated self-concepts will show considerable resistance to change, and handle incongruencies by means of defense mechanisms and general distortions of reality.

William James (1907) indicated, in his classical discussion of the self, that an individual may handle the problem of different social groups' evaluating him in different ways by developing a multiple self-concept. A person with such a self-concept will actually conceive of himself quite differently according to his momentary group associations. Thus the academically successful college student may perceive himself as a much more adequate and highly valued person on campus, in his own intellectual group, than in his home community, where his scholastic achievements are less well known and not so highly valued.

One's self-concept changes with age. For the young child, dependence and submissiveness to authority are praiseworthy traits and a means of ego-inflation. But in adolescence these same characteristics are less likely to be highly valued by one's peers. Physical prowess in the boy and youthful beauty in the girl are passports to social esteem more in adolescence than in middle age. Growing up is likely to involve a change in one's self-concept or, at least, a constant change in the nature of the support for one's self-concept. Attempts to re-establish old friendships after prolonged separations often point up the changes that have taken place in one and in one's own conception of himself. While the self-concept normally does have considerable stability, it is a social product and does change in accordance with consistent approvals and disapprovals in interpersonal relationships.

We would expect to find the stability of one's self-concept related to its positive-negative dimensions. This expectancy is supported by the research studies. For example, it has been shown that adolescents with initially positive self-concepts were much more stable over a period of time in their conceptions of themselves than were comparable individuals with initially negative self-concepts (*Engel, 1959*).

### SUMMARY

Defense mechanisms, attitudes, ideals, values, and the self constitute a hierarchy of organizational levels within the personality. This hierarchy represents a series of levels of increasing complexity and generality. Attitudes, ideals, and values also have an evaluative component.

An attitude is a relatively permanent tendency to act in certain ways with reference to given classes of objects or concepts. An attitude has overt behavioral, ideational, and emotional components. It represents a tendency to act, believe, and feel in certain ways toward a given class of perceptual or conceptual objects.

Ideals and values have these same characteristics except that they refer to broader areas of objects, concepts, and experience, and have more of an evaluative component. Ideals and values, like attitudes, are culturally induced. They are absorbed, largely without the individual's awareness, as a part of one's cultural heritage.

Attitudes, ideals, and values are culturally induced but become internalized determiners of behavior. They provide a certain consistency and continuity to one's behavior toward families of related objects, situations, and ideas. They constitute a person's own standards in terms of which his behavior and that of others is judged. These internalized attitudes, ideals, and values constitute important segments of one's "conscience."

The self is the highest level of personality organization. It is not an entity. It is a name given to one's current level of personality integration. There is never complete and perfect integration of the elements comprising the self. To some degree, everyone is a multiple self. Some poorly integrated or dissociated selves become genuine dual or multiple personalities.

One's self-concept develops as a result of the reflected evaluations of other people. A person's self-concept is largely his interpretation of what others think he is. The self-concept is the end product of a lifetime of experiences in which the individual learns to differentiate: (a) his physical self from the rest of the world, (b) among persons and things, (c) among different classes of people, and (d) among different individuals. As a result of his social interaction with the significant people in his life he develops a "social self" and a self-concept, and makes various extensions of his self. His self-concept, once established, becomes autonomous to a considerable degree and is defended against threat in various ways.

## REFERENCES

BROPHY, A. L. Self, role, and satisfaction. *Genet. Psychol. Monogr.*, 1959, **59**, 263–308.

CARTWRIGHT, D., and HARARY, F. Structural balance. *Psychol. Rev.*, 1956, **63**, 277–293.

COOLEY, C. H. *Human Nature and the Social Order.* New York: Scribner, 1907.

EISMAN, B. S. Attitude formation: the development of a color preference response through mediated generalization. *J. abnorm. soc. Psychol.*, 1955, **50**, 321–326.

ENGEL, M. The stability of the self-concept in adolescence. *J. abnorm. soc. Psychol.*, 1959, **58**, 211–215.

FESTINGER, L. *A Theory of Cognitive Dissonance.* Evanston, Ill.: Row, Peterson, 1957.

FISHER, S., and CLEVELAND, S. E. *Body Image and Personality.* New York: D. Van Nostrand, 1958.

HAVIGHURST, R. J., and TABA, H. *Adolescent Character and Personality.* New York: John Wiley and Sons, Inc., 1949.

HEIDER, F. *The Psychology of Interpersonal Relations.* New York: John Wiley and Sons, Inc., 1958.

HILLSON, J. S., and WORCHEL, P. Self-concept and defensive behavior in the maladjusted. *J. consult. Psychol.*, 1957, **21**, 83–88.

HSU, F. L. K. Personality Development in West Town. In Sanders, T. (ed.), *Societies Around the World*, Vol. 2. New York: Dryden Press, 1953.

JAMES, W. *Psychology.* New York: Henry Holt and Company, 1907.

KLAUSNER, S. Z. Social class and self-concept. *J. soc. Psychol.*, 1953, **38**, 201–205.

MASLOW, A. H. *Motivation and Personality.* New York: Harper & Brothers, 1954, 1965.

McCALL, R. J. Invested self-expression, a principle of human motivation. *Psychol. Rev.*, 1963, **70**, 289–303.

MUNN, N. L. *Psychology* (4th ed.). Boston: Houghton Mifflin Company, 1961.

OSGOOD, C. E., and TANNENBAUM, P. H. The principle of congruity in the prediction of attitude change. *Psychol. Rev.*, 1955, **62**, 42–55.

PAPAGEORGIS, D., and McGUIRE, W. J. The generality of immunity to persuasion produced by pre-exposure to weakened counter-arguments. *J. abnorm. soc. Psychol.*, 1961, **62**, 475–481.

RHINE, R. T., and SILUN, BETSY A. Acquisition and change of a concept attitude as a function of consistency of reinforcement. *J. exp. Psychol.*, 1958, **55**, 524–529.

ROGERS, C. R. The Actualization Tendency in Relation to Motives. In Jones, M. R. (ed.), Nebraska Symposium on Motivation. Lincoln: University of Nebraska Press, 1963.

SECORD, P. F., and BACKMAN, C. W. Personality theory and the problem of stability and change in individual behavior. *Psychol. Rev.*, 1961, **68**, 21–32.

SPITZ, R. The smiling response: a contribution to the ontogenesis of social relations. *Genet. Psychol. Monogr.*, 1946, **34**, 57–125.

STAATS, A. W., and STAATS, C. K. Attitudes established by classical conditioning. *J. abnorm. soc. Psychol.*, 1958, **57**, 37–40.

TACH, H., and CANTRIL, H. A preliminary inquiry into the learning of values. *J. educ. Psychol.*, 1957, **48**, 145–156.

WHITE, R. W. Motivation reconsidered: the concept of competence. *Psychol. Rev.*, 1959, **66**, 297–333.

WYLIE, RUTH C. Some relationships between defensiveness and self-concept discrepancies. *J. Pers.*, 1957, **25**, 600–616.

# Chapter 11

# Character and Personality

An INDIVIDUAL'S PERSONALITY represents the highest level of organization of his motives, habits, attitudes, and value systems. Dozens of definitions of personality have been formulated and while no one of these is universally acceptable, there are certain components of personality which are generally agreed upon.

## THE CONCEPT OF PERSONALITY

First, *personality has particular reference to the unique or distinctive characteristics of an individual.* Although we can hardly exclude from consideration those characteristics that are universal human traits, personality gives particular weight to those qualities or combinations of qualities which set one individual apart from others. A person's personality is not distinctively characterized by his being human, or possessing speech, or being normally gregarious. His personality is identified more in terms of how he deviates from the norm in these respects. The individual's personality is characterized by his *unique* organization of dynamic behavioral tendencies.

Second, *personality has a social reference.* It gives particular weight to those distinguishing qualities of an individual that characterize his social relations. Personality has reference to one's social habits and to those aspects of his nature that have developed in social interaction and relate to other people. In practice, personality refers largely to one's socially-relevant physical and behavioral characteristics.

Third, *personality has both a stimulus and a response aspect.* The stimulus component of personality is contained in the root meaning of the term. "Persona," in ancient Rome, was a theatrical mask that an actor wore in order to identify the part he was playing. Thus, personality refers to the socially perceived individual—the individual as he is experienced, evaluated, and responded to by other people. This component of personality is referred to as man's "social stimulus value." It is the impression one makes on other people.

When we describe a person as having a pleasing and gracious, or irritating and obnoxious personality, we are indicating the way the individual impresses other people. We are not describing how he acts, what he says, or his other characteristic reaction patterns. We are registering his effect either on us or on people in general. Personality has a social stimulus-value aspect.

We can also indicate a person's personality in terms of the way he characteristically acts in social situations. When we describe a person as dominant or submissive, aggressive or withdrawn, we are indicating how he characteristically responds in his relations with other people. Personality also has a social response aspect.

Fourth, *personality is a dynamic concept and has particular reference to social interaction.* Stimulus and response in social situations are matters of one's point of view. In social interaction, one person's response constitutes another person's stimulus. What one person says is his response, but it stimulates someone else who, in turn, responds. Personality refers particularly to the dynamics of social interaction.

We shall use the term personality to refer to the unique organization of stimulus and response characteristics and tendencies of the individual as they are dynamically involved in social situations.

### CHARACTER AND PERSONALITY

Character and personality cannot be sharply distinguished. Character refers to those socially relevant behavior trends that have particular moral and ethical implications. When we are concerned with behavior commonly labeled good or bad, and when activities are considered with reference to their moral and ethical implications, we speak of character rather than personality traits. Lying, cheating, and stealing are dominantly character traits, whereas dominance and submission, introversion and extroversion are personality characteristics. If we accept an idealistic conception of personality adjustment, personality traits also have evaluative dimensions and, within a given culture, are also considered good or bad, desirable or undesirable. This means that the distinction between character and personality is a relative and constantly shifting one.

Since the origin and development of character and personality traits are essentially alike, we shall sometimes use one term and sometimes the other depending upon our judgment as to the relative importance of the evaluative component, but we recognize that what we say about one applies to a large degree to the other as well.

### PERSONALITY AND PHYSIQUE

There have been many attempts to relate dimensions of body structure to personality characteristics. Bone structure, muscle distribution, and general bodily conformation have been considered either to determine or to be indicative of character and personality traits. The "man on the street" still entertains many of these beliefs—the big muscular man is dominant and aggressive, the fat person is jolly and easygoing, the frail person is tense and serious. Shakespeare said, "Let me have men about me that are fat, sleek-headed men, and such as sleep o'night. Yon Cassius has a lean and hungry look. He thinks too much. Such men are dangerous."

The most recent attempt to relate body build to personality is that of Sheldon and Stevens (1942). These workers propose a system of classification for constitutional (body) build and a parallel classification for temperament (a basic ingredient of personality). They also postulate a relation between the two. The authors avoid the simple type concept by dealing with components or dimensions of bodily structure and temperament. They postulate three such components of bodily build and three corresponding temperament components. The components of bodily build are *endomorphy*, the relative prominence of the abdomen and fatty tissue; *mesomorphy*, muscles, bones, and connective tissue; and *ectomorphy*, the relative fragility and "linearity" of body build. To indicate the extremes of the dimensions, the endomorphic individual is round and fat; the mesomorph is square and muscular; the ectomorph is tall and "skinny."

Each person can be given a quantitative rating for each of these bodily components. These ratings are obtained from a standard photograph of the person. For example, one person might be given a rating of two on endomorphy, five on mesomorphy, and four on ectomorphy (the range of values for each component is from one to seven). This constitutes the person's "somatotype." Each person is likewise given similar ratings on each of the three components of temperament—viscerotonia, somatotonia, and cerebrotonia. *Viscerotonia* refers to a love of physical comfort, slow reactions, indiscriminate amiability, and a relaxed posture. *Somatotonia* is characterized by love of physical adventure, competitive aggressiveness, general noisiness, a need for action, and assertiveness of posture. *Cerebrotonia* includes overly fast reactions, chronic fatigue, difficulties in sleeping, inhibited social responsiveness, need for solitude, restrained and tense posture. The authors postulate a causal relationship between the two variables, somatotype and temperament type. Using their own subjective ratings of temperament they report correlations around .90 between endomorphy and viscerotaonia, mesomorphy and somatotonia, and between ectomorphy and cerebrotonia. These relationships may be fictitiously high because of the possible contaminating influences of the raters' familiarity with the bodily variables and their expectations concerning the relationship between the somatotype and temperamental variables. Independent attempts to verify these relationships have given conflicting results, but the studies with the best controls report low but positive correlations between the organic and tempermanetal variables (*Tyler, 1956*).

Bodily handicaps and physical deformities have also been thought to determine personality. According to this conception, the absence of a body part or a major physical defect produces feelings of inferiority which may explain either the person's low self-concept and poor achievement or his compensatory high achievement. The psychoanalyst, Adler (*1929*), has advanced this claim most vigorously. According to him, man's feelings of inferiority derive principally from organic inferiorities and most of his defensive behavior represents attempts to compensate for his real or imaginary physical inadequacies.

Research studies quite regularly report a greater incidence of social withdrawal, personal unhappiness, and all types of defensive behavior among individuals who possess physical defects than among those who are closer to the group norm. Consistent, but low, positive correlations are also found between many dimensions of physique and various measures of personal and social adjustment; however, the assumption of a direct causal relationship between the two variables is questionable. It seems unlikely that the observed behavioral characteristics derive directly from the physical deviations. Occasionally both behavior and bodily deviation may arise from the same genetic or prenatal cause, but more often, the relationship between physique and behavior is the result of social intervening variables.

These social variables operate in the following way: A child who

*Figure 15.  Sheldon's concept of constitutional and temperamental types.*

deviates significantly from the culturally-approved norm is devalued by his associates. He finds that he is considered a less worthy individual than someone who has a more ideal physique. His devaluation is indicated by his being less sought after and less popular. He is rebuffed in his social overtures and is socially ostracized. He is also labeled as less worthy, to the degree that other people expect less from him than they expect from "normal" people. This social downgrading of the physically deviant individual may range from being slightly below average in social popularity to being treated as something less than human.

The individual who is devalued by his culture accepts as valid this social judgment. He internalizes the low-valued social judgment as he sees it reflected in the reactions of other people. This internalized cultural judgment becomes his own "self-concept."

Having internalized these social judgments in terms of a self-concept, the individual then feels obligated to act in accordance with others' expectations of him as well as with his own self-expectancies. The intervening variables involved in the conversion of a physical trait into a handicap are the social evaluations of the trait, and the individual's own acceptance and internalization of these social judgments.

The converse of this process operates with individuals whose physical deviations are in socially approved directions. Girls who are very attractive, boys who are superior in strength and "manliness," and people in general, who are rated as superior in "attractiveness" are found to be above average in social and personal adjustment (*Dimock, 1937; Silverman, 1945; Sawrey and Telford, 1964*).

The average person is unaware of the extent to which his own culture has conceptualized the ideal human physique. Each culture has rather specific conceptions of the ideal human form. Our traditions and folklore perpetuate these social stereotypes. Mass communication media—books, magazines, newpapers, radio, television, and the movies—help inculcate, perpetuate, and stereotype our conceptions of the ideal body-build and appearance. Americans annually spend billions of dollars and tremendous amounts of time and effort in order to bring themselves as close as possible to the culturally specified ideal male and female types. The use of "make-up," foundation garments, shoulder pads, "lifts," elevator shoes, bustles, "falsies," toupees, hair dyes, tints, bleaches, artificial eyelashes, eye shadow, and colored contact lenses; the bewildering array of machines, medicines, diets, and systems for either reducing or increasing weight, in general or in specific body parts; facial creams and lotions whose types—foundation, vanishing, theatrical, lubricating, moisturizing and hormonal—are limited only by the ad writer's vocabulary; are all evidences of a widespread concern with the problem of a set of less-than-ideal physical attributes. Of course, the prevailing conception of what constitutes the ideal in human form varies from culture to culture, from generation to generation within the same culture, and to a lesser extent, from one chronological age group to another within the same culture and generation. In certain primitive African tribes, in order to be desirable as a prospective bride, a girl must be big, strong, and preferably weigh at least two-hundred pounds. Consequently, the girls and women are fed large quantities of curdled milk in order to fatten them (*Wood, 1873, Thomas, 1937*). These women also scarify their bodies from the breast to the pit of the stomach and on the forehead in such a way as to produce rows of small almond-shaped swellings. The members of other African tribes chip or file their front teeth to sharp points for beauty and distinction. In other tribes no young woman thinks herself beautiful until she has removed the upper incisors (*Thomas, 1937*). All of these physical characteristics are far from the American ideal of the sylphlike female figure with unblemished skin and intact, perfectly matched teeth. The saber cut on the cheek of the pre-war German college student was a mark of honor, while the same cut on an American college boy would only be a facial disfigurement. There are tremendous cultural differences with reference to the ideal physical form.

The hourglass figure of the 1890's was the ideal female profile of that era. It gave way to the straight boyish figure of the 1920's when the breasts were bound and compressed so as to diminish their apparent size. In the 1950's a fully developed breast became the ideal and this was achieved, when necessary, through the use of "falsies."

Parents are perpetually surprised and disturbed to find that their children's conceptions of what is proper and desirable in dress and body-build differ in many respects from their own.

Body physique and general "looks" are matters of considerable personal and social significance in most cultures but the standards of beauty vary tremendously. The important thing is not the absence or presence of a given physical characteristic but the significance attached to it first by society and then by the individual himself. A physical defect is often not a thing in itself so much as it is a cultural evaluation of the developmental deviation. Physique has an effect on personality but the influence is largely indirect rather than direct.

Another indirect influence of physique on behavior may be via a person's anxiety level. A person with a socially defined physical handicap is more vulnerable to anxiety than the average person. He feels more threatened by the ordinary demands of his culture. When such threats produce high levels of anxiety, there occurs a decrease in the individual's ability to deal adequately and constructively with his environment. Rigid, constricted, compulsive, or impulsive, and fragmented solutions to problems tend to develop. The high anxiety levels of the deviant individual may result in a high incidence of socially unacceptable and blind-alley solutions to life's problems.

The physically handicapped anxious individual may also restrict his activities, maintain a lower level of aspiration, and persist in an unrealistic minimal self-definition as a defense against the threat of failure and increased anxiety. When a person has had a great deal done for him, when he has not been required to develop competences and to display initiative as much as the normal person, and when he has lived in a greatly simplified world, he has a tendency to remain in such a situation or to regress to such a condition when stresses become too great and anxiety mounts (*Wenar, 1953, 1954*).

### PERSONALITY AND "CHEMIQUE"[1]

To what extent does the chemistry of the body determine personality? The ancients typed people on the basis of "four temperaments." The sanguine individual had a surplus of blood, the choleric a surplus of bile, the phlegmatic, an excess of phlegm (mucus), and the melancholic too much spleen. Sometimes a fifth, "nervous temperament" was added which was supposed to be the result of a surplus of "nerve fluid" (*Woodworth and Marquis, 1947*). While this classification of temperaments based on bodily fluids or "humors" is purely of historical interest, there have been much more recent attempts to explain personality largely on the basis of glandular functioning.

In a book entitled *The Glands Regulating Personality*, Berman (1928) attempts to account for personality almost entirely in terms of the functioning of the endocrine glands. The pugnacious individual has overactive adrenal glands and the tense nervous individual is so because of oversecretion of the thyroid. The individual is at the mercy of his glands. While no one today would agree with this extreme position, one's body chemistry cannot be entirely ignored as a personality determiner.

---

[1] A term apparently coined by Woodworth and Marquis (1947) to refer to a person's biochemical and glandular characteristics.

Almost all of the evidence relating to the glandular determinants of personality comes from studies of the lower animals and has only inferential bearing on the question of the determination of the personality of humans. By selective breeding, strains of animals have been developed which differ markedly in activity level (*Rundquist, 1933; Brody, 1942*) and emotionality (*Hall, 1941*). Natural selection and domestication seem to have developed strains of animals differing widely in wildness, savageness, aggressiveness, timidity, and emotionality (*Dawson, 1932; Hall and Klein, 1942; Mahut, 1958*). These studies indicate that certain components of "temperament" are of genetic origin.

Studies of the glandular systems of those strains of animals which differ in temperamental characteristics disclose some systematic anatomical differences. Emotional strains of rats have larger adrenal, thyroid, and pituitary glands than do comparable nonemotional strains (*Yeakel and Rhoades, 1941*). Wild Norway rats have larger adrenal glands than do tame strains of Norway rats (*Rogers and Richter, 1948*). Stockard *et al.* (*1941*) have related the lethargy of certain breeds of dogs such as Basset Hounds to their relatively inactive thyroid glands and low metabolic rates as contrasted with the alertness and high activity of Salukis and German Shepherds who have more active thyroids and higher metabolic rates. These physiological differences seem to be genetically determined. These studies provide interesting suggestions as to the part that inheritance plays in endocrine gland functioning that determines the temperamental traits of the lower animals. It seems likely that similar genetic and biochemical factors play a part in human behavior.

## CONCEPTS OF CHARACTER AND PERSONALITY ORGANIZATION

### The Concept of Distinct Personality Types

The notion that people can usefully and validly be classified into a limited, and preferably small, number of categories in terms of their personality and character traits is an intriguing one. People have always categorized others in terms of classes, castes, or types. Despite its questionable validity, people will undoubtedly continue to deal with others within a conceptual framework of classes or types.

Pigeonholing people according to types is an attempt to simplify the complexities of life and reduce the amount of decison-making involved in relating to others. If I know that a person is a Democrat, I can, without knowing him personally, predict with some degree of accuracy his political beliefs and behaviors. Knowing that someone is a Baptist implies something concerning his "religious beliefs and practices." Similarly, there are certain group differences in limited areas of belief and practice between employers and employees, the wealthy and the poor, tradesmen and professional people, northerners and southerners, adults and children. Many people also believe that there are significant emotional and behavioral differences between fat and thin people, between men and women, and between blonds and brunettes.

The type concept goes beyond a belief in the existence of *group differences* between these various categories of people. The type concept assumes that people assigned to a certain category on the basis of one of these variables are *alike* in many other socially-significant ways. Differences between types are often thought to be qualitative rather than quantitative in nature. When they are recognized as quantitative, the differences between types are considered to be large with no overlapping between the contrasting types; the populations are thought to be mutually exclusive.

### CRITICISM OF THE TYPE CONCEPT

The type concept implies either a bi-modal or a multi-modal distribution of human traits. For example, introverts as a type should all be found close together at the extreme end of a scale of introversion; extroverts should cluster at the opposite end. However, in practically every measurable human trait, people are arranged in a uni-modal distribution approximating a normal bell-shaped curve. When people are measured on any socially significant trait they do not arrange themselves in ways which are consistent with the type concept.

The pure type is the exception rather than the rule. Most people are neither pure extroverts nor introverts. They possess mixtures of these traits in varying degrees. The so-called type represents the extreme end of a continuum of individuals without any breaks or discontinuities anywhere along the line. In a normal distribution, the bulk of the individuals are closely grouped around a central point with progressively fewer and fewer individuals farther and farther removed from this central point. If we consider those individuals farthest removed from the norm as the *purest types*, there will be relatively few such people. The person fitting the pure type is an atypical individual.

When we try to place people in relatively few distinct categories, we force them into an oversimplified and artificial arrangement. Having once classified people we are likely to overgeneralize our categories. We categorize and classify in terms of one variable and then ignore the hundreds of other equally significant attributes in which those individuals in any single category differ widely. We assume that all the people in one typological category are the same not only in respect to the single attribute but in respect to all other attributes.

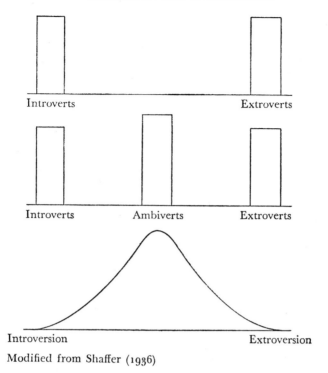

Introverts                              Extroverts

Introverts          Ambiverts         Extroverts

Introversion                       Extroversion

Modified from Shaffer (1936)

*Figure 16.   Diagrammatic representation of a pure dichotomous type of concept (introverts-extroverts), a modified type of concept (introverts-ambiverts-extroverts), and the concept of a continuum.*

Although the typing of people will probably always be with us in our systematic attempts to understand human nature, there is very little to recommend it. This does not mean that artificial and arbitrary classifications may not have some usefulness. Such groupings often represent heuristic fictions (untrue but useful "as ifs"). For example, if for certain practical or research purposes we want two groups of people differing markedly in height (the tall and the short), we may decide that we will call "short" any male below five feet four inches in height, and "tall" anyone above six feet one inch in height. These limits are purely arbitrary. Many individuals will fall right on our division point. If we measure the same individual at different times of day he may shift from above to below our division point. By making a series of arbitrary rules, we can find two non-overlapping groups of "tall" and "short" male "types." As long as people know and accept our definition of these types, no one is misled by the names. However, if we generalize from our groups and assume that all men can legitimately and in some absolute sense be classified as either tall or short we are greatly oversimplifying the facts of life. By arbitrary definition such categories as "mentally retarded," "mentally normal," and "mentally gifted" can be useful for the educational grouping of children, but this does not mean that these groups represent homogenous and discrete classes or "types" of individuals.

## Concept of Stages of Character Development (Erikson)

To some degree the concept of levels or stages of personality and character development is analogous to the type concept. When we speak of the infantile stage of personality development we seem to refer to a distinct chronological age range characterized by a unique set of personality characteristics that give way at a critical age to a different constellation of traits. When we describe an adult as having an infantile personality we imply that he has retained that set of behavioral traits characteristic of infants.

If we arbitrarily divide development into "ages" or "stages" and stereotype the characters and personalities of the individuals included within the defined limits, we are resorting to another form of typing. Differences among individuals, all of whom are of the same chronological age or are in the same developmental "stage," will still be tremendous and the typing tends to either neglect or minimize these differences.

Many theoretical conceptions of character and personality take man as he is and deal with him as a completed product. Other theories consider character and personality developmentally. Freud's concept of stages of psycho-sexual development, Piaget's stages of cognitive or intellectual development, and Erikson's phases of psycho-social development are examples of the developmental approach. Since Erikson's concept of development is broader than either Freud's or Piaget's and has been worked out in more detail, we shall summarize his concept of developmental sequences or phases.

The development of character and personality is conceived of as a continuous and sequential process. While Erikson is concerned primarily with emotional and motivational development, the entire process involves a sequence of biological, psychological, and social processes that is divided into eight stages. The first five stages constitute an extension and a reformulation of Freud's stages of psycho-sexual development, to which Erikson has added three adult phases. Development is a continuous process with each phase constituting a part of a continuum. Each phase begins in and grows out of the preceding phases and it, in turn, merges with and lives on in all subsequent phases. Erikson places less emphasis on the three phases of adulthood then on the first five phases covering the periods of infancy, childhood, and adolescence. Whereas Erikson's first five phases of psycho-social development correspond to Freud's five stages of psychosexual development, classical psychoanalysis does not recognize any corresponding stages of adult development.

Each phase is characterized by a phase-specific developmental task that must be mastered if subsequent development is to proceed normally. However, preparation for each task occurs in previous phases and is worked out more fully in subsequent ones. For example, the struggle for autonomy is present from the beginning and manifests itself in such things as the infant's wriggling his arms free when they are tightly held. However, it is normally between the second and the fourth year that the issue of autonomy vs. dependency becomes critical. The sequence of phases is considered to be universal but the typical ways of mastering each developmental task vary from culture to culture. While culture does not determine the sequence of development, it does influence the manner in which the developmental tasks are mastered. The course of development is irreversible but the rate and pattern of each individual's growth represents the response of his biological makeup to the particular familial-cultural influences of his life. Erikson conceives of development as the adaptation of the biological man within a socio-cultural context.

There are successful and unsuccessful methods of handling the developmental tasks, or, rather, each person has varying degrees of success in mastering the developmental tasks. In reality, each person achieves somewhere along a continuum between extremes. Thus we have eight dimensions or areas of development with each person achieving a status somewhere between extremes in each dimension. These dimensions are called (1) basic trust vs. mistrust, (2) autonomy vs. shame or doubt, (3) initiative vs. guilt, (4) industry vs. inferiority, (5) identity vs. identity diffusion, (6) intimacy vs. isolation, (7) generativity vs. stagnation, and (8) integrity vs. despair. Each individual acquires a certain ratio between the positive (the first member of each pair) and the negative traits (the second member of each pair). To the degree that the balance is toward the positive end of each continuum the individual has a better chance for unimpaired total development.

The basic processes involved in psychopathology are the same as those found in normal development. Pathological development represents only a different configuration or balance of the same developmental processes that are found in a healthy personality. Erikson asumes a universal value system based on the developmental sequences of human growth, the prerequisites of optimal development, and the common elements in social systems. He takes for granted a dovetailing of the positive components of the developmental dimensions with an "average expectable environment." Erikson, unlike Freud, sees human nature as originally neither good or bad but as having the potential for either. A healthy mature personality, for him, achieves personal happiness and responsible social effectiveness by maintaining a position well toward the positive end of the continuum of each of the dimensions of development. We shall describe each of these eight developmental phases as Erikson has interpreted them in various contexts. We shall also make some extrapolations and applications of our own (*Erikson, 1959a, 1959b, 1963, 1964; Maier, 1965*).

## 1. ACHIEVING A SENSE OF BASIC TRUST

Erikson considers a sense of basic trust the cornerstone of a healthy personality. Others have called this same characteristic "confidence." It is the principal component of a feeling of security and forms the basis for all later phases but most importantly for the sense of identity which develops in adolescence. A sense of trust represents a basic attitude toward one's world—particularly one's social world, and is thought to develop in the first two years of life. It is only partly conscious.

When the infant's physiological needs are regularly satisfied, the child comes to associate his inner sense of well-being with the consistent behavior of the persons who care for him. A reasonably consistent confirmation of the child's expectations leads to a trust in other people and in the world. Trust in one's world grows out of a certain rhythm and regularity to the infant's life. A continuity—first of food, warmth, and sleep, and later of attention and affection—is required for the child to develop expectancies, the realization of which establishes and sustains a sense of trust.

The sense of trust is nourished by care that is sensitive to the child's individual needs and the parent's feeling of self-confidence in his dealing with the child within the framework of the culture's dominant "life style." When the parent's belief conflict with those of the dominant culture or with those of the "experts," when father and mother display divergent patterns of child care, or when the parents are unsure of themselves and the appropriateness of their own patterns of life, the child will reflect these ambiguities in displaying a feeling of distrust.

Erikson attaches more significance to the underlying emotional and attitudinal themes that underly the parental handling, care, and training of the child than to their specific child-rearing practices and skills. A sense of trust seems to derive more from the nature and "quality" of parent-child relationships than from sheer quantity of attention and maternal care. The sense of trust is mutual. Parental uncertainties and distrusts are transmitted to the child in many subtle ways and instill in him a reciprocal sense of distrust. Freud called this the "oral stage" of psycho-sexual development, and Erikson follows Freud in postulating that "oral gratification" for the infant is essential for the development of a basic sense of trust.

Many adults obtain a reinforcement for their sense of basic trust from religion and tradition. Traditional beliefs are important carriers of a faith and conviction that serve to support and maintain the individual's basic trust in the meaning and trustworthiness of the universe. More and more people derive a feeling of confidence and trust from their immersion in scientific and artistic pursuits, personal service, and in social action programs. A profound and passionate belief with some degree of social support provides a meaning to life and instills a feeling of trust in oneself and in the universe quite apart from the validity of the belief. A high level of basic trust makes it possible for the individual to grow personally and socially, to seek out, and to accept new experiences. Every reinforcement of one's trust produces an additional increment of it.

Erikson perceives the crisis of this developmental phase to occur when the mother turns from the baby as the primary focus of her attention to other pursuits given up during pregnancy and early postnatal life of the child. The infant becomes increasingly aware of himself as a distinct person and sudden changes in his relations with the significant people in his environment threaten his basic sense of trust. Erikson believes that the extreme regressions seen in neurotic behavior and in psychotic states represent reactions to profound feelings of distrust. He points out that in psychotherapy people in these states must be convinced that they can first trust the therapist and then trust themselves and finally come to trust the world.

## 2.   ACHIEVING A SENSE OF AUTONOMY

Erikson considers the critical period for the child's achieving a sense of autonomy to be between eighteen months and four years. Prior to this period, the child is in a state of extreme dependency. The forces that control and direct his behavior are largely external to him. However, when the child learns to walk and to talk, he is able to explore his world more independently. He accomplishes new feats and discovers that he can initiate his own activities and control his own behavior. Having developed a sense of trust in the first developmental phase, the child is ready in the second to break away from the dependencies of the earlier period and establish his individual autonomy.

"Let me do it," becomes the dominant theme of the second developmental phase. The child is anxious to feed and dress himself, to walk and talk, to open and shut doors, and to explore the world outside. He tries to expand his world, to set his own limits, and to do things on his own terms. Each new skill acquired brings with it an increment of autonomy. For example, when the child learns to walk, he has not only perfected a means of locomotion, he has also achieved a new status in the eyes of his culture and in his own eyes. "One who can walk" also means, "one who can go far," "one who can achieve great things," and "one who is now independent."

Satisfactorily meeting the challenge of this period depends primarily on the parent's ability to gradually grant the child freedom in appropriate and safe areas while maintaining control in others. A firm maintenance of limits in some areas must be counterbalanced by a comfortable acceptance of the child's autonomy in others. Trust and autonomy interact. The child who has not attained an adequate sense of trust is hesitant to strive for autonomy. He feels a need for dependency and is fearful of striking out on his own. Conversely, the way in which adult restraints are maintained and relinquished has considerable influence on the child's feel of trust and self-confidence acquired in the earlier period of life. The child's sense of autonomy and feeling of pride in independent endeavor developed in the second period also have considerable influence on his attitudes toward social mores and cultural norms later in life.

Extent of mutual trust and degree of autonomy interact as the child is permitted different degrees of freedom by different adults. As the child learns to relate to and to trust each adult individually, he is able to adjust his degree and extent of autonomy differentially to different people. To the degree that the child is able to modify the exercise of his newly gained independence according to the amount of autonomy each adult can permit him, his sense of basic trust, his feeling of self-confidence, and his sense of autonomy are not threatened by the failure of all adults to permit him to exercise his autonomy to its maximum. To the extent that the child is able to utilize to his own advantage adult differences in the degree of autonomy they are willing to grant him, he gains an increasing sense of autonomy.

Excessive feelings of shame, self-doubt, and personal inadequacy result from failures to develop adequate autonomy. The child's condition of dependency is perpetuated by his doubts concerning his capacity to function as an independent being. Because he does not trust himself he continues to permit and to encourage others to do things for him.

To recapitulate: An adequate sense of trust is necessary in order to develop autonomy and a well developed sense of autonomy contributes to one's feeling of trust. The child's social world must support and encourage him in his striving for autonomy lest he become paralyzed either by his fear of possible failure or by his feelings of shame at having violated the mutual trust implied in his earlier dependency. Achieving autonomy and at the same time accepting a delimitation of that autonomy by the adult world prepares the child for a life of "law and order" in which privileges carry their obligations and individual rights are always limited. A lawful independence permitted and maintained with a firm dignity by trusting and trusted parents prepares the child for the acceptance of a limited autonomy in adulthood. Social organizations and cultural mores define the privileges and obligations of conduct and require the acceptance of certain limitations on behavior as the price for autonomy and self-determination in other areas. The increasing complications and mechanization of life in industrialized nations greatly increase the interdependence of people, and the autonomy of the individual is of necessity circumscribed. This situation often arouses anxieties concerning the loss of one's autonomy. Fears of having one's independence of action restricted by the increasing complexities and interdependence of contemporary economic and social organizations has contributed to the rise and maintenance of social movements with a "back to nature" theme. Social action involving a search for the old or "lost" values or roots often represent individual and/or group attempts to reduce the uncertainties and dilution of individual autonomy that occur in an industrialized and automated society.

3. DEVELOPING A SENSE OF INITIATIVE

The primary developmental tasks of this phase are two. The first and foremost is that of conscience development. The second task is that of establishing an appropriate sex role. Having attained a sense of trust and a measure of autonomy in the earlier years, the child moves outward during the next years (roughly from four to seven) into larger social and geographic regions. His newly found autonomy challenges him to move out into the world and to master new tasks. The child's increased language and locomotor facility makes it possible for him to expand his activities beyond his family and his immediate home environment. This is the time when the child, having turned from a close attachment to his parents, must bring his new-found autonomy under the control of his own conscience. In the absence of immediate parental control, the inner voice of the child's own conscience replaces the parental voice in supporting and/or directing his behavior.

It is during this period that the child normally becomes aware of sex differences and establishes his appropriate sex role. Freud called this the genital stage, and it is during this time that the Oedipus Complex was alleged to develop. Freud conceived of the Oedipus Complex as distinctively sexual in nature and as referring specifically to the desire of the boy for his mother with hostility toward the father because the like-sex parent is perceived as a rival for the mother's affection. The corresponding relationship between father and daughter is technically the Electra Complex, although in practice the term "Oedipus Complex" is used to represent the desire of either the boy or the girl for the parent of the opposite sex. Erikson's conception of these relationships is less specifically sexual in nature than Freud's. He believes that both the boy and the girl become emotionally attached to the mother because she has most consistently provided them comfort. While the boy is becoming emotionally attached to his mother he is also identifying with his father in establishing his sex role as a male. Conflict arises from the fact that the father, as the primary object of sex-role identification, is also the person with whom the boy must compete for his mother's affections. The girl's first affectional attachments and sex-role identifications are to the same person—the mother—and she experiences conflict only when she must compete with her mother for her father's attentions. The rivalry of the child and his like-sex parent for the affections of the opposite sex parent is resolved by the turning of the child's affections to other persons. When the parent of the opposite sex is successfully replaced as the immediate object of the child's romantic interest, the like-sex parent is enhanced as the object of identification and the child is freed to facilitate the establishment of his appropriate sex role in this way. Erikson believes that only the child who has fully developed his basic sense of trust and has successfully achieved autonomy can relinquish his romantic fixation on the parent.

Failure to resolve the conflicts of this period results in a sense of guilt. The sense of guilt arises out of the persistence of a romantic attachment to an inappropriate person (the parent) and the child's failure to establish an appropriate sex role.

## 4. ACHIEVING A SENSE OF INDUSTRY

This is the age when the child goes to school and learns to get busy as others are busy. The child is for the first time presented with social tasks, which he is expected to handle. In all cultures, at this age, children receive some systematic instruction. Failure to master the developmental tasks expected by one's culture gives rise to feelings of inferiority. In preliterate people the education of children is fairly straightforward and socially relevant. In primitive cultures the child's systematic instruction is related to the skills required to handle the utensils, tools, and weapons used by adults. On the other hand, in cultures with a written language, the child is first taught to be literate. He is given the tools of literacy which, in turn, will make it possible for him to acquire the informational and technological skills of a wide variety of possible occupations and activities. The more literate and industrialized societies, in contrast with primitive societies, have more indistinct educational goals. These goals are remote in time, and their relevance to the ultimate educational endeavors is not obvious. Because of this, the school comes to be a world by itself, with its own goals. In this phase the child's sense of competence and industry is derived dominantly from his educational achievements.

In this phase, peers assume an increasing importance as measures of the child's own success or failure. The focus shifts from dependence upon the parents as the major influence in the child's life to dependence upon one's peers and social institutions. Erikson believes that many of the individual's attitudes toward work as well as the individual's habits of industry originate in this period. The person who successfully meets the challenges of this phase acquires what Erikson calls a "sense of industry" and avoids an excessive "sense of inferiority."

A sense of industry involves more than educational and occupational competence. It includes a feeling of interpersonal competence—the confidence that he can exert a positive influence on his social environment in pursuit of meaningful social and personal goals.

### 5. ACQUIRING A SENSE OF IDENTITY

This is the last phase of childhood and youth, and it is in this period that the individual acquires a sense of identity, which is essential for meeting the challenges of adulthood. Erikson's own interest in adolescence and public preoccupation with the problems of this period lead him to present a more comprehensive discussion of this phase than of any other stage of development. A sense of identity, according to Erikson, has many roots and many dimensions. In its simplest form an adequate sense of identity, as contrasted with "a sense of identity diffusion," involves (1) the development and maintenance of a feeling of "inner sameness and continuity," which is matched by the sameness and continuity of one's meaning for others; (2) a conviction that the individual's way of achieving in the personal and vocational areas are successful variants of the way other significant people in his culture achieve these goals and provide recognition for such achievement; (3) the feeling that one is learning effective social skills and developing a unique personality with reference to a tangible future within a social context that he understands. The youth's development of an adequate sense of identity requires him to work through and integrate himself in the following seven dimensions or areas:

### A. Time perspective

With inappropriate time perspective, the youth may either demand immediate action and prompt solutions to life's problems or be so unaware of the reality of the limitations of time that he perpetually proscrastinates in the hope either that time will stand still or that time itself will solve his problems. A realistic time perspective is a prerequesite to a full sense of identity. Failure to develop an adequate time perspective results in "time diffusion," according to Erikson.

A sense of identity requires that the individual maintain an awareness of personal continuity, despite change over time. The individual needs to either say or feel that "Although I used to be that way, and this is the way I am now, and I expect to change in the future, I am still the same person and other people perceive me as the same." A certain amount of regularity in one's life, an organized pattern of existence within which expectancies develop and are confirmed, is necessary for the development of adequate time perspective just as it is for the inculcation of a sense of trust. Trust has temporal dimension and implies that yesterday's events are related to what is happening today and that today's occurrences have a meaningful reference to what will happen tomorrow. Lacking this sense of continuity over time, the individual becomes preoccupied with activities that give him the most intense immediate experiences of being alive.

### B. Self-certainty

A congruence of one's self-concept with the impression he conveys to others contributes to one's sense of identity. Feelings of doubt and confusion concerning one's self-concept and one's "social image" militate against a sense of identity.

### C. Role experimentation

Experimentation with a wide variety of roles is a prerequisite to identification with a role appropriate to the individual. The ultimate goal of experimentation with many different roles is identification with a positive ideal. A failure in role experimentation results in "negative identity."

### D. Anticipation of achievement

Persistence and integration of effort with the expectations that one's efforts will be productive are essential for establishing an occupational identity. Expectations of nonachievement result in "work paralysis."

### E. Sexual identity

The establishment of an appropriate sex role is necessary for a sense of identity. Seeing oneself as wholly male or female and feeling comfortable in his contacts with members of both sexes contributes to a sense of identity. Inappropriate or inadequate sexual identity results in "bisexual diffusion."

F.  Leadership polarization

A realistic appraisal of authority, with a willingness to both lead and follow in appropriate situations, contributes to a positive identity. Failures in this area take the form of "authority diffusion."

G.  Ideological polarization

An anchoring trust in life, which may be partially supplied by a religious, ideological, philosophical, or social action commitment, as indicated earlier, contributes to one's sense of identity. Youth searches for certainties. It looks for something and somebody to be "true." The failure to find enduring values in one's culture, religion, or philosophy results in a "diffusion of ideals."

*Characteristics of the alienated.* Extreme identity diffusion has been given several names—alienation, estrangement, noninvolvement, detachment, and anomie. Alienation results from failure of the individual to satisfactorily work through the developmental tasks of any or all of the preceding phases. These failures manifest themselves in inadequacies in any or all of the seven dimensions previously listed.

Filled with distrust, the alienated individual expects only punishment from his fellow men. Human relations are perceived as based on mutual exploitation. Men are separated from each other by their self-centeredness and their inability to understand each other. In modern society intimacy is impossible. All appearances of sincerity are suspect. A deeper probing of friendly intent always discloses the underlying themes of chicanery, hypocrisy, and deceit. The universe is inherently chaotic and unpredictable just as are human relations. Social institutions, cultural mores, and political activities are all artificial games played by the common man to cover up the contradictions and absurdities of the world. Initial distrust develops into an intense repudiation of the world. This complete repudiation represents the all-or-none attitude of childhood—an inability to repudiate selectively. The whole world is perceived as a huge, impersonal machine, devoid of understanding, sympathy or compassion.

Failure to develop a sense of autonomy and adequacy often takes the form of a glorification of the experiences of childhood—the "Old Oaken Bucket" delusion. Since the universe is not intelligible and neither are human relations, the only realities of life are the simple sensous satisfactions and direct perceptivity of childhood. The masses of humanity stifle life. Modern society over-stimulates and stultifies man. Early infancy, with its passivity, security, and effortless gratification, is idealized. A high value is placed on childlike modes of experiencing. Unreflective physical existence with an intensification of immediate sensory experience or increased introspective awareness of oneself are the primary sources of satisfaction.

At a less acute level, the alienated individual has diffuse parental images and ambivalent attitudes toward authority. Parental figures are either hostile and threatening or weak and passive. One can never be sure which they are and that they will remain unchanged. Nurturant women become possessive and controlling and apparently strong men are basically weak and fraudulent.

Diffuse parental imagery is a part of diffuse sexuality. Doubts concerning one's sexual adequacy result in either under- or over-valuation of sex. Impulsive sexual experiences are idealized as primitive or childlike sensory experiences, which are glorified as the expression of the "free man."

Most of the characteristics of alienated youth can be perceived as the manifestation of a crushing sense of inferiority. The distrust and pessimism, the feeling of distance from others, and the perception of the universe as chaotic and without meaning are all manifestations of profound feelings of inadequacy.

Alienated youth has failed to develop and maintain that feeling of an inner sameness and self-continuity that is recognized as valued by others. He does not feel that he is achieving in the social and vocational areas in a personally and culturally significant way. He feels that what he is learning is not relevant to a tangible future within a meaningful social context. He feels inadequate and inferior. He is thus failing to meet the simplest requirements for developing a sense of identity.

The susceptibility of youth to the stresses of rapid social change is a well documented phenomenon. The adolescent seems to have a lowered threshold for all things relating to the broad area of adjustment covered by Erikson's "sense of identity." The 1960's have witnessed an apparent increased interest in political and social problems on the part of youth in America. This is, of course, not a new phenomenon. In Europe, youth movements of this type go back to the 19th century. Whereas many of the youth movements in Europe during the 19th century and in Latin America and Africa during the 20th century have been revolutionary in nature and directed at overthrowing the existing social or governmental structures, the student movements of the 20th century in the United States have been more concerned with the issues of personal identity as defined by Erikson. As a specific application of Erikson's concepts, we shall interpret contemporary social action movements within his framework. We are indebted to Erikson (1964), Fishman and Solomon (1964), Solomon and Fishman (1964), and Gelineau and Kantor (1964) for many of these ideas.

Youth movements in the United States born of single specific issues such as the draft, free speech, voting rights, school integration, or inadequate housing have expanded to include the larger issues of peace, civil rights, racial discrimination, and economic injustices, and have finally proceeded to broad moralistic, humanistic, and personal principles involving a relatively unstructured world outlook encompassing the entire range of human endeavor. Follow-up studies of the personnel make-up of these various movements show great crossover and overlap of people involved in these activities (*Fishman and Solomon, 1964*). The social action movements of the 1960's in the United States are not aimed at overthrowing the existing political, economic, or social structure of the country. They are aimed at reforming, modifying, and purifying the existing organizations in order to bring practice more into line with their alleged aims and purposes.

There is much in the social action movements of youth that can be interpreted as a search for identity. The youth of this generation are learning that values and knowledge are becoming increasingly relative. They are told that knowledge that used to double in millenia or centuries is now doubling every decade. Old conceptions are being replaced by newer ones at an ever-increasing rate. Students are reminded that much of what they are now learning will be out of date by the time they are ready to use it. Many of the occupations in which they will find employment are not yet in existence. Rapid social and economic change always contribute to a sense of uncertainty and discontinuity. Much in the social action movements of youth is suggestive of a restless seeking for that sense of continuity between past, present, and future which is considered to be a crucial ingredient of a healthy personality.

A dominant theme in the social action youth movements of the 1960's is a search for the old or "lost" values. These movements attempt to overcome the uncertainties and diffusion of ideals of the present by a return to earlier values and simpler ways of life. The tremendous appeal of folk music, the return to "nature," the revived interest in Thoreau and Rousseau, and the glorification of the "noble savage" all suggest a nostalgia for the simpler cultural roots and traditions.

Attempts to return to earlier values are discernible in the youth movements of other countries. The Nazi youth's fascination with traditions of the powerful old gods and the tribal hordes, the Italian fascist youth's identification with the earlier traditions of a powerful Rome, and the Zionist youth's searching for their biblical roots, which antedated the degradations of the ghetto, all represent glorifications of the past and contrast with the depravity and powerlessness of modern man. In order to give meaning to current social action movements, attempts are made to link the glories of the past with "the cause" and to extract from these continuities inferences and mandates for the future. Commitment to the cause identifies one with persistent and universal values beyond the present and beyond the self. From this commitment a sense of meaning, a feeling of continuity, and a feeling of importance are obtained. Nationalistic movements in the newer countries of Asia and Africa and in the more closed communistic nations may serve the same function for youth as do the social action youth movements in the United States. They provide a means of striving for autonomy and identity.

Many of these youth movements sponsor an over-simplified and even childlike view of good and evil. The magical and omnipotent slogans not only represent over-simplified solutions to social problems; they also increase personal commitment, create an exaggerated sense of rightness and invulnerability, and rationalize many forms of behavior that would otherwise be shunned. Public demonstrations, parades, picketing and chanting, ceremonies, rituals, and distinctive garb—whether formal uniforms, leather jackets, or beatnik attire—contribute to the participant's feeling of identity and power. Public pronouncements, press conferences, and T.V. appearances all contribute to the individual's feeling of importance and power.

For the individual who has failed to achieve an adequate sense of autonomy, social movements constitute vehicles for accelerating the breakaway from childhood dependencies with the help of a dedicated peer group. Involvement in political and social movements contribute to one's feeling of importance and power suggestive of adulthood.

Many individuals rationalize their search for identity and autonomy by perceiving themselves as acting in the interest of personal ideals, the social good, and the general interests of mankind. Illegal activities are justified in terms of a "higher law" or a "greater good." Sincerity of purpose and feeling are contrasted with the social, political, and personal hypocrisy of the adult world and produce a feeling of invulnerability and an assurance of ultimate success. The physical discomforts, self-sacrifice, dramatic renunciation and even burning oneself to death in public are perceived as evidence of the intensity of commitment as well as acts of purification reminiscent of the asceticism of certain religious orders. The heroic deed somehow imbues the doer with the fantasied power to change the course of world events. The lesser sacrificial deed shows up the banality and mediocrity of middle-class existence and is in contrast to the hypocrisies and inconsistencies of the adult world.

The appeal to sincerity of belief and depth of conviction as an index of the "right" represents a return to a belief in an infallible conscience as the proper guide to conduct. One youth group of the '60's dedicated to social action called itself "Conscience." The ethic of social relativism does not provide a firm basis for youth in search of certainties in an unstable and constantly changing world. A return to the belief in an infallible conscience provides this certainty and makes it possible for the individual to sustain and validate his own unique identity and enhance his feeling of individuality and autonomy. If each individual's conscience is unique as each person is unique, validating deviant behavior in terms of sincerity of motive and feeling makes each person a law unto himself.

Thus we are presented with the paradox of youth in search of autonomy and individual identity joining up with kindred souls to form groups within which there is great pressure for conformity. The values and patterns of the larger society are either deprecated or rejected, but the group often becomes more relentlessly intolerant of unaffiliated youth and of lack of dedicated commitment by its members than it is of the outside world.

While the social action movements of youth may at times become destructive, there is evidence that social protest movements may have at least short-term effects in reducing crime and mental illness (*Solomon et al., 1965; Fishman and Solomon, 1964*). Social action perceived as consonant with one's beliefs, and which provides some promise of redress of one's grievances, may reduce the motivation for acting out in more personally and socially destructive ways. For individuals participating in such movements, the issues of ideological commitment, leadership, self-certainty, and the anticipation of achievement may be at least temporarily solved. The feelings of alienation and exile that result from a failure to develop an adequate sense of identity and that at times may lead to delinquency and crime and at other times to introspection, moodiness, or a kind of existential pessimism, may be alleviated to some degree by the intellectual rationalizations, the personal commitments, impulsive actions, risk-taking, and suffering characteristic of certain social action programs.

6. ACQUIRING A SENSE OF INTIMACY AND SOLIDARITY

The primary problems of the first period of adulthood are those of marriage and a career. Graduation from adolescence to adulthood requires a sense of individual identity, and graduation from the first to the second phase of adulthood requires the finding and development of a sense of shared identity. The person who is not sure of his individual identity is unable to establish the comfortable interpersonal intimacies that are essential to the establishment of an adequate sense of shared identity. The surer one is of himself the more he is free to seek out and accept mutual friendship and love. Erikson sees much of the adolescent heterosexual behavior that persists into adulthood as the individual's continued attempt to define his individual identity. Adequate meeting of the tasks of the first period of adulthood assumes a psychological readiness for the mutual trust and intimacy of marriage. To the degree that each person has developed a satisfactory personalized pattern of life that guarantees him an individual identity, he is able to accept the joint intimacies and responsibilities of marriage.

The second developmental task of this period is finding a job and working in a socially useful and personally satisfying vocation. Successful pursuit of a career is dependent upon the prior establishment of adequate trust and autonomy, but more particularly, adequate initiative, industry, and personal identity. Psychological adulthood requires continued learning and vocational development within the realm of work. The sharing of affection, love, and work serves as the foundation for the rearing of mentally healthy offspring, which is the primary task of the second phase of adulthood.

Failure to acquire the sense of intimacy and solidarity that is essential for satisfactorily meeting the problems of love and work in adulthood results in feelings of isolation and "social emptiness." The inability to establish intimate personal relations results either in social isolation or the development of purely formal and stereotyped forms of interpersonal relations. The person who has not found himself in the occupational realm has a feeling of being an isolated unit enduring the punishment of futile and meaningless labor.

### 7. ACQUIRING A SENSE OF GENERATIVITY

The primary task of the second phase of adulthood is establishing a family and rearing one's offspring. This involves embarking on the second round of the eight phases of development in which the parents accept the challenge of their responsibility for developing trust, autonomy, initiative, industry, and a sense of identity in the next generation. Adequately meeting the problems involved in the production and rearing of one's offspring provides an increment to one's feeling of adequacy, an additional type of intimacy, and a feeling of accomplishment through vicarious participation in the achievements of one's children.

Failures in meeting the challenges of this phase of adulthood produce a developmental arrest—a feeling of personal stagnation and a withdrawal from interpersonal intimacies. The individual who fails in this phase of adulthood often turns to self-indulgence and self-absorption, which further estrange him from his family and his community.

### 8. ACQUIRING A SENSE OF INTEGRITY

Adequately meeting the problems of this, the last phase of adulthood, is probably not so much an acquisition of this period as it is a reaping of the harvest of all of the preceding phases. The person who has worked through the critical problems of the earlier phases enters this last period of life with a sense of integrity. This phase had its most fundamental roots in the first. Out of a profound feeling of trust the individual, even in the waning periods of life, has an assured feeling of reliance upon himself and upon others. In old age the individual derives a feeling of security from a philosophy of life that extends beyond the life cycle of the individual. Such a philosophy involves an acceptance of and a feeling of satisfaction with one's own life. It also involves a commonality of feeling with men and women of distant times, of other countries, and of different pursuits. It includes a prideful identification with one's children and grandchildren.

Just as mentally healthy children do not fear life, people in the last phase of life do not fear death. Either in terms of a personal identity, or vicariously through their offspring and/or their own accomplishments, they expect to live on through eternity.

The lack of a sense of integrity is signified by despair—a feeling of irrevocable failure, and a fear of death. Two moods alternate: regret that one cannot start life again and find a different route to trust and integrity, and rejection of the fact of failure through a projection of the causes of one's deficiencies onto the outside world.

## The Trait Cluster or "Dominant Component" Concept

The most recent attempts at character and personality description are quantitative and statistical in nature. Starting with a large number of measurements and ratings of personally and socially relevant behavioral traits, intercorrelations among all these variables are computed. From these intercorrelations, clusters of traits and stable syndromes are identified. These trait syndromes are represented by a set of test scores that intercorrelate highly with each other and still correlate very low or not at all with the other measures of trait clusters. Having found such stable groupings of test scores, the elements common to each group are extracted and named. These statistically isolated components are considered to represent personality or character "factors." In this manner, a very large number of character and personality trait measures can be reduced to and explained in terms of a relatively small number of components or factors. Personality and character can then presumably be described in terms of the *relative strengths* of these various components.

One attempt to study character in this way has found six major components (vectors or factors) contributing to over-all "maturity of character" (*Peck et al.*, 1960). These six components are: (1) moral stability (the following of the moral code, willingly and with satisfaction), (2) ego strength (perceptual accuracy, insight, rational judgment, and appropriate affect), (3) superego strength (the degree of inner control over behavior or conscience), (4) spontaneity (direct expression of feelings and wishes), (5) friendliness (generalized warmth of feeling for others), and (6) hostility-guilt complex (strong feelings of hostility and guilt).[1]

Moral stability, ego strength, superego strength, and friendliness are all positively correlated with general "maturity of character." Spontaneity shows a curious relationship to maturity of character. People at both extremes of the maturity scale are high in spontaneity while those of intermediate maturity of character are low in spontaneity. This means that high spontaneity goes with either very high maturity or extreme immaturity of character development. The hostility-guilt component is negatively correlated with maturity of character.

On the basis of the relative strengths of these six factors, five personality patterns were found. These five characteristic patterns of character organization were called "types" and named: (1) the amoral type (weak in ego strength, moral stability, superego strength, and friendliness; high in spontaneity and hostility-guilt), (2) the expedient type (below average in ego strength, superego strength, moral stability, and friendliness; high in spontaneity and hostility-guilt), (3) the conforming type (moderate ego, superego strength, and friendliness; low in moral stability, spontaneity, and hostility-guilt), (4) the irrational conscientious type (weak to moderate ego strength; low in friendliness; high in hostility-guilt, superego strength, and moral stability), (5) the rational-altruistic type (high in ego and superego strength, moral stability, spontaneity, and friendliness; low in hostility guilt). These character types can be considered as occupying points along a normal developmental scale of character maturation.

### THE AMORAL INDIVIDUAL

The infant begins as an amoral individual. He displays inaccurate perceptions, labile emotionality, and an absence of self-control. He is entirely lacking in moral principles, or inner direction of behavior. He is impulsive and spontaneous in his activity. Any behavior controls established during this period are by means of physical rewards and punishments and a limited degree of anticipation of such rewards and punishments. In psychoanalytic terms the infant is controlled by the "id" (his instinctive tendencies) and lacks an ego or superego. The infant gets hungry and cries; he is fed and becomes quiescent. The discomfort of thirst, colic, un-

---

[1] The most extensive factorial studies of personality are those of Cattell (1957), Eysenck (1953), and Guilford (1959). These studies are more elaborate and attempt to attain a much higher level of systematization than we are attempting. Interested readers are referred to these studies.

favorable temperature conditions, and sticking pins produces diffuse, chaotic squirming, twisting, and thrashing about, which persists until the discomfort subsides. Because the sight, sound, and contact with other people regularly precedes the removal of noxious stimulation, the appearance of another person may come to have a quieting effect on the child because of his anticipation of an improvement of his physical conditions.

As the child gets older he may direct his responses to noxious stimulation or threats of noxious stimulation in purposive ways as indicated in an earlier chapter; however, his behavior is largely impulsive, and directed to immediate concrete situations and short-time consequences. The young child is not concerned with social consequences nor does he possess inner behavior controls. He is an amoral person.

The adult amoral character type has become arrested at the infantile stage of development. This arrested development may be the result of lack of capacity for learning (the severely mentally retarded), or being raised in an environment so fluid and contradictory in its demands and its reinforcements that no stable patterns of socially-appropriate behavior have developed. In many respects the adult "psychopathic personality" is of this type. The symptoms commonly said to characterize the psychopathic personality are:

(1) Failure to understand and/or accept ordinary ethical values or to strive for socially acceptable goals.

(2) Impulsive, irresponsible behavior.

(3) A lack of conscience development despite average or superior abstract intelligence.

(4) A marked discrepancy between an apparent inability to profit by social experiences and a general level of measured intelligence.

(5) A tendency to live in the immediate present; an inability to work for delayed satisfactions.

(6) Ability to assume a role and put on a "good front" in order to deceive and take advantage of others.

(7) High level of hostility toward authority and rejection of discipline.

(8) Well-developed defensive behavior and lack of insight (*Coleman, 1964*).

Most of these characteristics represent the persistence of childish and immature ways of acting. A typical example of an amoral adult (psychopathic personality) may help delineate the type:

A 20-year-old boy (John) was referred to one of the writers for psychological study by the district court. The immediate cause of his detention was forging his father's name on a check. The boy's social history disclosed a pattern of defiance of authority, a violent temper resulting in perpetual impulsive, irresponsible behavior, a lack of concern for the consequences of his acts coupled with the ability to talk himself out of difficult situations. He was a chronic liar. Sometimes he seemed to lie when the truth would be more advantageous to him. His school records showed superior academic aptitude (IQ's 120–135) but a series of school failures. Reports of chronic truancy, running away from home, and defiance of authority were scattered all through the school records. John dropped out of school on completion of the eighth grade, left home, and had been in contact with his family only occasionally since that time. His contacts were usually occasioned by a bank check showing up with either his father's or his brother's name forged on it. Prior to his most recent offense his family had always covered the checks and did not press charges against him.

About a year before his present trouble John had married an eighteen-year-old girl whom he had known only a week. After about four months of married life John got on a freight train and left town one morning following a quarrel with his wife. He said he was going to look for a job. He had made no contact with either his wife or his family until another forged check showed up. This time John's father had him traced and held for trial.

An interview with John disclosed a personable young man with considerable verbal fluency and superior general intelligence. He would alternate between maintaining a "poker face" and being noncommittal on the one hand, and being affable and fabricating the tallest tales and most ingenious rationalizations of his behavior on the other.

Some reasons for John's behavior were obtained from the other members of his family. He was the youngest of four boys—ten years younger than his next older brother. He apparently was an unwanted and rejected child who was alternately neglected and over-indulged. As a child John never experienced any clear-cut or consistent discipline.

The brothers and father constituted a well known and very successful law firm. John had apparently been pampered and over-indulged from infancy. The family's account of John's early life sounded like that of the typical "spoiled" child. His parents and brothers "covered" for him and protected him from punishment for minor misdeeds, and were able to prevent any legal actions against him for his more serious crimes, until the present.

It seemed that John had been deprived of all opportunities for reality testing. He never really suffered the consequences of his many violations of the ethical and moral codes of his culture. He had never learned to anticipate social punishments and rewards for conforming to social expectancies and consequently never had an opportunity to develop a conscience. At 22 years of age he was still an "amoral" or, at most, a mixture of the amoral and the "expedient" personality types.

## THE "EXPEDIENT" INDIVIDUAL

The expedient type is typified by those young children who have learned something about the social punishment-reward patterns of their culture and are controlled by their immediate consequences. The behavior controls of these children have shifted from the dominantly physical to the social level. Their behavior is controlled largely either by the immediate social consequences of their acts or their anticipation of such consequences. They are primarily self-centered. Their honesty and dishonesty depend upon the situation and the apparent relative advantages of either. For example, when children below the ages of eight or nine were asked if and under what circumstances they were sorry that they had told someone a lie, most of them indicated that they were sorry concerning the lie that did not work. The undetected lie, the one which apparently worked to their advantage, was not regretted (*Macaulay and Watkins, 1926*). The older children often regretted lies which "worked." When asked why they regretted having told such lies these children indicated that they felt that they had violated a confidence with someone else or they just did not feel right about it afterwards.

The adult who becomes arrested at this developmental stage retains many of these same characteristics. He may act honestly because it is good business to have a truth-telling reputation. It is to his advantage for people to have confidence in him. However, when the probable rewards become sufficiently large or if he thinks he can avoid detection and censure, he will be dishonest. He conforms to social expectancies in order to achieve personal advantages. He has not internalized a set of ideals; he has no conscience or superego.

The socially-expedient adult is essentially the "other-directed" person popularized by Reisman *et al.* (1950). An example may help delineate this type.

> Harold, a 20-year-old law student, is of this type. He is a self-satisfied, fairly capable student who rooms alone and has a reputation as a "smooth operator." With other people, he is affable and pleasant and on occasions can be self-ingratiating. He makes many superficial, short-term friendships, but has never established any lasting emotional attachments to the members of either sex. He is wary of over-attachments and deep emotional involvements.
>
> He is a better-than-average student but works part-time and misses many classes. He systematically asks other students to make carbon copies of

their class notes and give him one. As he never reciprocates, eventually all the members of his class refuse to do these favors for him. He never gives up and seldom takes offense when rebuffed. His usual response to a refusal for help is a shrug of the shoulders and an "all right," as if to say, "well, it didn't hurt to try," and he goes on to ask someone else.

Harold started out in school in business administration. He later shifted to law, not because he intended to practice law but because he only wished to know enough about law to "keep out of trouble," and to be able to operate on the borders of the law without detection or conviction. He does small favors for people who are in a position to reciprocate. His reputation for honesty is very low. He is willing to be dishonest if some personal advantage will result.

Harold was the only child of middle-class parents who allowed him indiscriminate freedom to do largely as he pleased. They were overindulgent and overprotective. He never learned any clear picture of a moral code. He did largely what he wanted to, since, by a judicious use of threats and tears, he could always get his own way. He learned to control adults and whenever others exerted pressure on him, his parents would support and protect him. Harold grew up considering himself and his own immediate needs as first and foremost.

### THE CONFORMER

The conforming pattern of social behavior is most characteristic of the child in middle and late childhood. It may develop at the same time and as an alternate to the "irrational-conscientious" type of adjustment. At this stage of character development the conforming child has internalized one general principle of behavior. This principle is to do what one "should," and one should conform to the rules of his group. He strives to avoid the shame of social disapproval by doing as others do. He differs from the "other-directed" expedient individual who plays each situation "by ear" trying to pick up relevant social cues and guiding himself accordingly, in that he learns the rules and then tries to act in accordance with these rules. He is polite and considerate in conventional ways. The conformist is controlled by external sanctions and experiences shame when he departs from social mores. "Right" is acting according to the rules, and he is uncomfortable when he violates these rules. He never generalizes the abstract principles of honesty or dependability to the extent that he feels right about violating formal rules of conduct in order to be true to his own internalized ideals of conduct.

The following case is an example of the conformist individual:

Monroe, at ten years of age, was rated as a superior individual by his parents, teachers, and peers. He was very responsible. He always finished tasks on time, always did his share of co-operative projects, was polite, honest, and well controlled. The only misgivings others had concerning him centered around his inability to deviate from what others were doing or to take criticism or disapproval from others.

At this age "being good" for Monroe consisted in "minding father and mother," "being neat and clean," "helping father and mother," and "being nice to little sister." "Being bad" involved "not doing things father and mother tell you to do," "talking out loud in school," "talking back to teacher," and "being untidy."

By the time he was fifteen, Monroe's popularity had declined considerably. He was not as much unpopular as he was simply ignored by his peer group. He did associate with two boys who were considerably like him. He still retained many of his "Little Lord Fauntleroy" characteristics. At fifteen years he was seen as a passive, slightly feminine, and dependent person. He was considered lacking in assertiveness, over-anxious to please, and over-concerned lest he make mistakes. Monroe did not change as much between the ages of ten and fifteen as did the frame of reference within which he was judged. The pattern of conforming behavior that was considered meritorious at ten had remained unchanged and was now an evidence of immaturity and arrested development.

Monroe's behavior was rigid rather than spontaneous. He had a good deal of social anxiety lest he not do all the right things, but he experienced very little personal guilt. His compulsive conformity protected him from neurotic anxiety. Monroe admitted to no dislike of other people. He likewise claimed to "like" everyone but actually seemed unable to feel or display any depth of feeling toward others.

Monroe was the oldest of three children. His father was a steel mill employee, a skilled laborer. His family was lower middle class. Monroe's father was described as a "benevolent despot." He was a strict disciplinarian who "stood for no nonsense" from the children. He had never had any trouble with Monroe, but the younger boy had been somewhat defiant of his father's authority. Monroe's mother was a very efficient but passive person. Both parents attended church regularly and belonged to, but were largely passive members of, the PTA.

Monroe's home was a rigid, impersonal, restrictive one that fostered dependency and conformity. Spontaneity, self-expression, and rationality were neither encouraged nor rewarded. Monroe's personality reflected these influences.

## THE IRRATIONAL-CONSCIENTIOUS PERSONALITY

The irrational-conscientious person has internalized a behavioral code that he strongly believes and that guides his behavior. If such a person sees an act as honest he carries it out irrespective of whether or not other people approve and irrespective of its effects on others. When his acts conflict with his code he feels guilty; he violates his own integrity.

Of course, the internalization of a set of ideals is a stage in normal development. It is one characteristic of maturity. However, the irrational component of this syndrome constitutes a blind-alley, restrictive influence. The irrational-conscientious individual has internalized a rigid, logic-tight system that functions autonomously and without regard to its social consequences. Acts are good or bad in a kind of absolute way because of their self-evident nature or because one's conscience tells him so. Such people do not recognize that the rules and principles which they have internalized were originally man-made and are intended to serve humane and altruistic purposes. When adherence to the "letter of the law" defeats the "spirit" and interest of the social mores, departures from the code are in order. The irrational-conscientious person is unable to do this. He is rigid and inflexible in his judgments and acts. In psychoanalytic terms, he has a blind and rigid superego.

The following case has a large irrational-conscientious character component.

> Mrs. H. came from a deeply religious family. Her father and two uncles were ministers; two elder brothers were missionaries in South Africa. Both parents and all of the children were college graduates. One brother attended medical school to prepare himself as a medical missionary, but was dropped from medical school at the end of his first year because of poor scholarship. Mrs. H. was the only girl in her family.
>
> Mrs. H. was never really interested in the opposite sex, but married because she felt it was her duty to do so and have children. After three miscarriages she had a baby girl who is now seven years old. Mrs. H. is thirty-two.
>
> Mrs. H. is very punctilious in her religious duties and is insistent that her husband and daughter follow her example. In addition to having held a series of offices in her church organizations, she is now president of the PTA and a member of the governing board of the local Community Chest.
>
> Mr. H. is a skilled tradesman with a modest but steady income. He plays a passive role in the household. Mrs. H. runs a "tight household." Her house is kept scrupulously clean. Everything has a place and is always in its place. Household expenses are budgeted and the budget is rigidly adhered to. She cannot "understand" why intelligent people "live beyond their means," and "let their children run wild." Mrs. H. insists that all "normal" people know what is right and wrong and she cannot understand why they do such foolish things. She feels that right and wrong are self-evident and she is always on the side of the "right."
>
> Other people find Mrs. H. a "difficult person." They perceive her as extremely opinionated and bigoted. She is unable to co-operate with others because of her inability to compromise or make concessions of any sort.

There is only one "right way"—her way, and that is how things must be done. Mrs. H. is a fairly typical irrational-conscientious individual.

## THE RATIONAL-ALTRUISTIC INDIVIDUAL

In Western culture the rational-altruistic is considered the highest level of character development. Persons attaining this level of development have a set of socially appropriate internalized moral principles but these internalized values constitute an "open" rather than a closed system. These principles are subject to modification and the individual's behavior is determined not only by his own conscience but also by his judgment of its effects on others. Such an individual is honest and loyal because such behavior contributes to the welfare of others. It is also consistent with his own convictions.

The rational-altruistic person is rational because he evaluates conduct realistically in terms of its probable consequences instead of acting either impulsively and irrationally in a stimulus-bound fashion or compulsively in a constricted and rigid way. Such a person is altruistic because he considers the welfare of others as well as himself. He does not blindly follow his internalized rules of conduct without regard to the social effects of his acts. The rational-altruistic person maintains a constant interaction between his own values and the requirements of the situation as he evaluates them. The individual is sufficiently flexible for his behavior to be guided by the "spirit" rather than by the "letter" of the law. He is consistent in the principles for which he stands but is not rigid in his behavior.

Ralph H. approximates our conception of the rational-altruistic individual as described by Peck *et al.* (1960).

> At age seventeen, Ralph, a high-school senior, lives with his parents and a younger sister in a tract house in an area inhabited by lower middle class people. His father operates a service station. His mother keeps house and spends two hours a day keeping the books at the station. Since age twelve Ralph has worked with his father at the service station. His father is a friendly, relaxed type of person interested in his family, his work, and his community. He is considerate and self-assured as head of his family. He describes himself as a very fortunate average person. He is quite satisfied with himself and his status. "I've got a fine wife, two swell kids, and a good business—everything a man could wish for."
>
> Ralph and his father have always played and worked together. According to his father, Ralph is a "good worker." He can do anything around the station and he does it well. "I've always been proud of him," his father says.
>
> Ralph's mother is a good natured comfortable person who enjoys her family and her work. Except for attending occasional baseball games and

movies with her children, his mother's community contacts are minimal. Ralph's mother has as much confidence in him as does his father. She has permitted both children considerable freedom in selecting their own clothing and in choosing their own recreations. She seldom tells him what time he must be in at night.

Ralph and his younger sister Jane seem to get along well together. They occasionally go on a double date to a school dance. According to their mother, they sometimes fight but are really very fond of each other.

Ralph has a wide range of friends; most people like him. He has held a succession of class offices in school starting in the fourth grade and continuing to the present. Ralph has always been a good student. He has played on the basketball team for the past two years. While he has always liked school, he has also felt the pull of outside work. Several times he has spoken to his parents about dropping out of school and working full-time in the service station. Each time, his parents vigorously opposed the idea and he continued in school. He has had teachers whom he did not like and has criticized them to their faces and to his parents. This has never gained him the enmity of the teachers. At the present time he plans on going to college and studying engineering.

Ralph has never established any strong emotional attachments outside of his family. He is popular with the girls, always has dates for the school social functions, but continues to "play the field." He goes around with two other boys on the basketball team but views them with a critical eye. He has a strongly practical and realistic outlook on life. He is observant of the world, conversant with community and world affairs, but is not overly concerned about them. He takes people and the world as they are without trying to understand them completely. Ralph's conceptions of right and wrong are fairly clear and consistent. He displays considerable autonomy of judgment and is little swayed by the opinions of peers or adults. Although he tries to avoid conflicts with others, he stands up for what he believes to be right, and strongly defends anyone who is being mistreated. Ralph is a fairly typical rational-altruistic teen-age boy.

Although Peck and Havighurst's five character types are derived by factor analysis and are described as a "dominant component" form of characterization, they really constitute a developmental order of personality maturity. The least mature personality type is the amoral, followed by the expedient, the conforming, the irrational-conscientious, and finally the rational-altruistic.

## DEVELOPMENT OF MORAL CHARACTER

The principal contributions to the understanding of moral development prior to the 1950's were the theoretical conceptions of Freud (1938),

Piaget (1932), and Hartshorne and May (1928, 1929, 1930). These workers approached the problems of moral character and developed their theoretical formulations in very different ways. Freud's psychoanalytic conceptions were concerned primarily with the emotional and motivational components of morality. Piaget's interest focused on the cognitive aspects of the child's moral orientation. Hartshorne and May's researches and theoretical formulations dealt largely with moral conduct. During the 1950's and '60's there has occurred a resurgence of interest in the problems of the nature and origin of moral character. The bibliographies on the topic now list several hundred references. However, four comprehensive surveys and evaluations of the literature in the field have been published and we shall borrow heavily from these critical surveys for our purposes (*Hoffman, 1963; Kohlberg, 1963; Kohlberg, 1964; Brown, 1965*).

## Moral Conduct as a Composite of "Good Habits"

Moral character, like attitude, has a behavioral, an emotional, and a cognitive component, and each of the three approaches to morality listed above has concentrated on one of these. Hartshorne and May derived their conceptions of morality from their "Character Education Inquiry" of the late 1920's. Although these studies dealt with moral knowledge as well as with moral conduct, the primary emphasis was on the latter. These workers consider moral character to consist primarily of a general set of "good habits." Moral habits are presumably learned by associative processes just as other habits are learned. In order to derive moral character from specific habits it is assumed that direct training involving, first, physical rewards and punishments, and then social rewards and punishments, gradually generate expectations of a consistency of such reinforcements. Specific habits, which are originally situationally tied, generate generalized habits that persist throughout life. These habits transfer beyond the situations in which they originally developed and carry over into permissive situations. The regularities of reinforcement involved in learning are generalized into abstract principles and become internalized in terms of moral principles, which become consolidated into a conscience. According to this conception, conscience is the culmination of a hierarchy of reaction tendencies consisting of specific habits, generalized habits, the generalizations of principles derived from the patterns of reinforcement involved in the acquisition of these habits, the internalization of these principles so that they become determiners of behavior independent of external situations, and finally the consolidation of these internalized principles into a conscience. Conscience is considered to consist of internalized cultural values and rules of conduct.

While this interpretation of the origin of conscience has considerable appeal, the evidence in support of it is inconclusive. Studies of the consistency of moral behavior indicate that, in children at least, such behavior fails to show the predictability from situation to situation that such a conception seems to require. Hartshorne and May, in their classical study of the 1920's, investigated the moral behavior of some eleven thousand children in a variety of settings. These children were given opportunities to lie, cheat, and steal under circumstances where they believed themselves to be secure against discovery when in fact they were not. The children were studied in their regular classrooms, at home, in athletic contests, and in party games. The correlation between their lying, cheating and stealing in these varied circumstances averaged about .34. Even in closely related circumstances children showed considerable inconsistency. Not only might the child who cheated in classroom situations fail to cheat in athletic contests, but the child who cheated in arithmetic often failed to cheat in spelling. Recent studies have verified the comparatively low correlations between moral conduct as measured in different situations (*Rau, 1964; Burton, 1963*).

If conscience development as manifested in moral conduct were a simple process of social learning, we would expect it to continue at least to maturity. Studies on moral conduct have failed to find such a progressive development. Hartshorne and May (1928) found no grade differences in extent of lying, cheating, stealing with the exception of the school test where there was a steady increase in deception with increase in school grade. In the classroom situations, age was slightly negatively correlated with honesty. Other experimental studies of resistance to temptation to cheat or steal fail to show significant increases of this resistance from nursery school to high school (*Grinder, 1963; Rau, 1964; Kohlberg, 1964*). The failure of measures of overt indices of resistance-to-temptation to show a positive relationship to age indicates either that general morality is not being measured by these simple devices or that moral character is not the product of age-related learning. We shall return to this question later.

### Morality and the Superego

Superego is a psychoanalytic term roughly synonymous with conscience. A simplification of Freud's psychoanalytic conception of the origin of the superego is as follows: The parent frustrates the child's activities and this generates hostility in the child toward the parent. The child represses his hostility toward the parent because of his fear of loss of parental love and the anticipation of counterhostility from the parent. The child incorporates (internalizes) the parent's prohibitions and punishes himself when he violates or is tempted to violate these mandates. This results in the child's modeling his behavior after that of his parents. The self-punishing superego is conceived of as a turning inward on himself of the child's hostility which was originally directed outward toward the parent. Self-punishment following transgression takes the form of guilt feelings, which substitute for the fear of punishment or withdrawal of love by the parent. The child avoids guilt by acting in accordance with the incorporated parental prohibitions. The process by which the child derives his superego from his parents by the incorporation of their prohibitions is called "identification." The content of the superego derives from the culture that the parent represents. The norms and values of one's culture are thus considered to be internalized through identification with one's parents and operate as a socializing and moral force—the superego.

Although the terminology of the social learning and the psychoanalytic concepts are different and the levels of their explanations may differ, both accept the same basic premise that modes of conduct, moral standards, and values that are originally externally enforced become part of the child's own set of standards and values. Whereas social learning theorists make use of the concepts of conscience and guilt as intervening variables, and tend to concentrate on overt behavior, the psychoanalysts conceive of morality in terms of superego strength and the strength of the superego is, in turn, indicated by the degree of guilt engendered by transgression. It is further assumed that the stronger one's superego (the stricter his conscience) the more righteous he will be.

What have the research studies disclosed about the relation of guilt to moral behavior? One of the first studies on the problem was patterned after the Hartshorne and May research already described (*MacKinnon, 1938*). College students were given opportunities to cheat under circumstances where they did not know that they could be observed. Out of a group of 93 students, 43 were identified as "violators," and 50 were labeled "nonviolators." Four weeks later each subject was asked in private if he had cheated. Those who had not, simply said so. Of those who had cheated, 22 denied it while the remaining 21 confessed to varying degrees. The confessed cheaters were then asked if they had felt guilty about their violations. The violators who lied and the non-cheaters were asked whether they thought they would have felt guilty if they had cheated. An equal proportion (25 percent) of those who had cheated and confessed and those who had cheated and denied it reported that they had either felt guilty or would have felt guilty. Of those who had not cheated 84 percent said that they would have felt guilty if they had cheated. When asked, "Do you, in everyday life, often feel guilty about things you have done or have not done?" 75 percent of the non-violators answered in the affirmative whereas only 29 percent of the violators said they did. These findings are at least consistent with predictions made on the basis of psychoanalytic theory. "The more righteous a man, the stronger will be his superego," or, conversely, "a strong superego operates to prevent wrongdoing."

When these same subjects were asked to check from a list of common forms of punishment those most frequently employed by each of their parents, 28 percent of the violators and 48 percent of the non-violators checked physical punishments. Psychological punishments (making the child feel that he has fallen short of an ideal, has hurt his parent's feelings, and lost their love) were checked by 52 percent of the non-violators and only 22 percent of the violators. These results suggest that loss or threatened loss of parental love is a more potent determiner of conscience than is fear of counterhostility from the parent.

Despite extensive and intensive work on the relationships between the child-rearing practices of parents and the behavioral traits of their children, very few reliable relationships have been established. However, the three associations that seem to have been most consistently found are: (1) Persistent withdrawal of love as punishment for wrongdoing by parents having a "warm" relationship with their children is associated with strong conscience development in the offspring. (2) The use of physical forms of punishment in disciplining children and a permissive attitude toward aggressive behavior are associated with aggressive behavior and low levels of conscience development in the children. (3) There is considerable support for an association between parental stress on early independence training and strong achievement motivation in the child. We are now concerned with only the first two of these relationships.

It is axiomatic in psychology that an association or correlation establishes neither the existence nor the direction of cause-and-effect relationships. While it may be that parental practices cause the child's characteristics, the relationship could conceivably be reversed. For example, inherently aggressive children may provoke their parents into beating them, while mild mannered children do not. Likewise while the use of "psychological" forms of punishment by "warm" parents may be conducive to the development of socially conforming children with highly developed superegos, it is also conceivable that children with highly developed consciences are more likeable and encourage emotional warmth on the part of their parents. Of course, it is possible for the causal relationships to work both ways and to be mutually reinforcing. The likeable child invites emotional warmth and the emotional warmth, in turn, sustains and reinforces those characteristics which make the child likeable. Similarly, the initially aggressive child incites counteraggressive behavior in the parent that, in ways that we will describe later, may accentuate the child's aggressiveness. However, what evidence we have indicates that the cause and effect relationships probably operate in the direction that common sense would seem to indicate—that the parental behavior is primarily the cause rather than the result of the child's activities although it is undoubtedly true that the two interact. For example, Bandura, Ross, and Ross (1961) have shown that the fathers of hyperaggressive boys had been rejecting long before their sons became noticeably aggressive although the two variables finally constitute a mutually reinforcing system.

Although the original psychoanalytic conceptions of the nature and origin of conscience (the superego) were developed by Freud, and most of the extensions and modifications of the original theory have been made by the neo-Freudians, the next steps forward, as typified by the studies cited above, were made by contemporary empirical psychology working principally within a social-learning frame-of-reference. The following seem to be the generalizations that have been derived from the empirical studies of conscience:

(1) The more "psychological" techniques of discipline (praise, isolation, and the withdrawal of love) are positively associated with the development of conscience.

(2) It is generally the "warm" parents who use the withdrawal of love as a major disciplinary technique.

(3) The withdrawal of love by parents judged to be "cold" in their parent-child relationships does not seem to produce children with strong consciences.

(4) The use of physical disciplinary techniques (physical punishments and the bestowal or withholding of tangible rewards) is negatively associated with conscience development.

Although only indirectly related to conscience development, the following additional generalizations seem to have been established:

(1) Severe physical punishment is associated with high levels of aggressive behavior in children.

(2) High level of parental permissiveness about aggression is associated with hyperaggressiveness in the children.

These relationships are usually rationalized in the following ways: The warm, nurturant parent establishes strong emotional ties with his offspring. When the child's transgression brings tears to the mother's eyes, the "hurt look" in her face, the quaver in her voice, the brusqueness in her manner, and an interruption of communication, the child feels either shame or guilt. Presumably emotional warmth is necessary for the withdrawal or threat of withdrawal of love to be effective. That which has never been given cannot be withdrawn. The withdrawal or threat of withdrawal is proportionate to the value of that which has been given.

One type of behavior that parents universally disapprove of is aggression directed against parents. Children should not attack or be impertinent to their parents! In order to discourage such aggressive behavior, children are often physically punished. How well does physical punishment work as a deterrent to aggression? Apparently, not very well. As previously indicated, parents who have aggressive children have used physical punishment as the dominant means of discipline. Severe physical punishment is one of the most consistent correlates of delinquency in boys. Experimental studies indicate that physical punishment does not decrease aggressiveness. Why does punishment fail to function to discourage the activities which it follows as it should according to both common sense and the conventional laws of learning?

Punishment for aggression has an interesting property. It is itself an instance of the behavior it is designed to eradicate. Punishment of an act of aggression constitutes counteraggression. To the degree that the child rationalizes the relationship between his aggressiveness and his punishment he learns to be discriminating in the object of his aggressive behavior. He learns that it is not healthy to aggressively attack parents, other adults, or people who are bigger or stronger than he is, but it is all right to be aggressive to those smaller or weaker or subordinate to him—as parents successfully do. This is a subtle type of learning but there is nothing unique about it. It is largely a matter of stimulus discrimination. Essentially the child learns to discriminate between "aggression-upward" and "aggression-downward." Thus the child learns to inhibit physically aggressive responses toward parents, while physical aggression toward siblings and peers is much more freely expressed.

In addition to ordinary discrimination learning, physical punishment by parents may engender aggression because it constitutes a prestigeful model with which the child identifies. The development of morality involves selective reinforcement, but it also involves imitation and identification. As pointed out in an earlier chapter, identification is a general or over-all modeling process, whereas imitation is more a piecemeal process and involves the copying of more specific acts. Learning by identification means imitation of a very general nature. Learning which involves imitation and/or identification is also called "role learning."

The fact that children do imitate and model their behavior on the basis of examples set for them by others requires no experimental verification. However, such experimental verification is abundantly available and an impressive series of studies carried out by Bandura and others have thrown considerable light on the determinants of imitations and identification (*Bandura and Walters, 1963; Bandura, 1965*). These experiments have involved the manipulation of the subjects serving as models, the acts performed by the models, and the consequences of the activities both to the model and to others. To illustrate: different groups of children observed either live models, the same models presented in films, or cartoon figures performing the same unique strikingly aggressive acts. In some situations the aggressive behavior was punished, in others the same behavior was rewarded, and in still other situations the behavior had no particular consequences. In the post-exposure situation the children were given access to the same materials in the same setting that they had previously observed. In this instance, the children who had seen the aggressive acts punished imitated the behavior least. The children who had seen the behavior rewarded displayed more imitative responses than either of the other two groups, although the difference between the effect of "response–punished" and "responses–no consequences" was not significant. Cartoon subjects and filmed presentations were as effective as were real live models in producing imitative responses in these children. Some additional findings disclosed by these and similar studies are as follows:

(1) Behavior that is sex-role appropriate for the model is imitated more than sexually inappropriate activities (aggressive behavior performed by a male model was imitated more than was the same behavior performed by a female model).

(2) Behavior appropriate to the sex-role of the child is imitated more than behavior less appropriate to the sex of the child (boys imitate physically aggressive behavior more than girls do).

(3) A model who is powerful or who possesses "rewarding power" is imitated more than a comparable model lacking these characteristics.

(4) Models with whom the children have had previous pleasant associations are imitated more than the same models with whom the children have had the same amount of contact of an affectionally neutral type.

(5) Children reinforced for matching a model's moral judgments significantly alter their moral orientations in the direction of that of the model.

In some cases, the experiments that demonstrated these relationships did not end with the first post-exposure test of imitation. The children were subsequently offered attractive incentives if they were able to reproduce the behavior they had seen. In many cases the differences previously found in the spontaneous imitative responses of the different groups of children were completely wiped out. It was also found that the children could describe or relate accurately what the models had done *even though they had failed to imitate the behavior.* Because of the discrepancies between what the children *were able to do and what they had done* in the initial post-exposure tests, these experimenters make a distinction between that which is learned and that which is performed. Many of the variables manipulated have differential effects on performance but not on learning. This may have some significance for the distinction between morality as conformity behavior or as conscience and morality as moral judgment to be made later.

Parents influence the morality of children by the patterns of reinforcement (rewards and punishments) they afford and by serving as models for imitation and identification. The fact that punishment does not seem to produce guilt directly has been interpreted as indicating that identification is required to transform punishment-anxiety into internalized guilt. In this context, identification means taking on the role of the person who punishes, reproves, and/or praises. The child taking on the role of the punishing parent criticizes or punishes himself for transgressions. Workers trying to systematize this concept have found it necessary to distinguish between *personal identification*—the desire and attempt to be like the parent as an individual—and *positional identification*—the desire to occupy the parent's status as authority or family and sex role as powerful figures or as controllers of resources. Research findings indicate that personal identification is related to moral development, while positional identification is not (*Kohlberg 1964; Hoffman, 1963*).

Personal warmth would be expected to increase personal identification, and this seems to be the case. Parental warmth and personal identification with the parent have been found to relate to internalized moral judgment, to guilt, and to nondelinquency (*Kohlberg, 1964*). The child of emotionally warm parents becomes anxious over possible loss of the parent's love. To assure himself of the parent's continued love and to reduce anxiety, the child strives to become like the parent and incorporates his moral standards and values. This interpretation is supported by studies indicating that degree of father identification is positively related to the father's warmth and affection toward the child as rated by the mother. The further finding that degree of identification, as indicated by the extent to which boys and their fathers respond to personality and attitude tests, correlates positively with the boys' perception of their fathers as "helpful" and "kind" is consistent with this interpretation (*Hoffman, 1963*). Discipline by a loving father is assumed to be more likely to elicit anxiety over love withdrawal than is discipline by a nonloving father.

Father-son similarities and differences certainly result from more than simple parental identification. For example, boys whose fathers are criminals are *less apt* to become criminals if accepted by their fathers than if rejected by them. Parental warmth may lead to identification with a parental ideal rather than with the parental model when the parental model is opposed to the norms of the larger society (*Hoffman, 1963*).

In contrast to personal identification, positional identification as indicated by identification with like-sex parent and with adult authority and power is unrelated to moral conduct, moral judgment, or to guilt (*Rau, 1964; Kohlberg, 1964; Hoffman, 1963*).

During childhood, personal identification and moral role taking focus primarily upon the parents. As the adolescent moves out of the family circle into the more equalitarian peer group, the parents as models for role taking and identification are largely replaced by various individuals and groups and morality becomes more a matter of moral principles and social relevance than of fixed internalized superego or of identification with the real or idealized parent.

## Moral Ideology and Judgment

The cognitive component of morality was almost completely disregarded by the original psychoanalytic conceptions of the superego. It was recognized only in the form of "moral knowledge" in the classical studies of Hartshorne and May (*1928, 1929, 1930*). However, prior to these developments, there was a tradition that related morality to "strength of will" and to practical judgment (*Webb, 1915; Sidgwick, 1901*). More recent statistical studies have given support to the belief that there is a strong "will factor" in personality which includes some moral traits (*Cattell, 1950; Peck and Havighurst, 1960; Kohlberg, 1964*). Psychoanalytic writers are giving increasing importance to "ego strength" as contrasted with "super-ego strength" as the important determiner of moral conduct (*Redl and Wineman, 1952; Hartmann, 1960; Erikson, 1963; Loevinger, 1966*).

Kohlberg (*1964*) lists five "ego strength" variables that have been shown to be related to moral conduct. These are (1) general intelligence, (2) the tendency to anticipate future events and to choose the greater remote outcome over the lesser immediate reward, (3) the capacity to maintain stable, focused attention, (4) the capacity to control unsocialized fantasies, and (5) self-esteem or satisfaction with the self and with the world. These relationships imply that the major consistencies of individual morality may be found in the judgmental and decision-making characteristics of the individual rather than in the supposedly rather fixed moral habits or super-ego strength of the individual.

The classical studies of moral ideology and judgment were those of

Piaget (1932). To obtain an understanding of the child's moral concepts Piaget told children little stories matched in most ways but differing at critical points and the child was asked to indicate which of the two paired stories described the "naughtier" action and tell why the chosen one was the "naughtier" of the two. For example: In one story, Marie, wanting to give her mother a pleasant surprise, cut out a piece of sewing for her, but while doing so cut a *big hole* in her own dress. In the paired story, Margaret took her mother's scissors while her mother was out, played with them and then because she didn't know how to use them properly cut a *small* hole in her dress. Piaget discovered that the younger children thought Marie's actions to be naughtier since she had done the greater damage whereas the older children considered Margaret's behavior to be the more reprehensible because they considered the child's motives to be the crux of the matter.

Piaget summarized his findings in terms of what he calls two moralities. The one morality Piaget called *heteronomous* (subject to another's law). This he designated as the characteristic morality of the child below the age of eight. The second morality, which normally develops after the age of eight, was called *autonomous* (subject to one's own law). Piaget indicated eleven different aspects of the development of moral judgment which show characteristic differences corresponding to these two general moralities. Six of these eleven aspects have proven to be stable differences as indicated by replication of his findings using children of various nationalities (English, Spanish, Swiss, Belgian, American), social classes, and religions. The observed age-related differences also seem to be independent of the particular stories used or types of situations depicted.

The six aspects of the development of moral judgment that have held up and that can be considered components of Piaget's heteronomous-autonomous dichotomy are:

(1) Intentionality in judgment. Young children judge an act as bad in terms of its actual physical consequences, whereas older children judge an act as bad in terms of the intent of the person. For example, when asked which was worse—a child who broke five cups while helping his mother set the table or a child who broke one cup while stealing some jam, almost all four-year-olds selected the child who broke the five cups, whereas the majority of nine-year-olds said the "thief" was worse and the proportion of children selecting the child who broke the one cup while stealing as worse regularly increased with chronological age.

(2) Relativism in judgment. The young child sees acts as either totally right or totally wrong and believes that everyone views them in the same way. The adult's view is the right one. The older child, on the

other hand, is aware of a diversity of views of right and wrong. In one story a lazy student is forbidden by his teacher to get any help with his homework. A friendly classmate helps the student. The children are asked whether the friendly classmate thinks he did right or wrong in helping the lazy student, whether the lazy student thinks he is right or wrong for helping, what the teacher would think, etc. Most six-year-olds expected only one judgment, on which all would agree, whereas by nine years a majority of the children recognized that there would be more than one moral view of the situation.

(3) Independence of sanctions. For the young child, an act is bad if it elicits punishment, while the older child perceives an act as bad because it violates a rule or does harm to oneself or to others. When asked to explain a situation in which a boy who attentively watched his baby brother while his mother was away was spanked by the mother on her return, most four-year-olds simply say that the boy was bad because he got punished. They completely ignore his obedient behavior. The five-year-olds say that the boy was bad because he must have done something wrong in order for him to be punished. They postulate a misdeed to account for his punishment. Most seven-year-olds say that the boy was good even though he was punished. Punishment and wrongdoing are separated by the older children.

(4) Use of reciprocity. Children below eight seldom use reciprocity as a reason for being considerate of others, whereas older children often do. When asked "What would the Golden Rule say to do if a boy came up and hit you?" even most ten-year-olds interpreted the Rule in terms of concrete reciprocity: "Hit him back." "Do unto others as they do unto you." Between ten and thirteen most children begin to judge clearly in terms of an ideal reciprocity, putting oneself in someone else's position, and in terms of more abstract ideals of conduct.

(5) The use of punishment as restitution and reform. Young children sanction severe and arbitrary punishment of misdeeds, whereas older children increasingly favor milder punishment as well as acts of restitution to the victim and reform of the culprit.

(6) Naturalistic views of misfortune. Young children view accidents and misfortunes occurring after misdeeds as punishments meted out by a deity or by "nature" (immanent justice). Older children do not interpret accidents and natural misfortunes as punishment for misdeeds.

The remaining five aspects of moral development listed by Piaget, which have not held up under independent replication, are:

(7) Modification of obedience to rules or authority because of situational demands or human needs.

(8) Maintaining peer loyalty demands as opposed to obedience to authority.

(9) Favoring direct retaliation by the victim rather than punishment by authority.

(10) Favoring equality of treatment rather than differential reward for virtue or for conformity to authority.

(11) Punishment based only on active individual responsibility rather than on collective responsibility.

The six dimensions of moral judgment (particularly the first four, which have been well supported by other studies) primarily reflect cognitive development. All of them are positively related to I.Q. as well as to mean chronological age. In contrast with these six, the remaining five aspects, which do not follow Piaget's stage theory, are primarily emotional-social in nature. The related studies do not support Piaget's conception that there is a general trend from an authoritarian to a democratic ethic during childhood, although they do indicate that the child's earliest morality is oriented toward obedience, arbitrary punishment, and impersonal forces, and that it develops toward more relative, internal, and subjective values.

The research studies have also further qualified Piaget's "stage" interpretation of his dimensions of moral development. His dimensions do not represent precise unitary stages that cut across the separate aspects of moral judgment. Any individual child will show considerable irregularity as he develops within each of these dimensions. It is unusual for a child to pass from the heteronomous to the autonomous stages in all dimensions simultaneously. While the Piaget-related studies have only partially supported his theories, they have supported the notion of the existence of basic trends in the development of the cognitive aspects of moral development.

KOHLBERG'S STUDY OF MORAL JUDGMENT

One of the most extensive studies of moral thought and judgment carried out in the Piaget tradition is that of Kohlberg (1963, 1964). This study deals primarily with the individual's moral values. Kohlberg's stories are of his own invention, and typically present moral dilemmas such as the man in a civilian air-defense post who has to decide, after a heavy bombing raid that may have endangered his family, whether he should stay at his post or go to his family. After analyzing the responses of a hundred boys between the ages of seven and seventeen, who came from different social classes and some of whom were officially delinquent, Kohlberg distinguishes six developmental stages and thirty aspects of morality. This yields a complex matrix of 180 categories. The six developmental stages were characterized by the following types of moral judgment:

(Type 1) Punishment and obedience orientation.

(Type 2) Native instrumental hedonism.

(Type 3) "Good-boy morality" of maintaining good relations, approval of others.

(Type 4) Authority maintaining morality.

(Type 5) Morality of contract, of individual rights, and of democratically accepted laws.

(Type 6) Morality of individual principles of conscience.

Kohlberg labels the first two types of moral judgment as "Premoral," the second two as "Morality of Conventional Role-Conformity," and the last two types as "Morality of Self-Accepted Moral Principles." Kohlberg finds that the first two types decrease with age, the next two increase with age up to thirteen and then stabilize, whereas, the last two types continue to increase through age sixteen. These stages, like Piaget's, are seen as representing the products of the child's efforts to make sense out of his experiences in a complex social world, each arising sequentially from its predecessor.

It is obvious that these developmental stages are similar in many ways to Piaget's conception of the child's progress from a heteronomous to an autonomous morality. Kohlberg and Piaget both agree that the successive moralities of the child are not the outcomes of a series of lessons taught by adults, but are the result of the child's spontaneous restructuring of life's experiences that are fairly universal and inevitable. Kohlberg seems to perceive moral development as much more complex than does Piaget. It involves more than passing from heteronomous to autonomous morality.

It should be pointed out that Kohlberg's last developmental stage is more than the psychoanalytic superego development. Explanation of one's moral behavior in terms of a conscience goes considerably beyond the possession of a conscience. The internal agency can be present long before the individual explains or rationalizes his activities in terms of such an agency.

## The Specificity and Generality of Moral Character

Prior to systematic study of the topic, most people assume that morality is unitary. When we state that a person is of "good moral character" or when we describe a "psychopath" as a person lacking in moral values we feel sure that we are saying something meaningful concerning these individuals. We observe specific acts having some moral implications and assume that these specific acts are a representative sampling of the individual's behavior from which predictions can be made concerning future behavior. When we conceptualize morality as having a conduct, a feeling, and an ideational component, we are likely to think of these as three faces of a single system each manifesting the same underlying trait in various ways.

As soon as the studies of moral character left the general observational and armchair speculative levels and became quantitative, the evidence for specificity rather than generality became overwhelming. Whether the question of generality is raised with reference to moral character as a whole or whether it is raised with reference to each of the three dimensions of morality (conduct, feeling, and knowledge) the data seem to indicate specificity rather than generality to be the rule. Hartshorne and May (1927, 1928, 1929) emphasized the specificity of moral conduct because they were surprised by their own data. They had expected much more consistency. More recently, Burton (1963) has argued that the many low positive correlations between different situations do indicate the existence of a weak factor of general morality. The picture of moral conduct derived from the relevant research studies is one of positive but low correlations between moral conduct in one situation and moral conduct in another situation (Brown, 1965; Rau, 1964). In terms of our usual conceptions of morality, the young child's development in the area of moral conduct while having a small degree of inner congruity is predominantly uneven.

The evidence relative to the generality of moral feelings (conscience or superego) is of a similar nature and shows only slightly more consistency. After summarizing the related studies and studying the guilt reactions of over a hundred teenage boys, Allinsmith (1960) concluded that the person with a fully generalized conscience was a statistical rarity. It is necessary to speak of "guilts" rather than of "guilt" to make any sense out of the complexities of moral learning and conscience as manifested by feelings of guilt.

Moral thought and moral judgment show greater consistency than does either conduct or guilt but even here there is considerable inconsistency. Piaget explicitly states that there was too much inconsistency in the moral judgments of children to justify the presumption of stages in the usual sense. However, Kohlberg reports a developmental progression with some degree of individual consistency. While in all three dimensions—conduct, feelings, and cognitions—morality seems to be more specific than general, the extent of trait generality does increase in the order listed.

Trait consistency is, of course, a relative thing and has been shown to be related to several variables. There seems to be an increase in the consistency of attitudes and moral conduct with age (*Burton, 1963*). Horowitz (*1936*) found a gradual consolidation of specific attitudes into more generalized ones as children progress from the kindergarten through the eighth grade. For example, he showed that the attitudes and behavior of white children toward Negroes were extremely variable from situation to situation at the kindergarten level but showed regular increases in consistency through the following eight years. The child comes to be freer of the influence of the specific situation or circumstance and builds up more generalized attitudes and ways of acting as he gets older. Cognitive moral development shows the highest positive correlations with age, and experimental studies show that verbal and cognitive controls of overt behavior increase with age (*Kendler et al., 1960; Burton, 1963*).

There is a tendency for high consistency to go with high honesty and for low consistency to be associated with dishonesty. A correlation of .776 between honesty and consistency has been reported (*Hartshorne and May, 1928*). Inconsistency seems to be associated with being labeled a "problem child" (*Newcomb, 1929*). These relationships may mean that "dishonest children" and "problem children" are more "stimulus tied" in their behavior. In contrast with the more honest and more normal children they respond largely in terms of the stresses and demands of the immediate situation. When children have been classified according to social class it is found that both groups become more consistent in moral behavior as they get older but the higher social class children become more honest while the lower social class children become more dishonest (*Hartshorne et al., 1930*).

The interaction of character and personality traits may also account for some of the apparent inconsistencies of moral conduct and conceal the existence of an underlying core of generalized traits and behavior trends. The manifestation of one trait, which by itself may be quite consistent from time to time and from situation to situation, is influenced by the simultaneous operation of other traits. For example, timidity may interact with dishonesty in such a way that a person may cheat whenever the probability of detection is low and fail to do so when the likelihood of detection is high. The less timid but equally dishonest individual may cheat in a wide variety of circumstances because he is less concerned about the possibility of detection. Trait interaction may lower the predictive value of single indices of moral behavior because such behavior is the result of the combined operation of many interacting traits.

Behavior which seems inconsistent from an external point of view may be quite consistent in terms of the individual's self-concept. A boy may act consistently within his own frame of reference when he cheats in the classroom but be quite honest in athletic contests. In the classroom situation, cheating is perceived as outwitting a person in authority—an enemy —whereas cheating in athletic contests is taking advantage of a member of the in-group—a friend.

There is evidence that the determiners of knowledge (moral judgment) are often not the same as the determinants of feelings (conscience), and behavior (moral conduct) may not necessarily reflect either moral judgment or conscience or both combined. It is hardly necessary to document the fact that a person may see quite clearly that a course of action is immoral and still choose to follow it. Bandura (*1961, 1963, 1965*) has shown that young children *while imitating destructively aggressive-behavior* of a rewarded model make strong negative evaluations of the acts. The prospect of rewards to follow the activity outweighed the child's disapproval of the behavior. When children who had not imitated the aggressive behavior were asked to comment on the model's behavior, they could describe the entire behavioral sequence with considerable accuracy. They had learned the ideational equivalents of the model's behavior without translating it into action. When children making up three experimental groups differing in the behavioral sequences they had observed the models perform (aggressive model-rewarded, aggressive model-punished, and aggressive model–no-consequences) were offered highly attractive incentives contingent upon their reproducing the model's responses, the previously observed performance differences were entirely wiped out. Even though the children in the model-punished condition had performed significantly fewer imitative responses than had the children in either the model-rewarded or the no-consequences group, they all had acquired the same information and all were able to perform the acts equally well when sufficiently motivated. The observed differences were primarily differences in performance rather than differences in either knowledge or feelings. Moral behavior is not a reliable index of either conscience or moral judgment.

Moral judgment and conscience interact with aesthetic, economic, scientific, and personal (affiliation, prestige, survival) values to form in each person an idiosyncratic pattern of valences which manifest themselves in behavior.

The moralization of the individual is much more than the simple incorporation of the parents' superego as the psychoanalysts have suggested. It also involves more than the abstraction and internalization of the patterns of social reinforcement provided by one's culture, as an oversimplified social learning conception would indicate. The moralization of the individual also involves more than a computer-like programming of the culturally defined rules of conduct as an extreme cognitive theorist might insist. Moralities are diverse and dynamic. They undoubtedly involve components of all of the above and much more to produce a dynamic matrix of factors with a small core of common elements that produces some degree of both internal and external consistency. They also interact with situational, motivational, and various nonmoral beliefs, feelings, habits resulting in many apparent and/or real behavioral inconsistencies.

The longitudinal studies of the consistency of character and personality traits disclosed quite a different picture. In these studies a relatively small number of subjects were studied over a period of years and the consistency of their behavioral characteristics during this time interval was determined. The longitudinal studies found considerable consistency in the individuals' behavioral trends over a period of years (*Peck et al.*, 1960; *White*, 1952).

In the Peck *et al.* (1960) study, 36 children were studied intensively from age ten through seventeen. This study disclosed that each child showed a fairly stable and predictable pattern of moral character over this period of time. While the details of overt behavior changed as they matured, each child maintained a characteristic pattern of feelings and attitudes toward life.

Quantitative evidence in support of his contention consists of correlations among measures and ratings of these individuals on various moral values and character traits obtained at ten, thirteen, and sixteen years of age. The average correlations between such measures obtained at ten and sixteen years is .70. The corresponding value for ten and thirteen years is .78 and for the years thirteen and sixteen the average correlation is .92 (*Peck et al.*, 1960). Three facts are made clear by these correlations. First, the shorter the interval between measures, the greater the similarity (the three-year intervals give correlations of .92 and .78; the six-year interval .70). Second, the older the subjects, the higher the correlations between successive ratings (ten to thirteen years gives .78; thirteen to sixteen years gives .92). Third, all of the correlations are high for measurements and ratings of this type (the over-all average correlation is .80). These data indicate the persistence of personality and character traits over a period of years. The pattern of character and personality structure that a child displays at ten years of age will very likely be displayed in late adolescence.

It is obvious that an individual's consistency of behavior over time is in a different dimension than is his consistency from situation to situation at a given period in his life. For example, the expedient child of sixteen has learned more and better ways of expediency than has the same child six years before, but at each time in life he is still behaving expediently. He is consistent over time in his expediency. However, at any point in time, and from the standpoint of another person, his behavior varies from situation to situation in an apparently inconsistent manner. He is honest at one time and dishonest at another; he is belligerent with one person and ingratiating with another according to his own interpretation of their relative advantages to him. The overt surface inconsistency belies the underlying consistency of motive-pattern. The expedient individual's inconsistency follows a predictable pattern.

The individual high in conformity displays uniform patterns of behavior from one social situation to another insofar as his associates expect and approve his behavioral uniformities. The underlying behavioral consistency derives from his pattern of conformity. His overt behavior will be as consistent or inconsistent as the behavior and social expectancies of the groups of people with whom he affiliates.

The irrational-conscientious individual, whose behavior is largely inner-directed, is consistent over time *and* consistent from situation to situation. Having internalized and encapsulated a set of values, he maintains these relatively unchanged and is driven to act in accordance with the values irrespective of the external situation or the social consequences of his behavior.

The rational-altruistic person as defined by Peck *et al.* (1960) is intermediate between the expedient and conforming types, on the one hand, and the irrational-conscientious type, on the other, in the consistency of his patterns of overt behavior. The rational-altruistic person is neither stimulus-tied nor other-directed as are the expedient and conforming types, nor is he compulsively driven to act in accordance with an internalized moral code as is the irrational-conscientious person.

The question of consistency involves some apparent paradoxes. We have the seeming contradiction of a consistency of personality patterns despite the inevitable growth changes which occur. We also have the apparent contradiction of a consistency of underlying motivational patterns with *either* consistency or inconsistency of overt behavior. Some people's personality make-ups require that they be overtly consistent, while others require inconsistency. However, the latter are consistent in the pattern and form of their inconsistency.

### SUMMARY

Personality is not an entity in itself. It is the name given to the highest level of organization of one's motives, habits, attitudes, and value systems. Personality refers to the individual's unique organization of response tendencies as they are involved in social interactions. Personality has both stimulus and response aspects. "Character" refers to those socially relevant behavior trends which have particular moral and ethical implications.

Physique contributes to the stimulus-value aspect of personality. The effects of physique on one's behavior are more often indirect than direct. Physique affects one's personality largely via the social evaluation of the individual in the light of his physical characteristics. The person tends to accept society's evaluation of him and proceeds to act in accordance with these social judgments. The person who deviates from the socially approved norm is prone to anxiety concerning his status. His high anxiety level may also be conducive to the development of personally and socially handicapping behavior mechanisms.

Levels of endocrine gland functioning may affect physique, activity level, responsiveness, and general temperament.

The personality and character type concept has very limited scientific usefulness; however, the notion of characteristic *patterns* of organization of character and personality components does seem to have some validity and may prove to be useful. One recent analysis of character based on statistical analysis finds the following dominant components: (1) moral stability, (2) ego strength, (3) superego strength, (4) spontaneity, (5) friendliness, and (6) a hostility-guilt complex. Based on the relative strengths of these six components, five characteristic patterns of character organization are described. These five are the amoral, expedient, conforming, irrational-conscientious, and the rational-altruistic personalities.

Erikson's developmental phases of character development involve the achieving of a position somewhere along a continuum between extremes in each of the following eight areas: (1) Basic trust vs. distrust, (2) Autonomy vs. shame or doubt, (3) Initiative vs. guilt, (4) Industry vs. inferiority, (5) Identity vs. identity diffusion, (6) Intimacy vs. isolation, (7) Generativity vs. stagnation, (8) Integrity vs. despair.

Moral character has a behavioral, an emotional, and a cognitive component. Hartshorne and May have studied moral conduct from a social-learning point of view. Psychoanalysts have been concerned primarily with the emotional component. Piaget's interest has focused on the cognitive aspects of the child's moral orientation. Moral development involves all of the above and much more to produce a dynamic matrix of factors with a small core of common elements that yield some degree of internal and external consistency.

Cross-sectional studies have found character and personality to be very low in consistency as indicated by the low correlations between traits as they manifest themselves in different situations. Longitudinal studies of the same individual have shown a fairly high consistency in the patterns of character and personality traits as determined at different times during the person's lifetime.

## REFERENCES

ADLER, ALFRED. *The Practice and Theory of Individual Psychology.* New York: Harcourt, Brace and Company, 1929.

ALLINSMITH, W. Moral Standards. In Miller, D. R., and Swanson, G. E. (eds.) *Inner Conflict and Defense.* New York: Henry Holt & Co., 1960.

BANDURA, A., Ross, D., and Ross, S. A. Transmission of aggression through imitation of aggressive models. *J. abnorm. soc. Psychol.,* 1961, **63**, 575–582.

BANDURA, A., and WALTERS, R. H. Aggression. In *Child Psychology: The Sixty-second Yearbook of the National Society for the Study of Education.* Part I. Chicago: The National Society for the Study of Education, 1963.

BANDURA, A. Vicarious Processes: A Case of No-Trial Learning. In Berkowitz, L. (ed.), *Advances in Experimental Social Psychology.* New York: Academic Press, 1965.

BERMAN, LOUIS. *The Glands Regulating Personality* (2d ed.). New York: The Macmillan Company, 1928.

BRODY, E. G. Genetic basis of spontaneous activity in the albino rat. *Comp. Psychol. Monog.,* 1942, **17**, No. 5, 1–24.

BROWN, R. *Social Psychology.* New York: The Free Press, 1965.

BURTON, R. U. Generality of honesty reconsidered. *Psychol. Rev.,* 1963, **70**, 481–499.

CATTELL, R. B. *Personality: A Systematic Theoretical and Factual Study.* New York: McGraw-Hill Book Company, 1950.

CATTELL, R. B. *Personality and Motivation Structure and Measurement.* New York: World Book Company, 1957.

COLEMAN, JAMES C. *Abnormal Psychology and Modern Life* (3d ed.). Chicago: Scott, Foresman, 1964.

DAWSON, W. M. Inheritance of wildness and tameness in mice. *Genetics,* 1932, **17**, 296–326.

DIMOCK, H. S. *Rediscovering the Adolescent.* New York: Association Press, 1937.

ERIKSON, E. H. The Problem of Ego Identity. In Klein, G. S. (ed.), *Psychological Issues.* New York: International Universities Press, 1959.

ERIKSON, E. H. Growth and Crises of the Healthy Personality. In Klein, G. S. (ed.), *Psychological Issues.* New York: International Universities Press, 1959.

ERIKSON, E. H. Ego Development and Historical Change. In Klein, G. S. (ed.), *Psychological Issues.* New York: International Universities Press, 1959.

ERIKSON, E. H. A memorandum on identity and Negro youth. *J. soc. Issues,* 1964, **20**, 29–42.

ERIKSON, E. H. *Childhood and Society* (2d ed.). New York: W. W. Norton and Company, 1963.

EYSENCK, H. H. *The Structure of Human Personality.* New York: John Wiley and Sons, Inc., 1953.

FISHMAN, J. R., and SOLOMON, F. Youth and social action. *J. soc. Issues,* 1964, **20**, 1–27.

FREUD, S. *New Introductory Lectures on Psychoanalysis.* New York: W. W. Norton and Company, 1933.

GELINEAU, V. A. and KANTOR, D. Pro-social commitment among college students. *J. soc. Issues,* 1964, **20**, 112–130.

GRINDER, R. Parental child-rearing practices, conscience, and resistance to temptation of sixth grade children. *Child Development*, 1962, **33**, 802–820.

GUILFORD, J. P. *Personality*. New York: McGraw-Hill Book Company, 1959.

HALL, C. S. Temperament: a survey of animal studies. *Psychol. Bull.*, 1941, **38**, 909–943.

HALL, C. S., and KLEIN, S. J. Individual differences in aggressiveness in rats. *J. comp. Psychol.*, 1942, **33**, 371–383.

HARTMANN, H. *Psychoanalysis and Moral Values*. New York: International Universities Press, 1960.

HARTSHORNE, H., and MAY, M. A. *Studies in the Nature of Character:* Vol. I. Studies in Deceit. New York: The Macmillan Company, 1929.

HARTSHORNE, H., MAY, M. A., and SHUTTLEWORTH, F. K. *Studies in the Nature of Character:* Vol. II. Studies in Self-Control. New York: The Macmillan Company, 1928.

HARTSHORNE, H., MAY, M. A., and SHUTTLEWORTH, F. K. *Studies in the Nature of Character:* Vol. III. Studies in the Organization of Character. New York: The Macmillan Company, 1930.

HOFFMAN, M. L. Child rearing practices and moral development: generalizations from empirical research. *Child Development*, 1963, **34**, 295–318.

HOROWITZ, E. L. The development of attitudes toward the Negro. *Arch. Psychol.*, 1936, **27**, No. 194, 1–93.

KENDLER, T. S., KENDLER, H. H. and WELLS, D. Reversal and non-reversal shifts in nursery school children. *J. comp. physiol. Psychol.*, 1960, **53**, 83–88.

KOHLBERG, L. Development of Moral Character and Moral Ideology. In Hoffman, M. L., and Hoffman, L. W. (eds.). *Review of Child Development Research*. New York: Russell Sage Foundation, 1964.

KOHLBERG, L. Moral Development and Identification. In Stevenson, H. W., *Child Psychology*, The Sixty-second Yearbook of the National Society for the Study of Education. Part I. Chicago: The National Society for the Study of Education, 1963.

LOEVINGER, J. The meaning and measurement of ego development. *Amer. Psychol.*, 1966, **21**, 195–206.

MACAULAY, E., and WATKINS, S. H. An investigation into the development of the moral conceptions of children. *Forum Educ.*, 1926, **4**, 13–33, 92–108.

MACKINNON, D. W. Violation and Prohibitions. In Murray, H. A., *Explorations in Personality*. New York: Oxford University Press, 1938.

MAHUT, H. Breed differences in the dog's emotional behavior. *Canad. J. Psychol.*, 1953, **12**, 35–44.

MAIER, H. W. *Three Theories of Child Development*. New York: Harper and Row, 1965.

NEWCOMB, T. M. The consistency of certain extrovert-introvert behavior patterns in 51 problem boys. *Teach. coll. contrib. Educ.*, 1929, No. 382.

PECK, R. F., and HAVIGHURST, R. J. *The Psychology of Character Development*. New York: John Wiley and Sons, Inc., 1960.

PIAGET, J. *The Moral Judgment of the Child*. Glencoe, Illinois: Free Press, 1948 (originally published in 1932).

RAU, L. Conscience and Identification. In Sears, R. R., Alpert, R., and Rau, L. (eds.), *Identification in Children*. Stanford Calif.: Stanford University Press, 1964.

REDL, F. and WINEMAN, D. *Controls from Within*. Glencoe, Illinois: Free Press, 1952.

RIESMAN, DAVID, and ASSOCIATES. *The Lonely Crowd*. New Haven: Yale University Press, 1950.

RHINE, RAMON J. A concept-formation approach to attitude acquisition. *Psychol. Rev.*, 1958, **65**, 362–370.

ROGERS, P. V., and RICHTER, C. P. Anatomical comparison between the adrenal glands of wild Norway, wild Alexandrine, and domestic Norway rats. *Endocrinology*, 1948, **42**, 46–55.

RUNDQUIST, E. A. The inheritance of spontaneous activity in rats. *J. comp. Psychol.*, 1933, **16**, 415–438.

SAWREY, J. M., and TELFORD, C. W. *Educational Psychology* (Rev. ed.). Boston: Allyn and Bacon, Inc., 1964.

SHELDON, W. H., and STEVENS, S. S. *The Varieties of Temperament*. New York: Harper & Brothers, 1942.

SIDGWICK, H. *Methods of Ethics*. London: The Macmillan Company, 1901.

SILVERMAN, S. S. Clothing and appearance: their psychological implications for teen-age girls. *Teach. Coll. Contr. Educ.*, 1945, No. 912.

SOLOMON, F., and FISHMAN, J. R. Youth and peace. *J. soc. Issues*, 1964, **20**, 54–73.

SOLOMON, F., WALKER, W. L., O'CONNOR, G. J., and FISHMAN, J. R. Civil rights activity and reduction in crime among Negroes. *Arch. Psychiat.*, 1965, **12**, 227–236.

STOCKARD, C. R., ANDERSON, O. D., and JAMES, W. T. *Genetic and Endocrine Basis for Differences in Form and Behavior*. Philadelphia: Wistar Institute of Anatomy and Biology, 1941.

THOMAS, WM. I. *Primitive Behavior*. New York: McGraw-Hill Book Company, 1937.

TYLER, L. E. *The Psychology of Human Differences*. New York: Appleton-Century-Crofts, 1956.

WEBB, E. Character and intelligence. *Brit. J. Psychol. Monogr. Suppl.*, 1915, **1**, No. 3.

WENAR, CHARLES. The effects of a motor handicap on personality: I. The effects on level of aspiration. *Child Developm.*, 1953, **24**, 123–130.

WENAR, CHARLES. The effects of a motor handicap on personality: II. The effects on integrative ability. *Child Developm.*, 1954, **25**, 287–294.

WHITE, R. W. *Lives in Progress*. New York: Dryden Press, 1952.

WOOD, J. A. *The Uncivilized Races of Man*. Hartford: J. B. Burr and Hyde, 1872.

WOODWORTH, R. S., and MARQUIS, D. G. *Psychology* (5th ed.). New York: Henry Holt and Company, 1947.

YEAKEL, E. H., and RHOADES, R. P. A comparison of the body and endocrine gland weights of emotional and nonemotional rats. *Endocrinology*, 1941, **28**, 337–340.

# Chapter 12

# Personality Theories

PERSONALITY IS AN OMNIBUS CONCEPT and one that has been defined in many different ways. The many different definitions of personality stem from the generality of the concept itself. In the English language alone, eighteen thousand terms were found that were used to describe human characteristics (*Allport and Odert, 1936*). Some years ago, Allport (1937) found almost 50 different definitions of personality. More have been added to the list since that time. Personality is an inference made from behavior. The particular behaviors that are observed by the person defining personality will determine, in part, the nature of his definition. The experiences that the definer has had that have molded his own personality will be further determinants in that these experiences will have been important in determining the selection of behaviors for observation that are deemed relevant to personality.

## *INTRODUCTION*

Personality theories are general theories of behavior. Our knowledge of human behavior currently tends to be segmental in nature. Specific aspects of behavior have been studied, and great quantities of information have been accumulated about them. The formulation of global concepts that will account for all of the possible behaviors of man is an imposing task. Frequently, theories of personality have been lacking in precision, predictiveness, and testability demanded by theorists in the more specific areas of psychology. Many theories of perception, learning, and motivation have been developed, but such theories typically do not purport to deal with the totality of behavior. Competing theories exist because of the complexity of the problems even in these more limited areas. The theories in these areas conform more adequately to the characteristics of theory that are demanded by science than do the theoretical formulations in the area of personality.

Theories of personality attempt to deal with the vast array of behaviors, structures, and events of significance for the individual. Competing personality theories do not necessarily represent mutually incompatible formulations. Some of the theories represent modifications of earlier ones and hold much in common with those from which they derive. Differences can be accounted for, at least partially, in terms of emphasis. Some theories emphasize the *acquisition of behavior* and attempt to describe in considerable detail how the behavior itself is acquired. Such theories tend to be historical in nature, and heredity, development, and learning play prominent roles. In other theories the acquisition of behavior is assumed and little attention is paid to whether or not the behavior is a function of heredity, growth, learning, or some combination of these factors. The behavior is accepted as the way the organism is behaving under particular circumstances and the relationship between the *organism and its current environment* becomes the focus of attention.

No theory of personality has been devised that is completely satisfactory as far as formal theory building is concerned or as far as psychologists themselves are concerned. No theory has been accepted universally or even nearly so. Many theorists are interested in helping others to live more adequate lives and their theories grow out of their work with neurotic or deviant personalities. Others are concerned with the understanding of normal behavior. Some of the more influential positions are described and discussed in this chapter. The description of the various positions is inadequate and some injustice is done to the formulations. Limitations imposed by the nature of this text, the space available, and the authors' limitations in terms of preferences and biases are freely acknowledged. Theories are grouped under three different headings according to the dominant characteristics of each theory. *Psychoanalytic, phenomenological, and learning* approaches to the problems of personality are the gross classifications employed. The various theories are presented in brief, and statements that superficially appear to be presented as facts are facts only insofar as the theory or position is concerned. These statements may or may not express the position of psychologists in general or of the authors of this text.

## PSYCHOANALYTIC APPROACHES

Psychoanalytic approaches to personality have been either formulations made popular by Freud (1933, 1938, 1943, 1949, 1953) or changes in emphasis of the Freudian approach. Freud was trained in medicine, as were many of the subsequent personality theorists. His was the first comprehensive theory of personality and it derived from his interest in the treatment of nervous disorders. The people who broke away from him and formulated theories of their own carried with them much of the flavor and general orientation of Freud's psychoanalytic approach. Some have made lesser changes or have added to and enriched psychoanalytic theory but still operate within the same general frame of reference as Freud. These *neo-Freudian* positions will be given brief mention in this chapter.

## Freud's Psychoanalytic Position

The following account of Freud's ideas is limited to an overview of those matters that pertain to his theory of personality.

There are three major systems within personality as presented by Freud. These systems are called the *id*, the *ego*, and the *superego*. They do not usually operate independently of each other, although they may. Behavior is nearly always the result of interaction among the three systems.

### THE ID

The id is the source of energy for all three psychic processes, the more primitive of the three, and the only one of the three that is present at birth. The contents of the id are inherited from the ancestors as are the instincts. The id has no social values or morals. Operating on a primitive basis, it is ignorant of social restraint and reason. It is the original and basic system of the personality, and derives its energy from the body processes. When a high energy level is experienced by the id as uncomfortable tension, the id operates to discharge the tension immediately and reduce the energy to a lower, more comfortable level. This tension-reduction principle by which the id operates is called the *pleasure principle*. That is, when tension is too high the organism feels unpleasant. The id then functions to return the organism to a more pleasant state or condition. It can accomplish this through either reflex action or the *primary process* (fantasy). The primary process is a psychological process by which energy is discharged through creating an image of whatever will remove the tension. Dreams, hallucinations, and images qualify as products of the primary process. These images serve as signals for other psychological structures to commence operation in order to reduce the tension.

## THE EGO

The ego develops as a result of the infant's inability to reduce tension by the primary process. Hall and Lindzey (1957) have pointed out that the hungry person cannot be satisfied by images of food, and thus the primary process is not by itself capable of reducing tension. The needs of the organism must be satisfied by contact with the outside environment. If food is to be obtained, the hungry person has to differentiate between a memory image of food and an actual perception of food. He must learn to get and eat food before the tension can be reduced. The image of food must become a perception of food by locating food in the environment so the sensory organs can convey the real image to replace the mental image. The ego distinguishes between things in the mind and things in the external world, whereas the id can know only the subjective reality of the mind.

Where the operations of the id are said to follow the pleasure principle, the ego obeys the *reality principle*. The purpose of the ego is to make possible the discharge of tension and restore inner equilibrium, and to protect the individual against dangers that arise in the external world. The aim of the reality principle is to prevent the discharge of tension until an object that will satisfy the need has been found. When the object is discovered, the pleasure principle is then served. The reality principle temporarily suspends the pleasure principle and thus makes delay in satisfaction possible. The reality principle seeks verification of whether or not an experience has external existence. It compares the products of mental activity (images, judgments) with what actually takes place in experience. This is called *reality testing*.

The ego is in charge of all the intellective processes such as thinking, learning, reasoning, perception, and memory. The *secondary process* of utilization of these cognitive processes in order to satisfy the needs is the domain of the ego. The ego determines which instincts will be satisfied by traffic with the outside world, when they will be satisfied, and the manner of their satisfaction. The ego can be said to be the executive of the personality, but authority still resides with the major stockholder, the id. The ego comes into existence in order to advance the aims of the id and not to impede them. It derives its power from the id and has no existence apart from its identification with it. Its functions are to mediate between the instincts and the environment, to maintain the existence of the individual, and to see that reproduction occurs in order to maintain the species.

## THE SUPEREGO

The third major system of personality, the *superego*, is the last to be developed. It develops out of the rewards and punishments that come to the child from his parents. The child soon learns to behave in conformity with the desires of the parents. The cultural ideas of right and wrong, good and bad, sinful and virtuous are thus acquired by the child. The internal representation of the values and ideals of the culture as presented by parents comprise the superego. It has been called the moral arm of personality. It does not necessarily reflect reality; rather, it represents the ideal situation. It strives for perfection rather than for pleasure and thus is in opposition to the id.

The superego is divided into two subsystems. The first of these is called *conscience* and is derived from the things that parents say are wrong and for which the child is punished. The other subsystem is that of the child's *ego-ideal*. This subsystem derives from whatever the parents approve of and reward. The conscience can cause the individual to feel guilty for not behaving in accordance with internalized values and is thus a punishing agent. The ego-ideal serves a rewarding function by making the individual feel proud when his behavior is appropriate to the cultural standards. Self-control is substituted for parental control when the superego has fully developed.

To the superego goes the task of keeping the id under control. The impulses of the id that give rise to aggressiveness and sexual expression are of great concern because the expression of these impulses is strongly restricted and regulated by society. It further has the task of trying to modify the realistic goals of the ego in a perfectionistic direction. Moral goals could be substituted for realistic ones entirely as far as the superego is concerned. It would block instinctual satisfaction permanently and not just postpone or delay it, as the ego does.

The personality functions as a whole with the integration of these three systems. The id, the ego, and the superego ordinarily do not come into serious conflict, and calm and rational behavior prevails as long as the ego maintains sufficient strength.

## DYNAMICS

The energy that furnishes the power for thinking, reasoning, and other psychic processes is no different from the energy provided by biological processes to insure the continuous physiological functioning of the person. The portion of the available supply of energy that is devoted to the psychological processes is termed *psychic energy*. The id and its instincts are the reservoir of energy for the personality.

An instinct is a psychological representation of a bodily or internal source of excitation. The instincts are inborn and primitive in nature. They derive from body excitations called *needs*, which are reflected psychologically as *wishes*. The psychic energy of the id is composed of all of the instincts in combination. The id is the dynamic center of the personality.

The energy of the id is discharged in a diffuse manner through the general activity of the infant before it has an opportunity to accumulate. When the general activity of an organism is blocked or partially blocked in some manner, the energy is not immediately discharged but accumulates and flows into various psychological systems; these systems, containing percepts, memories, and ideas, become energized. An object that permits the discharge of this energy is said to be *cathected*. The energy has become invested in an image that serves to motivate behavior by increasing the person's sensitivity to particular objects in the external environment.

The characteristic features of an instinct are said to be four in number: source, aim, object, and impetus. The source of the instinct is a bodily condition or a need. The aim is the removal of the excitation deriving from this need or its psychological reflecting wish. The object refers to all of the activity and conditions that are involved in the satisfaction of the need or in wish-fulfillment. The impetus of the instinct has reference to its strength, which is a function of the intensity of the need.

The number of instincts is unknown, and Freud made no attempt to list all of the possible instincts that could derive from bodily states. He made no pretense of knowing the number of instincts but assumed that all were classifiable under the heading of either *life* instincts (*Freud, 1955*) or *death* instincts (*Freud, 1953*).

Hunger, thirst, and sex are life instincts. Life instincts serve the purpose of survival of the organism and racial propagation. The force or energy by which these life instincts perform their work is called *libido*.

Great importance is attached to the life instinct of sex, which is a broadly conceived instinct deriving from a number of separate bodily needs and giving rise to erotic wishes. Certain areas of the body when stimulated give rise to pleasurable feelings: sucking gives rise to oral pleasure; elimination, anal pleasure; and rubbing, genital pleasure. The pleasurable feelings deriving from the stimulation of these areas are the sources for erotic wishes.

Freud assumed that every person had an unconscious wish to die. He believed that there exists in living organisms a compulsion to return to the organic state out of which life was formed. The various destructive and aggressive behaviors are said to derive from the *death instinct*. In man the death instinct is referred to as a "death wish." This fits in with the general conception of behavior of the Freudian position. That is, the master plan for activity revolves around a kind of tension-reduction or return-to-stability hypothesis. A person is activated by internal irritants and the activity subsides when the irritant is removed by appropriate behavior. This procedure is a constant one wherein tension is generated, then is reduced. The cycle is repeated over and over (*repetition compulsion*). A state of equilibrium is thus constantly restored. If an organic state (death) is viewed as relatively constant, and living, as a state of tension and activity, the same general principle is operative on a broader scale by the operation of the life instincts and death instincts. All living organisms, thus, tend to return to the stability of the inorganic world.

The energy of the death instinct can be turned away from self-destruction and directed toward the outside world. This leads to quarreling and fighting with others or to aggression. The death instinct has not been as well accepted by others as have many of Freud's other concepts; however, he was convinced of its importance. The life and death instincts are in constant opposition, and much behavior is a product of the interaction between these two.

CONTROL OF ENERGY

The id is the original controller of all of the psychic energy and uses it in reflex action and wish-fulfillment. The energy of the id is fluid in nature; that is, it can be directed from one image to another. This state of flux results from the id's inability to form discriminations among objects or even between real objects and images. No distinction is made among perceptions, memory images, and hallucinations. A cathexis may be formed for either a wish-fulfilling memory image or for a realistic perception. The ego has the capacity for making those distinctions that the id cannot make and thereby causes objects or events to be approached that can reduce the instinctual tensions. It uses some of the energy of the id for this purpose. The processes of the ego are more successful in tension-reduction than those of the id. More and more energy is diverted to the functioning of the ego as long as it continues to satisfy the instincts. Some of this energy is then available for use in bringing the psychological processes to a higher level and to restrain the id from irrational behavior. If the id becomes too threatening, the ego builds defenses against its forces. This requires energy. (The various ego defenses were treated from a different point of view when defense mechanisms were discussed in an earlier section of this book.)

Among the earliest of the child's tension reducers are his parents (*cathexis*). The infant is completely dependent upon the parent for the satisfaction of his needs, and so parent cathexis develops very early. The rewards and punishments meted out by parents act as decreasers and increasers of tension. The child soon learns to match his behavior to the behavior rewarded by the parents (identification). He cathects their ideals and their prohibitions. The superego thus gets energy from the id by means of the child's identification with his parents.

The interaction of the driving forces of the id and the restraining forces of the superego mediated by the ego comprises the dynamics of personality.

ANXIETY

Anxiety develops as a consequence of transactions with the outer world that are necessary in order to satisfy the instincts. The role of anxiety is to warn the person of impending danger and it motivates him to do something. It operates as a signal to the ego that action must be taken. Anxiety is a state of tension that operates as a drive but arises from external stimuli.

Three types of anxiety are differentiated according to their source. The types are objective anxiety, neurotic anxiety, and moral anxiety.

Objective anxiety has to do with the ego and its relation to the outer world. This is basic anxiety from which the other two are derived. Objective anxiety represents fears produced by the environmental situation. Birth trauma is said to give rise to the original fear or anxiety. Neurotic anxiety derives from the relation of the ego to the id. It involves the fear that the ego will lose control of the instincts. It results in the person's engaging in behavior that will be harmful to him or that he will be punished for doing. Neurotic anxiety can take the form of a general apprehensiveness, or it can be attached to some environmental circumstance. Moral anxiety evolves from the relation of the ego to the superego. When the ego reacts in a situation in a manner that conflicts with the superego, the person feels guilty. Moral anxiety is actually a fear of the conscience. Feelings of guilt are to be avoided, and if the superego is overdeveloped the person may suffer from chronic guilt feelings.

The individual learns various ways of reducing tension. The ego must develop ways of discharging energy and in doing so it acquires a number of mechanisms by which it can operate. One of these is the previously mentioned *identification* procedure by which a child identifies with his parents. Other objects for identification are developed in the course of living. *Displacement* is the mechanism whereby the energy of an instinctual impulse becomes attached to a secondary object that will permit the reduction of tension when the original choice cannot be maintained because of external forces or ego controls. When the substitute activity has socially desirable implications, it is called *sublimation*. Identification and displacement are considered to be normal and not harmful to the individual. Other mechanisms are considered likely to lead to psychopathology. They have been called ego-defensive mechanisms.

### REPRESSION

Repression is considered the most important of the defense mechanisms described by Freud. It blocks the discharge of an instinct so that it cannot become conscious; hence, no reduction in tension is permitted. The repressed impulses are unconscious and neurotic symptoms are their manifestations.

Defensive behavior and defense mechanisms were discussed in considerable detail in Chapters Two, Three, and Four of this book. The reader is referred to those chapters for consideration of the numerous defenses that develop.

### PERSONALITY DEVELOPMENT

Freud gave considerable attention to the manner by which adult personality developed. The primary and fundamental instinct was sex, and the infant was born with a certain amount of sexual energy. The central nature of sex energy (libido) in Freud's system was indicated by his theory of psycho-sexual development.

Freud indicated that there are four universal stages of psycho-sexual development. He considered the early years of life to be of tremendous importance in the formation of personality and he paid particular attention to them. The first three stages of development normally occur during the first five years of life; the fourth stage represents the attainment of maturity. The middle years between the age of five and early adulthood are relatively less involved in personality development and this period has been called the *latency period*.

The three stages of development during the first five years of life have been designated the *oral* stage, the *anal* stage, and the *phallic* stage. The names of these stages derive from the parts of the body whose stimulation makes possible the discharge of libido.

The earliest of the three is the *oral* stage. This is the stage in development when the child's principal sources of pleasure center around the mouth. He is nourished through sucking to reduce his hunger, and the manipulation of his mouth provides pleasure. The child puts his hands and other objects in his mouth and the mouth becomes the focus for the discharge of sexual energy. Pleasure is derived from the intake of food and from biting. Character traits develop from this incorporation of material.

Later acquisitiveness is supposedly based on the pleasures of incorporation, and oral aggression in the form of sarcasm displaces biting activity. By displacement or through sublimation, oral functions provide the basis for the development of many attitudes and interests. Feelings of dependency develop from the nursing situation, and many residuals of these feelings may be life-long in duration. Freud believed that the most extreme form of dependency was represented by a desire to return to the womb.

The focus of libidinal discharge gradually shifts from the mouth to the anal region. The child's first real experience with external regulation of instinctive impulses is presented by the toilet-training situation. This anal stage is considered important in the development of later personality characteristics. If the toilet-training methods are harsh, the child may hold back his feces. If this tendency to withhold generalizes to other ways of behaving, the child may become obstinate and stingy or he may expel his feces in rage at inappropriate times. This is the prototype for a variety of expulsive traits such as temper tantrums and destructiveness. A number of other traits, including generosity and productivity, are said to derive from training during the anal stage of development.

The sex organs progressively become the seat for stimulation that results in the discharge of sexual energy. This leads to the phallic stage of psycho-sexual development. The physical exploration and the fantasy life of the child that accompany autoerotic activity give rise to the *Oedipus complex*. The Oedipal situation is characterized by the mother's becoming the object of the boy's sexual desires, and the father's becoming the object of the girl's desires. (The latter is also more specifically called the Electra complex.) The boy's incestuous craving for the mother and his resentment of the father produces conflict with his father. He fears that his father is going to harm him by removing his genitals. This is called *castration anxiety*. In the girl, the love for her father is accompanied by envy because he possesses something she does not have. *Penis envy* is the female version of castration anxiety in the boy. *Castration complex* is the label applied to these phenomena in general. The Oedipus complex and the castration complex are reputed to have far-reaching effects on subsequent personality.

The fourth and final stage of psycho-sexual development is called the genital stage. It is characterized by mature and responsible sexual-social relationships and derives from the other stages of development. It is essentially an adolescent and post-adolescent phenomena.

COMMENT

The Freudian position has been the focal point for much subsequent theorising about personality. It has been praised and condemned. The point to be made here, however, is that its influence has been widely felt. Therefore, we have devoted more space to it here than will be given to many of the positions. Those positions that follow will be described more briefly because they mostly represent modifications of the Freudian view.

## Jung's Analytic Psychology

Jung was an early associate of Freud's, but later broke away from him both intellectually and personally. One area of disagreement between them was Freud's insistence on the centrality of sexuality in his developmental theory. Jung's theory is distinguished by its strong emphasis on racial and phylogenetic foundations of personality. For Jung the individual is not only the product but also the container of his ancestral history. Whereas Freud stresses the importance of early childhood in personality development, Jung emphasizes its racial origins. According to this position many predispositions to respond in particular ways are the product of ancestral heritage. Only the briefest of outlines, in an attempt to give the flavor of his theory, will be presented. The personality consists of a number of separate but interacting systems (*Jung, 1916, 1928, 1933*). This complex interacting system is called the *psyche*.

### THE UNCONSCIOUS

There are two major parts of the unconscious structure of personality. The unconsicous plays a most important role in analytic psychology.

The first major portion of the unconscious is the *personal* unconscious. It is composed of experiences in the life of the individual that have been conscious at one time but are no longer available to consciousness. The personal unconscious is composed of *complexes*, which are constellations of feelings, thoughts, memories, and perceptions. The center or nucleus of a complex is built up from personal experiences and from inherited racial experiences. These complexes play an important part in guiding our behavior. Jung developed means of discovering the nature of the complexes of individuals. He developed the word-association technique, in which a word is given to the subject and he is asked to respond, as quickly as he can, with the first association that comes to mind. This and other means of getting at the complexes were developed.

The second major portion of the unconscious is termed the *collective unconscious*. The collective unconscious is an important part of personality and at times it may tend to dominate the individual as it does in mental disorders. The collective unconscious is universal and consists of latent memories that are a part of ancestral heritage, including man as a species and his phylogenetic ancestry. The collective unconscious is basically the same for all people because of their biological similarity and the communality of ancestral experience. Everyone has had a mother and as a result all infants are predisposed to perceive a mother and to react to her. Certain of our fears are said to be racial in origin. The concept of the inheritance of racial experience has been an important barrier to the acceptance of this theory. Even though experiences as such are not said to be heritable, it is contended that we inherit the possibility of reviving experiences of past generations. Such concepts usually are regarded as mystical and foreign to empirical science. The collective unconscious is the inherited, racial basis of the structure of the psyche. The ego, which for Jung is the conscious mind, is erected upon it as is the personal unconscious.

The collective unconscious is composed of structures called *archetypes*. These are universal ideas containing a considerable amount of emotion. For example, the infant inherits a pre-formed conception of the universal mother (the archetype), which determines how he will perceive his own mother. The archetypes are said to be numerous. Some of the ones that have been identified are birth, death, God, power, the wise man, the earth mother, and the child. Some archetypes have been considered so important that they constitute almost separate systems of the personality.

The *persona*, which is the public personality, is a mask that is worn by the person because of social pressures and traditions. It demonstrates that he is playing the role assigned to him by society even though it may contrast with his own private personality.

The *animus* and the *anima* have reference to the maculine and feminine characteristics of men and women. The feminine archetype in man is called the anima, the masculine archetype in women is called the animus. By constant association with the opposite sex down through the ages, men have become feminized and women have become masculinized. These archetypes act as collective images that motivate each sex to respond to members of the opposite sex. That is, man understands woman by the nature of his anima and woman understands man by the nature of her animus.

The *shadow* is the animal instinct that man inherited during the process of his evolution from lower forms of life. The shadow archetype produces socially unacceptable thoughts and feelings. It permeates the ego as well as the personal unconscious, and gives life and robustness to the personality. The *self*, though earlier considered as equivalent to the psyche, was later regarded as representing man striving for unity. The self holds the other systems of the psyche together and provides the structure with equilibrium and stability.

Two major, over-all orientations of personality are said to be *introversion* and *extroversion*. Both are present in the same personality but one of them is usually dominant.

Jung describes personality in terms of opposing tendencies within the organism, and interaction among the personality systems. Opposition and conflict are necessary within the personality because the tensions created by them are the essence of life. For Jung, man is constantly trying to move from a less complete to a more complete stage of development. This is an attempt to attain self-actualization, which represents the most complete differentiation and organization of all aspects of man's personality.

## Adler's Individual Psychology

Alfred Adler was the first of Freud's associates to break away from him. He developed a system of psychology that is commonly called "individual psychology." This system may belong as logically in the next section of this chapter (phenomenological approaches) as it does in this one. Adler is included here because of his early close associations with Freud.

The emphasis in individual psychology (*Adler, 1927*) is social. It is contended that man is a social creature and that his principal motivation derives from social urges. Social interests are considered inborn and only the specific interactions with people are determined by the nature of society itself. This emphasis on the social side of personality is a major contribution to personality theory. It is in sharp contrast with Freud's thinking, although Freud's emphasis on the biological determination of the nature of personality is comparable. But in general, the Freudian emphasis is on sex and the Adlerian emphasis is on social interest.

A further contribution to personality and psychoanalytic theory is the concept of the *creative self* (*Adler, 1935*). The self is conceived as a subjective, highly personalized system that interprets and organizes the experiences of the organism. It searches for those experiences that will help in fulfilling the person's unique *style of life*. Human aims are said to be fundamentally alike and it is considered that an over-all tendency of man is to strive for superiority. The different means whereby this superiority is attained represent the person's "style of life" around which all aspects of life are organized. The superiority is not necessarily objective superiority, but is represented as a movement from below to above. A great deal of emphasis is placed on the uniqueness of the individual and the uniqueness of his life style. The creative self affords a new dimension to the dynamics of personality. The self has occupied an increasingly important role in personality theories over the years.

Adler believes that man is motivated more by his expectations of future happenings than he is by experiences of the past. The expectations exist subjectively as strivings or ideals that affect present behavior. His conceptions of the general nature of personality endow man with creativity, individuality, sociability, and a striving for superiority, which coincide with many of the popular notions held about the nature of man.

Childhood experiences are recognized as being of some importance in the formation of adult personality. Factors that tend to produce a faulty style of life are considered to be organic infirmity, pampering, and rejection. Adler believes that children with mental or physical incapacities are likely to feel inadequate and consider themselves failures. This could be avoided by understanding, encouraging parents who would help them compensate for their infirmities. The pampering of children is strongly opposed by Adler. Pampered children do not develop social sensitivity; they become despots who expect society to cater to their self-centered wishes. Pampered children represent, for him, the potentially most dangerous class of society. Rejected, neglected, and badly treated children become enemies of society as adults because their style of life is centered around revenge.

Adler's social emphasis in the dynamics of personality and his concept of the creative self have had a good deal of influence on subsequent formulations relative to personality.

## Rank's Theory of Separation

Otto Rank was another individual theorist who was associated and identified with Freud. Like Adler and Jung he became critical of some of the Freudian concepts and developed his own views (*Rank, 1945, 1952*).

A salient feature of Rank's position is his emphasis on the strivings of people to break with the past in order to live independently of it in the present. He stresses the constructive strivings of men in the social milieu. His theory is not a grandiose one, but it has some distinctive features that will be briefly presented.

Rank borrows the concept of birth trauma from Freud's early theorizing and increases its stature to that of being the primary source of anxiety. Birth is considered to be the first real stressful situation encountered by the child. The trauma of birth serves as the basis for later signals of danger. The child is depicted as being expelled from the protected, sheltered, intra-uterine environment, where it has lived a parasitic existence, into a world where, by itself, it is ill-equipped to survive. The child must breathe for itself and is exposed to irritants of various kinds. The trauma of birth is the universal source of *primal anxiety*. The goal of human existence is to re-establish the contentments and satisfactions of the prenatal period. The greatest source of human fear is *separation.* The primary conflict of man is between the wish to return to the womb (a state of blissful contentment) and the fear of the uterine existence deriving from the trauma of birth. If birth trauma is viewed figuratively rather than literally, the universal problem of man is separation, which starts with the separation at birth.

Primal anxiety is considered to be the basis of life itself, and serves as the fundamental human drive. The fear of giving up conditions of security and protection in order to attain independent status (*life fear*) and the fear of the loss of individuality (*death fear*) represent the principal conflicts within each person. The death fear impels the individual to strive for individuality and separation from dependency on others. The life fear pushes the person toward dependent relationships similar to those of prenatal existence. The major ideal of the human race is the constructive and creative integration of these conflicting trends.

Rank considers *will* the integrative power of the personality. The process of separation is treated as a conflict of wills. The child must assert himself and resist the parent in order to become an independent person. Self-assertion by the child results in a clash of wills between it and the parent. The child's will really starts out as counterwill to the will of the parent, and because the child is dependent upon the parent, the counterwill becomes a source of guilt that is inherent in the child's attempt to become separate. This guilt is termed ethical guilt. The guilt deriving from behaving in a manner disapproved by society is called moralistic guilt.

The three principal ways of dealing with the union-separation or dependence-independence problem and its associated guilt are found in the *average man, the neurotic,* and the *artistic man.*

The average man fails to assert his will. He conforms to, and never actually becomes separated from, the society in which he lives. He never really becomes an individual. He has little conflict and is more a reflection of the culture than he is an individual.

The neurotic man develops to a point where he must assert himself but is unable to do so because of fear and guilt. He achieves a sense of separateness that is so strong that he cannot accept the union with society. He has a strong counterwill, which results in social hostility that prevents him from attaining the union that will absolve much of the guilt.

The artist also achieves separation, but he does it more adeptly. He successfully integrates his separate will and his need for union. This integrative solution is a unique and creative process on the part of the person.

Rank emphasizes forces in the individual that guide and impel him toward individuation and positive growth. All people are attributed tendencies for positive development.

## Later Social Psychological Emphasis

The rapid development of sociology and anthropology in this century has served to redirect the exploration of personality. The early Freudian and Jungian emphasis on the biological basis of man's strivings has been modified to a considerable degree by workers in the field of personality who have been impressed by the extent to which the behavior of man is affected by his social environment. The emphasis on the importance of man's interaction with man has resulted in interpretations of personality that emphasize its social, as opposed to its biological, nature. Adler (1927), whose position was described earlier, has given a social orientation to his interpretations.

Within the framework of psychoanalytic theory there have been a number of individuals who have shifted the emphasis from a biological to a social direction. It should be understood that interpretations emphasizing social processes have been advanced by people who have not been so closely identified with early psychoanalytic theory as those to whom we now turn our attention.

### ERIKSON

The contributions of Erikson (1946, 1950, 1959) to the development of personality theory have been extensive, and of considerable importance. He emphasizes personal-social, as opposed to psychosexual, stages of personality development, and extends the stages of personal-social development to cover a much broader portion of life than was characteristic of other theorists. Ego development is closely tied in with social-cultural factors in the life history of the individual. Another contribution of Erikson has been his emphasis on the development and function of the healthy personality. The Freudian emphasis grew out of concern for the treatment of neurotics. The emphasis on the healthy personality as opposed to the personalities of inadequate or inappropriately functioning people has been well received by workers in the field of mental health. Erikson has concerned himself, too, with problems of ego identity, and emphasizes the importance of the attainment of identity by individuals in society. The social-cultural emphasis does not represent an abandonment of the significance of inheritable structures and functions, but gives a realistic emphasis to cultural factors, which had not received adequate attention within early psychoanalytic theory.

### FROMM

The position taken by Fromm (1941) emphasizes the social side of a portion of the formulations that are also stressed by Rank (1945). His emphasis can be considered as a shift within the psychoanalytic position. Fromm believes that man has a basic nature that can be warped by society. He stresses man's potentialities for certain types of growth. Pathology results from a society's not permitting this growth. He postulates five basic needs of man: belongingness or relatedness, transcendence (to become a creative person), rootedness (to be a part of the world), identity or individuality, and a frame of reference (a consistent way of perceiving the world).

Central to this position is the struggle or conflict between feelings of isolation from striving for identity and freedom, and the desire for freedom and growth. The means of resolution of this conflict is, in large part, a function of the nature of the society in which the individual lives. Children's character must be shaped to fit the needs of society if the society is to function properly.

### HORNEY

Horney (1937, 1945) attempts to modify psychoanalytic theory in a social direction and to de-emphasize certain Freudian concepts. She rejects Freud's instincts and his emphasis on sexuality. Her position represents a shift in emphasis from the historical to the current adjustment processes of the individual.

*Basic anxiety* is the principal concept of Horney's position. This is described as the "feeling a child has of being isolated and helpless in a potentially hostile world." The child develops various ways of coping with this basic anxiety and the strategies for doing so may become relatively permanent fixtures in the personality. The importance of providing an appropriate social climate in order to reduce conflict and to prevent the development of neurotic tendencies is central to her position.

The neurotic needs of the individual have been classified in general as excess need for love, excess need for independence, and excess need for power.

### SULLIVAN

Sullivan (1947, 1953), though giving great emphasis to social factors as determinants of personality, still maintains a strong developmental orientation. For Sullivan, *all* behavior is interpersonal and the unit of study is the interpersonal situation, not the person. Personality is a hypothetical entity that can be studied only in terms of interpersonal action. Tension and means of tension-reduction constitute the basic dynamics of the system. Tensions derive from the needs of the organism and from anxiety. Sullivan rejects the idea that the instincts are important sources of energy and direction. People behave in particular ways because they have learned to do so as the result of interactions with people rather than because of innately determined predispositions to particular behaviors.

## Comment on Psychoanalytic Approaches

In general, the impact of Freudian theory on personality theory has been extremely powerful. Although literal followers of the doctrine of Freud have not been as prominent as those who initiated or attempted to initiate modifications of his position, the doctrine still stands as authoritative for a great number of people. Its emphasis on the role of motivation, the importance of early childhood experiences in the formation of adult personality, and the role of sexual factors in the lives of men represent distinct contributions of the position to psychology. Much of the language of Freud permeates the field of personality theory and psychology. The defense mechanisms, for example, have become the common property of professionals and laymen alike.

Psychoanalytic approaches to personality are bitterly attacked and enthusiastically defended. Many of the early formulations are so loose as to be untestable as hypotheses; others do not fit in with the scientific view of man. That the theory derives from the behavior of mentally disturbed persons is objectionable to many. The later modifications in terms of emphasis on environmental conditions and personal interactions have increased the palatability of the terminology and enhanced the flavor of the entire orientation for a great number of psychologists. The position still remains controversial and interesting as an approach to the problem of understanding man's behavior.

### PHENOMENOLOGICAL APPROACHES

This section of the chapter will describe a group of theories that can be described only loosely as "phenomenological." Without attempting to define phenomenology, those theories that are characterized by emphasis on the importance of the manner in which the environment is perceived, as opposed to the objective reality of stimulating conditions, have been included.

For the most part, the phenomenological positions do not place much emphasis on the historical aspects or derivatives of behavior. The emphasis is primarily on understanding the relationship of the individual to his environment as the individual now exists and perceives his world. The complexity of the personality and the "whole person" as a perceiving, feeling, thinking, responding unit are properties that are stressed rather consistently. Although other theorists are concerned about the whole person and convinced of the complexity of personality, these features have not been the focus of their theorizing.

The phenomenological approaches emphasize the understanding of personality from a different point of view or frame of reference than do some of the others. The emphasis on the whole person reacting as an integrated organism may stem from the concern that bits of knowledge discerned from atomistic approaches to behavior cannot be successfully pieced together to make a meaningful pattern. The whole personality has an element of unity that cannot be derived from the piecing together of fractionated or isolated behaviors.

The choice of a phenomenological approach to understanding personality may stem from the beliefs that the whole cannot be understood by understanding its components, or that the perceived world is the "real" one for the individual. The emphasis on the importance of the current perception of the present environment may derive from a belief in the relative unimportance of the means by which predispositions to respond or behavior are acquired. Such emphasis may stem, too, from the conviction that, as far as personality is concerned, historical considerations are factors that are common to many aspects of existence, but that the overwhelming considerations are in the here and the now.

It has been suggested that ahistorical theoretical formulations are more characteristic of professional people who are concerned about helping people with immediate personal problems deriving from the immediate environment than they are of those interested in a theoretical or academic understanding of behavioral phenomena. Whatever the reasons for the choice of a phenomenological approach to the problem of personality, a number of differing but somewhat comparable orientations have been advanced. Some of the more distinctive positions of this approach will be sketched in brief form.

## Field Theory

The application of field theory to the understanding of human behavior was initiated by the Gestalt psychologists. Field theory as a concept was borrowed from the physical sciences. As applied in psychology, field theory emphasizes that the way in which an object is perceived is determined by the context or configuration of the total situation. The importance of the relationship among the components of the perceptual field rather than the characteristics of the component parts is emphasized as the determiner of perception.

Lewin's (1935, 1951) field theory consists of a set of concepts used to represent psychological reality. The individual is conceived of as being differentiated from the rest of the world while remaining an integral part of it.

The psychological environment that contains the individual himself is termed the *life space*. The person is defined as a differentiated region within the life space. The life space is indispensable to the understanding of behavior because behavior is a function of the life space. The psychological environment is that portion of the physical world that is perceived by the individual. These perceptions are psychological reality; it is in relationship to these perceptions that behavior must be understood. The area of the environment not included in the life space (not perceived) may influence perception. The area outside the life space is designated as the *foreign hull*. In psychological investigation it is necessary to determine the nature of the facts that exist at the boundary of the life space. These facts are determinants of what happens in the life space. There is an interaction between the life space and the outer world. Lewin represents the boundary between the life space and the outer world as *permeable*. The permeability of this boundary is of great significance. A fact in the outer world may change the structure of events in the life space; therefore, these nonpsychological factors can become indirect determiners of behavior through influencing the life space. Psychological laws alone thus will not be adequate mediators of behavior. Any number of events may occur to disrupt or alter the life space of the individual. Lewin emphasizes that it is more feasible for psychologists to attempt to understand the immediate psychological situation by describing it in field-theoretical terms than it is for them to try to predict how a person will behave at some future time.

As far as the individual is concerned, his environment is a constantly changing one. Certain regions of the environment are predominant in the perceptions of the person at one moment and other regions are predominant at another. Psychological reality is a continually changing phenomenon, which is a powerful behavior determinant. The emphasis on environmental forces operating at the particular moment of behavior is referred to by Lewin as *systematic causation* as opposed to *historical causation*. The field of forces operating at the instant of action is all that need be known, in spite of the fact that these forces are influenced by past history.

The hypothetical construct of *force* is comparable to the usual motivational aspects of behavior. A force produces reactions and has such qualities as strength, direction, and region of application. Forces are inferred from movements toward or away from objects or by tensions within the individual. The apparent attractiveness of objects or events in the environment is described in terms of *valence*. Valence can be either positive or negative depending upon the desirability or undesirability of the object or situation involved. A valence is not a force. It has a steering function in the direction of behavior, but it does not supply the power for movement. Force or vector produces locomotion. A movement toward or away from any object or event occurs whenever a force of sufficient strength acts on the person in conjunction with objects of appropriate valence.

The concept of need holds a central position in Lewin's theorizing. Although this concept is criticized by Lewin, it is never really adequately described in his work. Increases in tension and the release of energy are caused by the arousal of need. Need tends to be a motivational concept of a pluralistic nature. The number and nature of needs are treated as manifold and almost any want, wish, or desire can be a need. The needs of a person are determined in large degree by social factors (*Lewin, 1951*). Much of behavior is designed for the purpose of reducing tension and satisfying needs.

The behavior of the individual is a consequence of forces operating at any given moment in time. The behavior is directed toward psychological regions having the strongest positive valence and away from regions having negative valence.

Conflict can be produced when both positive and negative valence are involved in a given action tendency. The varieties of conflictual situations described by Lewin are discussed in Chapter Nine of this book. They comprise an important part of Lewin's writings, but they will not be given further attention at this time. The reader is encouraged to reread the section of the previous chapter dealing with varieties of conflictual situations.

The field theory approach to the understanding of personality emphasizes the life space as a field of forces within which the individual exists. Lewin, however, writes a great deal about the internal organization or structure of the person. The development of the individual is given a good deal of attention and analysis in terms of field theory. The number of behavior possibilities increases with maturation and experience. The adult has more tension systems than the child. The psychological environment becomes more differentiated with age. Time, for example, becomes differentiated into a present, a future, a near past, and a remote past. As development occurs, the parts of the personality structure become more discernible and more adequately organized and integrated. As the child develops he learns, too, to differentiate between what is real and what is imaginary. Development of behavior is a function of both the person and the psychological environment.

Lewin attempts to present his theory spatially and he makes extensive use of charts and diagrams to illustrate the structural as well as the dynamic nature of personality. His use of terms to designate concepts is borrowed in great part from physical sciences. His ahistorical account of behavior and his emphasis on the importance of the current and momentary field give his theory a distinctive Gestalt flavor.

## Organismic Theory

The organismic point of view is closely related to Lewinian field theory and to Gestalt theory. The perceptions of the individual are the center of focus for understanding behavior. The perceptual field is divided into figure and background; the properties of both of these subdivisions and their interactions are investigated. The organismic point of view differs from the conventional Gestalt position in that the latter restricts concern very largely to the phenomenon of conscious awareness. Organismic theory shares this concern but has extended the general Gestalt position to include the organism and the personality as a whole.

Organismic theory emphasizes the unity and consistency of the entire personality. Disorganization or inconsistency is a pathological state largely produced by the impact of a threatening environment. Although the organism must be viewed as an integrated whole or organized system, the components of this whole may be differentiated and analyzed. This analysis, however, is always in terms of the organized system. The function of the whole personality cannot be understood by the study of its components because the whole functions according to laws that cannot be discerned by the study of its parts.

The motivational aspects of organismic theory revolve around the single concept of *self-actualization*. This is the all-important motive that gives direction and unity to the life of the individual. (A presentation and critique of adjustment as self-realization can be found in Chapter One of this book. The reader is encouraged to reread that section.) Inherent in the organismic system is a tendency toward positive growth or toward self-realization. The natural unfolding of the potentials of the organism produces a healthy integrated personality. Oppressive environmental forces may warp development of the individual's personality and deny the person the opportunity to behave in accordance with his nature, but if the organism is permitted its natural growth, it will develop wholesomely. Such a position has been described as a "Mammy Yokum philosophy"; that is, good will triumph over bad because good is better than bad.

Organismic theorists feel that there is more to be learned from intensive study of a single person than from an extensive investigation of isolated psychological functions (such as learning, motivation, and perception) among many individuals. Clinical psychologists who are concerned with assisting the total individual to live more adequately have found organismic theory quite attractive. A good concise treatment of organismic theory can be found in *Theories of Personality* by Hall and Lindzey (1957).

Some of the dominant characteristics of particular organismic theories will be discussed. These positions share in common the general features of organismic theory. In addition to these general features, each has its own distinctive characteristics. It is to some of these distinctive characteristics that we now turn our attention.

### GOLDSTEIN

Kurt Goldstein (1940) conceives of the individual as an integrated whole composed of a number of differentiated structures, which remain integrated unless abnormal conditions prevail. He views the organization of the various structures in terms of figure and ground. The figure in the experience of the individual is that on which his activity and awareness are focused. The activity of the organism changes as figure-ground relationships change in the stimulus world of the person. The figure-ground relationship is a constantly changing one.

The dynamic aspects of the theory are essentially homeostatic in nature. A constant amount of energy is assumed to be evenly distributed throughout the organism. This distribution represents the normal tension state. The energy distribution is constantly being disturbed by both personal and environmental circumstance. The ensuing behavior serves to redistribute or equalize the energy state. This is termed the *equalization process*. Disturbances in the normal tension state produce activity that is designed to restore equilibrium. In development, certain mechanisms appear that tend to serve as devices for the maintenance of the normal tension state of the individual.

What may appear to be different drives are only mainfestations of the all-inclusive motive of self-actualization. The innate potentialities of the individual are important determinants of the direction of behavior. There is an interaction between the organism and its environment. The person must "come to terms" with his environment in order to master it and further self-realization. Goldstein sees man as striving for self-actualization, which includes mastery of the forces of the environment that might hinder self-realization.

### MASLOW

Maslow (1954) contends that psychology has concerned itself too much with the negative side of man's nature and not enough with the positive side. He attempts to provide explanations for behavior with a positive affective approach rather than accounting for behavior as a result of conflict, misery, and guilt. He is concerned with the healthy personality and the understanding of it in terms other than comparison with the mentally ill.

Maslow emphasizes the inherent goodness of man's nature in contrast to other positions that emphasize the necessity for socialization in order to produce "good" behavior. Aggression and destructiveness are not an inherent part of man's nature. He may become destructive when his inner nature is warped or frustrated by a corrupting environment.

A system of human motivation based on a hierarchy of needs has been developed by Maslow. His classification of needs that man strives to fulfill is as follows: physiological needs, safety needs, needs for belonging and love, esteem needs, needs for self-actualization, cognitive needs, and aesthetic needs. These are arranged in a hierarchy of prepotence. When the most prepotent needs become satisfied, lesser needs emerge and press for satisfaction. This hierarchy is not a rigid one, although certain needs do take precedence over others under normal conditions. The most demanding need at one time may be satisfied and be quite unimportant at another time. When fulfillment of man's inborn needs is denied, he may become antisocial.

The emphasis on normal personality, on positive growth characteristics, and on a hierarchy of needs as a motivational system gives Maslow's position a unique flavor.

LECKY

Prescott Lecky (1945) maintains that personality is the organizer of behavior and that psychological phenomena are the expressions of a unified personality. The source of psychological motivation for Lecky is the need to maintain *self-consistency*. Man's efforts are constantly directed toward the maintenance of a harmonious, organized personality structure. This structure largely consists of values that are consistent with each other.

He views man as a problem solver who seeks to *maintain and produce tension*. This is in sharp contrast with tension-reduction theories that have been advocated by others.

## Self Theory

Self theory has a great deal in common with organismic theory and is clearly phenomenological in nature. Self theory is very appealing to the lay person because the language used in the description of the theory is the language of subjective experience. In the past decade, self theory has become very popular with certain clinical and social psychologists. William James (1890), in an early treatment of the concept of self, describes it as the "Empirical Me," or all that a man is and has. The word *self* is currently used in two different senses (*Hall and Lindzey, 1957*). One use of the word is to refer to a person's feelings toward and evaluations of himself as an *object*. The other meaning is used when referring to self as a *process*. When self is referred to as the governing process of the organism, self as a process is being employed. No current theorist thinks of self as an entity, that is, as a "man within man" that guides, directs, and determines behavior. When self as a process is discussed it is frequently called *ego*; the words have been used interchangeably with some confusion resulting from this practice.

### ROGERS

Foremost among contemporary self theorists is Carl Rogers. His self theory (*1951*) combines features of organismic theory with Freudian theory, while maintaining a distinctly phenomenological orientation. He emphasizes the current situation as perceived by the individual as the causal agent in behavior. The current situation as perceived by the individual is called the *phenomenal field*. The self is a differentiated part of the phenomenal field and consists of the conscious perceptions and values of the I or me. The *self-concept* includes the picture of what I am as a person.

Although there are a number of specific needs, there is only one basic motive; that is, to *actualize, maintain, and enhance the self*. The organism reacts as a unified whole to the phenomenal field in order to satisfy its needs. The self-concept develops from the organism's interaction with its environment and is subject to alteration. The self strives for consistency; experiences that are not consistent with the self-concept represent threats and produce emotional disturbances. A person whose self-concept is essentially realistic is free of the conflicts that would restrict the individual in his positive growth.

Development of the self-concept occurs through organization and reorganization of the perceptual field. Changes in the self-concept occur in the same manner. In addition to the self-concept as a behavior-regulating agency, the biological urges of the organism are recognized as playing a partial role in the determination of behavior.

For Rogers, the way to find out about the nature of a person's self-concept is for the individual to report the manner of his feelings. These personal, phenomenological reports comprise the basic data of the system. Introspective reports are of prime importance to the understanding, by an objective observer, of the structure of one's self-concept.

### SNYGG AND COMBS

The term *phenomenal field* is used by Snygg and Combs (*1949*) in essentially the same manner that Rogers uses it. For them, *all* behavior is determined by and related to the phenomenal field of the individual. The biologic or organic determinants of behavior are not given the considera- tion in this system that they are by Rogers. The phenomenal field of the organism changes with changing needs and with external conditions. It is divided into the phenomenal self and the self-concept. The phenomenal self "includes all those parts of its phenomenal field which the individual experiences as part or characteristic of himself" (1949, p. 58). The self- concept is composed of parts of the phenomenal field that have been differentiated by the person as characteristics of himself.

The introspective data is derived in a different fashion than that of Rogers. The introspection that yields meaningful material for Snygg and Combs is the introspection of the observer, who relates the client's reports to his own feelings and to his information relative to personality function; thus, the nature of the self-concept of another is understood through the personal frame of reference of the observer rather than from the objective evaluation of the report.

AN OBSERVATION

The concept of self has become an increasingly popular one in psychology. The self as an organizing process has gained a certain respectability among those interested in personality theory and development. Many psycholo- gists have difficulty accepting the introspective reports of a person as being actually reflective of how the person does feel, think, or reason. The phenomenology of Snygg and Combs, which depends upon the observer's subjective evaluation of verbal reports, introduces still another variable into the study of the phenomenal field of another person.

Self theory has been most popular among and most utilized by clinical psychologists who have been interested in assisting another person to live more adequately. Whether or not self theory will become sufficiently more rigorous and more subject to empirical evaluation to become attractive to more objectively oriented behavioral scientists is difficult to predict. It is certainly true that modern self theory has been productive in research and has produced systematic attempts to measure the self-concept and changes that tend to occur in it as the result of therapy or other experiences.

## Biosocial Theory

The principal proponent of the so-called biosocial theory of personality is Gardner Murphy (1947, 1958). Murphy's book Personality: A Biosocial Approach to Origins and Structures (1947) utilizes field concepts, organ- ismic concepts, and associative learning theory in its presentation. His position has been described as eclectic because of his apparent willingness to adapt, from various theoretical positions, ideas and orientations that are representative of American psychology in general.

The predominant emphases in Murphy's theory are field-theoretical, phenomenological, and organismic. Associative learning theory is used only slightly in the development of his position. The position is eclectic, and therefore is hard to force into any particular classification. The "best fit" would appear to be under the phenomenological classification.

The "bio" portion of this biosocial theory is represented by an emphasis on physiological predispositions or *organic traits*. These are tissue tensions that are expressed as symbolic traits as the result of learning. The individual learns to associate certain symbols or thoughts with original tissue condition and can thus learn to respond appropriately to the symbolic representation of the organic tissue condition. These organic traits can be directed or channeled by social pressure and experience into specific varieties of behavior. This process is called *canalization*.

Murphy uses the concept of *self* to indicate a person's perceptions and conceptions of himself as a person. The *ego* is used as a controlling or regulating process. *Role* represents the ways of behaving under particular circumstances that are imposed by society. Roles eventually become a part of the personality of the individual and reflect the impact of society on the personality. The term *cognitive habits* is used to cover the functions and operations of self, ego, and role.

Murphy's biosocial theory basically treats motive as an organic or tissue-tension gradient. Tension-reduction produces satisfaction and tension-increase produces discomfort. He rejects the notion that complex motives derive from primary drives and emphasizes that any motive is a part of a total motivational state and must be understood within that context. Biological and social needs do not constitute separate categories. Murphy accounts for the apparent active seeking of certain stimuli in terms of the nature of human sense organs. The organism has certain *sensory and activity needs* that do not depend upon learning but are characteristic of our biological structure. Certain tastes, sounds, and pressures are satisfying in nature without the organism's having had previous training.

Personality and culture cannot be independently defined. Appeal to one must be made for the definition of the other. The personality is dependent upon the culture, and the culture cannot be thought of independently of the personality of its members.

Murphy's biosocial theory has had a broad acceptance. Hall and Lindzey (1957) suggest that this is so partly because the theory is so soundly based on accepted psychological principles.

## Comment on Phenomenological Approaches

The field-theory approach to the study of personality as represented by Lewin (1935, 1951) is thoroughly psychological. More recent theoretical formulations in field theory pay more attention to nonpsychological factors or the life space (*Escalona, 1954*). The objective environment probably cannot be given so little importance as it is by Lewin. Leeper (1943) and Tolman (1948) are both critical of the formulations of Lewin for the small emphasis given the role of the physical environment.

The essentially ahistorical nature of Lewinian theory is the object of attack by many psychologists who believe that man is a product of heredity, maturation, and learning.

Lewin's formulations tend to give scientific respectability to the subjective frame of reference. He treats man as a complex organism with psychological systems that emphasize man's nature as a living human being and minimize his mechanical and behavioristic sides.

Organismic theory emphasizes the unitary nature of the individual. Conceiving of the individual as a whole, integrated, and functioning organism is an idea that is given psychological support and acceptance.

Rogers' acceptance of the usefulness of self-reports as direct sources of information about a person, and his emphasis on conscious processes as opposed to unconscious ones, has opened up the concept of self as an area for quantitative investigation. Self theory has many followers and their energy, ingenuity, and interest in devising techniques for the investigation of the self-concept has probably caused psychologists who have heretofore largely ignored such concepts to have another look at the utility of the concept of "self."

### LEARNING APPROACHES

Psychologists interested in theory construction have given a great amount of attention and effort to the building of behavior theories. Because of the objectivity of these approaches to behavior and their dependence upon laboratory findings, their utility for understanding personality has tended to become lost. Hull's (1943) book setting forth his position was entitled *Principles of Behavior*, and Tolman's (1932) book was entitled *Purposive Behavior in Animals and Men*. Both of these dealt with *behavior*. Because of the strong emphasis on those behaviors that appear to be learned and the emphasis on the manner of acquisition, these books have come to be regarded as books on *learning theory*. Early attempts were made to apply the principles of learning derived largely from laboratory experimentation to personal and social situations (*Guthrie, 1938*). The more recent efforts in this direction seem to have been better received than earlier ones. The work of psychologists exposed to the Hullian influence at Yale University has been outstanding in adapting learning theory to the understanding of human personality. Reinforcement theory (*Skinner, 1938*) has become increasingly important in personality and has been fostered by a number of people (*Krasner and Ullmann, 1965; Ullmann and Krasner, 1965*).

No attempt will be made to outline all of the possible ramifications of learning approaches to the study of personality. Only a few of the salient features of some of these approaches will be treated. Earlier chapters of this book sketch some principles of learning as they are used to account for adjustive behavior. This constitutes a learning approach to behavior. Learning approaches are more of an orientation or frame of reference than a theory.

## Learning-Psychoanalytic Approaches

The work of a number of psychologists has contributed to the application of learning principles to psychoanalytic concepts. Attempts to test the validity of certain psychoanalytic concepts have been made in psychological laboratories. As a result of these investigations, a number of the concepts have been utilized in formulating what are essentially learning approaches to the understanding of personality.

### DOLLARD AND MILLER

An early systematic attempt to apply learning principles to the acquisition of social and personal behavior was that of Miller and Dollard (*1941*) and Dollard and Miller (*1950*). They gave emphasis to the role of social learning and were concerned with personality and psychotherapy. Their position represents a kind of wedding of Freudian theory with general principles of learning.

The learning principles most fully exploited in this theory are those of drive, cue, response, and reward (*Miller and Dollard, 1941*). According to this position any strong stimulus, whether internally or externally instigated, can act as a *drive*. The stimulus itself has *cue* or distinctive characteristics that come to be identifiable by the person. Possessing drive, and the stimulus providing a cue, the individual makes *responses*. These responses are *rewarded* or reinforced and eventually become established as *habits*. Habit is a central construct in describing human behavior. It is a link between cue and response; habits form a major component of personality. The principles underlying the development of habits are the actual principles for the development of personality.

A drive is a stimulus that is strong enough to elicit some action on the part of the individual. It is an energizer of behavior. Certain drives such as pain, hunger, thirst, and sex refer or are linked to physiological processes and are called primary drives. Certain other drives are acquired on the basis of association with the primary drives. These drives are largely social in nature and are termed secondary or acquired drives. Learning consists primarily of developing behaviors (habits) that operate to reduce drive-stimuli.

The development of personality is of central importance in this approach to understanding human behavior. It recognizes that the infant possesses a small number of specific reflexes and that an *innate hierarchy of responses* exists. *Response hierarchy* refers to the tendency for certain stimuli to elicit certain responses rather than other responses. The hierarchy of particular responses may be either innate or acquired from experience through learning. These response hierarchies can be modified by learning. Using the principles of drive, reinforcement, extinction, generalization, or discrimination, crucial learning situations in the development of the child are analyzed.

Fear as an acquired drive (*Miller, 1948*) occupies an important role in this approach to the study of personality. Fear is considered a learned drive because the fear response can be attached to stimuli that were not previously fear-producing. The experimental evidence in support of this assumption has been described in earlier chapters and will not be repeated at this point.

In their analysis of the behaviors important to the concept of personality, Dollard and Miller (1950) account for the mechanism of repression in terms of the inhibition of cue-producing responses that mediate thinking and reasoning. Repression is the process of avoiding certain thoughts. Avoidance of thinking about certain things is learned in precisely the same manner as other responses. The response of not thinking of certain things is reinforcing because it leads to drive-reduction. The response of avoiding certain thoughts thus becomes a part of the general response repertoire of the individual. Those things that are unnconscious in the life of the individual constitute experiences that have not been verbally labeled.

The authors' treatment of conflict is in terms of gradients of approach and avoidance. This concept has been discussed previously in this book. For a comprehensive account of this position the reader is referred to Miller (1951). He describes this theory of conflict in detail and cites a number of experimental studies, the results of which lend strong support to the usefulness of the theory. The dynamics of conflict behavior are deduced from more basic principles of behavior. Conflicts leading to neuroses and characteristic of neurotic behavior are tied in with the general principles of learning.

The learning of neurotic behavior and the learning of symptoms are emphasized as obeying the same general laws and principles that are characteristic of the learning of more adaptive or integrative responses.

Dollard and Miller demonstrate how fear becomes attached to anger cues during the development of the child and how sibling rivalry leads to anger and consequent anxiety over feeling angry. Their explanation of emotional conflicts and the cultural conditions giving rise to conflicts in terms of established learning principles is a noteworthy effort.

SEARS

Of no less significance than the work of Dollard and Miller is the contribution of Sears (1948, 1951). It will be treated briefly here because it is much like that of the former.

The unique contributions of Sears have to do with the socialization process and psychological growth of the child (1948). He also emphasized the importance of studying individuals in situations involving groups of two or more. The behaviors that are of great personal-social significance are those that occur in such groups. He contends that psychology must be concerned with *behavior* and that socially significant behaviors are influenced by the social setting in which they occur (1951). His emphasis on social setting and on growth processes has had great influence on the study of personality development in children, and has contributed to the development of personality theory in general.

## Mowrer's Approach

Mowrer (1947) is an advocate of a dual theory of learning. In contrast with other reinforcement theorists, he contends that certain learning (problem solution) is direct and dependent upon reinforcement, and that only emotions are capable of being attached to new stimuli by conditioning principles. Emotions, particularly *fear*, then operate as intervening variables, the reduction of which serves to reinforce learning responses. Most learning situations are complex in nature and can be understood only by taking both of these forms of learning into account. Another variety of emotion, anticipation or *hope*, is learned in essentially the same way as fear and also becomes an intervening variable in learning. Hope causes organisms to seek out and remain in the presence of stimuli that have heretofore indicated that positive reinforcement was forthcoming. Thus, reward can be interpreted as establishing an emotional state of hope and anticipation in the same way that fear is a consequence of pain and punishment (*Mowrer, 1960*).

Mowrer (*1950*) studies, within a learning frame of reference, such psychoanalytic concepts as regression and the neurotic paradox. He deals with the treatment of enuresis by the application of learning theory, and demonstrates considerable ingenuity in applying learning principles to the realm of personality. Mowrer indicates that *how* one learns is the essential subject matter of learning and that as far as learning *theory* is concerned it makes little difference *what* one learns. *What* one learns in a personal-social behavioral sense comprises the bulk of what is known as personality. The use of learning principles to approach the problems of personality is encouraging, but Mowrer (*1960*) cautions against over-optimism about the contributions that can be made at this time.

### BEHAVIORAL APPROACHES

Behavioral approaches to the understanding of personality are many and varied. The various approaches, as far as personality theory is concerned, do share a number of common elements. Essentially, the workers in this area emphasize either implicitly or explicitly that personality is a deduction made from the observation of behavior. Unlike the learning approaches of Dollard, Miller, Mowrer, and Sears, investigators in this category virtually eliminate hypothetical concepts such as the unconscious, ego, and id. The personality of the individual is composed of what he does rather than of whatever internal dynamics might be producing the behavior. Indeed, the concept of inner dynamics as a director of behavior is relegated to a secondary or tertiary level of importance. Behavioral approaches are models that are basically *psychological* rather than *medical*. That is, they are concerned directly with *behavior* rather than with supposed "underlying" or disease factors that "cause" symptoms (behavior). Behavioral psychologists are concerned with investigating behavior through operationally defined and experimentally manipulable variables. Their orientation is an empirical one, concerned with the effects of environmental stimulation in the direction of the individual's behavior. Behavior is the consequence of reinforcement on the organism. The role of *social reinforcement* in the shaping of behavior is paramount. The fact that other people are significant sources of meaningful stimuli that alter, direct, and maintain the individual's behavior is focal for the understanding of the behavior from which "personality" is deduced.

In such a view, the concept of *personality* as a behavior determinant becomes superfluous and possibly detrimental to the scientific understanding of behavior. If the term is to be utilized, it must refer to the consistent modes of responding that are characteristic of a person or group of people. This position constitutes a rejection of the "inner dynamics" concept of personality, and emphasizes the role of reinforcement or stimulus functions (particularly social stimuli) in the behavior of the individual. Behavioral psychologists do not deny that behaviors, once established, constitute important variables in the determination of how the individual might behave in the future. But instead of attributing this fact to some internal or inferred process, they attribute it to the unique reinforcement history of the individual.

"Inner states" that are significant for behavior can be conceived of as responses. If one desires that a child "like" him, he must become associated with the positive reinforcements that the child receives. The child will then approach him and make the varieties of responses that have been reinforced previously. It is from these responses that the "liking" is inferred. These responses, once established and then reinforced, become persistent response systems and constitute portions of the child's "personality," i.e., he is likeable, friendly, outgoing, and approachable. If the reinforcement history of the child has been such that he does not approach adults, or actively avoids them, other responses constitute portions of his "personality," i.e., he is shy, withdrawn, and resistant. The "inner dynamic" approach would attribute the approach or avoidant behavior to the "liking" or the "shyness" of the individual. The behavioral approach attributes the approach or avoidant behavior to the reinforcement history of the individual. If the behavior is consistent and persistent it is due to the nature of the reinforcements and their scheduling.

The behavioral approach to personality cannot be attributed to any one individual. It has grown out of a concern on the part of experimentally oriented psychologists for the development of more scientific ways of dealing with behavior that is of personal-social significance. The work of many psychologists is involved in the development of behavioral thinking. The publications of Ullmann and Krasner (1965), Krasner and Ullmann (1965), Bandura (1965), and many others, to which the above refer, provide an excellent background of both theory and empirical support for behavioral approaches to the study of personality.

Lundin (1961, 1965) points out that even within the limits of lawful behavior, each person develops in a different set of circumstances and, as a result, develops a *unique* variety of behaviors. The unique behavioral patterns acquired by the individual are the behaviors peculiar to him and constitute *his* personality. Lundin gives great emphasis to the importance of understanding the unique circumstances under which one develops behavior in order to understand the behavior of the normal adult as well as the maladjusted. He further emphasizes the continuity of responses and their interdependence. Human responding is ordinarily integrated responding. Responses that are inappropriate to environmental circumstances are not usually exhibited.

When a person's behavior becomes grossly inappropriate to environmental demands, the behavior is recognized as pathological. The basic principles of learning still apply even when personal uniqueness is carried too far. The disturbed behavior of the individual results from his unusual reinforcement history and the unusual circumstances in which he has developed.

Lundin (1961) attempts to demonstrate that, by using empirical investigations as evidence, it is possible to develop a psychology of personality based on observable facts without resorting to the many intervening variables that are characteristic of other approaches. Using *reinforcement theory* as his principal frame of reference, he indicates how a unique personality comes into existence, what the person is like, and what environmental circumstances are operating to control him.

## An Evaluation

From earlier chapters in this book, the reader will, by now, have full knowledge that the preference of the authors is to use established principles of learning and motivation in accounting for the personal-social behaviors of man. This orientation should not be construed as the only reasonable or worthwhile approach to understanding personality.

Learning approaches to personality represent a very rapidly developing area in psychology. The volume of empirical research in the area grows with each issue of the psychological journals. Compared with other approaches to the problem of personality, research here has a great body of empirical data upon which to draw. Learning has been the topic of tremendous amounts of research effort, and a large body of empirical results is available for those who wish to relate their research findings to established psychological principles.

Research workers in this area have begun to deal with symbolically mediated behavior (*Bandura, 1965; Staats and Staats, 1964*) and other complex processes that emerge when behavior is viewed from the analytic frame of reference. Extension of learning principles to the understanding of complex human behaviors would seem to be a productive and promising approach to the study of personality.

## SUMMARY

Personality theories are essentially general theories of behavior. The concept of personality is such an inclusive one that hardly any aspect of the study of man and his behavior can be excluded.

Many of the personality theorists have been people strongly interested in assisting others in the problems of living. As a consequence, a great deal of attention has been focused on the behavior of the maladjusted or neurotic personality. No theory of personality has been devised that is completely satisfactory as far as formal theory building is concerned, or as far as psychologists are concerned. There has been universal acceptance of no personality theory to date. The likelihood of one's being developed in the near future that will have universal acceptance is extremely remote.

The theories presented in this chapter were divided into three general classifications: psychoanalytic approaches, phenomenological approaches, and learning approaches. The theories did not fit easily into such a scheme, and some forcing was required. Some of the salient features of the theories of various individuals were given in brief form and each of the three general classifications of theory received brief comment.

## REFERENCES

ADLER, A. *Practice and Theory of Individual Psychology*. New York: Harcourt, 1927.

ADLER, A. The fundamental views of individual psychology. *Int. J. indiv. Psychol.*, 1935, **1**, 5–8.

ALLPORT, G. W. *Personality: a Psychological Interpretation*. New York: Henry Holt and Company, 1937.

ALLPORT, G. W., and ODERT, H. S. Trait-names: a psycho-lexical study. *Psychol. Monogr.*, 1936, **47**, No. 211.

BANDURA, A. Vicarious Processes: A Case of No-Trial Learning. Vol. II. In Berkowitz, L. (ed.), *Advances in Experimental Social Psychology*. New York: Academic Press, 1965.

DOLLARD, J., and MILLER, N. E. *Personality and Psychotherapy*. New York: McGraw-Hill Book Company, 1950.

ERIKSON, E. H. Ego Development and Historical Change. In *The Psychoanalytic Study of the Child*. New York: International Universities Press, 1946, **2**, 359–396.

ERIKSON, E. H. *Childhood and Society*. New York: W. W. Norton and Company, 1950.

ERIKSON, E. H. Identity and the Life Cycle. In Klein, G. S. (ed.), *Psychological Issues*. New York: International Universities Press, 1959.

ESCALONA, S. The Influence of Topological and Vector Psychology upon Current Research in Child Development: An Addendum. In Carmichael, L. (ed.), *Manual of Child Psychology*. New York: John Wiley and Sons, Inc., 1954.

FREUD, S. *New Introductory Lectures on Psychoanalysis*. New York: W. W. Norton and Company, 1933.

FREUD, S. The Psychopathology of Everyday Life. In Brill, A. A. (ed.), *The Basic Writings of Sigmund Freud*. New York: Random House, 1938.

FREUD, S. *A General Introduction to Psychoanalysis*. Garden City, N.Y.: Garden City Publishing Company, 1943.

FREUD, S. *An Outline of Psychonalysis*. New York: W. W. Norton and Company, 1949.

FREUD, S. The Interpretation of Dreams. In Strachey, J. (ed.), *The Standard Edition of the Complete Psychological Works*. Vols. IV and V. London: Hogarth Press, 1953.

FREUD, S. Three Essays on Sexuality. In Strachey, J. (ed.), *The Standard Edition of the Complete Psychological Works*. Vol. VII. London: Hogarth Press, 1953.

FREUD, S. Beyond the Pleasure Principle. In Strachey, J. (ed.), *The Standard Edition of the Complete Psychological Works*. Vol. XVIII. London: Hogarth Press, 1955.

FREUD, S. *The Standard Edition of the Complete Psychological Works*. London: Hogarth Press, 1953–1959.

FROMM, E. *Escape from Freedom*. New York: Rinehart, 1941.

FROMM, E. *The Sane Society*. New York: Rinehart, 1955.

GOLDSTEIN, K. *Human Nature in the Light of Psychopathology*. Cambridge: Harvard University Press, 1940.

GUTHRIE, E. R. *The Psychology of Human Conflict*. New York: Harper & Brothers, 1938.

HALL, C. S., and LINDZEY, G. *Theories of Personality*. New York: John Wiley and Sons, Inc., 1957.

HORNEY, K. *The Neurotic Personality of Our Time*. New York: W. W. Norton and Company, 1937.

HORNEY, K. *Our Inner Conflicts*. New York: W. W. Norton and Company, 1945.

HULL, C. L. *Principles of Behavior*. New York: Appleton-Century-Crofts, 1943.

JAMES, W. *Principles of Psychology* (2 vols.). New York: Henry Holt and Company, 1890.

JUNG, C. G. *Analytic Psychology*. New York: Moffat Yard, 1916.

JUNG, C. G. *Contributions to Analytic Psychology*. New York: Harcourt, Brace, 1928.

JUNG, C. G. *Modern Man in Search of a Soul*. New York: Harcourt, Brace, 1933.

KRASNER, L., and ULLMANN, L. P. *Research in Behavior Modification*. New York: Holt, Rinehart and Winston, Inc. 1965.

LECKY, P. *Self-Consistency*. New York: Island Press, 1945.

LEEPER, R. W. Lewin's topological and vector psychology: a digest and critique. *Univ. Ore. Publ. Stud. Psychol.*, 1943, No. 1.

LEWIN, K. *A Dynamic Theory of Personality*. New York: McGraw-Hill Book Company, 1935.

LEWIN, K. *Field Theory in Social Science: Selected Theoretical Papers*. D. Cartwright (ed.). New York: Harper & Brothers, 1951.

LUNDIN, R. W. *Personality: An Experimental Approach*. New York: The Macmillan Company, 1961.

LUNDIN, R. W. *Principles of Psychopathology*. Columbus, Ohio: Charles E. Merrill Books, Inc., 1965.

MASLOW, A. H. *Motivation and Personality*. New York: Harper & Brothers, 1954.

MILLER, N. E. Studies of fear as an acquirable drive: fear as motivation and fear reduction as reinforcement in the learning of new responses. *J. exp. Psychol.*, 1948, **38**, 89–101.

MILLER, N. E. Comments on theoretical models: illustrated by the development of a theory of conflict behavior. *J. Pers.*, 1951, **20**, 82–100.

MILLER, N. E., and DOLLARD, J. *Social Learning and Imitation*. New Haven: Yale University Press, 1941.

MOWRER, O. H. On the dual nature of learning: a reinterpretation of conditioning and problem solving. *Harv. educ. Rev.*, 1947, **17**, 102–148.

MOWRER, O. H. *Learning Theory and Personality Dynamics*. New York: The Ronald Press Company, 1950.

MOWRER, O. H. *Learning Theory and the Symbolic Processes*. New York: John Wiley and Sons, Inc., 1960.

MURPHY, G. *Personality: A Biosocial Approach to Origins and Structure*. New York: Harper & Brothers, 1947.

MURPHY, G. *Human Potentialities*. New York: Basic Books, 1958.

RANK, O. *Will Therapy*. Trans. by Julia Taft. New York: Knopf. 1945.

RANK, O. *The Trauma of Birth*. New York: Brunner, 1952.

ROGERS, C. R. *Client-centered Therapy*. Boston: Houghton Mifflin Company, 1951.

SEARS, R. R. Personality development in contemporary culture. *Proc. Amer. Phil. Soc.*, 1948, **92**, 363–370.

SEARS, R. R. A theoretical framework for personality and social behavior. *Amer. Psychologist*, 1951, **6**, 476–482.

SKINNER, B. F. *The Behavior of Organisms: An Experimental Analysis*. New York: Appleton-Century, 1938.

SNYGG, D., and COMBS, A. W. *Individual Behavior*. New York: Harper & Brothers, 1949.

STAATS, A. W., and STAATS, C. K. *Complex Human Behavior*. New York: Holt, Rinehart and Winston, Inc., 1964.

SULLIVAN, H. S. *Conceptions of Modern Psychiatry*. Washington, D.C.: William Alanson White Psychiatric Foundation, 1947.

SULLIVAN, H. S. *The Interpersonal Theory of Psychiatry*. New York: W. W. Norton and Company, 1953.

TOLMAN, E. C. Kurt Lewin, 1890–1947. *Psychol. Rev.*, 1948, **55**, 1–4.

TOLMAN, E. C. *Purposive Behavior in Animals and Men*. New York: Appleton-Century, 1932.

ULLMANN, L. P. and KRASNER, L. *Case Studies in Behavior Modification*. New York: Holt, Rinehart and Winston, Inc., 1965.

Part IV

Mental Health

*Chapter* **13**

# Some Principles
# of Wholesome
# Personality Adjustment

UNTIL RECENTLY, clinical psychologists and mental hygienists have concerned themselves more with the maladjusted individual than with the person making a normal or above normal behavioral adjustment. People who achieve average or better than average levels of adjustment cause relatively few social problems. The processes of normal living seem to be self-evident, arouse little curiosity, and seldom become matters of social concern. However, when people depart markedly from the norm in their behavior, when their actions seem irrational and self-defeating, when they do foolish things and we feel that "they certainly know better," we begin to ask, "Why?" When deviant behavior becomes personally incapacitating, socially irritating, or dangerous to the individual or to others, it becomes a matter of public concern. Thus it is not surprising that the problems of behavioral maladjustment and mental illness have had a priority over the question of how the normal and above-normal individuals attain and maintain these functional levels.

### THE EMPHASIS ON PATHOLOGY

Because of our great concern with the "problem" individual, we now know much more about the symptoms, characteristics, personal histories, and family and social backgrounds of neurotics, psychotics, and social delinquents than we do about the bulk of the more normal people. It takes a fairly high level of sophistication to see problems in the commonplace. For example, to the average person, the problems of blindness and partial blindness are obvious and warrant individual attention and social help, but the question of how people with normal or supernormal vision see is relatively meaningless. The man on the street can understand efforts directed at the prevention or treatment of defective vision, but the facts of normal vision are thought to take care of themselves. This same attitude is even more prevalent concerning the problems of mental health and illness.

People who have treated the topic of behavioral adjustment *scientifically* have avoided the area of supernormal adjustment because by doing so they thought they could ignore the problem of values. However, we have already indicated that procedures designed to preserve one's life, prevent injury to oneself or others, decrease the level of social rejection, and increase the personal happiness and social effectiveness of people in trouble involve a series of value judgments just as truly as does trying to decide what changes should be effected in a "normal" individual to make him a still "better" person. The problems of mental health and mental illness necessarily consider personality within a value context. The value judgments involved in treating sick people are more universally accepted and less subject to question. The value judgments implied by efforts to help the mentally ill are of the order of: (1) it is better to live than to die; (2) it is better to be comfortable than to be in pain; (3) it is better to be accepted than to be rejected by one's culture; (4) it is better to be happy than unhappy. These values are so generally accepted that we are hardly aware of their existence.

When we ask, "In what direction should this reasonably normal individual change in order to be a still better adjusted person?" or "What is the ideal adjustment pattern for a given person?" we immediately become aware of the value judgments involved and enter a region of less universal agreement as to what is "best." Those workers who have tried to deal with adjustment problems within the framework of scientific methodology, which is supposedly nonevaluative and purely descriptive, have limited themselves to proposed programs for the prevention and treatment of mental illness and maladjustment because of their naive assumptions that they were being nonevaluative. It is becoming increasingly clear that any prescriptive or recommended program of remediation or personal betterment is value laden and culturally limited. While recognizing the necessarily culturally-valued nature of any proposed program of personal and social betterment, workers are becoming more willing to suggest principles and programs even within such a limited framework.

The serious limitation to any proposed list of principles or prescribed programs of positive mental hygiene is lack of information. Very few studies of the organic, social, and personal characteristics and antecedents of the "well-adjusted person" have been made. Two such studies (*Peck et al.*, 1960; *White*, 1952) were mentioned in the preceding chapter. In addition to these two longitudinal studies dealing with normal and above-normal people, some cross-sectional surveys, case studies, and general discussions have appeared (*Barron*, 1954; *Jahoda*, 1958; *Jourad*, 1958; *Maslow*, 1954, 1956; *Rogers*, 1961; *Smith*, 1959). Psychologists are becoming increasingly interested in the adjustment processes of the normal and superior individual.

### PRINCIPLES DERIVED FROM THE PROPOSED DIMENSIONS OF ADJUSTMENT

In Chapter One a multidimensional, idealistic concept of adjustment was proposed. It was there suggested that increasing adequacy of adjustment could be described as movement toward the most desirable regions of a scale representing these dimensions of adjustment. We will now see what principles of wholesome personality adjustment can be derived from this frame of reference. This development will involve some repetition of points discussed less fully in Chapter One.

## The Selective-Awareness Dimension

As indicated in Chapter One, the stimulus selectivity of an individual is partly a function of his organic make-up. Organic selectivity, in turn, is partly species-specific (not all types of animals are equally sensitive to various forms of stimulation), and partly peculiar to the individual (the color-blind person does not differentiate certain hues).

In addition to the organic determiners of stimulus-response selectivity, each person becomes selective as a result of learning; one's personal and social effectiveness are, in part, determined by the nature of these acquisitions. This acquired selectiveness affects perception and affection as well as ideational and overt motor activity.

Each individual begins life responding relatively indiscriminately to the environmental forces impinging upon him according to his organic sensitivity and the physical characteristics of the stimuli (intensity, size, duration, form) impinging on his senses. The infant responds promptly and involuntarily to immediate sensory stimulation. His attentive adjustments are extremely mobile. Attention shifts from object to object in a reflex sort of way. In a certain sense the infant, as William James (1907, *p.* 222) says, "seems to belong less to himself than to every object that happens to catch his notice." Attention seems to be determined largely by each object's intrinsic characteristics.

Learning produces changes in the child's responsiveness to his environment. As stimuli acquire meaning, the child shows increased responsiveness to some stimuli and decreased responsiveness to others. Modifications in the nature of his responses also occur. The child learns that certain stimuli or groups of stimuli have considerable significance for him and that other stimuli of equal innate stimulating power are of little significance. He learns to disregard the latter and to become increasingly concerned with the former. Learning seems to lower the thresholds of excitability and responsiveness for certain stimuli and heighten them for others.

Throughout life every person is continually bombarded by an ever-changing flow of stimuli, but because of limitations imposed by his attention span as well as by his available time and energy, he is continually selecting those to which he will respond. If he responds to A, he cannot respond to B. If he attends to this, he cannot attend to that. If he indulges one interest, a competing interest must be deprived.

If a person is perpetually concerned with trivia, he will never meet up with the more socially important and personally satisfying aspects of life. There was probably never before a time in which so many components of the universe were capable of making an impact on the individual. With space being compressed daily by airplanes, missiles, and satellites, with the barriers of distance eliminated by means of telephone, telegraph, radio, and television, the individual citizen is potentially "in touch" with a rapidly expanding environment.

As the result of increasing literacy in the general population, magazines, newspapers, books, and billboards are becoming increasingly important sources of stimuli competing for attention, time, and energy. Shrieking billboards, flashing lights, innumerable signs, as well as rapidly moving people and vehicles are additional stimuli bidding for our concern. Because of this perpetual bombardment of our senses by competing stimuli, it is essential that the well adjusted individual be a discriminating person. Survival and effective living require that the individual be sensitive to his environment, but maximum sensitivity to the significant aspects of one's universe requires selective unresponsiveness as well. A high level of attentive concentration on significant problems implies selective inattention as well. The selective responsive dimension may be extended to include what has been called the "efficient perception of reality" (*Maslow, 1956*). "Efficient perception of reality" as used by this author involves distinguishing the spurious from the real, the fake from the genuine, and the dishonest from the honest. Another characteristic of the psychologically healthy person is "the quality of detachment" (*Maslow, 1956*). This characteristic is defined more broadly by Maslow than is our selective stimulus-response dimension; it includes ability to concentrate, productive absent-mindedness, and the ability to be solitary without discomfort. These characteristics imply the presence of habits of responding and habits of not responding, habits of attending and habits of not attending, and the ability to discriminate between the essential and the nonessential elements of an environing complex. "Freedom to focus on main purposes" as one of the characteristics of well-adjusted people, is another name for this same quality (*Bond, 1952*). Rogers (*1961*) calls it an "openness to experience," but for most effective living this openness must be selective.

"Awareness" has an intensity as well as a quality dimension. Maslow (*1964*) has written extensively of the "peak" experience of highly self-actualizing people. "Level of awareness" is raised or lowered by emotional as well as by attentional processes. "Experiencing" is a term used by some to refer to a high level of feeling that is a component of experience. When "experiencing" at a high level, an unusual degree of concentration and emotional appreciation of the apparently commonplace occurs. Perception under threat is restricted and "self-centered." Selective awareness involves a dynamic interaction of ideational, emotional, perceptual components.

## The Tolerance Dimension

The tolerance adjustment component has several facets. It involves acceptance of one's self and others as well as the rest of the individual's entire phenomenal world. Cultures differ greatly in what they consider to be the optimal range along the acceptance-striving-for-change scale. The ancient Oriental cultures are alleged to have placed a high premium on acceptance and renunciation as personality characteristics. Whereas Western cultures typically strive for an "economy of abundance" in order to satisfy one's desires and attain a relative homeostasis, Oriental cultures strive for satisfaction by reducing one's wants. When an individual's "wants" are reduced to a very low level, his satisfaction can be attained by a minimum of material things. "Reduce your claims to a zero and you have the world under your feet!" It should be noted that some authorities believe that

Western cultures have exaggerated the Oriental emphasis on the virtues of acceptance, resignation, and renunciation. Early American Puritan-Protestant cultures also renounced pleasure-seeking as a worthwhile goal in life. They stressed individual salvation through hard work, thrift, and competitive success (*Weher, 1930*). The "from-rags-to-riches" frame of reference of the time stressed the virtues of the strenuous life as a means of personal salvation and social betterment. Although there is considerable evidence accumulating in support of the contention (*Reisman et al., 1950*) that there has been a shift from the earlier "inner direction" of the Protestant ethic to the "other direction" of the "social ethic" (*Whyte, 1956; DeCharms and Moeller, 1962*), the emphasis is still upon group achievement and creativeness. Increased productivity by means of technology is seen as a possible means of satisfying man's needs more abundantly and changing the world in ways that are personally and socially desirable.

It is still quite probable that the ideal American adjustment range will be closer to the rejection-of-the-status-quo end of a theoretical acceptance-striving-for-change scale than will be true of the Oriental cultures; however, within a given culture, each individual will function at some point or range on such a hypothetical continuum. Well-adjusted people have reasonably satisfactory self-concepts and accept themselves as they are without thinking very much about the matter. They recognize their own shortcomings without excessive concern. They strive for self-improvement but in doing so they remain problem-centered and are not defensive in their motivation. They feel sufficiently guilty concerning their improvable defects to do something about them, but they do not "spin their wheels" in the quagmire of self-incrimination and unproductive anxiety. The discrepancy between their self-concept and their concept of the ideal can be admitted without it constituting an excessive threat. Their self-satisfaction is such that they do not need to pose or be defensive (*Allport, 1961; Rogers, 1961; Maslow, 1956*).

The well adjusted person accepts other people. He sees human nature as it is, not as he would prefer it to be. He has a set of values and a moral code, but he can still accept, associate with, and even like people who violate that code. He may not approve of what others do; he tries to change them in ways that he considers desirable, but his concern for them as individuals worthy of consideration and help is contingent neither upon their being like him nor upon their conforming to his own conception of what is personally and socially desirable. The well adjusted person has an abiding faith in the improvability of people but he neither demands nor expects perfection. He can perceive the worst in human beings without feeling revolted or disgusted by it.

The well adjusted person finds the world a pretty good place in which to live but considers that it is still subject to improvement. He neither accepts the world as the best of all possible worlds nor does he perceive it as hopeless. He does not close his eyes to the world's imperfections and take refuge in passive contemplation nor does he believe in humble obedience to immutable cosmic purposes.

The ideally organized person is able to accept the gradual betterment of his world. He does not demand miracles. He is able to work with long-range plans. His outlook is hopeful and optimistic. His world is more one of promise than of threat.

A satisfactory position on the "tolerance" dimension requires a reasonably acceptable self-concept (self-acceptance), a high degree of acceptance of others, and of the realities of human nature, and a comfortable relation with reality. Perhaps acceptance and tolerance are not the best terms for this dimension for the ideal seems to demand a warm and profound relating of oneself to others (empathy). This involves an ego-extension and an identification with other people or even with mankind as a whole. According to Maslow (1964), the healthy personality has a strong sense of personal identity but also has "mystic" or "oceanic" experiences in which the individual identifies with other people to the point that he seems to merge with all mankind or even with all nature. These experiences go considerably beyond "acceptance" and "tolerance."

## The Autonomy Dimension

The autonomy dimension of adjustment is currently receiving a critical re-evaluation. Many people believe that social conformity has a stultifying effect on self-realization and creativity. The reaction against those social forces contributing to conformity has sometimes taken the form of a compulsive nonconformity. Nonconformity can become just as rigid and compulsive as social conformity as a way of life. Both of these extreme adjustment patterns are handicapping and maladaptive.

The over-conforming individual is excessively conservative. He has been punished for deviating from the socially approved patterns of behavior so much that even the perception of differentness either in himself or in others is threatening. His social anxiety keeps his behavior within such narrow limits that he is unable to be spontaneous and creative except in restricted socially approved ways.

The compulsive nonconformist is just as limited and socially determined in his behavior as is the extreme conformist. When the social norm dictates neatness, he must be slovenly; when others are serious, he becomes frivolous; when fashion demands formality, he must be casual. Such behavior is, of course, as rigid and socially determined as is that of the extreme conformist. The nonconformist lacks freedom, flexibility, rationality, and adaptability although he typically sees himself as free, independent, original, and creative.

Sometimes what passes for nonconformity within the larger cultural context is really conformity to the values and expectancies of a subculture or gang or clique. The adolescent may defy the social dictates of the dominant adult culture in order to be acceptable to a peer group whose approvals and disapprovals are more important to him. The "Bohemian" is a conformist within his Bohemian culture. Defiance of the broader social conventions may be the price of admittance to the inner circles which demand rigid conformity to their own code. This means that social conformity and nonconformity have to be judged within their appropriate contexts.

It seems that the optimum range for adjustment on the conformity-nonconformity dimension is somewhere between the two extremes. The well adjusted individual is both conforming and autonomous in discriminating and selective ways. Individual and social efficiency, productivity, and creativity require a large component of social conformity. As previously indicated, maximum concentration on significant problems requires an habitual "absent-mindedness" and disregard of irrelevant stimuli. Habituation of the tremendous number of daily activities relieves one of the necessity of making daily decisions concerning these acts, and leaves the person free to explore new approaches to significant problems in his special area of competence. Nonconformity is most likely to be productive in areas where an individual is most knowledgeable. To go off the beaten paths in all directions in the hope of becoming creatively productive is not a very fruitful procedure. The artist is most likely to produce promising innovations in the field of art. His attempt to produce advances in chemistry by randomly mixing solutions on the chance that something uniquely useful may be produced is not likely to be fruitful. Because a creative architect must deviate from conventional architectural forms to be productively creative, it does not follow that nonconformity in the way he dresses and talks, or in the kind of car he drives are equally promising forms of deviation.

Studies of creative people show that such people early in life possess the skills and interests necessary to their later achievements. Architects are good at drawing even in childhood. Creative mathematicians have a talent for mathematics. These creative individuals also have a very high level of interest in their special areas of competence (*Rowan, 1961*). Nonconformity in a person's special areas of competence is most likely to be creatively productive.

The emphasis placed by some workers on individual autonomy and self-direction as desirable personality traits may or may not be a plea for social nonconformity (*Maslow, 1956; Rogers, 1961; Allport, 1961*). The over-conscientious person has a high degree of individual autonomy and self-direction. He has internalized a moral code which functions in a very rigid, autonomous fashion. Such a person feels that he is entirely right in all that he does, but his autonomy is maintained at the expense of others' welfare and his own long-range social effectiveness. Self-direction is not an un-qualified good. Autonomy needs to be tempered with social sensitivity and social perceptiveness. The psychopath may be highly autonomous but he is not an effective social being. Healthy autonomy requires a *selective* detach-ment from one's culture.

## The Personal Integration Dimension

The ideal level of personality integration to be achieved is that of an intermediate position between the extremes of diffusion and disintegration, on the one hand, and rigidity, closure, and self-containment, on the other. The latter are characteristic of the partitioned existence of the neurotic-compulsive and the irrational-conscientious individuals. Lack of personal integration is characteristic of the expedient, the amoral, and the dis-associative-neurotic individuals. The well integrated personality functions as an articulated system with sufficient flexibility to interact appropriately with the ever-changing requirements of reality. Fact and value are satis-factorily integrated. Life is lived as a whole, with an encompassing view of one's own life and of one's culture. The capacity for change and flexibility of behavior are reconciled with the demands of stability and personal integrity. A unifying philosophy of life operates as a stabilizing influence and provides a continuing meaning to one's existence. An inner core of beliefs, socially relevant skills, and personally acceptable attitudes provides a consistency between the self-concept and external behavior. However, these personality components are not fused in such a way as to preclude the development of new configurations as the result of new experiences.

To be productively creative requires a certain "looseness" in one's personality structure. Creativity requires a degree of flexibility. It involves the interaction of fact with fantasy, and the capacity for perceiving the familiar in new ways. To be creative requires the individual to bring existing elements from varying contexts into new and unique relations with each other so as to form new configurations. This requires an openness to new experiences and ability to transform meanings. This openness to new experiences is enhanced by a certain amount of "looseness" and flexibility in one's personality make-up.

Creative activity requires the individual to tolerate ambiguity, conflict, and suspended judgment. The creative person is unfrightened by the mysterious or the unknown. He perceives the unknown as a challenge and is highly tolerant of tentativeness and uncertainty. He is not motivated to bring premature closure on problems. He is able to "regress" to the spontaneity of childhood and permit a free flow of ideas with an intermingling and interacting of autistic and reality-tied components without finding the experiences threatening (*Wild*, 1965). Uncritical regressive thought activity contributes to the inspirational component of creativity, but critical direction and control of thought is required by the final production. The elaborative aspect of creativity makes use of the conventional critical thought processes in which the processes of the products of inspiration are criticized, synthesized, and integrated.

Thus, creative activity requires both stability and instability of personality organization. It involves the capacity to engage in loose, unregulated thinking (divergent thinking) and the ability to return to critical and regulated thought (convergent thinking) as the occasion requires. Fanciful, unregulated thinking can occur only when the individual is free of the anxiety and guilt that such loose thinking commonly arouses. Creativity requires a well balanced and nicely modulated relating of reality-tied and autistic processes, in the same way that adjustment in general requires the balancing of stable and integrated personality components with flexible ones.

## The Self-Realization Dimension

Self-realization and self-actualization mean many things to different people. For some people self-realization is *a* motive; in fact, it is sometimes considered to be *the only motive* of the organism (*Goldstein*, 1940). For others it is just *one* of man's motives (*Rogers*, 1961; *Allport*, 1961).

Along with the belief in self-realization as a fundamental motive goes an implicit faith in the inherent goodness of human nature. The individual is thought to strive perpetually to realize his potential. Realizing one's potential as a unique human being is considered to be "a positive, constructive, realistic, trustworthy process" (*Rogers*, 1961, *p.* 187). A commitment to the self-realization concept requires that the individual develop a "trust in his organism." When he does this he finds that ". . . doing what 'feels right' proves to be a competent and trustworthy guide to behavior . . ." (*Rogers*, 1961, *p.* 191).

Such a point of view seems to imply a Rousseau-like faith in the goodness of man's inherent nature that, if permitted to unfold and blossom forth in terms of its own innate potential and self-contained motivating force, will result in optimum personal satisfaction and social effectiveness. Such a conception implies a kind of pre-established harmony between man's innate nature and his environmental demands.

In place of a pre-existing benign harmony between man and his environment which forms the basis of satisfactory adjustment, we conceive of man as possessing very few specific innate behavioral trends but possessing a very high capacity for learning. Man's inherent potential consists of his sensori-motor-glandular-neural mechanism which originally functions in a relatively diffuse and generalized way. Man's native behavior potentials are considered to be general rather than specific in nature and the channeling of these potentials is largely the result of environmentally directed learning.

This means that a very amorphous and generalized potential raised to a given activation level by the various sources of drive, described in an earlier chapter, finds outlets in and direction from its environment. This inherent behavior potential can express itself in an infinite number of possible ways. Some, but only some, of these ways lead to personal satisfaction and social effectiveness. Self-destruction and crime, thievery and homicide are among every individual's potential. Of the infinite number of ways in which the individual may realize his potential, only a relatively small number can be realized. The main purpose of this chapter is to indicate the directions in which one can realize his potential most effectively.

When the advocates of self-realization as the most significant dimension of adjustment speak of being ". . . that self which one most truly is," as the goal of life, and when individual improvement is indicated by the individual's moving ". . . toward *being*, knowingly and acceptingly, the process which he inwardly and actually is," (*Rogers, 1961, p. 187*) they leave unanswered the important question as to what makes man what he "most truly, inwardly, and actually is."

If we consider man at any moment to be what he is as the result of his inherited potential *plus* the experiences and events of his lifetime, his acquired tendencies are just as much a part of what he "really" is, as is his innate potential. Doing what "feels right," being "that self which one most truly is," and having a "trust in one's organism" probably means "acting consistently with one's previously acquired moral code," "behaving in keeping with one's self-concept," and "believing in the adequacy of one's training and the validity of one's value systems."

To self-actualize is to become a more adequate person to the extent that previous acquisitions contribute to movements along the other dimensions of adjustment in desirable directions.

The differences of opinion with respect to self-actualization do not have to do with either its existence or its importance but rather with its origin. Some workers (*Rogers, 1965; Maslow, 1964*) assume that the self-actualizing motive is inherent, basic, and primitive, whereas others, the authors included, think that they are derived by higher order conditioning from motives and drives of a lower order.

Self-actualization can be conceptualized as the reduction of the discrepancy between one's self-concept and one's ideal self-concept. When the discrepancy between what a person is and what he would like to become is being reduced, that person is achieving self-realization in personally valued ways. Behavior that brings the person closer to his ideal is positively self-reinforced and perpetuated. Activities that lower one's self-concept and thereby increase the disparity between self and ideal self are negatively reinforcing and consequently tend to be eliminated. Thus, self-actualization is motivational in the sense that the individual provides self-reinforcement for activities that reduce the discrepancy between self and ideal self—especially concerning the most highly valued components of the ideal self. To self-actualize is to move on each of the dimensions of adjustment, in directions that maximally reduce the perceived disparity between the "real" self and the ideal self. Self-actualization is a never-ending process to the degree that the ideal self as a goal is continually changing and always receding. This means that self-realization does not consist in attaining a fixed goal. The potency of the motivational aspect of self-actualization derives from the person's perception of progress in socially valued ways rather than from the achievement of a fixed goal. The satisfactions are derived from the processes of living and from achieving in personally and socially valued directions, rather than in the reaching of a static goal (*Rogers, 1965*). Although personal satisfaction and happiness are seldom listed as the criteria or dimensions of adjustment, no conception of the good life entirely disregards them. We conceive of happiness as the accompaniment or consequence of life processes functioning at optimum points in terms of the other dimensions of adjustment. Pleasure seeking as a life goal is universally belittled but personal satisfaction and happiness are considered to be the incidental outcome of activities directed at something quite different. The person who is appropriately selective in his responses to his environment, whose acceptance versus attempted-modification efforts are realistic, and whose self-realization motives are adequately met will be a happy person.

The person who is "open" to experience and who perceives the world as dominantly friendly; the person who is not afraid of his own thoughts and feelings, and maintains an openness to experiences of external reality will find life worth living. When an individual is adjusting more adequately, he moves toward the pleasant end of the theoretical pleasant-unpleasant continuum. The possibility that inappropriate and unrealistic euphoric states may exist throws some doubt on the desirability of un-qualified pleasantly-toned experiences. In the manic-psychotic state the individual is said to be perpetually elated and happy; everything is fine and he feels wonderful. He lives in the best of all possible worlds. If this is a genuinely happy state, it would not be indicative of superior adjusting in a more inclusive sense. Some workers believe that the manic individual is really trying to cover up, or deny, or compensate for anxieties that are threatening to engulf him. Since the question of the reality of the apparent manic-euphoric state is unsettled, we will have to leave the problem of whether the optimum level of pleasantness may be a medium between extremes or at the extreme pleasant end of the scale.

It seems certain that the presence of a reasonable level of physical, mental, and emotional well-being is an important component of "good adjustment." One's state of happiness must be judged within a social as well as a personal framework. A chronically unhappy disposition may be evidence of poor adjustment but unhappiness concerning social injustice, deprivation, and misfortune may not be. When Allport (1961) says that, among other things, the "mature personality" (1) is able to relate himself *warmly* to others, (2) possesses a fundamental *emotional security*, (3) perceives, thinks, and acts with *zest*, (4) is capable of *humor*, and (5) lives in *harmony* with a unifying philosophy of life, he is including an affective component in each of these elements.

While Rogers (1961) maintains a dominantly personal rather than a social emphasis in his treatment of the adjustment process, he does not equate adjustment with personal happiness. His list of four characteristics of the good life as a process are: (1) increasing openness to experience (for enjoyment as well as perceptual completeness); (2) increasing trust in one's organism (being able and willing to do what "feels right" as a guide to behavior which is truly satisfying); (3) increasing creativity as a means to personal satisfaction and social effectiveness; (4) existential living (living fully in each moment). It is obvious that an affective component is directly or inferentially present in each of these four characteristics.

### PRINCIPLES DERIVED FROM MOTIVATIONAL VARIABLES

## Optimal Levels of Motivation

There undoubtedly exists an optimal range of motivational intensity that is most favorable for personal and social adjustment. This range is some-where between two extremes. Activation level can range from apathy at the one extreme to behavioral disorganization and panic at the other. These

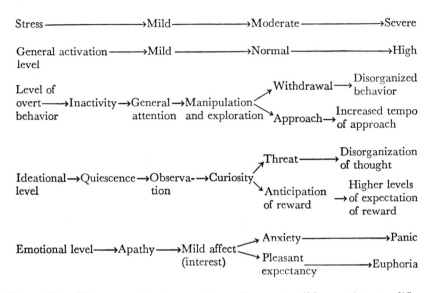

*Figure 17. Diagrammatic representation of some possible reactions to different degrees of stress.*

variations in activation level result from the summative effects of all the contributors to the drive state affecting the individual. The various sources of drive operate as stresses on the organism. These stresses are experienced by the individual as either threats (safety motivation) or promises (growth motivation or the anticipation of rewards).

When stress is either minimal or absent, the individual will be apathetic and inactive. With slightly increased stress, the person becomes attentive and alert and his activity level increases. With further increases in stress, the individual becomes either interested and curious or wary and cautious. Greater stresses result in emotional states of either an unpleasantly anxious or a pleasantly expectant type. When stresses become extreme, anxiety may mount until it threatens to overwhelm the individual and panic, with accompanying paralysis, flight, or attack may occur. If the situational stresses are perceived as extremely promising of reward, the effects of high motivational levels are less disruptive, but there are situations in which the possible rewards are valued so highly that excitement mounts to a point where it also becomes disruptive of ongoing activity.

With high levels of emotion, either disorganized or stereotyped responses appear, perceptual and ideational overgeneralization occurs, and the individual becomes less discriminating. It seems that personal and social adjustments are most adequate at intermediate motivational levels.

## Positive Versus Negative Motives

It is also probable that over-all adjustment will be facilitated by motivation that is dominantly positive (promise of success) rather than negative (fear of failure) oriented. Although we often list motives as either positive or negative, both aspects are usually present. On the physiological level, food-seeking may be dominantly a deficiency motive (hunger-relieving), but it also has pleasurable taste-seeking, exploratory, and curiosity components as well. Seeking the companionship of others may be for the reduction of loneliness or for pleasant social contacts. Competitive sports may represent an opportunity for one individual to demonstrate his competence and increase his prestige, while another individual may be motivated in competition dominantly by his fear of losing and the threat to his status.

The person's feelings of security in any given situation obviously affect his perception of that circumstance as either threatening or promising. When a person comes to a given situation with a high level of confidence, when his backlog of success experiences is such that he feels that he will either "win" or, at least perform creditably, or his status is such that one failure will not be serious, his motivation will be dominantly in terms of a promise-of-prestige-enhancement framework. Another person who feels insecure and is afraid of failure enters the same competitive situation with a dominant failure-avoidance motive. With most people, fear of failure and promise of success are both present.

For most adequate functioning, moderate levels of motivational intensity, dominantly positive (a pleasurable challenge) rather than negative (threatened failure) types of motivation, and reasonable feelings of security are required.

Adequacy of adjustment is related more to one's means of coping with stress than with the extent of stress. When threats to the individual arouse dominantly defensive and repressive (unconscious) mechanisms, neurotic and psychotic patterns of adjustment develop. So long as the individual's motives function on the conscious level, perceptual and ideational distortions will be minimal. When the individual functions dominantly as a "rational coper" (*Allport, 1961*), he is consciously in control of the situation. When ego-defensive devices dominate the individual and function largely on an unconscious level, we have a "poorly" organized individual who is incapable of coping rationally with his world.

## Time and Space Variables in Motivation

Time and space variables in motivation also have some important implications for adequate adjustment. Allport (*1961, p. 307*) says that the "mature personality" will have "a widely extended sense of self." By this, Allport means that one's self-concept includes all of the possible extensions enumerated in an earlier chapter. The person with an extensive self-concept identifies with a broad spectrum of people, an extensive set of beliefs and values, as well as a broad constellation of ideas. He is personally involved in a large segment of his world.

For maximum adjustment in most situations, a long-range time orientation is advantageous. A projection of the probable consequences of behavior into the future is necessary for most appropriately dealing with the here and now. The person who lives in the immediate and concrete present is likely to choose immediate satisfactions in place of greater delayed rewards. He may resort to blind-alley solutions to problems which are inappropriate within a larger context.

Motivation in terms of circumstances not immediately present; that is, striving for goals that are remote in time, make the individual relatively independent of his contemporary physical and social environment. It provides him with a measure of personal autonomy and a wider range of possible choices in deciding what is best for him to do.

## SOCIAL VARIABLES IN ADJUSTMENT

As was pointed out earlier, adjustment is a two-way process. It involves relating the individual most effectively to society; at the same time, society provides the means of realizing the individual's potential for perceiving, feeling, thinking, and creative activity including the changing of society itself. Since the person and society are reciprocally related, one cannot be considered except in relationship to the other. If an individual's behavior is evaluated within a mental hygiene context, a society or certain aspects of society must also be so evaluated. If our criteria of a "good" person is culturally limited, certainly our evaluation of a society is even more so. While we have neither the space nor the competence to fully describe a "good" society, we will try to indicate some of the cultural prerequisites for the development of an adequately adjusted individual within the framework already indicated.

As a general principle, the good society will permit, encourage, and reward the movement of individuals in the direction of optimum adjustment in each of the important adjustmental dimensions. Social acceptance, affection, prestige, esteem, and security will be bestowed by such a society consistently and uniformly for behavior which will ultimately produce a "good" individual. The good society will provide a set of built-in reinforcements for meritorious achievements rather than for caste, class, race, color, and irrelevant physical characteristics.

The good society contains a certain amount of "play" in its make-up. It has some degree of "looseness" in its social structure. It is an "open" rather than a "closed" system. By this, we mean that the system is tolerant of a wide range of behavior. The permissible range of behavior is limited only by the principle that one person's freedom does not unduly restrict another person's freedom.

The good society will provide a wide range of socially approved and prestigious roles for people for all ages, sexes, races, temperaments, and intelligence levels. Such a society will afford opportunities and stimulation sufficient for the utilization of each person's potential. Each individual will be judged not in terms of a set standard or in comparison with others, but rather according to the extent to which his potential has developed or is developing in the direction of social effectiveness and personal betterment. Such a person is a worthy person and all other "good" people are just as worthy as he is.

The good society will make it possible for each individual's basic physiological needs to be met at least on a minimal level, and still allow sufficient time and energy for his social, intellectual, and aesthetic motives and interests to express themselves. When people are chronically hungry, cold, and physically exhausted, social, intellectual, and aesthetic interests recede into the background. When economic insecurity looms large in a person's life, a high level of anxiety is likely to accompany it. In view of our popular philosophies of competitive success ("You can't keep a good man down"; "There is always room at the top"), poverty is generally perceived as a personal failure. Of course, hunger, cold, economic insecurity, and deprivation of all sorts are relative things which are evaluated in terms of one's own culture and subculture, as well as the individual's particular levels of aspiration and frame of reference.

The good society will provide a community of attitudes which places a high premium on those goals and activities which have maximum long-range values for the individual and society (facilitate discrimination and selectivity in terms of the selective stimulus-response dimension of adjustment). It will tolerate, encourage, and reward behavior which deviates from the norms in ways which promise to be productively creative. Conversely, it will enforce conformity where it is necessary for individual and public safety. It will encourage a selective and discriminating conformity-nonconformity pattern of behavior.

The good society will provide a minimum of threat and a maximum of promise for each individual. It will engender guilt and shame only in socially appropriate ways and these affective responses will be kept within manageable limits. Activation levels aroused by threat and promise will be sufficiently high for effective performance but below those levels which result in behavioral disorganization. A good society will induce anxieties concerning an individual's improvable shortcomings but will not maintain uniform, unrealistic perfectionistic standards for all.

We have already suggested the ideal role of society with reference to the self-realization dimension; that is, acceptance of a wide variety of self-expression; encouragement and reinforcement of a broad range of achievements; the maintenance of a friendly, permissive, open system with a minimum of required façades, "oughts," and unessential social expectancies. It will encourage a high level of self-direction and self-confidence.

## SUMMARY

One's concept of the "good life" is culturally limited and value-laden. Principles of wholesome personality adjustment attempt to bridge the gap between what is known concerning the processes of adjusting on the one hand and a given philosophy of life on the other. This presentation is limited to the Western and dominantly American cultural frame of reference, with an admixture of the authors' own value systems. Social and individual values are both deeply ingrained and pervasively influential in determining one's conception of the good life.

The "good life" is a process or set of processes rather than a state of being. It is characterized by movement or growth in certain directions along a number of different dimensions. We have listed these as (1) the selective stimulus-response dimension, (2) the acceptance variable, (3) the conformity-nonconformity dimension, (4) the affective (the pleasant-unpleasant feeling) variable, and (5) the self-realization component. We conceive of ideal adjustment as consisting of life processes operating within or moving toward the regions of optimum functioning in each of these variables. This is purely a theoretical framework for purposes of conceptualizing the good life.

This multiple dimensional concept implies the existence of an optimal functional syndrome (pattern of characteristics). This concept is not only complicated by the fact that the ideal is culturally limited, but it may vary at different stages of a person's development. The concept of an ideal syndrome means that optimal adjustment is not the same as maximum development of all the personality components.

Adequate adjustment is facilitated by motives that are of moderate levels of intensity, dominantly positive (satisfaction-seeking), and that include reasonable feelings of security. Motives with an extensive temporal and spatial frame of reference contribute to the good life.

Social circumstances that are conducive to the good life include:

(1) A certain degree of flexibility or looseness in organization.

(2) A fairly high level of acceptance and encouragement of variability of behavior.

(3) A broad spectrum of socially approved and prestigious roles for all people.

(4) Reinforcement of productive creativity and maximum self-realization of socially appropriate potential.

(5) Provisions for the satisfaction of one's organic needs.

(6) Provisions for optimal functioning of the individual in each of the five adjustmental variables.

## *REFERENCES*

ALLPORT, G. W. *Pattern and Growth in Personality.* New York: Holt, Rinehart and Winston, 1961.

BARRON, F. *Personal Soundness in University Graduate Students.* Berkeley: University of California Press, 1954.

BOND, E. D. The student council study: an approach to the normal. *Amer. J. Psychiat.,* 1952, **109**, 11–16.

DeCHARMS, R., and MOELLER, G. H. Values expressed in American readers: 1800–1950. *J. abnorm. soc. Psychol.,* 1962, **64**, 136–142.

GOLDSTEIN, K. *Human Nature in the Light of Psychopathology.* Cambridge: Harvard University Press, 1940.

JAHODA, MARIE. *Current Concepts of Positive Mental Health.* New York: Basic Books, 1958.

JAMES, W. *Psychology.* New York: Henry Holt and Company, 1907.

JOURAD, S. M. *Personal Adjustment.* New York: The Macmillan Company, 1958.

MASLOW, A. H. *Motivation and Personality.* New York: Harper & Brothers, 1954.

MASLOW, A. H. Self-actualizing People. In Moustakas, C. E. (ed.) *The Self.* New York: Harper & Brothers, 1956.

MASLOW, A. H. Further notes on the psychology of being. *J. Humanistic Psychol.,* 1964, **4**, 45–58.

MASLOW, A. H. *Religion, Values, and Peak Experiences.* Columbus, Ohio: Ohio State University Press, 1964.

PECK, R. F., HAVIGHURST, R. J., COOPER, R., LILIENTHAL, J., and MORE, J. *The Psychology of Character Development.* New York: John Wiley and Sons, Inc., 1960.

RIESMAN, D. GLAZER, N., and DENNEY, R. *The Lonely Crowd.* New Haven: Yale University Press, 1950.

ROGERS, C. R. *On Becoming a Person: A Therapist's View of Psychotherapy.* Boston: Houghton Mifflin Company, 1961.

ROGERS, C. R. Some questions and challenges facing a humanistic psychology. *J. Humanistic Psychol.,* 1965, **5**, 1–5.

ROWAN, HELEN (ed.). *Creativity. Carnegie Corporation of New York Quarterly,* 1961, **9**, No. 3, 1–7.

Smith, M. B. Research strategies toward a conception of positive mental health. *Amer. Psychologist,* 1959, **14,** 673–681.

Weber, M. *The Protestant Ethic.* Trans. by T. Parsons. New York: Scribners, 1930.

White, R. W. *Lives in Progress.* New York: Dryden Press, 1952.

Whyte, W. H. *The Organization Man.* Garden City: Doubleday, 1956.

Wild, C. Creativity and adaptive regression. *J. pers. soc. Psychol.,* 1965, **2,** 161–166.

*Chapter* 14

# Regaining Mental Health

IN RECENT YEARS there has been an increase in the number of professional psychologists who identify themselves with "clinical" psychology in one form or another. The number of psychologists involved in guidance, counseling, and psychotherapy has been increasing constantly. These psychologists have dedicated their efforts toward the prevention of mental illness and to the re-establishment of mental health for those who have already become so emotionally disturbed or personally disorganized that their functioning as effective members of the social community has been seriously impaired.

The increase in the number of psychologists identified with clinical areas of psychology has been partially a function of society's concern about mental health and mental illness. The number of professional people needed to work in the area of mental health is far greater than the number who are currently trained and employed in the field. A brief look at the frequency with which people become mentally ill will serve to indicate why this area of psychology is an expanding one.

### PSYCHOLOGICAL DISTURBANCES: THE PROBLEM

In earlier discussions in this book, psychological disturbances were treated as extensions, intensifications, or elaborations of behaviors that are common to most people. Extreme or extensive deviations from normal or usual behavior are commonly classified as mental illnesses. The label "mental illness," then, is used to encompass a variety of disturbances in the areas of emotion, motivation, perception, and personal-social behavior. It is highly questionable whether or not such disturbances should be considered mental illness. Typically, they are not the result of infectious or disease processes in the usual sense of the word, and it would probably be more appropriate to use some designation other than "illness." A variety of other labels are used, but the use of "mental illness" as a term persists in spite of its misleading connotations. In the following discussion, a variety of terms, including psychological disturbance, psychological disorder, behavior disorder, and mental illness will be employed synonymously. They will designate overt behavior, thought processes, and emotional reactions that are of such a socially-culturally deviant nature as to be of personal or societal concern.

The frequency of the occurrence of psychological disorders in our culture is difficult to determine with any great precision. This is because of several factors operating together. First of all, there is no general agreement on exactly what constitutes behavior that is indicative of mental illness. The criteria of mental illness are fluid and flexible. Behavior for some people under some circumstances would be considered disorganized and bizarre, while for other people in the same circumstances it would be considered normal, or not unusual. Behavior under a given set of circumstances may be extremely variable from person to person without any indication of behavior pathology. The demarcations between appropriate and inappropriate social responses are not clear and concise.

The ways by which data relative to the incidence of psychological disturbance are gathered are lacking in precision, and the data are not all representative of the same things. The generalizations made from the data are frequently more expansive than the manner of the obtaining of the data justifies. Most of the data relative to the frequency of mental illness are obtained from institutions for the care and treatment of the mentally ill. This means that a person must come to the attention of a responsible agency before he is classified as mentally ill and becomes a part of the data. Many seriously disturbed people do not come to the attention of such agencies. Furthermore there is little to lead one to believe that those who do come to the attention of responsible agencies are a representative sample of those who are mentally ill. The probability that the representation of various socio-economic groups, educational levels, marital status groups, ages, and sexes is proportional to the occurrence of mental illness in these groups is rather low. When community survey techniques are used and the behaviors found within the community are compared to a standard derived from a population other than that community, or a standard derived from the deliberations of psychologists or sociologists, the dangers of inappropriate evaluation are many. Such techniques can yield valuable descriptive data, but it is hazardous to designate persons or communities as mentally ill on such bases.

The picture of the incidence of psychological disorders derived from statistics on persons being treated by private and public agencies is insufficient. It is probable that the more severely disturbed persons are treated by public agencies, whereas the moderately disturbed seek help from private individual psychotherapists, and the milder cases go undetected and untreated.

## Some Data on Mental Illness

The National Committee Against Mental Illness (1961) and the Department of Health, Education, and Welfare (1960) have provided some data on the frequency of occurrence of psychological disorders in the United States. Unless otherwise indicated, the data reported in the following discussion are derived from these sources.

There are over 700,000 patients in psychiatric hospitals at any given time in the United States. Length of hospitalization for psychiatric patients tends to exceed that of patients hospitalized for physical illness. The average length of time that a psychiatric patient is hospitalized tends to run to weeks and months rather than days. There are approximately 763,000 hospital beds for psychiatric patients. It is estimated that roughly seventeen million Americans are mentally or emotionally disturbed and in need of psychiatric treatment. Assuming that one half of these people should be hospitalized and that a complete turnover of patients could be accomplished five times per year, less than one half of those requiring hospitalization can be accommodated. Actually, each year about 290,000 new patients are admitted to mental hospitals and psychiatric wards of general hospitals, and a total of about one million patients per year are treated in this way. During 1957, 2,500,000 individuals were treated for psychological disorders by the combined efforts of mental hospitals, psychiatric clinics, or by psychiatrists and clinical psychologists in private practice. If the estimate of seventeen million needing psychiatric treatment is anywhere near accurate, this means that about 15 percent of those needing psychiatric or psychological treatment actually obtain such treatment in a given year.

Of the one million patients treated in mental hospitals in a year, about 75 percent are severely disturbed. The most serious of the disorders, schizophrenia, accounts for 24 percent of new admissions to hospitals.

Because these patients are typically young and their period of hospitalization tends to be rather long, they account for one half of the institutionalized population. Another large segment of the institutional population is composed of the aged psychotics. They account for 27 percent of first admissions and tend to be hospitalized for long periods of time.

Minor behavioral disorders and emotional disturbances tend to be great in number. Roughly one half of the general medical practitioner's patients are said to suffer from some kind of emotional disturbance, and nearly one third of hospitalized medical and surgical patients are known to be either neurotic or psychosomatic cases.

It is reported in the Midtown Manhattan study (*Srole et al., 1962*) that only about one out of every five adults between the ages of 20 and 59 living in that area can be considered essentially well in terms of mental health. The area studied contains 175,000 people of various socio-economic levels, educational backgrounds, national origins, and religious preferences.

## Personal and Social Implications

In addition to the numbers of people who are severely disturbed to the extent that they can be recognized as such by laymen and professionals, there are many people who suffer from less severe and less obviously incapacitating frustrations, conflicts, and anxieties. Some people who on the surface seem to be reasonably happy, well integrated persons are really suffering psychologically and are in need of help. Under the surface, many persons carry with them burdens of personal feelings of inadequacy, fear, sorrow, and discontent that make their personal lives miserable and their social utility extremely limited. They may behave in only slightly eccentric ways, and their basic unhappiness and unproductiveness goes unnoticed by friends and associates.

The "hail-fellow-well-met" and the "shy" may both be in need of professional help if they are eventually to live complete and full lives. The aggressively hostile, the seclusive and fearful, the depressed, the anxious, the woman-hater, the man-hater, the boisterous, the sensitive, the heavy drinker, the antisocial, the chronically fatigued, the self-disparaging, and other individuals displaying behaviors of an asocial or antisocial nature are frequently not recognized as in need of psychological help.

Emotional stress, of course, is a part of life. It is probable that most people learn to live with emotional stress quite adequately. When emotional stress becomes excessive or when the means of coping with it have not been acquired, serious problems may arise. Personal relationships may suffer, inefficient work habits may develop, personality traits that are socially handicapping may appear, and the emotional stress becomes greater and greater. In attempts at problem solution more emotional stress is generated. Very frequently people in such situations need the help of a professional psychologist or psychiatrist to establish effective means of dealing with their problems and to become reasonably happy and competent individuals.

Being born into and reared in our culture presents problems that must be resolved. Ours is a highly competitive culture and many of its aspects pose problems in personal adjustment for great numbers of people. The ramifications of prestige in our culture may lead people to dissatisfaction, discouragement, and discontent. Ours is a vigorous culture that results in a high level of economic productivity and, at the same time, leaves its trail of despair for those who for one reason or another become too absorbed in the competitive race for superiority, for tangible goods, for high levels of education, for gadgets, for friends, for recognition, and for security.

Unsatisfactory home life exacts a toll of psychological distress for some people. Unloved, neglected, over-protected, and "spoiled" children have a difficult time adjusting to the demands of society when they reach adulthood. Families where quarrelling, rivalry, and bitterness prevail provide a very difficult environment for the growth of compassion, happiness, and contentment. Families that are so close-knit as to discourage the development of individuality and independence can be equally damaging to the growth of wholesome personality characteristics. Schools that place too great an emphasis on academic achievement, neglect individual differences, impose rigid rules of conduct, and fail to recognize that children and young people have lives to live beyond that of the school create stress and anxiety that contributes to the development of unfortunate behavior.

Inadequate opportunity to obtain an education or to secure employment and plan a safe economic future is a problem for some people. Inadequate housing, unemployment, inadequate funds, and the absence of recreational facilities can contribute to the development of behavior disorders. Mental health becomes a matter of concern not only for the individual but for the family, the community, and the nation in general. The loss, both economic and social, due to behavior disorders is a great one and one that receives but a small amount of financial attention in comparison with certain physical illnesses.

There is one psychiatrist for about every 19,000 people in the United States and one clinical psychologist for about every 38,000 people. This number is totally inadequate to meet the need for competent therapists (*Hoch et al.*, 1966). The cost of providing adequately trained persons and adequately equipped facilities is high, but the cost of not providing adequate psychological and psychiatric services may be even higher in economic and social loss as well as in terms of human suffering. A great

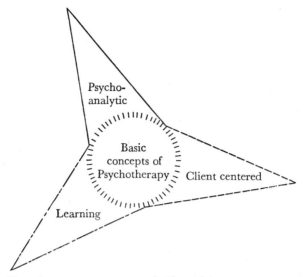

*Figure 18. Shared concepts among psychotherapists.*

deal of research effort and study has gone into attempts to develop effective ways for the restoration of mental health. A great deal more effort must be devoted to this enterprise if significant advancements are to be made.

Counseling and psychotherapy are available to most college students through either institutional provision or private facilities. These services are of tremendous value to the individual and to the community. We now turn our attention to the nature of counseling and psychotherapy as it functions in preventing psychological disorders and re-establishing mental health.

### PSYCHOTHERAPY: ITS GENERAL NATURE

Professional psychotherapists differ rather markedly in their approaches to psychology and in their theoretical orientations within personality theory. With such a complexity of personality theories, it is often wondered how a system of psychotherapy based on a particular theory might differ from a system of psychotherapy deriving from another theory of personality. That differences in procedure do occur is undeniable, but psychotherapists have a great deal in common and many of their procedures are functionally the same. The differences in psychotherapy are as likely to be functions of the personality of the therapist as of his theoretical orientation.

Therapists share the broad goals and intended outcomes of psychotherapy (*Gardner, 1964*). The professional therapist is interested in being of assistance in creating a more abundant existence for his client, regardless of his theoretical orientation. Human behavior is exceedingly complex and there is more than one way by which changes in thinking, feeling, and behaving can occur. It is true that some persons may make more progress in therapy with a particular therapist or even with a therapist of a particular theoretical orientation while others find other therapists and orientations more suitable for them. There will always be individual differences in therapists and, given the complexity of the human organism and our current state of knowledge, differing theories of personality are likely to exist for some time to come.

Theoretical orientations are important in the training of psychotherapists, and students of professional psychology should become aware of these differences. But for most people seeing or needing to see a therapist the theoretical orientation is probably of little consequence. Successes and failures are experienced by all responsible psychotherapists. The person seeking psychotherapeutic services should contact a professionally trained and responsible person.

## People with Problems

Professional help is sought by great numbers of people who have a tremendous variety of problems. The range of problems for which professional help is sought runs from students who have difficulty studying to those with severe neurotic or psychotic problems. It is a common misconception that only people who are seriously disturbed seek or need psychotherapy. On the contrary, many people use psychotherapy as a means of dealing with problems that are completely rational in nature but for which they have been unable to find solutions. Others may contact a psychotherapist about a problem that is of minor importance but causes them discomfort or inconvenience.

People with problems that center around feelings of inadequacy, inability to concentrate or study, irrational fears, social incompetence, marriage, parent-child or child-parent relationships, sex, money, feelings of depression, inability to make friends, compulsive behavior, nightmares, insomnia, psychosomatic reactions, tics, delusions, hallucinations, and a host of other personal and interpersonal factors comprise the clientele of any psychotherapeutic clinic. A few examples may serve to illustrate the variety of problems for which professional psychotherapy is sought.

Mrs. J. came to the clinic to talk to someone about her seven-year-old son. He was a fine boy, she explained, and she loved him dearly. He was a bit sensitive, perhaps, and a little over-active, but he was "all boy." The problem presented was that of bed wetting. She had been unable to get him to spend dry nights, and the medical doctor had assured her that no organic difficulty was responsible for this behavior. She felt she had failed the boy in some way and wanted to see a therapist and have her son see someone, too.

Don F., a senior in high school, had very little idea what he wanted to do after graduation. He was certain that he did not want to enter his father's business, but beyond that he had no plans. His parents were very concerned about his apparent lack of purpose, and his father contacted a psychotherapist to seek help for his son.

A young lady, Mary M., went to see a clinical psychologist at the college counseling center. She had difficulty in talking about her problem, but finally indicated that she had a younger sister at home with whom she had never gotten on very well. As a matter of fact they appeared to dislike each other intensely. Mary felt guilty for not liking her sister and angry at the same time. The younger sister was going to be a freshman at the college the next semester, and their parents wanted the two girls to share a small apartment. This presented an almost intolerable situation for Mary. She wanted to talk about her relationship with her sister and with her parents.

A young man, Jerry T., sought help with a problem that made him feel inadequate and was embarrassing. He thought that he might be a homosexual but had had no homosexual experiences. He was unable to be comfortable with a girl on a date. He had quit dating because he felt frightened and guilty whenever he found himself alone with a woman. His friends were constantly trying to "line him up" with a date. He felt he must have some help with this problem.

Betty L., a college sophomore, was a good student. She had studied diligently her first year at college and had earned good grades. She started her second year in the same fashion but became very interested in a young man with whom she started keeping company. He was a senior and wanted to marry her. Betty felt that she should finish college, but she had been getting poor grades since she started to "go steady" with this young man. She was afraid that she would be a bitter disappointment to her family if she did not finish college. She also felt that if she did not marry this young man she would be unhappy. She sought the help of a psychotherapist.

Kathleen A. sought help with the following problem. She was the daughter of an industrial executive. Most of her childhood had been spent in the care of a nurse or governess and, later, at boarding schools and summer camps. Her younger brother, whom she barely knew, had been treated similarly. He was now in a military school for boys. Kathleen and her brother, who was now fifteen years old, had corresponded rather regularly for the past year and a half. They had both looked forward to spending the Christmas holidays at home, but the parents had decided that they would take a trip to Mexico for the holidays and had informed the children that they should not come home for Christmas. Kathleen had then asked that her brother come to visit her for Christmas. This was arranged. During the time that they spent together it became obvious to both Kathleen and her younger brother that they did not know or like their parents very much. After her brother had returned to school, Kathleen thought about her brother and herself a great deal. She came to the conclusion that neither she nor her brother was loved by the parents. This, she decided, she could live with, without too much difficulty. Her concern was that she herself might become like her parents. She said she had never felt any great fondness for anyone and wondered if she were capable of ever loving anyone. She said she would not want to have children and treat them as shoddily as she felt she had been treated. Her father had been married previously and she was born to his first wife. She had never really known her real mother; she also said that she was quite certain her mother was pregnant with her before she was married and that her father may or may not have been her real father. She was unhappy, confused, and angry that she and her younger brother were in the situation in which they found themselves.

If one reads "between the lines" in the cases that have just been presented, it becomes apparent that the problems brought to a psychotherapist are many times more complex than they appear to be initially. Mrs. J. and her son both had problems, the basic nature of which were serious. Bed wetting was a serious behavior problem, but other things were not well in the family. Don's lack of purpose and desire to avoid involvement in his father's business was confirmed. He was very bitter toward his father and his own adjustments were very precarious. Mary's problems were no less serious than Don's. Jerry's problems reflected his own feelings of guilt for some earlier behavior with women and an unfortunate attitude toward sex. His case turned out to be quite an involved one. Betty and Kathleen both had serious problems involving parental relationships. They were quite different problems, but both were serious and complex.

The examples that have been presented do not represent bizarre or unusual cases. More serious cases of disorganized behavior, from sexually deviant involvements to referred cases of individuals who compulsively set fires, steal, or commit other crimes, come to the attention of psychotherapists. Fully developed neurotic and psychotic patients are, of course, a part of the clientele, but patients of this nature are frequently thought to comprise the majority of psychiatric patients. Cases like the ones that have been described are probably more representative of the patients seen in an outpatient clinic than are the more seriously disorganized. The very seriously disturbed frequently need the protection provided by a hospital and require constant supervision, care, and treatment.

## Characteristics of the Psychotherapist

In trying to describe what a psychotherapist is like, there is the problem of avoiding stereotyping. Therapists are certainly not all alike. They do have some elements in common and some characteristics are more typical of them as a group than others. If one is going to consult a psychotherapist, the probability is high that he will discover in his therapist many of the characteristics we are about to discuss. The professional psychotherapist is well above average in intelligence; he is technically competent; he is well educated; he is sincere, friendly, understanding, and genuinely interested in his client's welfare.

### EDUCATION AND TRAINING

The education and training programs for psychotherapists are rather lengthy. The psychiatrist is trained as a medical doctor and then receives further training in psychiatry. The clinical psychologist is trained as a psychologist and then receives further training in clinical psychology. The educational background of psychotherapists, then, indicates that they are quite intelligent. In addition to a high initial level of intelligence they typically have a broad educational background. They know something of anthropology and of sociology. They develop considerable cultural sophistication because it is their professional responsibility to know and understand the divergent cultural backgrounds of their clients. They are exposed to a broad variety of experiences in their education and training. They develop wide cultural understandings along with professional knowledge of human behavior and technical skills.

The licensing of psychiatrists and certification of clinical psychologists make it possible for the interested person to determine whether he is consulting with a duly licensed or certified psychotherapist. Local medical or psychological associations can be contacted in order to determine the status of any of their members.

### ETHICAL STANDARDS

Because of the intimately personal nature of the psychotherapeutic relationship and the likelihood that matters will be discussed that are highly personal, a concern for the safeguarding of information divulged in therapy has developed. Both the professions of psychiatry and psychology have established codes of ethics to which they prescribe. These codes provide a good deal of assurance to the client that he will be treated with integrity and confidence. The American Psychological Association publication *Ethical Standards for Psychologists* (1953), is a detailed presentation of what is considered ethical pratice and what is not.

Psychotherapists take their ethical and professional responsibilities very seriously. A great deal of time and energy has been devoted to the development of ethical standards. These standards are zealously maintained by professional psychotherapists. The professional psychotherapist treats information in confidence. He discusses aspects of his client's case only with other professional persons who can be of assistance in helping his client. Any information that is shared with another person is shared with the consent of the client. The professional psychotherapist does not attempt to deal with problems that are outside his realm of competence.

The codes of ethics for psychologists and psychiatrists are extensive; no attempt will be made to present a detailed discussion of them here. In addition to the codes of ethical behavior, the psychotherapist is governed in his relationship to his client by his own personal values, which are those of a person dedicated to assisting his client (*Wrenn, 1958*).

UNDERSTANDING

People who are about to consult a psychotherapist frequently feel that their problems are unique and are doubtful that they will be understood by an outsider. The business of understanding is an important function of the professional psychotherapist. He is specifically trained to intellectually understand the client's behavior. This type of understanding is expected by the client. But the type of understanding about which he is likely to be concerned is not intellectual understanding but emotional understanding. Will the therapist be able to see the client as the client sees himself? The former type of understanding has been termed *diagnostic understanding* and the latter has been called *therapeutic understanding* (*Porter, 1949*).

Therapeutic understanding refers to the feeling reactions of the therapist that cause the client to feel that he is being understood and accepted. The client needs to feel that he is accepted and respected as a person and that the therapist really understands what is going on within him. Rogers (1951) has referred to this as the internal frame of reference. The therapist tries to think *with* his patient rather than *about* his patient. He attempts to view the problem as it is understood by the client. Most therapists are very much concerned with therapeutic understanding, and try to adopt an internal frame of reference in order to understand the problems as they are understood by the client. This is not always an easy thing to do, and most therapists devote considerable effort to assure a maximum understanding of the patient and his problems.

The prospective client may anticipate that the therapist will be a cold, logical, machine-like person who performs in a rigid, perfunctory, and impersonal manner. This is precisely the image that the professional psychotherapist *does not* want to create. Most therapists are sincerely concerned about the welfare of their clients and are genuinely warm and friendly. The psychotherapist tries to provide a friendly atmosphere in which the patient will feel comfortable and accepted as a person of integrity. Far from being cold and machine-like in their procedures, they are typically pleasant, dynamic, and spontaneous in their responses to the person who has come to confer with them. Most therapists do not behave in a sterile, routine, predetermined manner in their relationships with clients. Their professional training and personal interests in the problems of people have combined in the production of a professionally competent person who is an understanding and accepting human being.

Acceptance of the client as a person with problems has received a great deal of attention from clinical theorists who believe that the client should experience acceptance as a feeling of being unconditionally liked, understood, and accepted (*Brammer and Shostrom, 1960*). Acceptance or altruistic love as therapeutic agents have considerable support in the writing and work of psychotherapists (*Fromm, 1956; May, 1953*). Concern for the welfare of the patient is a natural development from the basic attitudes and personality of the therapist. The therapist is nonjudgmental as far as the attitudes expressed by the patient are concerned. He is interested in the patient's attitudes and values, but he need neither approve nor disapprove of them. He simply accepts them as being those of his client, whom he is trying to and is expected to help. The dignity and personal worth of the patient are respected, as are the patient's rights to make his own decisions and live his own life. Some psychologists believe that each individual possesses creative growth forces that, when released through acceptance, assist in his becoming a more adequately functioning individual (*Rogers, 1951*).

Although the psychotherapist is in a role of authority, he does not behave in an authoritarian manner. The client is free to discuss what he wishes to discuss without fear of offending the therapist and experiencing rejection. Permissiveness varies from one therapist to another. Some allow almost complete freedom to discuss anything, while others feel free to direct the flow of conversation back to channels that they feel will prove more fruitful for the advancement of the therapy. There is disagreement as to how permissive the therapy situation should be. Some workers feel that permissiveness is a part of accepting the patient, while others believe that the setting of certain limits in psychotherapy is a part of reality to which the patient must learn to adapt himself. These people argue that, in real life, limits are set by social convention and legal structure, and that complete permissiveness in therapy is too far from the reality that the client must eventually face. The counterargument runs that therapy is the place in the patient's life where he experiences the most permissiveness and acceptance, and that such an atmosphere allows him to work through his problems more readily.

### THE COURSE OF PSYCHOTHERAPY

There are a great number of psychotherapeutic systems or approaches to psychotherapy (*Snyder, 1947; Harper, 1959*). The approaches to psychotherapy derived from differing theories of personality that have been discussed in a previous chapter. Psychoanalytic therapy of various kinds, relationship therapy, client-centered therapy, re-educative therapy, directive therapy, and behavior modification are all currently being employed. Research results tend to show that similar changes occur in various kinds of psychotherapy (*Heine, 1953; Gardner, 1964*). In spite of the differences in procedure, some common aspects of the psychotherapeutic process can be indicated.

Psychotherapy is usually instituted because a patient comes to a therapist for help with a problem. The problem presented by the patient is usually some symptom that is disturbing to him. The patient initially seeks professional help as a means of curing the symptom or alleviating his distress. Frequently it is discerned that the patient's complaints are simply symptoms; that is, they are indications that something is wrong, but the basic cause of the difficulty may not be known to the patient. The symptoms may range from mild to severe and cover a tremendous variety of difficulties.

The patient typically relates to the therapist the nature of his difficulty, or the nature of the problem as he sees it. Some therapists allow the patient to relate his difficulties and describe his symptoms in his own way and at his own rate; others may ask specific questions.

The patient typically wants to know what is wrong with him, if the therapist can help him, how long therapy will take, and how much it will cost. The first interview and perhaps part of the first few interviews may be used in description of symtoms and dealing with the above mentioned details of the therapy. In most circumstances, the early questions of the client cannot be answered with any precision. How long therapy will take is difficult to determine in a few interviews. Also, determining what is wrong with the patient is one of the goals of therapy that may take considerable time. Psychotherapists cannot ethically promise complete or quick cures. This matter is usually discussed at an early interview, during which time the patient begins to learn what is expected of him in therapy.

During the first few interviews, a typical procedure is to obtain some kind of case history and evaluation of the patient. This may all be done by interview, whether through direct query or volunteered by the patient. In some instances psychodiagnostic and personality tests may be administered. During the first few interviews, the therapist may decide that he can treat the patient effectively, or he may make a referral, or recommend hospitalization for a severely disturbed patient. If, after the first few interviews, therapist and client are in agreement that the therapy should proceed, arrangements are made for the continuation of the sessions.

The role of the therapist is a complex one in which he performs unique functions. His association with his client is on a professional basis, and the only reason for this association is to help his patient to live more effectively. In this way he is different from any other person in the life of the patient. He is an educated, trained, and responsible person with knowledge of human problems and characteristics, and experienced with dealing with the problems of people. The patient is provided an opportunity to discuss many facets of his existence that he would not feel free to discuss with friends or with parents.

### VARIETIES OF PSYCHOTHERAPY

The various theories of personality have been generated in large part from the experiences of psychotherapists in dealing with clients and their problems. In that the clinical practice and observations of the psychotherapists evolve into points of view relative to personality, it can readily be understood that personality theories and psychotherapeutic procedures are closely allied. A general orientation to some of the various procedures will be presented in the discussion that follows.

## Psychoanalytic Approaches

In psychoanalytic approaches to psychotherapy, concepts of levels of awareness are significant for therapy. The conscious level consists of those thoughts and ideas of which the person is aware at the moment. The preconscious is composed of those ideas of which the individual is not aware at the moment but that can be voluntarily recalled. The unconscious consists of memories and ideas that the individual has forgotten and cannot deliberately recall. The unconscious was perceived by Freud (1920) as comprising the bulk of the personality, and much of the forgotten material had a strong motivational influence on the individual's behavior. Psychoanalysis emphasizes the importance of the previous experiences of the individual, with particular regard for his psychosexual development. Instincts or genetically determined impulses to actions are directing agents for the libido, or life energy. Much of the early experience of the individual is unconscious but still remains motivational in character.

Great emphasis has been placed on the motivational aspect of the unconscious, which contains much forgotten and repressed material. Techniques for uncovering the repressed material of the unconscious and bringing it into consciousness have been developed. Much time is devoted to these processes in psychoanalysis. The recall of much unconscious material may be psychologically painful for the patient, and he may resist attempts to bring some of it into consciousness. *Resistance* designates both an inability to recall repressed desires and ideas and a reluctance to do so. Freud developed psychoanalysis to overcome resistance and bring the patient's conflicts and anxieties into consciousness. The overcoming of resistance was viewed by Freud (1920) as the key factor in bringing about permanent changes in the psychic life of the patient.

Prominent among the techniques for uncovering repressed material from the unconscious is the method of *free association*. In using free association the patient lies on a couch and relaxes. The therapist is typically behind the patient and out of his view. In this relaxed state the patient is told to relate everything that comes to his mind. The psychoanalyst urges the patient to tell everything that comes to his mind because one association leads to another that is deeper in the unconscious. The associations that are reported are interpreted as disguised expressions of repressed ideas and urges. The analyst uses his training, experience, and imagination in interpreting the associations of the patient. Resistance is encountered when the patient hesitates or does not want to relate certain ideas because of their personal nature or presumed unimportance. An effective relationship with the analyst must be established in order to overcome resistance.

The *transference* relationship evolves when the patient develops an emotional attachment for the analyst. Freud believed that transference was based on the patient's need to find a love object in order to express his repressed love longings. Ordinarily the love object would be a parent of the opposite sex. The psychoanaylst serves in the capacity of a substitute parent in such a situation. The establishment of transference helps to overcome resistance, so that progress in therapy can continue.

Another technique of psychoanalysis is that of *dream analysis*. The content of dreams as they are reported to the analyst is analyzed. Some of the content of dreams is said to be in universal symbols that can readily be understood and interpreted by the analyst. The latent content of dreams is penetrated and interpreted by the expert analyst; this latent content contains the real meanings that must be derived for the welfare of the patient. Dream interpretation may be used to break down resistance. Used in this way, it becomes a part of the free associations of the patient. Theoretically, when the patient understands the nature of his unconscious and the infantile nature of the causes of his symptoms, he is well on the road to recovery. The theory is that once the life energy (libido) is freed by the uncovering of repressed unconscious ideas, the ego will become strong enough to cast off the symptoms and the patient will be able to solve his problems of adjustment without further analytic assistance.

Psychoanalysts have modified some of the Freudian concepts and abandoned others. Jung (1928) emphasized that the patient must acquire something to replace his neuroses and that he must "build" a unique self. Jung placed great value on religion and philosophy in the building and integration of self. He rejected the Freudian couch and placed emphasis on the value of the face-to-face contact of therapist and patient. It has been found that the presence of the analyst in the room during free association does alter the content of the associations (Colby, 1960). Perhaps real differences could be found between face-to-face situations and the conventional out-of-sight arrangement for the analyst. Jung placed less emphasis on the sex life of his patients, emphasized the uniqueness of human motives, and postulated a striving toward individuation.

Adler (1927) emphasized power and status motives as being more significant in the life of the individual than the sexual motives. He emphasized the "life style" of the individual and his social striving. Assisting the patient to become more aware of his unique life style, his ideals, and his self-image is an important aspect of Adlerian therapy.

Rank (1945) placed considerable importance on the positive motivations of his clients. His theoretical differences with Freud have been indicated in the previous discussion of psychoanalytic theories of personality. Rank cast the therapist in a more personalized role, and he believed strongly that the therapist should avoid forcing his own values on the client. Rank emphasized the importance of child growth and development in the development of feelings of independence and security in adulthood. In therapy, he believed in establishing limits within which the client must function. The imposition of limits on client behavior was believed to help the patient gain feelings of security. Rank insisted that there was great therapeutic power in the patient-therapist relationship itself; thus, the personality and attitudes of the therapist became of central concern.

Fromm (*1941*), Sullivan (*1953*), and Horney (*1950*) have made significant changes in psychoanalytic theory. All three have given much more attention to the influences of the culture on personality. Fromm stressed the importance of ethical conflicts and the necessity for loving and being loved. Sullivan placed great emphasis on the importance of "relationship" in therapy. Horney emphasized the competing and contradictory demands of our culture upon the person, and the resolution of conflicts deriving from feelings of affection and dependence one has for parents and the feelings of hostility one has toward them for having to be dependent upon them. Assisting the patient in the resolution of his conflicts by making him aware of them is a basic part of the therapist's task.

A great deal of research needs to be done in order to evaluate the effects of psychoanalytic therapy. It has been reported that little movement in therapy was found to take place from one psychoanalytic session to another (*Bellak and Smith, 1956*). Eysenck (*1952*) reports that the analytic treatment of mental patients resulted in no greater recovery rate than was characteristic of patients receiving little or no treatment. The Eysenck reports created a great deal of interest in the problems of the evaluation of psychotherapy. Criticisms of the Eysenck reports (*Rosensweig, 1954*) have appeared in the literature, and the reports have also been defended (*Eysenck, 1961*).

## Client-Centered Therapy

Client-centered therapy (*Rogers, 1951*) has also been termed "phenomenological," "self theory," and "nondirective." The system is based on a phenomenological point of view and on confidence that the individual has within him the capacity for growth or self-actualization. The work of therapy is designed, then, to release the patient from threat and conflict and to permit growth to occur. Emphasis is placed on the differences between the client's perceived self and his behavior. When the individual begins to perceive himself as behaving in a manner consistent with his self-concepts, he begins to feel more secure, and more adequate. If the discrepancy between the perceived self and behavior becomes too great, it creates threat. The individual may protect himself against this threat through the use of defense mechanisms.

*Congruence* between awareness and experience is emphasized by Rogers (*1951*). In therapy, if a client is aware of communicating a feeling that he is actually experiencing, his behavior is said to be congruent. The client must eventually face the incongruence between his awareness and his experience, so that his communication of real experiences is in full awareness and not distorted in a defensive manner.

The client in client-centered therapy is presumed to have the capacity for growth toward becoming self-actualizing. The client becomes the center of the process. The attitude of the therapist is permissive and accepting in order to reduce threat to a minimum. The therapist is neither coercive nor authoritarian. Rogers (1961) emphasizes the importance of the attitudes of the therapist and indicates that they are more important than techniques. In the absence of threat, the client is able to accept parts of himself that he previously could not accept or of which he was unaware. In accepting himself more realistically, he is more capable of accepting others, and of fuller growth toward becoming a more self-actualizing person.

Emphasis in therapy is upon freedom for the client to discuss those facets of his problem or personality that he wishes to discuss. The therapist assists in this matter by trying to reflect the feelings of the client. The therapist attempts to understand and view the world as the client does. This is called an *internal frame of reference*.

The climate of the therapeutic situation is of vital importance and is characterized by the therapist's sincerity, warmth, acceptance of the client, regard for the client as a human being, and sensitive understanding. The therapeutic relationship is of greater importance than the direction of the discussions that take place. When the client's perceptions of himself as a person become more adequately differentiated, behavioral changes in socially desirable directions occur. The client possesses the capacity for positive growth, and the climate of the therapeutic situation permits such growth to occur. A great amount of responsibility for the progress of therapy is placed upon the client. It is he who has the problem, and a climate conducive to solution of the problem or resolution of the conflict is provided. The positive growth tendencies of the individual are depended upon for the occurrence of behavioral changes.

Various self theorists have been active in the development of therapeutic procedures. There are differences among self theorists, but the basic principle of self-actualization is typically central to their procedures. Maslow (1954) combines the self-actualization principle with his concept of basic human needs. Psychotherapy becomes, then, a procedure for systematic need satisfaction in order to permit the self-actualization of the patient. Other phenomenological and self theorists have made distinct contributions to the literature of psychotherapy (*Pepinsky and Pepinsky, 1954*). Self-theory approaches to personality and psychotherapy have been vigorously supported by a large number of psychologists.

Of particular significance have been the research efforts that have gone into the evaluation of therapy by self theorists. The results of therapy are difficult to evaluate, but sincere effort and considerable progress have been made by this group (*Rogers and Diamond, 1954*).

## Learning Theory Approaches

A number of psychologists have developed systems of psychotherapy from the general background of learning theory. These psychologists differ in their orientations to learning theory, but are in agreement that maladaptive behaviors are acquired through learning and that psychotherapy is essentially relearning. A brief look at a sample of learning approaches to psychotherapy will be presented. No attempt will be made to discuss all of the variations in procedure. The work of some psychologists who have made significant contributions to the field (*Mowrer, 1950; Rotter, 1954*) will not be given specific treatment. The following discussions should be adequate to give the general flavor of learning approaches.

### DOLLARD AND MILLER

Dollard and Miller (1950) depict the patient's neuroses as the creation of the conditions of his earlier life. In other words, neurotic behavior patterns are the products of social learning. People who seek the services of a psychotherapist in order to help solve their problems and alleviate their misery have not learned adequate ways of dealing with fears, conflicts, and the demands of social convention. People who have failed to solve their problems have typically met with rejection in various subtle and obvious forms from relatives, friends, and associates. They have attempted numerous ways of alleviating their distress and have lost confidence. The patient feels that no one understands or accepts him and that he does not understand himself. The neurotic has failed to solve his emotional and environmental problems. Some new conditions for learning must be provided by the therapeutic situation if better adjustments are to be learned. The organization and essential content of the following discussion is taken from Dollard and Miller's discussion of the main factors in therapy.

The patient finds that the therapist is someone with prestige who holds out hope for him by having enough faith in an eventual cure to attempt treatment. The therapist pays noncritical attention to the patient, listens sympathetically, and is very permissive. Being in an uncritical, nonmoralistic environment is a new situation for most clients. The patient is encouraged to express his feelings in speech in the therapeutic situation. The therapist does not condemn, and is accepting of the discussion of matters that have produced anxiety or disgust in the patient's friends. The therapist's acceptance, calmness, and composure tend to be imitated by the anxious patient. The patient experiences reassurance in the attitude of the therapist, which is markedly different from the reactions of his friends who have disapproved, condemned, or become disgusted. Considerable relief is experienced by the patient.

The free discussion of problems and conflicts in a pleasant and accepting climate is supplemented by the use of other procedures such as free association. In directing the client to say everything that comes to his mind, the therapist sets the patient free from the restraints imposed by logic. The therapist does not cross-question the free associations of the patient, and thus the arousal of additional anxiety is avoided. By encouraging the patient to talk, and consistently failing to punish him for the content of his verbalizations, a social learning situation is created that is the exact opposite of the situations in which he originally learned to attach strong fear to talking and thinking. The patient talks of situations that to him are frightening; since he is not punished for speaking of these frightening things, his fears gradually become extinguished. This extinction generalizes and weakens the motivation to repress other related topics so that they, too, can be dealt with.

Some topics have heretofore been too frightening for the person to discuss or even to think about. When the patient has difficulty in expressing himself, the therapist may help by supplying verbal labels to the emotions being experienced. A verbal label can serve as a tool in expediting communication as well as in thinking about the labeled feeling.

The therapist lends considerable assistance to the patient in making discriminations. He helps the patient uncover the nature of his problems by indicating that hopes for miracles are quite unrealistic, and subtly making clear that the efforts of the patient are imperative to his recovery. Differences between unrealistic fears and inappropriate behavior and the realities of the nature and demands of the situation are pointed out by the therapist. An important contrast is made between the helpless past conditions of childhood, in which fears were learned and behaviors acquired, and the current social conditions of the patient.

Through reassurance, the process of extinction, and the development of adequate discriminations, the fears of the client are reduced and the motivation for repression diminishes. The patient is encouraged to think about his problems and to try tentative solutions; thus the intellectual life of the patient is intensified and expanded to include previously avoided areas. Fears become extinguished in this process. When the patient becomes clearly aware of the nature of his problems and of the unrealistic basis of his fears, he is motivated to try new modes of behavior. The new modes of thinking and acting produce more satisfactory drive-reduction than did the old habits. The reduction in drive acts as a strong reinforcer for these new behaviors, and they tend to replace the older more futile ways of feeling and acting.

During the course of therapy the patient is really confronted with a graded series of learning situations. In the permissive atmosphere of the therapeutic situation the patient learns to solve problems and to make new responses. The new habits of reacting without fear, making adequate discriminations, and dealing with problems in a more realistic fashion are reinforced and tend to generalize from the verbal and feeling situations of therapy to the world of reality outside of the clinic.

## Behavior Modification

Modification of behavior through conditioning procedures has received a great deal of investigative attention in recent years. Training in behavior modification theory and technique has been recommended for inclusion in the training program for clinical psychologists (*Hoch et al., 1966*), and behavior therapy has become an important area of research (*Krasner and Ullmann, 1965*).

The program for changing behavior developed by Wolpe (*1958*) has created a great deal of interest and has led to many further developments in the field.

Wolpe (*1958*) modeled a system of psychotherapy following the results of laboratory research with cats. Cats were given electric shock in their feeding cages and it was observed that following this treatment they would refuse to eat in other areas of the experimental room. This behavior was interpreted as comparable to the generalization of anxiety in human patients. Anxiety, conditioned to the feeding cages, generalized and con-flicted with the eating response outside the cages. The cats were then treated by feeding them within the laboratory a considerable distance from the room in which they had been shocked. Anxiety reactions were in-hibited by eating at a sufficient distance from the cages. The feeding of the animals was gradually brought closer and closer to the original place where they had been shocked. The gradual nature of the approach to the feeding cages was maintained in order not to upset the eating responses. Eventually the animals were capable of eating within the room where they had previously been shocked and finally within the original feeding cages. The cats were "cured" of their neuroses in this manner. By strengthening the eating response, the response of anxiety was inhibited. Wolpe described this process as one of *reciprocal inhibition*.

Therapy sessions have been organized for human patients according to the same principle used with the cats. Through interview, a hierarchy of situations that produce anxiety in the patient is established. Starting with those situations that produce but little anxiety, the situation is arranged so that some positive response takes place; anxiety is replaced by this positive response. The patient works up through the hierarchy of anxiety-arousing situations by making some positive response in them until eventually he is able to replace his irrational neurotic responses with appropriate ones even in the heretofore most disturbing of circumstances. Investigations have reported considerable success in the use of conditioning procedures in psychiatry (*Wolpe et al., 1964; Ban, 1964; Eysenck, 1963; Wolpe, 1961*).

Eysenck and Wolpe are in agreement with other investigators in this area with their emphasis on behavior modification as the focus of remedial efforts. They have employed a behavior model that makes use of such constructs as inhibition and drive. Another group of investigators have followed Skinner's (*1953*) lead in rejecting the use of such constructs. Skinner (*1953*) attacked the assumption that behavior disorders were a reflection of some internal conflict or sickness.

So-called "neurotic behavior" is conceived of as maladaptive behavior that is acquired through a process of conditioning and is capable of being modified by a number of laboratory techniques of demonstrated effectiveness. There is *no complex, no illness*, and treatment is directed entirely toward *the behavior* of the individual. This is in sharp contrast with dynamic psychotherapy, with its emphasis on hypothetical underlying complexes, disease processes, and illness. Behavior therapy constitutes a rejection of traditional psychodynamic personality theories. Conceptions such as insight, lifting of repression, and unconscious processes and urges are rejected as unnecessary to the modification of behavior. The treatment problem becomes one of altering the reinforcing environment so that adequate behaviors are maintained, effective new behaviors learned, and inadequate behaviors extinguished. Behavior therapy consists of the application of principles of learning to the treatment of disordered behavior. This has been accomplished in a wide variety of areas using a variety of techniques (*Grossberg, 1964*).

Counterconditioning (*Bandura, 1961*), response inhibition (*Eysenck, 1960*), operant conditioning with positive reinforcement, social reinforcement, avoidance conditioning, and extinction have all been employed as procedures for the modification of maladaptive behavior. When the focus of attention is on the modification of disordered behavior, it has traditionally been held that the immediate behavior could be altered or the sympton alleviated but that when this happened other inappropriate behaviors would occur. This is known as symptom substitution. Contrary to the prediction, there is little evidence that this actually happens (*Grossberg, 1964*).

The number of psychologists contributing to this expanding area of investigation is imposing, and a great amount of research is being reported in the psychological literature. Emphasis on the utility of social reinforcers in the development and modification of behavior (*Krasner and Ullmann, 1965; Bandura and Walters, 1963; Rotter, 1954*) has led to extensive investigations of various social reinforcements in the modification of behavior. Child behavior has come under intensive investigation (*Bijou, 1965; Patterson, 1965*) through the use of reinforcement techniques. Speech problems and stuttering have received extensive investigation (*Goldiamond, 1965*). The problems treated by behavior modification procedures also include those of developing more appropriate behavior in mentally retarded children (*Bijou and Orlando, 1961*) and sex problems (*Feldman, 1966; Lazarus, 1963*), in addition to the usual neurotic and severely disturbed behaviors, including schizophrenia and autistic children (*Wolf et al., 1964*). Case studies in behavior modification are available in great number (*Ullmann and Krasner, 1965*).

The behavior therapies are being expanded continuously, and their success has created challenging new possibilities for the effective treatment of behavior disorders using scientific procedures. The science of psychology and the practice of clinical psychology are becoming more mutually supportive and interdependent.

### CHARACTERISTIC PROBLEMS IN PSYCHOTHERAPY

Whether psychotherapy is conducted from the frame of reference of psychoanalysis, self theory, or learning theory, there are certain problems that tend to occur during the course of the therapy.

The problem of establishing a satisfactory working relationship between therapist and client is one that is common to psychotherapeutic methods. When any person is dealing intimately with the life and problems of another, the situation is always a delicate one. Feelings of mutual respect must be engendered and an atmosphere must be created wherein the patient has confidence in the integrity and competence of the therapist. The patient must feel free to discuss himself and the nature of his problems in intimate detail. The establishment of such circumstances is called the establishment of *rapport*, a comfortable relationship between therapist and client.

Practical understandings must be established about what is to transpire in therapy and what the responsibilities of the patient and the therapist are. Arrangements as to time and place for the therapeutic sessions must be made, and agreements relative to procedures, the role of the client, the role of the therapist, and fees must be accomplished. The client typically does not know exactly what is expected of him or how he is to proceed. These practical matters pose problems for a therapist and client and must be clarified before very much can be done.

In the new, accepting, and understanding atmosphere of therapy, patients frequently make rapid initial progress toward the resolution of their problems. This is a very satisfactory early experience for the client. However, the relief from anxiety and the improved feeling of well-being that occur are likely to produce some difficulty. The patient may feel so well that he regards therapy as complete. He may want to terminate the therapeutic relationship, or he may relax in the comfort of his new insights and cease devoting adequate effort to the psychotherapeutic sessions even though they are continued. The initial rapid progress in therapy is usually at a rather superficial level. If therapy is terminated at this point the patient usually experiences no long-lasting improvement in his basic feelings or actions. The partial understandings that may be mistaken for revelation and clear evidence of dramatic and significant improvement may not be so rapidly followed by deeper understanding and clearly significant changes in the life of the client. Patients can become discouraged about therapy when progress bogs down after the initial rapid advances.

It sometimes happens that a client, in his eagerness to make rapid progress in therapy, will discuss facets of his existence that are highly personal and that he will shortly resent having divulged. When this happens the relationship between the therapist and the client tends to become somewhat strained, and the previously good relationship has to be re-established .When a patient presents material that he really is not emotionally ready to discuss, either out of eagerness to make progress in therapy or to please the therapist, actual progress may be impeded.

A problem for both patient and therapist may develop in the form of patient dependence upon the therapist. It sometimes happens that the patient incorporates into his general pattern of living the habit of spending his hour per week with the therapist. The security and support provided by the sessions with the therapist become an essential part of the patient's life; as long as this arrangement is not interrupted, the patient's motives to make further progress in therapy are not very impelling. Obviously, such a situation is not desirable and may pose a serious obstacle to patient recovery.

A problem growing out of the warm and accepting atmosphere of the therapy situation may be in the area of affection. The therapist is a "good" person and one that is trusted, respected, and liked. In some situations the affectional attachments of the patient for his therapist may become so strong that the patient identifies with the therapist in personal matters and feels strong emotion in the form of love for him. This phenomena is called *transference* by some psycho-therapists. If transference becomes too great, the emotional involvement may prevent realistic handling of the problems of the patient in therapy. A feeling of warmth, understanding, and respect may be mistaken for personal love by the patient. The complications of such a situation may pose serious obstacles to progress in therapy.

### FURTHER THERAPEUTIC PROCEDURES

Many means have been devised to assist people who have become mentally ill or emotionally disturbed to try to regain adequate mental health. Some of these procedures are used by psychotherapists as a routine matter; others are designed for special purposes and special problems. Occupational therapy and physiotherapy are valuable adjunctive services in psychotherapy. These adjunctive services are areas of specialization that are used for many purposes other than psychotherapy and will not be discussed further here.

The problem of the shortage of adequately trained psychotherapists has led to a number of innovations in therapy. One such innovation has been that of limiting the time that the patient may see his therapist. Patient improvement in time-limited therapy has been reported to be favorable (*Muench, 1965*). However, most attempts to find answers to the perennial problem of clinic waiting lists and therapist shortages have depended upon the treatment of patients in groups.

## Group Therapy

The procedures known as group therapy have developed out of the scarcity of trained psychotherapists, the great number of individuals seeking assistance, and the belief on the part of some psychotherapists that working through one's problems within a group rather than in an individual therapy situation provides a more real, life-like atmosphere in which the patient can interact with others.

Two of the principal obstacles to adequate personal adjustment are excessive conflict with feelings of tension, anxiety, and helplessness, and isolation from other people, with feelings of loneliness and rejection (*Hilgard, 1962*). The work of the psychotherapist is dedicated to the resolution of conflict and the assistance of people to develop more satisfactory interpersonal relations. Therapy with individuals functioning in a group affords opportunity for practice in interaction with more than one person; then, too, the interaction is with people who, like the patient, are untrained in psychotherapy. The situation represents a practice ground for the development of social skills as well as a place for the resolution of conflicts and the solution of problems.

In group therapy a psychotherapist can see more than one patient at a time, and thus the patient-hours of contact with a professional therapist are vastly expanded. Interaction with other people in a situation designed to be therapeutic may serve a real function other than that of simply providing a laboratory for the trial and practice of social interaction techniques. It is possible that the security provided by a group of individuals may be enough so that certain patients who would have extreme difficulty in relating to a professional psychotherapist in a one-to-one relationship may be able to function in a group and derive psychological benefits that would take a great deal more time and effort in individual therapy. In other circumstances a patient may be seen on an individual basis until he is emotionally strong enough to function in a group, at which time he may be transferred to a group therapy session. Combining individual therapy with group therapy has some unique features and may prove to be a valuable therapeutic device. Some patients may make better progress in individual therapy as a result of their experiences in the group, and better progress in group therapy as a function of being in an individual therapy program.

The evaluation of group therapy is a fertile area for research, as is the scientific study of the methods of group psychotherapy. Such studies have been reported (*Powdermaker and Frank, 1953*), and further research is in constant progress. Group therapy represents a promising area of development in psychotherapy.

FAMILY THERAPY

The treatment of people with problems is often difficult because the family situation within which the patient must live or to which the patient must return is quite unsatisfactory. When this is the instance, the progress of therapy can be slow and tenuous. In recognition of the familial-social nature of many problems of behavior, some therapists have turned to the task of working with whole families rather than only with the psychologically referred member.

In conventional psychotherapy, attempts on the part of relatives of the patient to contact the therapist have been discouraged. Psychotherapy was considered a highly personal relationship that might be seriously threatened by contacts with the family. When behavior is viewed as a result of interactional experience, the necessity for understanding familial interactional processes becomes rather self-evident (*Handel, 1965*). There are a variety of approaches to family therapy. They may range from working exclusively with the family as a unit, through working with the referred patient alone plus working with the family, to working with a number of families at the same time. Landes and Winter (1966) have reported on a program of communal therapy for a group of families. In this procedure, the patient families lived with the psychotherapists and their families for a 48-hour weekend. Although family therapy is a relatively recent development, there is a great deal of interest and effort being devoted to its development and evaluation (*Haley, 1962; Satir, 1964*). The journal *Family Process* is devoted to the understanding and treatment of the families of psychiatric patients. This journal provides a source of current information on developments in this area. The interested student will find it informative and provocative.

PSYCHODRAMA

One of the techniques of group therapy that has been considerably developed is the psychodrama (*Moreno, 1946*). In the psychodrama patients are encouraged to "act out" their problems and fantasies on a stage. The dramatic re-enactment of events of significance in the life of the individual and of experiences related to his emotional difficulties is used as a therapeutic procedure. The patient may play the role of himself in a psychodrama with other patients or therapists playing supporting roles. On other occasions he may become a spectator while someone else plays his role. This gives an opportunity for the patient to observe the mechanisms of his own behavior being portrayed by someone else. This vicarious view of himself may have the effect of increasing the objectivity of his own self-evaluations. Almost any life-like situation can be recreated on the stage, and the actors (other therapists or clinic staff members) can be directed to behave in the ways that will be most beneficial to the patient.

Through the psychodrama a patient begins to realize the nature of his problems and fantasies as he portrays these on the stage. Emotional acceptance and understanding of the patient's own life situation and the situations of those with whom he interacts are enhanced. Eventually, the patient comes to interact more effectively in real life with people whom he has interacted with through fantasy in psychodrama.

## Therapy with Children

The goals of psychotherapy with children are essentially the same as those for adults. Special techniques for working with emotionally disturbed children have been developed because of these children's lack of insight into their own problems and the fact that they are typically unaware of their need for therapy. In order for real help to be given to a child, the psychotherapist usually has to work with both the parents and the child. Direct therapy with the child is designed to accomplish appropriate changes within the child himself. Changes in attitude, feelings about others, feelings about himself, and changes in behavior are usually indicated. In dealing with the parents, where the child is the principal area of psychological concern, the efforts are devoted to bringing about changes in the child's psychological (and sometimes physical) environment. In so doing, it may become necessary to engage in intensive psychotherapy with the parents as well as the child.

PLAY THERAPY

One of the methods frequently used with children is play therapy. Psychotherapy conducted in a playroom offers some features that are not practical for the conventional office procedure.

Toys, clay, paints, a sandbox, dolls, and various other items that can be handled or manipulated are provided. The items provided for play are used to get the child to express his hostility and his conflicts while engaged in a permissive atmosphere of play. Children frequently produce their own psychodrama in play therapy. In such a situation the child may gain in feelings of security and develop a positive relationship with the therapist. The playroom facilities may be used for diagnostic purposes as well as to provide a situation wherein pent-up tensions may be released and catharsis may take place.

A good relationship between the therapist and the child patient is particularly vital. The child must develop confidence that the therapist is a real friend and that this friend is a nonpunishing, accepting person. When he has this confidence the child will feel more free to talk about his fears, hates, resentments, wishes, wants, and desires; thus progress in psychotherapy can come about with greater facility and speed.

## Medical Treatment

Advances in the field of medical treatment of emotional disturbances have been particularly noticeable in recent years. Biochemical and pharmacological treatment has received more recent attention than any other medical approach. Some drugs have been developed that have been particularly effective with tense, anxious patients. A variety of drugs is now available for the treatment of patients with psychological problems.

The use of drugs has reduced the frequency with which surgery for the relief of symptoms in psychiatric patients is performed. Shock therapy in the form of electric, insulin, or Metrazol shock has been used less frequently since the advent of tranquilizing drugs.

The drugs most frequently used in the treatment of behavior disorders are the tranquilizing drugs (*Katz and Lewis, 1961*); these are used extensively in the control and treatment of patients in mental hospitals. Their use for outpatients in both medical and psychiatric institutions has become a rather common practice. It is probable that these drugs in and of themselves have no real influence on the causative factors in emotional disturbance, but they are very effective in the relief of symptoms (*Hutt and Gibby, 1957*). Certain patients that would not otherwise be amenable to psychotherapy can be so treated after the administration of drugs.

Drugs that have exciting or arousing effects are used with other psychiatric patients. Considerable effort has gone into the development and evaluation of use of these drugs with psychiatric patients.

Certain drugs are used in analysis in order to permit the patient to express feelings that he ordinarily would be afraid to express, such as deeply repressed experiences and feelings. Hypnosis is used for the same purpose by some psychotherapists.

### SUMMARY

The importance of psychological disorder in our culture and the difficulties of determining its extent were discussed in the early part of this chapter. The study of the incidence of mental illness in our culture presents interesting problems. Data relative to the frequency of mental illness are derived from the study of the incidence of persons who are treated for emotional or behavioral disorders by public agencies or private individuals. Practically nothing is known of the actual incidence of psychological disorder. Estimates based on institutional data have been made, as have estimates based on sociological-psychological surveys.

Emotional stress is a part of living. When stress becomes too great or tolerance for stress becomes impaired, disturbed behavior may ensue. The time, money, and effort expended in preventing mental illness and in restoring mental health are all of considerable magnitude.

Many cases of people's problems of a minor nature come to the attention of psychotherapists. The intensive educational and training background of professional psychotherapists qualifies them to assist people with minor difficulties in effective living as well as to help clients for whom these minor problems are actually only symptoms of more severe disorders.

What goes on in psychotherapy is frequently regarded as mysterious. The warmth and permissiveness characteristic of most psychotherapeutic situations is a new and refreshing experience for most patients.

The varieties of psychotherapy stemming from different orientations to personality are not to be construed as right or wrong approaches. The various procedures have sufficient characteristics in common that successful therapy can be reported from all the legitimate procedures.

Regardless of methods employed in psychotherapy, certain problems arise in the therapeutic relationship. The same general problems of therapist-patient relationships tend to appear for most methods of therapy.

Group therapy has become increasingly popular as a result of the scarcity of qualified psychotherapists and the abundance of patients. Group therapy is a promising development in psychotherapy, and efforts to improve techniques and evaluate results are being expanded.

The use of drugs in the control, treatment, and rehabilitation of mental patients is a common practice. Psychopharmacological developments have been rapid in recent years. Tranquilizing drugs are generally regarded as effective in the relief of symptoms, and certain patients become amenable to psychological treatment as the result of the administration of drugs.

Research in the areas of sociology, anthropology, biology, psychiatry, and psychology is being accomplished. The knowledge gained from these and other areas of investigation contributes to the health and well-being of people in general.

## REFERENCES

Adler, A. *Practice and Theory of Individual Psychology.* New York: Harcourt, 1927.

American Psychological Association. *Ethical Standards of Psychologists.* Washington, D.C.: American Psychological Association, 1953.

Ban, T. A. *Conditioning and Psychiatry.* Chicago: Aldine Publishing Co., 1964.

Bandura, A., and Walters, R. H. *Social Learning and Personality Development.* New York: Holt, Rinehart and Winston, Inc., 1963.

Bandura, A. Psychotherapy as a learning process. *Psychol. Bull.,* 1961, **58,** 143–157.

Bellak, L., and Smith, M. B. An experimental exploration of the psychoanalytic process: exemplification of a method. *Psychoanal. Quart.,* 1956, **25,** 385–414.

Bijou, S. W., and Orlando, R. Rapid development of multiple-schedule performances with retarded children. *J. exp. anal. Behavior,* 1961, 4, 7–16.

Bijou, S. W. Experimental Studies of Child Behavior, Normal and Deviant. In Krasner, L., and Ullmann, L. P. (eds.), *Research in Behavior Modification.* New York: Holt, Rinehart and Winston, Inc., 1965.

Brammer, L. M. and Shostrom, E. L. *Therapeutic Psychology.* Englewood Cliffs, N.J.: Prentice-Hall, 1960.

COLBY, K. M. *An Introduction to Psychoanalytic Research.* New York: Basic Books, 1960.

DEPARTMENT OF HEALTH, EDUCATION, AND WELFARE. *Patients in Mental Institutions, 1957.* Washington, D.C.: U.S. Government Printing Office, 1960.

DOLLARD, J., and MILLER, N. E. *Personality and Psychotherapy.* New York: McGraw-Hill Book Company, 1950.

EYSENCK, H. J. The effects of psychotherapy: an evaluation. *J. consult. Psychol.,* 1952, **16**, 319–324.

EYSENCK, H. J. (ed.). *Behavior Therapy and the Neuroses.* New York: Pergamon Press, 1960.

EYSENCK, H. J. The Effects of Psychotherapy. In Eysenck, H. J. (ed.), *Handbook of Abnormal Psychology.* New York: Basic Books, 1961.

EYSENCK, H. J. Behavior therapy, extinction and relapse in neurosis. *Brit. J. Psychol.,* 1963, **109**, 12–18.

FELDMAN, M. P. Aversion therapy for sexual deviation: a critical review. *Psychol. Bull.,* 1966, **65**, 65–79.

FROMM, E. *Escape from Freedom.* New York: Rinehart, 1941.

FROMM, E. *The Art of Loving.* New York: Harper & Brothers,1956.

FREUD, S. A. *General Introduction to Psychoanalysis.* New York: Liveright Publishing Corporation, 1920.

GARDNER, G. G. The psychotherapeutic relationship. *Psychol. Bull.,* 1964, **61**, 426–437.

GOLDIAMOND, I. Stuttering and Fluency as Manipulatable Operant Response Classes. In Krasner, L., and Ullmann, L. P. (eds.), *Research in Behavior Modification.* New York: Holt, Rinehart and Winston, Inc., 1965.

GROSSBERG, J. M. Behavior therapy: a review. *Psychol. Bull.,* 1964, **62**, 73–88.

HALEY, J. Whither family therapy? *Fam. Proc.,* 1962, **1**, 69–103.

HANDEL, G. Psychological study of whole families. *Psychol. Bull.,* 1965, **63**, 19–41.

HARPER, R. A. *Psychoanalysis and Psychotherapy: Thirty-Six Systems.* Englewood Cliffs, N.J.: Prentice-Hall, 1959.

HEINE, R. W. A comparison of patient's reports on psychotherapeutic experience with psychoanalytic, nondirective and Adlerian therapists. *Amer. J. Psychother.,* 1953, **7**, 16–23.

HILGARD, E. R. *Introduction to Psychology* (3d ed.). New York: Harcourt, Brace and Company, 1962.

HOCH, E. L., Ross, A. O., and WINDER, C. L. Conference on the professional preparation of clinical psychologists: a summary. *Amer. Psychologist,* 1966, **1**, 42–51.

HORNEY, K. *Neurosis and Human Growth.* New York: W. W. Norton and Company, 1950.

HUTT, M. L., and GIBBY, R. G. *Patterns of Abnormal Behavior.* Boston: Allyn and Bacon, Inc., 1957.

JUNG, C. G. *Contributions to Analytic Psychology.* New York: Harcourt, Brace and Company, 1928.

KATZ, B., and LEWIS, R. T. *The Psychology of Abnormal Behavior.* New York: The Ronald Press Company, 1961.

KRASNER, L., and ULLMANN, L. P. *Research in Behavior Modification.* New York: Holt, Rinehart and Winston, Inc., 1965.

LANDES, J., and WINTER, W. A new strategy for treating disintegrating families. *Fam. Proc.*, 1966, **5**, 1–20.

LAZARUS, A. A. The treatment of chronic frigidity by systematic sensitization. *J. nerv. ment. Dis.*, 1963, **136**, 272–278.

MASLOW, A. H. *Motivation and Personality.* New York: Harper & Brothers, 1954.

MAY, R. *Man's Search for Himself.* New York: W. W. Norton and Company, 1953.

MORENO, J. L. *Psychodrama.* New York: Beacon House, 1946.

MOWRER, O. H. *Learning Theory and Personality Dynamics.* New York: The Ronald Press Company, 1950.

MUENCH, G. A. An investigation of the efficacy of time-limited psychotherapy. *J. counsel. Psychol.*, 1965, **12**, 294–299.

NATIONAL COMMITTEE AGAINST MENTAL ILLNESS. *What Are the Facts about Mental Illness?* Washington, D.C.: 1961.

PATTERSON, G. R. Responsiveness to Social Stimuli. In Krasner, L., and Ullmann, L. P. (eds.), *Research in Behavior Modification.* New York: Holt, Rinehart and Winston, Inc., 1965.

PEPINSKY, H. B., and PEPINSKY, P. N. *Counseling Theory and Practice.* New York: The Ronald Press Company, 1954.

PORTER, E. H., JR. Understanding Diagnostically and Understanding Therapeutically. In Williamson, E. G. (ed.), *Trends in Student Personnel Work.* Minneapolis: University of Minnesota Press, 1949, 113–119.

POWDERMAKER, F., and FRANK, J. *Group Psychotherapy.* Cambridge: Harvard University Press, 1953.

RANK, O. *Will Therapy.* Trans. by Julia Taft. New York: Knopf, 1945.

ROGERS, C. R. *Client-centered Therapy.* Boston: Houghton Mifflin Company, 1951.

ROGERS, C. R. *On Becoming a Person: A Therapist's View of Psychotherapy.* Boston: Houghton Mifflin Company, 1961.

ROGERS, C. R., and DIAMOND, R. F. *Psychotherapy and Personality Change.* Chicago: University of Chicago Press, 1954.

ROSENZWEIG, S. A transvaluation of psychotherapy: a reply to Hans Eysenck. *J. abnorm. soc. Psychol.*, 1954, **49**, 298–304.

ROTTER, J. B. *Social Learning and Clinical Psychology.* Englewood Cliffs, N.J.: Prentice-Hall, 1954.

SATIR, V. M. *Conjoint Family Therapy.* Palo Alto, Calif.: Science and Behavior Books, Inc., 1964.

SKINNER, B. F. *Science and Human Behavior.* New York: The Macmillan Company, 1953.

SNYDER, W. U. The present status of psychotherapeutic counseling. *Psychol. Bull.*, 1947, **44**, 297–386.

SROLE, L., LANGER, T. S., MICHAEL, S. T., OPLER, M. K., and RENNIE, T. A. C. *Mental Health in the Metropolis: The Midtown Manhattan Study.* Vol. I. New York: McGraw-Hill Book Company, 1962.

SULLIVAN, H. S. *The Interpersonal Theory of Psychiatry.* New York: W. W. Norton and Company, 1953.

ULLMANN, L. P., and KRASSNER, L. *Case Studies in Behavior Modification.* New York: Holt, Rinehart and Winston, Inc., 1965.

WOLF, M. M., RISLEY, T., and MEES, H. Application of operant conditioning procedures to the behavior problems of an autistic child. *Behavior res. and Therapy*, 1964, **1**, 305–312.

WOLPE, J. *Psychotherapy by Reciprocal Inhibition.* Stanford, Calif.: Stanford University Press, 1958.

WOLPE, J. The prognosis in unpsychoanalyzed recovery from neurosis. *Amer. J. Psychiat.*, 1961, **117**, 35–39.

WOLPE, J., SALTER, A., and REYNA, L. J. *The Conditioning Therapies.* New York: Holt, Rinehart and Winston, Inc., 1964.

WRENN, C. G. Psychology, Religion, and Values for the Counselor, Part III, in the symposium, The Counselor and His Religion. *Personnel guid. J.*, 1958, **36**, 326–334.

452

# Index of Names

# Index of Subjects